Against the Grain

Against the Grain

Colonel Henry M. Lazelle and the U.S. Army

James Carson

Number 9 in the North Texas Military Biography and Memoir Series

Denton, Texas

Printed in the United States of America.

10 9 8 7 6 5 4 3 2 1

Permissions:

University of North Texas Press
1155 Union Circle #311336
Denton, TX 76203-5017

The paper used in this book meets the minimum requirements of the American National Standard for Permanence of Paper for Printed Library Materials, z39.48.1984. Binding materials have been chosen for durability.

Library of Congress Cataloging-in-Publication Data

Carson, James O., 1944- author.

Against the grain : Colonel Henry M. Lazelle and the U.S. Army / James O. Carson.

pages cm. -- (Number 9 in the North Texas Military military biography and memoir series)
Includes bibliographical references and index.

ISBN 978-1-57441-611-4 (cloth : alk. paper) –

978-1-57441-625-1 (ebook)

1. Lazelle, H. M. (Henry Martyn), 1832-1917. 2. United States. Army--Officers--Biography. 3. Generals--United States--Biography. 4. Authors, American--Biography. 5. United States--History--Civil War, 1861-1865--Regimental histories. I. Title. II. Series: North Texas military biography and memoir series ; no. 9.

E467.1.L35C37 2015
355.0092--dc23

[B]

2015034548

Against the Grain: Colonel Henry M. Lazelle and the U.S. Army is Number 9 in the North Texas Military Biography and Memoir Series

The electronic edition of this book was made possible by the support of the Vick Family Foundation.

The Officer's Oath

I do solemnly swear that I will support and defend the Constitution of the United States against all enemies, foreign and domestic; that I will bear true faith and allegiance to the same; that I take this obligation freely, without any mental reservation or purpose of evasion; and that I will well and faithfully discharge the office upon which I am about to enter. So help me God.

Table of Contents

List of Maps

List of Photos

Preface

It was a sunny morning, unusually warm for early June in Quebec, just across the border from Vermont. Brigadier General Henry M. Lazelle, US Army, Retired, stood on the porch of his rough-hewn log cabin and let the sun soak through his night shirt. He marveled once again at the beauty of the woods and the trillium plants that carpeted the glade around the cabin. On another early June day in 1850, he had stood on the Hudson River landing at West Point, an apprehensive 17-year-old wondering what lay ahead.

In February, he had written his son that, at 84, he looked "old and worn." This morning, however, one of his first back "at camp" for the summer, he somehow felt younger, more energized, despite the chest pain that seemed his constant companion.

Henry enjoyed his winter home in Winchester, Massachusetts, both for the friendships he had made there and its proximity to Boston. Winchester also provided many pleasant diversions for his second wife, Emilie. Nearly 40 years his junior, she brought joy and a degree of peace into the life of a long-troubled widower. However, Lake Memphremagog had become their real home, one they longed to return to in the spring.

For Henry, especially, there was a quiet and calm at "Wake Robin" cabin after 40 years of adventure, and often hardship, in the Army.

Less than a month after Henry and Emilie's return to the cabin in June 1917, his son, Dr. Horace Lazelle, received a cryptic telegram from "Lazelle" in Magog, Quebec: "Father passed away at three thirty this AM." According to the death certificate, the cause was arterial sclerosis. Horace wondered, however, whether his father's wounds as a young lieutenant in Texas, where he was "shot through the lungs" in a fight with Mescalero Apaches, compounded by the stress of several controversial events during his Army career, ultimately contributed to the decline in his health in his sixties and seventies.

Henry Martyn Lazelle, born in Enfield, Massachusetts, in 1832, the son of a farmer, was orphaned at the age of four and raised by a succession of relatives and family friends. Accepted into the U.S. Military Academy in 1850, he was suspended two years later, in part for poor academics but also because of numerous disciplinary infractions, many of them in concert with his roommate, the future American artist James Abbott McNeill Whistler. Graduating near the bottom of his class in 1855, he would eventually return as Commandant of the Corps of Cadets, the only disciplinary five-year man to do so.

In many respects, Lazelle's career is the story of the United States Army during the second half of the nineteenth century, from the early settling of the West, through the tumultuous years of the Civil War and Reconstruction, to the final ravaging of the great Indian nations. Along his path from lieutenant to general, he served with or under some of the giants of American history, and participated in events and campaigns that forged the nation.

Initially assigned to the 8th Infantry Regiment at Fort Bliss, Texas, the newly minted lieutenant served under future Confederate General James Longstreet, scouted with Kit Carson, and was seriously wounded fighting Mescalero Apaches in New Mexico's Guadalupe Mountains. Recovering from his wounds, he and his company chased the ever-elusive Apaches over broad swaths of southwestern Texas and New Mexico. After all Federal forces in Texas were surrendered to now-Confederate state authorities in 1861, Lazelle spent nearly a year as a "paroled" prisoner-of-war.

Eventually making his way to Washington, D.C., Captain Lazelle was exchanged for a Confederate officer and assigned to the Commissary General of Prisoners, responsible for inspecting military prisons and camps for paroled enlisted men and overseeing a major exchange of Federal and Confederate prisoners at Vicksburg, Mississippi. The young officer soon tired of staff duty. In the fall of 1863, he secured command of the 16th New York Volunteer Cavalry Regiment, assigned to the defenses of northern Virginia.

The 16th, an ill-fated amalgamation of several partially formed New York units, spent most of its time in futile pursuit of Confederate "ranger" John Mosby and his band of guerrillas. After a year of frustration upon frustration and failure upon failure, Lazelle resigned his volunteer colonel's commission and returned to his old regiment, once again a captain.

With the end of the Civil War, Lazelle and his regiment moved to the Carolinas, responsible for the administration of law and order, governance, and public services under Reconstruction. There they remained until late 1870, when the regiment was sent west again, this time into the tribal hunting grounds of the Sioux and Cheyenne, supporting the Yellowstone Expeditions for the Northern Pacific Railroad and the opening of the Black Hills to settlers and prospectors.

In December 1874, after a ten-year wait, Lazelle was promoted to major with the 1st Infantry Regiment at Fort Sully, South Dakota. There, in the spring and summer of 1877, he and a battalion's worth of infantry and cavalry troops operated against the remnants of Sioux Chief Sitting Bull's warriors along the Tongue, Powder, and Little Missouri Rivers and into the Black Hills.

The following year, he was ordered away from Fort Sully once more, to establish Fort Meade in the eastern Black Hills. His family joined him there the winter of 1879, in a four-room log cabin. That June, the family prepared to move again, this time to West Point, with Lazelle appointed Commandant of Cadets.

Throughout his career, there was an independent streak in Henry Lazelle, born of necessity in his youth as he shuttled from one guardian to another and took on jobs to help support the relatives who took him in. As he moved into adulthood, his sense of self-reliance and assurance, combined with unusually strong intellectual curiosity, were manifested in occasional challenges to authority. In the civilian world, self-confidence and disdain for authority often are the marks of entrepreneurial greatness. In the United States Army, these personal traits can lead to controversy. In the case of Henry Lazelle, they made for a number of newspaper-worthy stories.

The first of these emerged in the wake of one of the most damning incidents in the early history of African American cadets at West Point, when Cadet Johnson Chestnut Whittaker, a former slave from South Carolina, was attacked in his room, allegedly by masked strangers. Lazelle and West Point Superintendent General John Schofield quickly concluded, and a Court Martial agreed, that Whittaker had contrived the incident. President Chester A. Arthur eventually overturned the verdict, but the die had been cast. Cadet Whittaker was dismissed after failing one of his examinations.

The Whittaker affair cost General Schofield his job, tarnished Lazelle's image, and brought General Oliver Otis Howard, intent on reforming the West Point disciplinary system, to the Academy as Superintendent. Almost immediately, he and Lazelle clashed over policy and command issues. Lazelle won a few battles, but in the end he lost the war and was dismissed from the Commandant's position a year short of tour.

During the Whittaker controversy and prior to his battles with Howard, Lazelle had been promoted to lieutenant colonel. However, he still began his next assignment with the 23rd Infantry Regiment in purgatory at Fort Craig, New Mexico, one of the most desolate Army posts in the country. Rescued in 1884, in part by ill health at Fort Craig's high altitude, and reassigned to the Military Division of the Pacific as Assistant Inspector General, Lazelle moved his family from its rough adobe cabin to more opulent quarters, first at the Presidio of San Francisco and then at Vancouver Barracks in Washington State. In the fall of 1885, he was selected to attend British military maneuvers in India as the American representative.

Returning from India in early 1887, Lazelle once again received new orders, this time back to Washington D.C. to oversee publication of the Official Records of the War of Rebellion. He was almost immediately caught up in intense partisan political maneuvering by Republicans intent on unseating Grover Cleveland, the first Democrat elected to the Presidency since before the Civil War. Seizing on allegations in the press that Lazelle had purposely allowed non-official information to be inserted in the Official Records, the Republicans launched Congressional investigations and hearings. After nearly a year, Lazelle was fully exonerated, but the damage had been done. Once again he was dismissed short of tour.

In October 1889, Lazelle and his family returned to Texas for his final assignment as Colonel of the 18th U.S. Infantry, stationed first at Fort Clark and eventually, shortly before his retirement in 1894, at Fort Bliss, where his Army career had begun 38 years earlier.

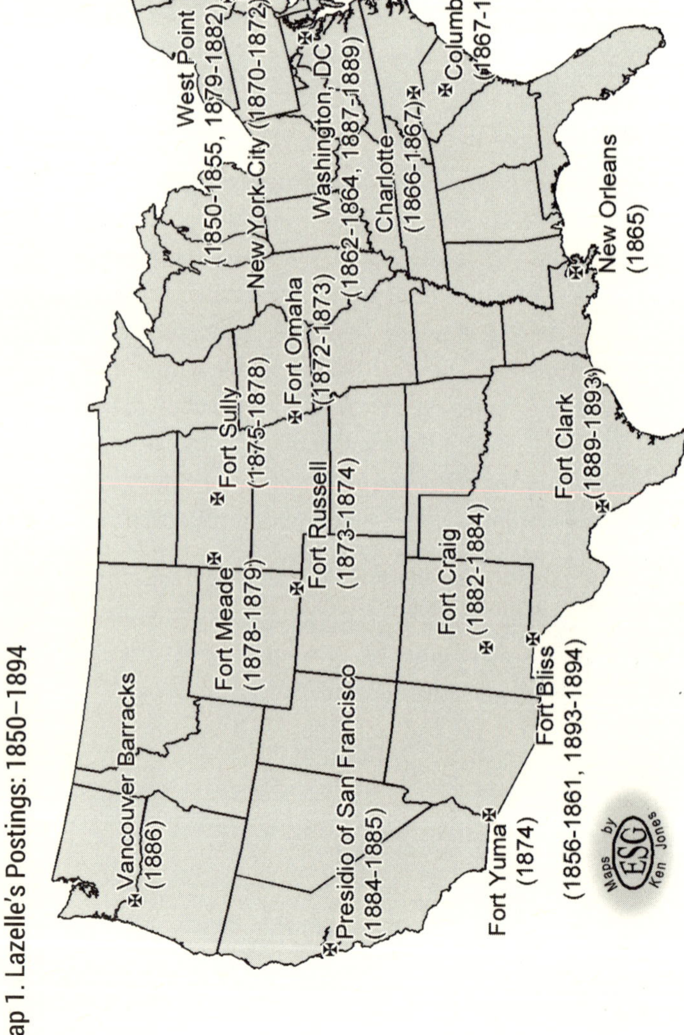

Map 1. Lazelle's Postings: 1850–1894

Photo 1. Colonel Henry M. Lazelle

As his career progressed, Lazelle authored articles on military strategy and tactics, challenging Maj. Gen. Emory Upton, the "father" of post-Civil

War U.S. Army tactics, and winning the Military Service Institution's coveted Gold Medal for an 1882 essay on improvements in the art of war. He also took up spiritualism and scientific inquiry, publishing books on force theory and the relationship between science and theology. In 1904, he was promoted, in retirement, to Brigadier General.

In the later years of his career, Lazelle proved to be a very complex and, at times, highly conflicted man. He lost Rebecca, his wife and the mother of his two boys, to gall bladder disease in 1893. Coming from a prominent Maryland banking family, she had shared years of hardship and sacrifice with him in the far West and the Dakotas, along with brief periods of "high living." Five years later, his eldest son, Jacob, who followed in his father's footsteps at West Point, was taken by encephalitis as a still-young first lieutenant on his way to the Philippines. After Rebecca's and Jacob's deaths, Lazelle became somewhat a lost soul, roaming from place to place, never quite able to settle down, and, after marrying his second wife, becoming distant from Horace, his surviving younger son.

It was this older, more troubled man that his only grandchild, Barbara Hollingsworth Lazelle, came to know, but only briefly and from afar. She was just ten years old when her grandfather died, and she had never met him. Yet, she developed a vivid picture of him from her father's stories, family photos, letters, and keepsakes.

Intrigued with her grandfather while growing up in Seattle, Barbara spent hours looking over albums of pictures he had sent from his travels abroad and duty on the western frontier. Through these family treasures, she remembered him as "a very handsome man in his full dress Army uniform—epaulettes, saber and plumed helmet. White hair, beard and violet blue eyes. Tall, slim, erect—a soldier from head to toe. I wish I might have seen and known him, for he loved children dearly. This was evident from the many anecdotes my father told me over the years about his own childhood and experiences with his Dad."

Late in her life Barbara began to write about her grandfather, especially stories her father told her of growing up on America's frontiers. She wanted to pass on this family history to her sons and grandchildren. She gathered a good deal of information and family records but, even by age 97, had not lived long enough to finish the story.

This biography was inspired by Barbara Lazelle's efforts, and it draws upon her extensive files and records. The author also researched files at the U.S. Military Academy, U.S. Institute of Military History at Carlisle Barracks, the U.S. National Archives, and Library of Congress, and conducted extensive searches of records and information available on the internet. Other important resources included the *New York Times*' digital archive, *Newspapers.com* and *Fold3.com.* The author also benefited from research done by the late Peggy Hoffman, a family friend and writer who began, but did not finish, a historical novel based on Lazelle's life.

By chance, the author, Lazelle's great-grandson, lives in Vienna, Virginia, approximately one mile from the Civil War encampment of the 16th New York Cavalry, which then-Colonel Lazelle, U.S. Volunteers, commanded in 1863 and 1864.

Acknowledgements

This book is dedicated to my wife, Margaret Kress Carson, my constant companion, advisor, and reviewer, as I have worked on my great-grandfather's story. She has walked the grounds of forts and battlefields, plowed through volumes of research materials, and gently offered criticism and editorial advice. It is largely because of her support and encouragement that this project has been completed.

I am also grateful to the following individuals and institutions for their guidance and research assistance: the Research Staffs of the U.S. National Archives and the Library of Congress Manuscript Reading Room and Law Library, Washington, D.C.; Alicia Mauldin-Ware, Archive Curator, Special Collections and Archives, U.S. Military Academy Library; Wanda Kienzle, Curator, Old Fort Bliss Museum, Fort Bliss, Texas; Jennifer Nielsen, Curator, Fort Bliss and Old Ironsides Museum; Steve Moore, Georgeville Historical Society, Quebec Province, Canada; Jim Lewis, author and historian, Hunter Mill Defense League, Oakton, Virginia; and William F. Haenn, author and historian, Fort Clark, Texas.

I also am especially indebted to Mr. James Breig, who provided extensive editorial assistance and advice and who introduced me to additional information resources through which I found new stories and anecdotes to enrich the Lazelle history, and to Mr. Ken Jones of Midlothian, Virginia, for his outstanding work in preparing the maps. Two close friends, both Civil War historians, Thomas Boltz of Reston, Virginia, and John Fincham of Winchester, Virginia, also provided invaluable advice, counsel and support throughout this project.

Against the Grain

Chapter 1

A Five-Year Man

On a warm afternoon in early June 1850, Henry M. Lazell[1] arrived at the Hudson River's West Point landing on a steamboat from New York City. His first view of the Academy was from Highland Gorge. Some years earlier, another newly arrived cadet, Horatio G. Wright, remembered that he felt as if "the rugged granite walls of the Highland gorge frowned down upon my eager eyes with that cold, hard frown which they have worn through the last four ages. Break-Neck Hill, Bull Hill, Butter Hill and Crow's Nest, brood in silent quaternion over the peaceful Hudson, as if in some mnemonic reveries of those Titans whose giant strength clave asunder their native union 'in the old time before.'"[2]

As Henry stared up at the imposing fortress-like walls of the United States Military Academy, he wondered nervously whether this really was his destiny. Close to six feet tall, lean but solidly built, with deep blue eyes and sharp features, Henry knew he could handle the physical rigors of cadet life. But could the orphaned son of a poor Massachusetts farmer compete with the cream of society and really become an officer of the United States Army?

Like so many New Englanders in the early nineteenth century, Henry came from "fighting" stock. His great-grandfather, William Lazell, had served in the French and Indian War in the 1750s. And his grandfather, Jacob Lazell, a tenant farmer, was a private during the Revolutionary War in Col. David Brewer's 9th Continental Regiment, mustered in Ware in 1775. Still, Henry questioned this next step in what had already been a somewhat turbulent first 17 years.

Henry and his twin brother, George, were born in Enfield, Massachusetts, on September 8, 1832. Four years later, their father died at the age of 43, followed soon after by their mother. At the time of his parents' deaths, Henry's brothers and sisters ranged in age from 19 to two. The youngest orphans were sent to be raised by older siblings, relatives, or family friends. Henry initially went to his 19-year-old sister, Mary Ann, newly married to John Hurlburt. Later, he moved in with another older sister, Priscilla, and her husband Calvin Brooks, and then, for 15 months while in high school, with the Newton family of Worcester, Massachusetts. At the time of Henry's appointment to the Military Academy, Calvin Brooks served as his legal guardian.

Henry had limited formal schooling in his early years, instead helping out with family businesses. Well before high school, while living with another older sister, Martha, he worked in the Worcester rope factory owned by her husband, Luther Slater. Luther's father, Captain Peter Slater, said to have been, at 13, the youngest participant in the Boston Tea Party, had moved to Worcester in 1775 and established the factory on Main Street in 1806.[3]

The factory—or rope walk—was a long, alley-like place, like a bowling alley, in which the child workers stretched out strands of roping and twisted them at the end of the alley, feeding them onto a roller which rolled the rope into a finished strand. As he walked onto the landing at West Point, Henry remembered how tired he had been after long hours in the factory and guessed he could probably handle cadet life as well.

Henry also had worked for an Irishman in a machine shop. He remembered making fun of the Irishman's pronunciation and trying to teach him to say "hair," which came out as "here." While teaching him to pronounce this correctly, something they were turning on a lathe went haywire, and the Irishman was furious. Henry later told his sons, "Never again was there any kidding about pronunciation." Henry doubted there would be much kidding at West Point.

Despite his childhood labor, Henry eventually completed his high school education in Worcester, living with the Newtons and Calvin and Priscilla Brooks. Then a Worcester lawyer with political connections, Brooks had encouraged Henry to apply for an appointment to the Military Academy through Congressman Charles Allen of the 5th Congressional District. Henry, at loose ends and wishing a more secure future, decided to try for it. His teachers at Worcester's Classical and English High School sent off recommendations, one of them, Warren Hazell, writing:

> Having been requested to state to you what I know of Henry M. Lazell with reference to his fitness for entering West Point; I will say that I have been acquainted with him for five or six years; that he was under my instruction, as nearly as I can recollect, about one year, and that during that time his deportment was invariably correct. He was of industrious and studious habits, and his proficiency was respectable.
>
> I have known but little about him for the last two or three years; but that little has been favorable to his character and talents, and to his standing as a member of our Classical and English High School. My impression is, that he would sustain himself well in the Institution, to which he desires admission. [4]

On April 23, 1850, with apologies for his tardiness due to unforeseen circumstances, Congressman Allen formally nominated Henry, at the last minute. Allen acknowledged receipt of the appointment in an April 25 letter to the Chief of Engineers (who had administrative responsibility in Washington for the Academy), and Henry signed an official acceptance of his appointment on May 5. Several weeks later, he boarded a steamer in New York City for the trip up the Hudson.

WELCOME TO WEST POINT

As 17-year-old Henry stood apprehensively on the Academy's river landing, he and his fellow newly appointed cadets were greeted by an Army sergeant who led them "up to the plateau, where they registered, deposited their money, and marched off to the barracks to be greeted by a cadet officer. 'Stand attention!' he bellowed. 'Hats off! Hands close upon your pants! Stand erect! Hold up your head! Draw in your chin! Throw out your chest!' They then followed the officer into the building and received uniforms, temporary room assignments, and regulation haircuts."[5]

The "plebes" (as the brand-new cadets were called) were then subjected to three weeks of basic military training known as squad drills, essentially basic marching; a formal "candidate examination" covering reading, writing, and arithmetic; and a medical examination. Until they passed the acceptance examination, they were "candidates" and wore a black probationary uniform. During this initial period, the plebes quickly learned that they were members of the lowest family of the human species:

> Instead of receiving kind hospitality, he becomes for a time one of an inferior caste, towards whom too often the finger of derision is pointed, and over whom the fourth class [*sic*] drill-master flourishes with too snobbish zeal his new-born authority. ... to be called "a conditional thing,"... to be crowded five in a room, with the floor and a blanket for a bed; to be twice or thrice a day squad-drilled in "eyes right" and "left face," in "forward march," and in the intricate achievement of "about face;" to be drummed up in the morning, and drummed to meals, and drummed to bed, all with arithmetic for chief diversion; this is indeed a severe ordeal for a young man who is not blessed with good nature and good sense, but with these excellent endowments it soon and smoothly glides on into a harmless memory.[6]

Founded during the Thomas Jefferson administration by an act of Congress in 1802, West Point was the nation's first chartered military academy and remains the oldest continuously occupied military post in America. During the Revolutionary War, General George Washington considered West Point one of the country's most important strategic positions because of its ability to control passage on the Hudson. Designed in 1778 by Thaddeus Kosciuszko, one of the heroes of the Battle of Saratoga, West Point's fortifications were never captured by the British.[7]

Following the Revolutionary War, a number of political and military leaders, looking to reduce America's wartime reliance on foreign engineers and artillerists, pushed for an institution of higher learning that would be devoted to both classical education and to the science and practice of warfare. Colonel Sylvanus Thayer, known as the "father of the Military Academy," was Superintendent from 1817 to 1833. Under his guidance, its academic standards were upgraded to the challenging coursework that Henry faced. Thayer also "instilled military discipline and emphasized honorable conduct. Aware of our young nation's need for engineers, Thayer made civil engineering the foundation of the curriculum."[8]

In 1850, when Henry arrived, West Point still was the primary source of officers for the U.S. Army, although state schools such as Virginia Military Institute (founded in 1839) and The Citadel in South Carolina (founded in 1842) served as secondary sources of commissioned officers. The U.S. Naval Academy at Annapolis, Maryland, had just been established in 1845.

The Corps of Cadets into which Cadet Lazelle was inducted numbered about 250 and was organized into a battalion of four companies, all officered by cadets. The Commandant of Cadets, an Army captain, commanded the battalion, and Army lieutenants were in charge of each company as "Assistant Instructors of Tactics." Some of the First Class cadets (seniors) served as the battalion's cadet captains and lieutenants; some Second Class (juniors) as cadet sergeants; and some Third Class (sophomores) as cadet corporals. All other cadets served as privates.

Squad drills were conducted by Third Class cadets, usually corporals; company drills by the Assistant Instructor of Tactics; and battalion drills by the Commandant of Cadets or an assistant from the tactics department. In ordinary roll calls, marching to meals, and other non-academic activity, the cadet officers were in charge.

FROM CANDIDATE TO CADET

In late June, following end-of-year examinations for existing cadets (and the plebes' three-week introductory training and candidate exams), the annual "marching into camp" was performed during which the Corps of Cadets (including the third classmen and new plebes but absent the first class and second classmen on furlough) encamped on a portion of "The Plain," a large, level field adjacent to the barracks and parade ground. During the encampment, drill training continued, with two formal parades daily at 8:00 a.m. and sunset. Plebes also had to put in the required hours standing watch. The encampment continued through the summer months, ending in late August when the cadets returned to their barracks.

Having passed the candidate exam, Henry was "found qualified for admission to the Military Academy" on June 24, 1850, was officially "admitted" on July 1, and began wearing the cadet uniform.[9] With his formal "appointment," Lazelle, like all cadets, was considered a regular Army "warrant officer," a special grade from which he would be promoted to second lieutenant upon graduation. As such, the cadets were fully subject to the rules and articles of war, and incurred a contractual obligation to serve a minimum of four years in the Army in return for their education.

The West Point record books provided detailed information on each entering plebe regarding his family situation and economic circumstances, including parents and their relative wealth (indigent, reduced, moderate or affluent); whether they came from a city, town or the countryside;

and the father's occupation. Henry was identified as an orphan from the countryside, whose father had been a farmer of "moderate" circumstances. His roommate, Oliver Otis Howard, had an almost identical background, except his mother was still alive. Of the 63 in his class, twenty had fathers who were farmers. Another fourteen fathers were lawyers, ten merchants, six doctors, nine Army or Navy officers, and two each clergymen and teachers.[10]

Henry's other classmates included George Washington Custis Lee and James E. B. Stuart. Lee was the eldest son of Robert E. Lee, who would become Superintendent of the Academy in September of 1852 and would later command the Confederate Army of Northern Virginia during the Civil War. The young Lee would graduate and, like his father, go on to serve as a Confederate general. Eventually, he succeeded his father as president of Washington and Lee University in Lexington, Virginia. J.E.B. Stuart also would achieve fame as a Confederate cavalry commander. He would die at the Battle of Yellow Tavern near Richmond in May 1864.

Henry would much later cross paths with Howard, who also rose to the rank of general during the Civil War and went on to found Howard University. They would lock horns over cadet discipline while Howard served as Superintendent and Henry as Commandant of Cadets at West Point in 1882.

Henry evidently was lax in corresponding with his family during his first months at West Point. In a letter dated July 19, 1850, to his twin, George, Academy Superintendent Captain Henry Brewerton, Corps of Engineers, wrote: "Your letter of the 16th Inst.[11] making inquiries relative to your brother Cadet H. M. Lazelle has been received. I am happy to inform you that your brother passed his examinations last month and is now in the performance of his military duties in camp. He is in good health and has promised me he will write to you without delay."[12]

Although Cadet Lazelle's records of academic achievement and disciplinary infractions during his plebe year are incomplete, Oliver Howard claimed, both in his autobiography and in an early letter home to his mother, that Henry and his other roommates were serious students:

> When we first went into quarters, the room to which I was assigned was in what was called the Old South Barracks, a very large room without alcoves. There were four separate iron bedsteads and four iron tables, with other meager furniture for four cadets. My mates were Thomas J. Treadwell, from New Hampshire, a student of Dartmouth; Levi R. Brown, from Maine, my own state; and Henry M. Lazelle, of Massachusetts. No young men were ever more studious or desirous to get a fair standing in the institution than we. [13]

Surviving records from that year suggest, however, that Henry, while at least a decent student, fell from disciplinary grace almost immediately, receiving his first demerit on July 3, only two days after donning the cadet uniform.

The record of each cadet's behavior was written meticulously in a large leather-bound book, with double columns on each page of 45 to 50 lines. The job of secretary-recorder went to a man with neat, legible penmanship. The pages were headed "Delinquencies," and when a cadet received his first demerit, a fresh page was begun for him: first the date, then the offense, then the number of demerit points. Few cadets survived an entire grueling year—even fewer a full four years—without a single misstep. Others, like Henry, were destined from the start to fill page upon page of double columns:

- July 3, Presenting arms incorrectly at drill, 1 demerit.
- July 6, Not rising at command, 1 demerit.
- July 7, Bedding not folded neatly at inspection, 1 demerit.
- July 17, Absent from reveille roll call, 1 demerit.

By the time the corps of cadets moved into barracks at the end of the summer, the page headed "Lazelle, Henry M. (Mass.)" was filling up relentlessly. Infractions ranged from "late turning out for officer of the day," to "not standing in front of tent at inspection," to "raising right hand before the command." Most of these were minor infractions—the honest mistakes in military practice and discipline of a new plebe still on the learning curve. Later, as he clearly began to challenge the system and his instructors—and fall under the spell of his second-year roommate, the future artist James Whistler—the infractions became more serious.

When the Corps of Cadets was encamped on The Plain that first summer, there were no academic classes, and the hours normally set aside for academic study were used for further drilling and "recreation." There was virtually no free time, and plebes were not allowed to attend the upperclassmen's "frolics" and dances at night. Henry still had to study dancing as part of his cadet training, but his partners the first year were other plebes, just as annoyed as he was to be spinning about the floor in the Fencing Academy building with their right hands gracefully supporting the shoulder blades of other cadets. Henry enjoyed the group singing in the early evenings, as the other plebes sprawled at ease under the stars, the one activity in which they could make a mistake without being punished. It was said that J. E. B. Stuart, called "Beauty" by his classmates, had the best singing voice.

Soon after they moved inside the barracks in September, the new cadets signed the oath of allegiance, although they remained on probation until January. A list of instructions on the barracks room door made settling in somewhat pro forma. Since they had only two blankets, a canvas bed cover, cot, chair, and desk, moving in was effortless. Their clothing consisted of four shirts, four pairs of woolen socks, two pairs of shoes, two pairs of silk socks, a dress uniform, and a fatigue uniform, plus two hats—a forage cap for the fatigues and a "flower-pot" leather dress hat with cockade, which required its own special box. Heavier underclothing and other winter necessities were soon added, along with a shoeshine kit and a shelf for books. Since each item had an assigned spot, setting up housekeeping was simple. Maintaining their rooms and keeping their modest possessions in proper order, on the other hand, were yet another source of demerits.

The winter schedule began immediately in September, with no break except for precious Saturday afternoons when Henry, sometimes with several other plebes and sometimes alone, explored the hills and the river, climbing up to the Crow's Nest and Fort Putnam or exploring caves along the water's edge. Fourth Class (plebe) cadets took three academic subjects: "Mathematics," including algebra, geometry and trigonometry; "French Language," including grammar and conversation; and "English Studies," including grammar, rhetoric and geography. Infantry training and artillery and cavalry instruction, which included light and heavy artillery practice and tactics, cavalry tactics, riding, broadsword, and fencing, were distributed throughout all four cadet years, in part to provide "healthful exercise and physical training." [14]

At the conclusion of his first academic year in June 1851, Henry had accumulated a total of 110 demerits (the highest in the class was 200 and the lowest 13). Overall, he stood 163rd out of 229 cadets in demerits. Academically, he placed roughly in the middle of his class (42nd in a class of 71): 45th in mathematics, 46th in French, and 22nd in English.[15]

French was very important, as almost all military textbooks of the nineteenth century were in that language, and the mathematics instruction was of French origin, in large part due to the influence of the Paris "Ecole Polytechnique" on former Superintendent Sylvanus Thayer. Dennis Hart Mahan, an 1824 academy graduate and professor of civil and military engineering, also had spent four years in France where he studied at the Military School of Application for Engineers and Artillerists at Metz. Any cadet who could not at least read French, regardless of his speaking skill, was in for a hard time academically.

Henry's class was divided into sections of 12 to 20 cadets each, the first cadet on each section roll assigned as "squad marcher" and responsible for his section's attendance and "deportment." The Academy used the "recitation" form of instruction, under which students were expected to have studied the material in advance. The instructor posed questions or problems which individual students or small groups would solve at the blackboard or answer orally.

Once the student had completed his response, the instructor would "examine him on such points as he has slighted or omitted, and on subjects connected with that discussed." The role of the instructor was more to "make sure of the cadet's thorough and accurate knowledge, to supply his deficiencies, and to amplify his conceptions, than directly to teach him the subject matter of the lesson. ... The instructor marks each recitation according to his estimate of its quality [on] a scale of valuation ranging from three, the maximum, for perfect, to zero, the minimum, for a total failure. ... At the end of each week these marks are aggregated, and on Monday, after dinner, the cadets, especially the doubtful 'plebes,' crowd the hall of the adjutant's office, where the weekly class reports are posted, eager to see the official estimate of their doings during the last week."[16]

Bad conduct demerits were given for various infractions of military and "police" regulations to which cadets were subject. Petty offenses and delinquencies—such as being late at roll-call, rusty belt plate, improperly polished shoes, inattention during drill, barracks room not swept at the proper time, using tobacco, neglect of duty or of study—were reported and, if there was an inadequate excuse, from one to a maximum of eight demerits were given for each offense. A cadet could be dismissed when he received over 100 demerits in six months or 200 in a year, and monthly reports of academic standing and conduct were regularly sent to parents or guardians.

Cadets were expected to "inform" on their compatriots, a system both reviled and defended by academy graduates. Horatio Wright believed it to be "fair and above board, and when justly acted out, it is certainly far better than any substitute," despite the fact that it sometimes produced "violent retchings [*sic*] of conscience and of friendship."[17]

WHISTLER ENTERS THE SCENE

Cadet Lazelle met his second-year roommate, James Abbott McNeill Whistler, of Pomfret, Connecticut, during the cadet corps' 1851 summer encampment. Henry described their first encounter in a 1915 magazine article he wrote about Whistler, who, by then, had become a world-renowned artist:

> My first vision of Whistler was at West Point when his bright, sunny face peered through the opening of my tent one rainy summer's day of our cadet camp life in 1851, asking if he might come in. He spent hours repeating the stories of his reading, and in describing with gleeful interest the various characters in them so graphically that one would know them if met on the street. And this was the beginning of our friendship of years of association and correspondence as classmates and roommates.[18]

Whistler was the son of Major George Washington Whistler, West Point Class of 1819, who had been called to Russia by Tsar Nicholas to build the railroad between Moscow and St. Petersburg, for which he received the Order of St. Anna. He and his family lived in St. Petersburg, where young James stood at the head of his class at the imperial Academy of Fine Arts. Returning to New England after his father's death, James was enrolled in, but quickly expelled from, the rather puritanical Christ Church Hall in Pomfret.

Using all the family connections she could muster, Whistler's mother enlisted the aid of Massachusetts Senator Daniel Webster in getting her son into the Military Academy, because she had heard so much of Robert Weir, professor of drawing there. Webster, possibly feeling that training in drawing was not quite as critically needed as some simple, old-fashioned discipline, recommended that President Millard Fillmore appoint James "at large." Young James's successful application, despite his poor eyesight, likely was also aided by the fact that his father was a well-known Academy graduate and because it was endorsed by a former Superintendent, Joseph Swift.

At any rate, Whistler passed the entrance examinations handily, and in 1851, ten days before his 17th birthday, became a full-fledged cadet. Around the time he entered the Academy, a cousin described him as "slight, with a pensive, delicate face, shaded by soft brown curls" with "a somewhat foreign appearance and manner, which, aided by natural abilities, made him very charming, even at that age."[19]

Whistler, by all accounts, was far from a serious student—except in drawing—and his disdain for serious study must have rubbed off on his roommate, Cadet Lazelle, who noted:

> He was one of the most indolent of mortals. But his was a most charming laziness, always doing that which was most agreeable to others and himself. He was far from studious. At West Point the evenings until ten o'clock were the hours for study. In our room we sat opposite each other, an iron table on which was an oil lamp between us. After an abstracted study of an hour or so I would look up, and almost invariably see the youthful Whistler, his head supported by one hand, fast asleep. He would rouse up for a little while, but the instant the half-past nine drum sounded, his bed was down and he very soon in it. Many hours during the day and evening, with lessons in prospect, he passed in etching, studying to accomplish by facial expression and attitude certain corresponding emotions. [20]

Benny Haven's

Early in his plebe year, Whistler discovered—and introduced his roommate to—the delights of Benny Haven's, a little tavern south of the Academy and a forbidden "haven" for wayward cadets. Benny's Dutch wife was an excellent cook, specializing in turkey, sausages, and buckwheat cakes, washed down with Benny's steamy rum flip. There were several "secret" paths through the woods to Benny's from the Academy grounds, great footwork being sometimes required, especially by plebes, to avoid detection.

In a letter to his sister, Nathaniel W. Hunter, who was at the bottom of his Class of 1833, attempted to explain the special appeal of Haven's tavern for the West Point cadet:

> We eat and drink (wine) moderately, talk of home of graduating and politics, toast the girls and return to barrack about 3 a.m. This helps very much to pass away the time until June or May when I intend to commence studying. I have told you of Benny's and of the many pleasant hours I have spent there. I hope yet to spend many more before I take my final *adieus*. However anxious I am to leave this place there are many things from which it will almost rend my heart to be separated forever and among these Benny's holds a very conspicuous place. The old man and his wife, and the chimney corner in which I have smoked many a pipe, and the blazing log fire, and the clean table and tablecloth, and buckwheat and butter cakes, and beef steaks, ham and eggs, all so much remind me of bygone and happier days that I would willingly cling to that forever.[21]

Although Henry had been able to resist the pull of this place during his first year, in part due to his poverty, he was no longer reluctant when Whistler added his persuasions. Soon the Lazelle record of delinquencies resembled that of his roommate: late at breakfast roll-call, absent from tattoo roll-call, inattention at ranks in drill, habitually gazing about at all ranks, laughing at inspection, not having gloves at church.

1852 was a rough year for Henry. He had entered the Academy a fairly serious student, having come from a more-or-less "straight-arrow" background of hard work and modest means. Whistler, with his disdain for authority and devil-may-care attitude, simply overwhelmed his less seasoned and more naïve roommate. Under his influence, Lazelle not only slipped in academic performance, but also suffered from numerous lapses in discipline.

He also began to display a growing predilection to challenge the system, which usually resulted in simple incidents being blown well out of proportion. A case in point occurred the night following the posting of the results of the January examinations. Henry and his roommate celebrated their passing marks by playing cards, which was strictly forbidden, after taps. Unfortunately, they were caught red-handed by that evening's inspecting officer. Years later, Henry wrote of the incident:

> Cards were forbidden in cadet barracks, but we had a pack, and one night long after "taps" (ten o'clock) we had been playing, and the cards laid carelessly aside, when we were surprised by the entrance of the inspecting officer, who spied the cards. We knew that the offense was a serious one against discipline, and considered whether we could properly ask that the report should read, "cards in possession," a lesser offense, instead of "playing with cards," as we were not playing when the inspector saw us. Whistler said, "No, we had been playing;" so we faced the music.[22]

In fact, the punishment was severe, and Henry was not willing to accept it without challenge. In a March 1852 report to the Chief of Engineers, who was in charge of West Point at the time, then-Superintendent Capt. Henry Brewerton described the incident and charges:

> On the night of the 3rd of January, First Lieut. E. W. Smith, one of the Asst. Instructors of Tactics, in making his inspection of the Cadet barracks about 11 o'clock, discovered Cadet Lazelle and his room mate seated at a table with cards before them—and with which they had no doubt been playing in violation of the 114 para of Academic regulations. The roommate of Cadet Lazelle was seated at the table with cards in his hands, fronting the inspecting officer as the latter entered the room. Immediately on perceiving the Inspector, the Cadet threw the cards on the table and endeavored to conceal them. At the same time, Cadet Lazelle, who was seated at the table with his back towards the Inspector, was observed to move his arms as if assisting his roommate to hide the cards.
>
> On these facts being made known to the Commdt of Cadets the next morning, the young gentlemen implicated were placed in arrest, charged with violation of the 114th Para Academic Regulations.[23]

At the time, it was the practice at West Point that, in disciplinary actions involving drinking or playing cards, classmates of an accused cadet could pledge, as a class, to abstain from committing the same offense and the cadet would be spared both the offense on his record and the punishment. All but three of Whistler's classmates signed such a pledge and he was "accordingly released from arrest and restored to duty—no notice being taken of his offense." For reasons unknown, Henry's classmates declined to sign such a pledge, and the Superintendent chose to impose punishment directly, instead of requesting a General Court Martial: deprivation of his summer furlough with his class and confinement to the limits of camp during the summer encampment period.

In what would not be his last challenge of authority either at West Point or during his career as an officer, Lazelle appealed his punishment in a letter to the Secretary of War. In his own report to the Chief of Engineers, the Superintendent refused to adjust the punishment, and his decision was upheld.[24]

This was not Henry's only offense. Among the many others for which he received demerits that year was a much more serious case of insubordination to his mathematics instructor, a second lieutenant, for which he was court-martialed in May. According to the charges, Lazelle

> did obstinately fail, and neglect, correctly to enunciate, as required by his Instructor, Lieut. M. Gogswell, 8th Infantry, a proposition contained in the recitation for the day—This after he, the said Cadet Henry M. Lazelle, had been repeatedly told the exact phraseology of the enunciation in question, and after he had been required, by said Instructor, to repeat after him the words of said enunciation, which he had been repeatedly and distinctly ordered to give.

Henry pled not guilty but was convicted by the Court Martial and sentenced to confinement to the limits of The Plain for thirty days and, during that time, to walk post, as a private sentinel, in front of the Cadet Barracks, from 2:00 p.m. until Retreat on four consecutive Saturdays, and to perform four extra tours of Sunday Guard Duty.[25]

Suspension

On August 2, Lazelle again was charged with insubordination for "unmilitary and discourteous conduct in persisting to speak to his company officer after having been forbidden and warned to desist." And on September 22, he was found guilty of further misconduct—"writing an improper excuse." That fall, the new Superintendent, Robert E. Lee, suspended him from the Academy for a full academic year.

At the time, the authorized rank for the positions of both the Superintendent and Commandant of Cadets was captain. Lee was a captain in the Corps of Engineers and a brevet colonel. "Brevet" was a temporary, usually honorary, rank of a higher grade than the officer's regular rank. Brevets often were awarded in recognition of meritorious conduct, especially during wartime. Lee had received his brevet promotions to major, lieutenant colonel and colonel for gallantry in battles during the war with Mexico between May and September 1847. Newly commissioned West Point cadets also were "breveted" as second lieutenants until they were appointed to a regiment, whereupon they received a date of rank as regular second lieutenants.

In commenting on Lazelle's suspension—and his appeal to the President of the United States requesting a "remission of a portion of the sentence of the General Court Martial that suspended him"—Lee noted that Lazelle's behavior during the year did "not appear to have been marked by subordination or at all times courtesy to his superior officers," that he stood at the bottom of his class academically, that it was "considered exceedingly doubtful by his Profs [*sic*] whether he was sufficiently proficient in his course of Phily [Philosophy]" to pass the examination, and that "unless a very great change should have taken place in his conduct, between this and June next, his amount of demerits would have exceeded 200, which would therefore have caused his dismissal."[26]

At this point in his West Point career, Henry—under the influence of his roommate Whistler—occupied the unenviable position of class "goat," at the bottom in academics (number 58 of 58 cadets), and only one member of his class had a greater number of demerits. Henry stood 56th in Mathematics, 55th in French, and 30th in Drawing—perhaps the only positive impact Whistler had on his academic performance.[27]

Henry Lazelle was not the only one of his contemporaries to face suspension. Two classes ahead of him, Philip Sheridan, who would become one of the Union Army's great generals and eventually be appointed Commanding General of the Army, was suspended for a year in September 1851 after attacking a cadet sergeant who, Sheridan felt, had wrongly reported him for a minor incident during a company formation. Like Lazelle, Sheridan at the time believed his suspension was "a very unfair punishment, that my conduct was justifiable and the authorities of the Academy all wrong."[28]

John M. Schofield, who graduated with the Class of 1853 and returned as Superintendent in 1876, narrowly avoided dismissal in June 1852. While he was helping prepare newly arrived plebes for the candidates' exam in mathematics, several of his classmates came into the classroom and engaged in "deviltry," for which Schofield was ultimately blamed. He was summarily dismissed by the Secretary of War, and only after the intervention of Senator Stephen A. Douglas was he eventually reinstated by a formal court of inquiry and court-martial.[29]

Henry most likely spent his suspension with his sister Priscilla and Calvin Brooks. His guardian would have been none too pleased, and Henry undoubtedly spent his time in purgatory engaged in some sort of "productive" activity and remedial academic studies.

When he returned to West Point the summer of 1853 for the annual "marching in," he was now a member of Whistler's class of 1855. His friend, however, was "absent with leave, on account of ill health," diagnosed by doctors in New York as "endocarditis." Whistler's year-end examinations had been postponed, as was, apparently, action on his demerits, which at 218 were sufficient for him to be dismissed on disciplinary grounds.

Sometime that summer, Whistler wrote Lazelle, asking for a summary list of his demerits and advice on applying for reinstatement. Henry wrote back in early August urging Whistler to carefully compose his request and to be prepared to appeal to the Secretary of War and President, if necessary:

> May Heaven or Haven (as it should be spelled) [a reference to Benny Haven's tavern] grant you success but Whistler don't be too confiding in men and their promises. I do not know your friend [not further identified] or upon what he founds your hopes but as you say no harm can be done by this proposition [not further identified], and if it fails why you still have at your disposal all those safe resources of attack left for the Secy of War, which you before used so successfully as almost to succeed and which I am confident you will now use with the most complete success. If you should fail in your missive to the President your experience and former arguments renewed will greatly aid you and you cannot —must not with them both to act on the President and then the Secty—this time fail.

Enclosed with the letter was a two-page list of demerits and a note confirming that it was "a most-painfully accurate mathematical account of these d___m (accursed?) demerits —you may rely upon it as correct in every particular as it corresponds precisely with the Adjutant's book as we have comprised balance sheets." Lazelle signed off hoping that "an exception will be taken to the general will that 'The prayers of the wicked availeth naught' and that mine may be answered. May God grant you success ... But 'Quad scriptum—scriptum est' [What is written, is written] !! You know my belief —you must however make the effort— and 'whistle' be it worthy of you."[30]

Whistler remained on convalescent leave until late August, and his application for reinstatement was successful. He returned to West Point August 28, promptly receiving a demerit for "reporting with long hair."[31] On August 31, having been "prevented by illness" from taking the June exams, he was found "qualified for advancement and assigned positions in his academic subjects."[32]

In a July 23, 1853, Post Order No. 80, Special Order 91, "the limits of Cadet Lazelle in arrest" were extended to the usual limits of cadets during the summer encampment, essentially completing his latest punishment. He finished the 1853–1854 (Second Class) academic year ranked 41st (out of 42) in Natural and Experimental Philosophy (which included Mechanics, Electricity and Magnetism, Acoustics and Optics, and Astronomy), 24th in Chemistry, and 8th in Drawing. Lazelle's high ranking in Drawing, no doubt the result of Whistler's influence, was his best rating in four years. Only once, in his plebe English studies when he ranked 22nd out of 71, had he been above the 50th percentile. Usually, he was found near the bottom of the list.

Henry's erstwhile roommate was among six members of the class found deficient and recommended for discharge. Whistler had 121 demerits and was near the bottom of his class in Philosophy, but he was number one in Drawing. By this time, Whistler had given up the idea of a military career and desired to leave West Point before his four years were up, but on academic rather than disciplinary grounds. And so, he failed Chemistry. As recalled and embellished somewhat by Lazelle:

> At the examination in the voluminous chemical course of the academy, at the end of his third year [his second year at the Academy, when he was a "third class" cadet], he was given the subject of silicon and its combinations. He utterly failed. He could not remember whether it was a gaseous or a solid substance. He wrongly guessed the former. He afterward said that if silicon had been a gas, he might have been a major-general. It is well that he was not, for he would have been a failure. [33]

At its June 20, 1854, meeting, the Academy's Academic Board formally took up Whistler's case and recommended him for discharge. Noting that he was then aged 19 years and eleven months, the Board cited him as "deficient in chemistry with an added notation of conduct," judged his aptitude as "good" but his study habits as "very idle" and his general conduct as "extremely inattentive to regulations" and demonstrating "very bad soldiership." He also had well above the maximum number of demerits allowed. [34]

Before he left West Point, Whistler gave his good friend several watercolors and drawings. The only one to survive the years is a copy of an 1836 Duffield Harding drawing of "Vicenza, North Italy," done in pencil, crayon, gouache, pen, and black ink on brown paper, and signed "JA Whistler." In December 1878, then-Major Lazelle of the 1st Infantry wrote Whistler that he still had the sketch. The drawing remains in the Lazelle family collection. [35]

Henry's deportment after his period of reflection while on suspension hardly improved, as he would not or could not conform to the expected norms of behavior. He was punished for not saluting officers, being late at roll calls, absences from meals, being inattentive in class, and walking away from cavalry drill. He had taken up with a group of town fellows, called "citizens," and received demerits several times for having them in his tent and carousing with them, "loitering behind the barracks," etc. He rarely got all of the parts of his uniform on, mended, polished and buttoned. He finished the year with a total of 200 demerits, the maximum allowed.[36]

Cadet Lazelle began his final year at West Point two months after most of his original classmates had graduated, with George Washington Custis Lee at the head of the class. He immediately continued his steady march to the bottom of the demerit list:

- June 22—Late at breakfast.
- June 25—Coat collar out of order at AM inspection.
- July 2—Not receiving officer in charge properly, 2 p.m.
- July 9—Absent from reveille.
- July 12—Outside of tent in shirtsleeves.

- July 15—Obtaining possession of Delinquent Books without authority.
- July 23—Citizen in tent about 6 p.m.

As classes began in the fall, the list continued to mount, with both minor infractions and more serious transgressions: failing to make proper recitation in artillery tactics, absent from drill, failure to make proper recitation in cavalry tactics, visiting at 2 and 2:30 p.m., visiting at 9:30 and 11 a.m., absent from quarters at 8 and 9 p.m., absent from parade, room out of order at morning inspection, and on and on to a total of 175 for the year.

On July 1, 1855, when he graduated and was commissioned a Brevet 2nd Lieutenant, Henry stood 30th in a class of 34. On the Conduct Roll, he stood 175th out of a total of 195 cadets; only four others in his graduating class had more demerits. This future regimental commander of infantry and cavalry troops and award-winning author of a treatise on strategy and tactics also did not exactly excel in his military subjects: 28th in Infantry Tactics, 24th in Artillery, 25th in Horsemanship and 29th in Cavalry Tactics.

With this rather dismal record in his military subjects, Henry would soon be tested on the Texas frontier with Mexico, where he would face cattle-rustling Mescalero Apaches and hungry grizzly bears, weeks of deprivation on the march, and in but a few years, prisoner-of-war status at the hands of the Confederate Army. In the meantime, he had to make his way from West Point to Fort Columbus in New York Harbor, where he would await orders to his first assignment as a second lieutenant.

Chapter 2

Operations Against the Apaches

When Cadet Henry M. Lazelle graduated from the United States Military Academy and was commissioned a Brevet (Bvt) 2nd Lieutenant of Infantry, officers were appointed to specific positions, carrying a specific grade, in specific units (e.g. 2nd Lieutenant, B Company, 1st Infantry Regiment). Academy graduates went into limbo status, as "brevetted" 2nd lieutenants, while awaiting "commissioning" as regular lieutenants in a unit with a vacant position. (Bvt) 2nd Lt. Lazelle, thus, was posted initially "in garrison" at Fort Columbus on Governors Island in New York Harbor.

For many years, Fort Columbus was the closest major Army post to West Point and served as a first posting or departure point for newly graduated cadets shipping out to posts along the Atlantic or Pacific coasts. Late that summer, Lazelle was assigned to the 8th Infantry Regiment and posted to Fort Bliss, Department of Texas, with a promotion date of October 9, 1855, as 2nd Lieutenant of Company "I." He did not formally join his regiment until March 18, 1856. Until then, he was officially "absent without leave," not a pejorative in today's sense of "AWOL," but rather more akin to "administrative leave status" or "in transit."[1]

At the time, Henry was one of just under 1,100 commissioned officers in the United States Army. In addition to his salary of $826 a year, he was entitled to an allowance for "servant's pay and clothing," and "commutation of subsistence and forage." Most of his fellow officers also were West Point graduates.

Following his departure from Fort Columbus, Lazelle made the long trip west by steamship—with stops in Savannah and New Orleans—by river packet, on horseback, and in an ambulance (a canvas-covered Army wagon). In his memoirs, Maj. Gen. Zenas R. Bliss,[2] West Point Class of 1854, described the 17-day voyage from Governors Island down the Atlantic coast, around the tip of Florida, and through the Gulf of Mexico to the Texas coast off Corpus Christi as "very pleasant on the whole," although they had many rough experiences, including "a mutiny, the ship caught fire, and we experienced a very severe norther."[3]

Off Corpus Christi, the officers and troops were first transferred to a steamer and eventually put ashore on St. Joseph's Island, described by Bliss as a "sand barrier some twenty-one miles long and five miles wide," on which the Army had maintained a presence since 1845. A day later, lighters[4] arrived to transport the troops to Corpus Christi, which Bliss described as "a small town of not more than 600 inhabitants and the principal depot for army supplies in Texas." There, Bliss had been "fitted out" for overland travel by wagon train to Fort Duncan, on the Rio Grande near the current town of Eagle Pass, some 500 miles southeast of El Paso.

Fort Bliss

The first U.S. troops to establish a presence in El Paso arrived in September 1849. Six rifle companies of the 3rd Infantry Regiment established a post known simply as "The Post Opposite El Paso," or the post opposite Paso del Norte, Mexico, a town that was later renamed Juarez. The post was situated on the Coons Smith Ranch and remained there until 1851, when it was abandoned. At that time, a chain of forts was being established between Santa Fe and San Antonio, and the El Paso garrison, except for a few men, was transferred to Fort Fillmore, about eight miles southeast of Las Cruces, New Mexico.

Taking advantage of the closure of the posts at El Paso and San Elizario to the south, local Indians increasingly made trouble between 1851 and 1853, raiding ranches, stealing cattle and mules, and generally making life miserable for the settlers. A number of stage routes, including the famous Butterfield Overland Stage, also ran through the area.

In December 1853, Jefferson Davis, Secretary of War under President Franklin Pierce, ordered a new military post at El Paso, and by Christmas, four companies of the 8th Infantry arrived from Fort Chadbourne, Texas. Lt. Col. Edmund B. Alexander commanded them and made the "Military Post of El Paso" official on January 11, 1854. Initially located on the ranch property of James Magoffin (Magoffinsville), the Post of El Paso officially became Fort Bliss on March 8, 1854, in memory of former President Zachary Taylor's son-in-law and Chief of Staff, Lt. Col. William Wallace Smith Bliss, who had died in 1853. Bliss graduated from West Point in 1833 and was on the Academy staff from 1834 to 1840. Later a hero of the 1846-1848 Mexican War, he was called "Perfect Bliss" behind his back when he was a cadet at the Academy.[5]

Photo 2. Fort Bliss, 1850s

W.W.H. Davis, "El Gringo," 1857, Courtesy of the University of Arizona Library, Books of the Southwest Collection

When Lazelle arrived at Fort Bliss in March 1856, the post was home to three companies of the 8th Infantry, with 12 officers, 237 enlisted men, and married officers' families. While Fort Bliss was no luxury post, and its desert, grass, and scrub brush environs were a far cry from the lush woodlands around West Point, it nonetheless was viewed by many officers and their wives as a highly desirable station. "There were dances and ranch parties and plenty of social life, for both officers and enlisted men. Grass grew in abundance on the mesa, and game abounded near the garrison. The Rio Grande was narrow, but full of water. Grain was processed at nearby Hart's Mill. News was brought by travelers, some of whom, according to their reports, were entertained at the fort with 'delightful courtesies.'"[6]

Lydia Spencer Lane, the wife of another 8th Infantry lieutenant who arrived at Fort Bliss three years later, described their three room adobe quarters, with a thatched roof and dirt floors as sounding "worse than it was, for the floor was hard as stone, almost; and with canvas nailed down first, and a carpet over that, we were well fixed. Some of the other quarters were more roomy and pleasant than ours; but we did not require anything better."

The "red, muddy waters" of the Rio Grande flowed close by, and Lane remarked that she saw fewer insects and snakes than in other places they had been posted:

> I only remember seeing one snake, and that was on the bedroom floor. When I awoke one morning I saw what I took to be a curiously striped piece of ribbon. My suspicions were aroused, however, and we soon found out what it was and killed it. We supposed it fell from the thatched roof to the floor. There was no ceiling in the rooms, so that the rafters and thatching were distinctly visible, and there was nothing to prevent a snake dropping in on us whenever he felt inclined.[7]

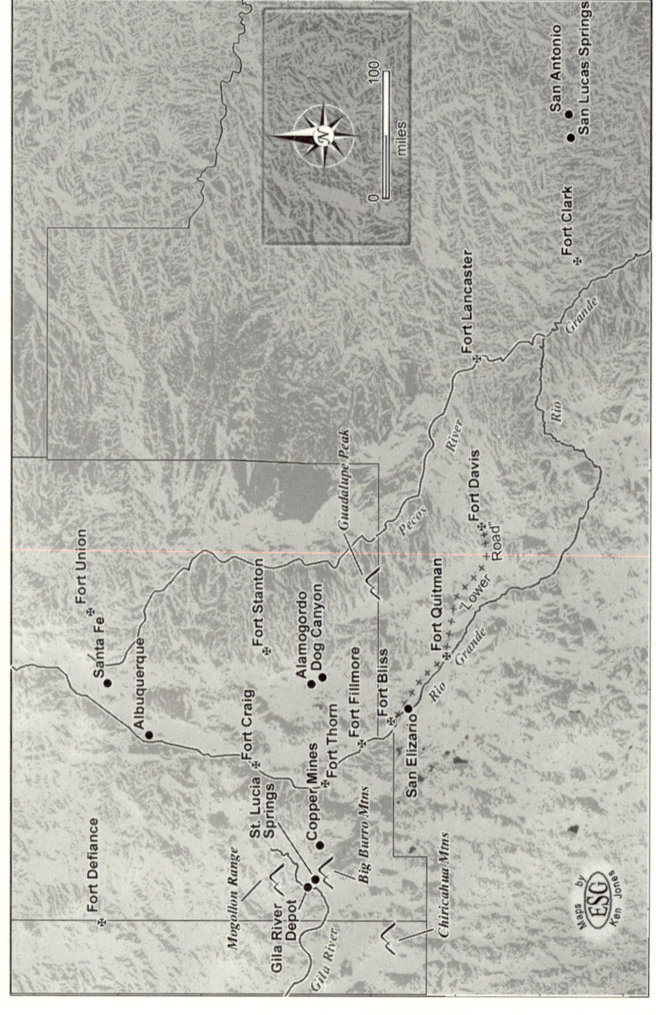

Map 2. Texas-New Mexico Territory: 1856-1861

The 8th US Infantry

At Fort Bliss, Lazelle joined a regiment, established in 1838, that already had seen a good deal of action. After its creation, the 8th served briefly on the country's northern frontier guarding against spill-over from anti-British rebellions in Upper and Lower Canada, before being transferred to Florida where it fought in the Second Seminole War. In 1846, on the eve of the war with Mexico, the regiment was transferred to Texas with Zachary Taylor's army. After the Treaty of Guadalupe Hidalgo in February 1848, which ended the war and established the Rio Grande as the border between the United States and Mexico, the 8th, with some 780 officers and men, remained in Texas and New Mexico, responsible primarily for the security of the trail between San Antonio and Santa Fe. Small detachments often were sent out in pursuit of "hostile" Indians, but minor skirmishes were "more common than pitched battles, and routine in-garrison duties dominated the daily lives of most of the regiment's military personnel."[8]

When Lazelle arrived on post, six companies of the 8th and its headquarters were stationed at Fort Davis—about halfway between El Paso and San Antonio. Another company, commanded by Capt. John Sprague —who would go on to serve as Adjutant General of the State of New York and appoint Lazelle as Colonel of a volunteer regiment during the Civil War—was stationed on temporary duty at Fort Stanton, between El Paso and Albuquerque. Lazelle's Company I and two other companies were at Fort Bliss, which was commanded by the senior company captain on post.

Other posts and camps temporarily occupied by troops of the 8th as they went about their duties securing the territory included Fort Inge, near the present-day town of Uvalde, Texas; Fort Clark and Fort Quitman, Texas; and Fort Fillmore and Fort Defiance, New Mexico. Most of the regiment's scouting operations were uneventful, but occasionally they led to real brushes with the Indians:

> Company K, First Lieutenant George L. Willard commanding, left Fort Stanton, New Mexico, on a scout on the 28th, arriving at camp near Sierra Gallina, New Mexico, the 31st of August [1858]. Left this place on the 1st, in pursuit of a band of Navajo Indians; killing two and wounding a number; recaptured 2500 sheep and 9 horses, arriving at Chusco Valley, New Mexico, the 28th of September.[9]

At the time, the troops of the 8th were equipped with horses for transporting officers and horses or mules for supplies. The enlisted men marched on foot. Generally, each infantry regiment had ten companies, with 64 privates in each company. A law of 1850 had authorized 74 privates to frontier companies, a total rarely reached. A captain, assisted by a first and second lieutenant and an orderly sergeant, commanded the company, and a sergeant and corporal were in charge of each of the company's four squads. On the frontier, regiments could theoretically have as many as 900 officers and men, but the usual average was 300-400.[10]

THE FORT BLISS FALCON CLUB

Having completed his first assignment by arriving alive at Fort Bliss in March 1856, Lazelle found himself under the command and tutelage of Capt. (Bvt. Major) James Longstreet, who was also serving as post commander. Longstreet, an Alabaman, was a member of the West Point Class of 1842, which included future Union Army Generals Henry Eustis, William Rosecrans, John Pope, Abner Doubleday, and George Sykes, and, in addition to Longstreet, future Confederate Generals Alexander Stewart, Daniel Hill, Richard Anderson, and Lafayette McLaws.

Like Lazelle, Longstreet had graduated near the bottom of his class (54th out of 56), and was well down on the "Conduct Roll" in his final year, 160th out of 217. The two apparently hit it off well from the very start, drawn to each other not only by their similar records at the Academy, but also reputedly by their respect for Robert E. Lee under whom Longstreet had served in Mexico.

In addition to his duties with Company I, Lazelle was assigned as Acting Assistant Quartermaster and Acting Assistant Chief of Staff of the regiment, duties apparently given to the junior-most lieutenant in the regiment. In his capacity as Acting Assistant Quartermaster, he wrote all contracts and bids for corn, firewood, hay, and other supplies procured locally.[11]

Lazelle also had a good deal in common with his company first lieutenant, Thomas K. Jackson, of South Carolina. Jackson had finished 25th out of 35 in the Class of 1848 at the Academy and had completed his final year with 169 demerits, standing 207th out of 230 cadets. Like Longstreet, he was a Southerner at heart and would resign his commission in 1861 to join the Confederate Army. Nonetheless, while at Fort Bliss, the two lieutenants shared a love of hunting, at which they and other officers spent many of their free hours, both for pleasure and to obtain fresh meat for the men of their company.

Along with several local citizens in 1857, Lazelle and Jackson formed a "Falcon Club" whose members competed regularly, with each shooter "selecting his own field for the day." Whoever brought down the greatest number of birds over an eight-hour period would win a ten dollar prize. According to one of the participants, hundreds of birds could be seen during the day "floating at random through the balmy air, like so many 'flakes' of cotton batting being wafted hither and thither by the gentle zephyrs that are continually in motion during the greater part of the year in that delightful and healthful climate."[12]

Jackson and Lazelle tied on the club's first outing, bringing down seven birds each. During the next day's competition, they placed a side bet on who would have the greatest luck, but by that afternoon they had again tied with five birds each. Now came the "tug of war," with the contestants widely separated from each other. Lieutenant Jackson had exhausted his supply of "patching," the cotton cloth wrapped around the ball in the "muzzle-loader" rifles they were using, and was forced to cut off a piece of his shirt tail which happened to have his name written in indelible ink.

This accident would prove to be fortuitous. Jackson hit his sixth bird with his final, jerry-rigged shot, but it continued flying far enough to reach the opposite bank of the Rio Grande before it came down. He watched it closely to see where the bird landed but was unable to make it across the river to retrieve his trophy. As luck would have it, the bird landed in a vineyard where a local worker found it, discovered a piece of patching in the bullet hole, recognized Jackson's name, and "hastened to the quarters of the club with the bird and to get his curiosity satisfied about the 'rag' with Jackson's name on it." Lazelle, who had refused to believe Jackson's account of his sixth bird, was forced to concede the contest.[13]

LAZELLE AND KIT CARSON

Sometime before the creation of the Falcon Club, and not long after his arrival on post, Lazelle had been dispatched on another type of hunting expedition—most likely as a training mission for him—with the now-famed Indian scout, Kit Carson. At the time, Carson had settled in Taos, New Mexico, north of Santa Fe, was engaged in ranching, and had been appointed Federal Indian Agent for northern New Mexico. In this capacity, he worked closely with Army units operating between El Paso and Santa Fe.

Carson often went out on scouting missions "in company with a single companion, being furnished by the government with a horse, arms and provisions." On one such mission, accompanied by Lazelle, "a fresh recruit from West Point," Carson experienced "one of the most perilous adventures of his whole frontier life."[14]

About three days into a week-long scout chasing a band of Apaches, and about 100 miles from Santa Fe, "in one of the most desolate and inhospitable parts of that uninviting wilderness," Lazelle and Carson came upon a band of "antelope" near a small spring, shot and killed one, and made camp. After a sumptuous supper, they secured their horses, and settled in for the night. Carson, fully aware that they could have visitors, proposed to the green lieutenant that they alternate standing guard every two hours since "they would probably witness the most stirring scenes of their lives toward the middle of the night, as that seemed to be a great resort for ferocious beasts for water and prey."[15]

Lazelle readily agreed to stand first watch, in great anticipation of something turning up. They had quartered the antelope and tied the best portions to a large cactus. This, Carson knew, would undoubtedly attract "the ravenous jaguar and panther, and perhaps the proud monarch of these canyons, the grizzly." Unfortunately, Lazelle, exhausted from twelve hours of riding with no food or water, and with his belly now full, soon fell fast asleep on first watch.

Their horses were the first to give the alarm as "hungry jaguars" approached the camp. Carson, "accustomed to sleep with one eye open," sprang into action firing his carbine and scaring the cats away. He became alarmed, however, when, upon looking around, he couldn't find his companion. To his surprise, the lieutenant had managed to climb a tall cactus from which he called out "Kit, did you kill anything?" Carson told him "no," but that he'd better come down because he also could hear a grizzly bear approaching.

Carson's rifle shots frightened all of the other animals away, but not the grizzly, which soon appeared "to the great consternation of the lieutenant." Kit later said that he felt "crowded closer" to the canyon wall than ever before, as the two of them stood their ground between their horses and the on-rushing bear. Lazelle jumped down and as the bear approached took the first shot, wounding it in the forearm. Carson took the second shot, into the other forearm, and crippled the beast sufficiently that they could finish him off.[16]

The Bonneville Campaign

By the time of Lazelle's first major operation against the Apaches in the spring of 1857, his experience with Carson and other short scouting missions with his company had removed the green edges and prepared him for an extended, two-column expedition known as "the Bonneville campaign." Long a "thorn in the side of the American and Mexican people," the Apaches of southwestern New Mexico and Texas Territory had been raiding settlements along the Rio Grande valley and into Mexico. Under the overall command of Benjamin L. E. Bonneville, Colonel of the 3rd Infantry Regiment and Acting Commander of the Department of New Mexico—a "hulking bag of wind in his dotage," known as "Old Bonny Clabber" to his subordinates—the Army launched a major, two-column campaign against them.[17] The northern column, commanded by Col. William Wing Loring, departed from Santa Fe moving southward. A detachment from Loring's command intercepted a band of Apaches on May 24, recovering about 1,000 stolen sheep, killing seven Indians, and capturing nine.[18]

The southern column, under command of Lt. Col. Dixon S. Miles, with about 400 men including Lazelle's company, set out to the west from Fort Thorn, New Mexico. It eventually encountered and fought Apache warriors on the Gila River in southwestern New Mexico. Twenty-four Indians, including five women, were killed, and 27 were captured.[19]

In a journal covering the period April 20 through June 13, 1857, Lazelle recounted his experiences and thoughts during the expedition. Although the journal ends before the Gila River action, it reflects much of his youthful character and fascination with the country in which he was operating, as well as his approach to military service and life on the western frontier. His penmanship is bold and clear, the mark of both his schooling and, perhaps, a growing level of self-confidence born of his recent experience. The journal clearly is the work of an educated and well-read romantic, replete with biblical references and literary quotations from the likes of Socrates, Lord Byron, Sir Francis Bacon, Goethe, Alexander Pope, Nathaniel Hawthorne, Charles Dickens, and Aesop's Fables. Indeed, in his final entry on June 13, he states that from then on he would "commence my journal in *rhyme*, so 'adios' to plain statements." Unfortunately, the rest of the journal is lost.[20]

The early portions are largely descriptive—sometimes ebullient, other times almost desperate—of the countryside and conditions on the trail, especially their impact on him personally and his health. Toward the end, however, a slightly more seasoned commentator starts to focus on tactical and operational issues. Lazelle begins:

> At the request of a dearly loved friend [we do not know to whom he refers], whose simplest wish is, and ever will be with me, a guiding point, these pages are rewritten. Hastily penned at first, during the leisure moments of an arduous and severe campaign, after the fatiguing marches of wearisome and sultry days. ... On the 20th day of April 1857, in obedience to orders previously received from Department Head Quarters, I left Fort Bliss, Texas, for the Gila river, attached as junior officer to a portion of Company K, Rgt. of Mounted Rifles. The Troops from that Post consisted of forty men from the company and Rgt. above mentioned under the command of Lieut. Du-Bois, and eighty Infantrymen, portions of Companies I and B, 8th Infantry. ... I, as part of the Staff, had the privilege (?) of riding in front as a sort of accompanying orderly to a simple, but kind old fellow named Simonson [a major], whom superior age (thanks to the wonderfully wise organization of our Army) had unfortunately placed in command. ... He is of great physical energy, but deficient in reason, cramped in his understanding, and warped in his judgment.

Here, Lazelle was acting in the fine tradition of junior officers—especially West Point graduates—who often had little good to say about their most immediate senior officers. However, his comments also reflected the frustration common among his contemporaries with a promotion system that rewarded seniority over competence. With no formal officer evaluation system, an officer of limited or no leadership ability could remain in his position and the service for years. Maj. John Simonson, for example, was not a West Point graduate. Rather, he had volunteered during the War of 1812, served in the war with Mexico, and had been promoted to major in September 1853.[21]

2nd Lt. John Van Deusen Du Bois, Company K of the 1st Regiment of Mounted Riflemen at Fort Bliss, a fellow 1855 graduate of West Point, also penned a journal covering the period of 1857 through 1861. His journal and letters enrich, and in many ways mirror, Lazelle's observations, especially in his disdain for incompetent senior officers. On April 29, 1857, Du Bois described the composition and character of the column with a level of disgust similar to that of his fellow lieutenant:

> The order of march is out. We start tomorrow. Our Rifle Company forms the advance guard, another the rear guard. The infantry companies do nothing.[22] The orders in reference to the mounted companies are very funny. Just think of being ordered to wash your horses' backs every night. They are only given "for grandma," however, and the cavalry officers will not probably be interfered with except to get double duty. Our column [has a total of] ten officers and 270 men—not a very large force to attack a nation who have been variously estimated to be able to bring into the field from eight to 2,000 warriors; but I predict now that we will never see an Indian except accident or some outside pressure forces our commandante to act. [23]

While both Lazelle and Du Bois had disparaging words for their more senior officers, Henry held one of the officers' wives in very high esteem, bordering on infatuation.

> April 29th—Received from the Major [Major Brice at Fort Bliss] a package from Mrs. Brice. It was a tobacco bag which she had promised to make for me, together with a handkerchief which she had not promised. So thoughtful she is, so kind, always giving, always pleasantly surprising. One of God's own handiworks as a woman, combining with a really brilliant intellect, enlarged understanding and power of thought which would do infinite credit to any man. ... May God grant me such a wife, beautiful in mind and person, and such as Heaven first formed her sex.

Was Mrs. Brice the "dearly beloved friend" to whom he seemed to dedicate his journal? Or was it some other lady? Whoever it was, she was significant enough in his life that he resolved, on her behalf, to give up drinking liquor and to stop swearing. Despite the frequent entreaties of his fellow officers to join them in drink, he was steadfast in refusing: "Thank Heaven for the influence of one dear, true, and esteemed friend, the dearest on earth, who had thus far restrained and saved me." The vow to avoid swearing apparently was more difficult to uphold. Early in the journal he confesses that he had "cursed but 800 times during the day, the average number being 500, per day."

In any case, Mrs. Brice and her gift meant so much to him that, ten days later, when he was in camp and discovered the tobacco pouch was missing at one a.m., he leapt on his horse and retraced his steps, in the middle of the night, alone and with no regard for his personal safety, in hopes of finding it. In his own words:

> Here I discovered, much to my vexation, that I had lost my tobacco bag (which had hung upon the pommel of my saddle) by the foolish frightened antics of my horse during the march. I determined immediately to go back, until it should be found, however far, and accordingly started alone. I had not occasion for quite so much courage and determination, however, for after a careful search of only about two miles, I discovered it lying on the trail. ... The morning of May the 10th found me benumbed, stiff and lame, in all my limbs, and with the most excruciating pain in the thighs and back.

Throughout his journal, Lazelle commented—richly but usually not positively—on the places he saw and the people he encountered, from American immigrants heading west, to local Indian and Mexican populations, and the Spanish who had first colonized the area.

> April 23rd—Passed through the miserably wretched villages of "Cruzes" and "Don Anna," which are Mexican collections of hovels, in perfect keeping, with the squalid filth and poverty, and accord

> well with the indolent worthlessness of their population, and the cursing idleness and superstition, of the whole degraded Mexican, or rather, Spanish, Mexico—Indian—Negro race—Incapable of further advancement and totally unconscious of their present degraded position.
>
> A succession of high toned, patriotic, energetic, indomitable and powerfully intellectual rulers, despotic in character, acting, with a singleness of purpose, and unity of object, through a series of generations, is the only form of government which in my judgment can save poor Mexico, develop her resources, elevate the minds and bring forth the energies of her people, so totally unfitted are they for self government, or control in its most limited form. This might relieve her from the terrible thralldom, which is imposed upon her people by superstition, ignorance, bigotry and falsehood, which is pressed upon her by the iron rule of the Roman Church—God forbid that those whom I may love, should be Roman-Catholics.[24]

Largely reflecting the racial prejudices of contemporary, middle-class, white New Englanders, Lazelle also may well have been influenced by the views of the Know-Nothings, a prominent political party during the late 1840s and the early 1850s whose adherents strongly opposed immigrants, especially followers of the Catholic Church. Many Protestants were wary of Catholics, and the Know-Nothings feared that they were more loyal to the Pope than to the United States. More radical members of the Know-Nothing Party believed that the Catholics intended to take over the country.[25]

While he had little positive to say about either the local Mexican population or the Catholic Church, the young lieutenant had a great deal of respect for the Indians that Bonneville's expedition was pursuing. Of them he wrote:

> April 30th—A pretty caricature of the respect which our crafty foe, who is moving, warily, but constantly, in thieving squads, and flying on wings of the wind, has, of our slow motioned and heavily laden Infantry, toilsomely dragging its lengthy and

> sluggish columns over the burning plains, its troops choking with dust finer than ashes, and its animals suffocating, and dying under their heavy burdens for want of water;—all much to the delight of these light footed, strolling, scattered vagabonds, who mockingly watch us from the mountains above.

Those "crafty" and "scattered vagabonds" struck that night, as reported by Du Bois:

> Last night about 2 o'clock 65 mules were stolen from the fort [Thorn]. Major Simonson & his command with Col. Bonneville had started for the Depot in charge of a large train carrying all our provisions etc. for four months. They could not have been more than a mile from the trail the Indians took with their stolen mules. The thing was the most audacious ever heard of in this country—within a half mile of where the Colonel of the Dept., the Colonel of the southern column, & over 500 men able to start in half an hour, were sleeping. The mules were considered so safe that the herders had all gone to sleep.[26]

Lazelle's journal continued:

> May 5th—At two p.m. we crossed the boundary line, which is marked by monuments, between the U. States and Mexico. The trail now took a direction toward Hannas [Janos], a town about sixty miles within the boundary of Mexico, and where we knew that Indian thieves were harboured, and a portion of the very tribe, with whom we were at war, were protected. At about 4 p.m. we arrived at "Lake Betra," which is about six miles from the line, in the territory of Mexico. We had traveled since leaving El Paso upwards of one hundred and seventy miles, and upon reaching this point, it was in a direct line, but sixty miles distant. The animals were crazy for water and in spite of all efforts of the men, many of them rushed into it, with packs and furniture on.

> May 7th–10th—The estimated distance marched today was thirty two miles, and the whole of it was dull, stupid, and devoid of incidents, if I might, [*sic*] except that of killing a rattle snake with my saber, the second one which I had seen during the Scout. ... The

> nights are excessively cold, freezing water to the depth of half an inch and for want of a sufficiency of blankets I have suffered much. ... We traveled until one o'clock on Sunday morning, following the trail by the light of a faded young moon. ... We then stopped, and picketing our animals and establishing guards, lay down to rest a few hours in a sort of ravine. ... We found here [in the afternoon at a water hole] a party of emigrants making their way to San Antonio Texas, from California. A harder looking, rougher, or more weather beaten assembly of white people I never saw. ... Here also we found the mail wagon from Teuson [Tucson] near Sonora, en route to Fort Thorn with its party in camp.

For the next several days, the column continued to march generally eastward toward the Burro mountains and then northeast toward St. Lucia Spring and eventually to the Gila River Depot, near the modern-day town of Cliff, New Mexico, which they reached on May 17. On the 15th, Lieutenant Du Bois had noted that the Indians were burning the countryside as they moved, in all likelihood to deprive the Federal troops of grass for their horses: "The Indians have burned the entire country about the Depot [Gila River Depot]. All the grass is gone. Fires are burning on every side of us. Each hill-top is a pillar of flame." [27]

Lazelle continued, noting on May 18 that after a month on the trail they had not even seen an Indian:

> nor heard of one having been seen, by any one else, since starting: with the exception of one whom our valiant commander—Col. Bonneville—thinks that he saw, from the window of his ambulance [wagon], while he was coming out here from Fort Thorn. ... Col. Loring's advanced guard of the "Northern Column" consisting of a company of Spies and guides, composed of rangers, woodsmen, and Navajo Indians, arrived last night, and report that Col. Loring's Column is one days march from the Depot [Gila]... His column has shared the same fate as our own, having seen no Indians, and with the exception of the severe sickness of Lieut. Tracy, have met with nothing unpleasant.

On May 21, Lazelle's column started out once again, this time "in hot search of a sheep trail," somewhere in the vicinity or leading out of the San Jacinto mountains, "made by some sheep, it is conjectured, which were stolen from a town called Secoro [Socorro] and distant from here about two hundred miles. These sheep were stolen about six weeks ago, and the 'trail' which our column of three hundred and fifty men !!!! are ordered to search for is reported by the guides to be two weeks old!!"

After four days, having traveled some 16 miles from "San Jacinto Springs" to the area of the "Copper Mines," they finally encountered a band of Apaches, or so they thought. Temporarily in command of the column's rear guard, Lazelle suddenly spied a lone rider dashing toward him at full speed. Reflecting his strong Protestant upbringing and familiarity with both the New and Old Testaments, Lazelle likened the unrushing soldier to "Jehu the son of Nimshi, for he rode furiously."[28]

> When near enough to be heard, he yelled out almost frantically, "The Indians are right ahead of the column, Sir!" This was indeed thrilling news, and threw my naturally excitable nerves into such a state of commotion, that I might fairly assert that my brains soon began to boil.

Lazelle quickly sent a non-commissioned officer and men back to bring up a disabled mule lagging behind, moved his rear-guard company up to join the column, and "tried to be cool, and perhaps outwardly was so." Convinced that they were about to engage a large number of Indians, there was great excitement throughout the Federal column, with "the commander galloping about and bawling for the bugler; men running; and 'Greasers' shouting in Spanish to the d---ed mules which I had to stay with, and protect."

Suddenly, however, all was quiet, "as silent as the grave at the head of the column, and this quiet feeling of mortifying disgust, gradually extended down through it to myself," as each man in succession learned that the hostiles they were about to encounter were actually a party of friendly Navaho scouts belonging to Colonel Loring's advance guard.

> And still worse than this. This small band of fifteen Indians, had, in the company of a few of the Guides of his column, on the day previous, met and defeated, the whole party of the famous Sheep Thieves, which "old Bonneville" had in his wisdom, sent two columns of eight hundred men against! All of the party with two exceptions were either killed or taken prisoners, we were told, and Col. Loring had, they said, gotten nearly all of the Sheep —about four hundred.

On May 28, Bonneville's Indian guides found yet another "fresh trail" of fifteen Indians leading in the direction of the Chiricahua Mountains. Lazelle jotted in his journal: "I suppose that a detachment will be sent to pursue it at least as far as the 'San Jacinto' Mountains about forty miles. I wish I could go, for I am sick of this 'Mutton track.'" Two days later, the track having gone cold, they returned to Gila Depot. They remained near the Depot, at "Camp Union," with orders to prepare to move out on June 10—with 30 days' rations per man—for the "Coyotero" country and then on to the "Chiricowa" (Chiricahua) Mountains en route back to Fort Thorne.

According to Du Bois's diary, the columns, with Bonneville and his staff in the lead, meandered to and fro for about two weeks, following the advice of Indian guides and scouts who, Du Bois was convinced, had no idea where they were going and "who together comprise as scoundrelly a set of cowards as ever betrayed Indians." On June 25, however, they came upon an Indian camp occupied by women and children whom they captured. The men were off hunting. With their captives, they continued on to the Gila Valley where, on June 27, they came upon a band of Coyotero and Mogollon Apaches and engaged the Indians, killing 24, taking 267 captive, and rescuing "a Mexican boy from captivity." During this engagement, "Lieut. Henry M. Lazelle, Eighth Infantry, was specially mentioned as charging with the Dragoons, shooting one Indian and cutting down another."[29]

Du Bois was thoroughly disgusted with the treatment of the captives, but complained only to his journal:

> One fine looking Indian brave was captured & by Col. Bonneville's desire, or express command, was taken out with his hands tied & shot like a dog by a Pueblo Indian [one of their guides]—not thirty yards from camp. May God grant that Indian fighting may never make me a brute or harden me so that I can act the coward in this way. Humanity, honor, a soldier's pride, every feeling of good in me was & is shocked by this one act. ...
>
> Some afflicting scenes occurred during the fight. An Indian was wounded and his wife carried him in her arms to the chaparral & was covering him with brush when the troops came upon them & killed them both. ...
>
> Walked over the field today. It was a sad sight. I could not avoid asking myself why we had killed these poor harmless savages. It is not pretended that they ever did any harm to us, never coming to the Rio Grande, & robbing only from the Mexicans of Sonora.[30]

The command returned to Gila River Depot on July 12, and on July 23 Du Bois received orders to accompany Colonel Miles back to Fort Thorne. He had nothing positive to say about either Bonneville or his grand "expedition."

> Col. Bonneville is still confident that the expedition is not broken up. He prates highly about another scout in the Chiricuhua Mts., but we younger subs know from the best authority that Gen. Garland [Department Commander] had not been in command one day before the scout was virtually ordered to be immediately put in irons & sent back home. It is lamentable that so good intentioned an old man [Bonneville] should be so weak on Indian affairs.[31]

Lessons Learned

Toward the end of his journal entries, well before the Gila Valley incident, Lazelle, the West Point graduate who did so poorly in his military subjects, finally focused on some operational and leadership lessons that could be gleaned from the Bonneville expedition. Later in his career, he would write extensively on military operations and tactics. This ill-conceived and—in his view—poorly implemented campaign already was shaping his views and would later influence his planning as a regimental commander during the Civil War.

With just a year's experience "on the ground," he was beginning to develop a more informed and mature appreciation for military operations and some of the key principles of warfare that had been addressed, as theory, at the Academy. In looking back on the early stages of the Bonneville operation, he focused on three key operational principles: "*Despatch* [promptness] in organization and arrangements, *Secrecy* [or surprise], and *Celerity* [speed] of movement," and the means by which these ends should be achieved. He gave Bonneville failing marks on all three.

Turning first to *secrecy*, Lazelle chastised Bonneville for signaling his intent months before launching the expedition "in the shape of a proclamation, beginning with the celebrated words, in worthy imitation, to a certain degree, of a nobler document. 'It becomes necessary to chastise the Indians.'" Forewarned by Bonneville's proclamation, the tribes against whom it stated the expedition was to be directed fled their normal hunting grounds, "leaving but a few light-footed warriors to provide for their decrepit old men and women," and setting fire to the prairie to impede the Army's advance.

The sin of giving advance warning to the Indians was, in Lazelle's view, compounded by the length of time it took to prepare the operation, a period of several months to concentrate troops and supplies. Characterizing the latter, as "slow, cumbrous and bungling," Lazelle was particularly derisive of Bonneville's "indulgence of a gastronomical propensity to collect an immense abundance of provisions." In his view, the time devoted to concentrating at the Gila River Depot, "long before they were needed, the most enormous supplies of stores entirely to the exclusion of pack-animals, for their transportation, for the troops who were to go into the field," was simply inexcusable.

Finally, he chastised Bonneville and his staff for failing to plan for and acquire a sufficient number of pack animals, which had a significant impact on *rapidity of movement,* which, he noted was particularly important "where operations are those of pursuit." At times, the cavalry was unable to pursue small bands of Indians because there were no replacements for horses lost. Moreover, the entire column was forced to stand down for two weeks due to "the state of health of our pack animals, the condition of their backs, etc., as there were none to replace the unserviceable animals."

Concluding his evaluation, Lazelle noted that as they were "trailing over a portion of country, by tedious marches and slowly moving columns, the Indians (if there were any) stepped aside, allowed us to pass quietly and then did as they pleased, as before." He conceded that the expedition did recover a number of stolen sheep and that "possibly a moral effect has been created," but he believed it "more probable that contempt, has, ere this, taken its place in the minds of the Indians. ... And if eventually, we are successful in this new territory where our coming has not been heralded, it will be the success of chance, not of intention and design."

While much of Lazelle's journal documented the daily pace and progress of military operations during the three-month period it covered, it also provided rich commentary on the rigors and occasional joys of life on the trail from the perspective of an as-yet unseasoned junior officer. It also reflected a certain sense of humor over the conditions of trail life, as well as, at times, a degree of melancholy. In short, he displayed a complicated personality with mood swings that would be seen again late in life.

> April 25th—It was very fortunate for us that the wind blew so severely today, or we should have been literally devoured by gnats, whose bites are very severe and much more unpleasant than those of their agreeable fellow-labourers, the mesquitoes [*sic*]. As it was, the moment that the wind lulled as it did, about four in the evening, they came in great clouds, causing every thing living, with a tender skin, either to suffer or run. ...
>
> May 5th—At "twilight" several of the officers, myself among the number, went down to the lake, half a mile to bathe. It had a steep bluff bank of limestone at this point, and the water was dark, but clear, and very deep. ... I stood upon the bank a moment, to feast my senses upon the delightful plunge, and then went headlong down, down into its cool fathomless depths. ... Its waters are warm, and delicious, and it was with the greatest reluctance, that I left it, not knowing when I should have the pleasure of feeling the surface of my own body again, so unsightly had we become from the accumulations of dusty marches.
>
> May 23rd—We have, today, traveled sixteen miles from the "San Jacinto springs," our last place of encampment, to The Copper Mines, so termed. The country passed through has indeed been beautiful. ... Clear lovely streams, of cold and pure, mountain water, dance merrily along, following the windings and turning of wooded glades, which are filled with an abundance of game inviting the hunter to the sport; while the air is swelling with the sounds of animal life many varieties of the feathered world.

During the rest of 1857 and 1858, Lazelle remained at Fort Bliss, assigned largely to garrison duties, but also engaging in short "scouts" and "escort" missions in Texas and New Mexico. For example, in August 1857, Lt. Du Bois, then still at Fort Thorn, wrote that on the evening of August 9, he, Dr. Haden, [Assistant Surgeon], and Lazelle "left Fort Thorn, crossed the river by moonlight & slept for three hours on the opposite bank. Breakfasted at Dona Ana and dined at Fort Fillmore—fifty miles in sixteen hours. Capt. Rhett gave us his ambulance & the next day we arrived at Fort Bliss."[32]

Again in November, Indians stole 25 mules from the fort. A local newspaper correspondent reported that Lazelle and Du Bois had gone in pursuit "with a company of Rifles and Infantry, but I am fearful they will not be able to overtake them." [33]

On April 24, 1858, Lazelle left Fort Bliss in command of an escort to Fort Davis, returning on May 8. Fort Davis had been established in 1854 and through the 1850s was garrisoned by Lt. Col. Washington Seawell and five to six companies of the 8th. The purpose of Lazelle's escort mission was not reported, but Fort Davis sat astride the main road between El Paso and San Antonio, which had seen an upsurge in travel following the discovery of gold in California. This coincided with an increase in Comanche, Kiowa, and Apache raids into Mexico from their tribal homelands to the north, incursions that threatened the security of emigrants, mail carriers and merchants along the road.

Lazelle's route of march probably would have taken him along the "Lower Road," which became the "Butterfield Overland Mail" route in 1859: from El Paso to Fort Quitman and on to Fort Davis through Eagle Springs, Van Horn Wells, El Muerto, and Barrel Springs.

Again, on October 2, 1858, Lazelle left post with his company "on a scout," arriving on October 31 at Agua Escondido, leaving the following day, and arriving at Fort Defiance, New Mexico, where the company remained through Thanksgiving and Christmas. From October 19 to November 18, Lazelle's company participated in a "campaign of 30 days in the enemy's country," as part of the second column of a "Navajo Expedition," commanded by 3rd Infantry Maj. Electus Backus. In all, the command covered 349 miles, killing four Indians and wounding four. Thirty-five Navajo horses were captured along with 278 goats and 22 sheep. Lazelle was among those singled out for commendation. [34]

On December 28, Company I, along with Company K, left Fort Defiance on a scout. Lazelle's Company I arrived at Camp Comfort on December 31, departed on New Years Day 1859, marched 400 miles, and arrived at Fort Bliss on January 18. [35]

Dog Canyon

Lazelle's second major operation against the Mescalero Apaches, one that would have a profound impact on his health for the rest of his life, took place later that month. Earlier in January, Mescaleros had raided a ranch near San Elizario, New Mexico, stealing several head of cattle and three mules. According to his official account, Lazelle took 30 infantry and mounted riflemen from Fort Bliss, chasing the cattle-stealing Indians for seven days before closing with them in Dog Canyon.[36]

Dog Canyon, a secluded, forested canyon on the north end of what is now Guadalupe Mountains National Park, lies at an elevation of 6,300 feet and is far removed from civilization even today. At the edge of the wilderness boundary of the park, it is some 110 miles east of El Paso and 12 miles south of Alamogordo, New Mexico. According to local lore, prehistoric Indians walked the trails of Dog Canyon more than 6,000 years ago, hunting animals, gathering plants, chipping stones into knives, scrapers, drills, and hammers, and leaving behind cylindrical holes created by the repeated grinding of seeds, such as those of the mesquite bush. These holes are known as mortars or "Indian wells" because they collect rainwater and a number of them can be found in the park. [37]

Archeologists believe the Apaches arrived in the area in the fifteenth century and took advantage of the reliable water source and lush vegetation found in the box canyon. Several Apache campsites lay within Dog Canyon. European settlers began moving into Apache territory in the mid-1800s. Apache raiding of wagon trains and homesteads prompted the U.S. Cavalry to take action. The Apache used the steep terrain of Dog Canyon as a stronghold in several skirmishes with the cavalry.

Lazelle's detachment left Fort Bliss January 31 and headed toward San Elizario, to follow the trail of the stolen cattle. Several citizens of that town, a guide, and an interpreter joined them. The Indians had a three-day head start, and their trail headed westward for about 30 miles, then turned toward the south and southwest over mountainous and rocky terrain for another 20 miles. Lazelle and his men turned northeast and after about 30 miles came upon a point of rocks "where the Indians, on their way to the settlements, had left some of their number to collect water in skins for whatever stock they might bring on their return."[38] The following days, the trail continued to lead generally toward the Sacramento Mountains and Dog Canyon.

After seven days and some 165 miles, the detachment made it to the entrance of the canyon. Following the Indians for two-and-a-half miles along a rock-strewn trail that was sometimes so narrow that men and horses could barely squeeze by in single file, the soldiers eventually emerged onto a broad flat plain. Lazelle described it as "surrounded by high and apparently inaccessible mountains ... interspersed with deep rocky ravines and steep hills, of various heights, with ragged stony sides." There, they encountered 30 armed Apaches, "painted and stripped," who raised a white flag and asked to talk.

The talks went nowhere. The Indians maintained that a few "bad men" had come with cattle, killed two of them, and then had been driven off by the Indians. Lazelle insisted on continuing to follow the trail to its end and moved forward another half mile, "the Indians constantly retreating from point to point, yet hovering on our flanks and in front of us." Finally, Lazelle and his men reached the edge of an encampment where the Indians insisted they advance no further. They now declared that all the cattle had been killed. Lazelle insisted on seeing the evidence:

> Upon this they sent one of their number to show us the spot, and there, laid upon the ground drying, were eleven perfectly green beef hides and two mule hides. The offal and refuse of the cattle were strewn about, and everything indicated that they had been recently slain.[39]

A quick search of the temporary encampment with "a large number of temporary and very recently erected lodges" indicated to Lazelle that "more than three Indians" had been involved and that all the women and children had been moved out. Determining also that "the head and flanks of our column, then in single file, were perfectly surrounded by them, while they were effectively sheltered by the rocks and possessed many natural advantages of position," Lazelle decided to move back down the trail about two miles and set up camp for the night.

Before daybreak, he took 22 men and moved "stealthily" back up the canyon to the Indian camp, only to discover they had moved even further up the canyon, had been reinforced, and now controlled the high ground. Lazelle forced the Indians from several positions but soon found he and his soldiers were facing high ground upon which was "a large collection of Indians, and their number was rapidly increasing."

> We attempted to gain its summit by advancing as skirmishers, and had nearly done so when about twenty Indians made a charge upon the center of our line, advancing very closely; for a moment considerable confusion prevailed. A steady fire, however, from the men who remained in their places soon checked the advance of the Indians, but they however were supported by others in their rear, and by considerable parties who were extending themselves to every available point on our flanks; we maintained our position for a considerable time, frequently advancing, when the Indians invariably gave way, but only to take up positions perhaps still more advantageous on our flanks or in the rear of us.[40]

One of Lazelle's men later wrote to a journalist friend, describing the intensity of the fighting. His account was reported in the national press:

> In the midst of the hardest fighting, I was taking aim over a rock, when a ball struck it not three inches from my face, and went whizzing by my ear so close that I felt the heat. I, however, picked off my Indian, and was taking another position, when a musket ball struck my forage cap and sent it whirling a rod [five yards] behind me. The concussion stunned me somewhat, but left no mark. While in the act of reloading, a large ball struck me in the right arm, midway between the shoulder and elbow, entering the fleshy part, just grazing the bone, but not breaking it. The rammer was jarred out of my hand, and fell at my feet. But I kept an eye on the Indian who shot me, finished loading, took deliberate aim,

> and sent a ball through his breast. He sprang high in the air, gave an unearthly yell, and fell dead.
>
> I then fell back and crept behind a large rock, where I performed a surgical operation on myself by pulling some cotton wadding out of my jacket, and stopping up the ball holes on each side of my arm. I then took my handkerchief off of my left arm, and tied it over the wound. While thus engaged, our men had begun to retreat down the hill, and I found myself midway between friends and foes. However, I loaded my rifle and gave the red devils a parting shot before following my comrades.[41]

Realizing his group of soldiers was greatly outnumbered and in danger of being outflanked, Lazelle ordered a withdrawal, taking the wounded with them. Private Newman had suffered a fractured thighbone, and four men had to carry him out. As Private Ogden helped transport Newman, he was shot and killed. Then Newman was shot in the head and killed, and Private Stampler was hit and died. As the retreat continued, several others were wounded, including Lazelle who was shot in the chest. According to the official battle account, published in November 1859 by Army Headquarters in New York, "Lieut. Lazelle gallantly continued in the action after he had been shot through the lungs, and until he had entirely extricated his command." [42]

Lazelle then sent a mounted trooper ahead to Fort Fillmore for assistance, and the detachment was met at San Agustin Springs by Maj. William Gordon and soldiers from the 3rd Infantry on the evening of the next day. In addition to the three killed, another seven men were injured, five of them, including Lazelle, severely. In his official report, he estimated the total Indian strength at 50 to 60. They were known to have lost nine killed and, he believed, a larger number were wounded.

Du Bois, learning of the incident at Dog Canyon while on extended duty at Fort Union, noted that there was "much indignation in the regiment at an infantry officer [Lazelle] having been sent in command [of a Mounted Rifles detachment] while the Rifle officer remained at post." However, on April 5, 1859, he also expressed relief that "Lazelle has recovered. I received a letter from him a few days ago. I am rejoiced to hear it. Two [West Point] classmates killed in one year is enough blood for us to offer in these insignificant Indian wars."[43]

Photo 3. Dog Canyon

Courtesy Andrew Stuart, *Hudspeth County Herald*

Photo 4. Lt. Henry M. Lazelle (circa 1861)

Courtesy Fort Bliss and Old Ironsides Museum

It took some time for Lazelle to recover sufficiently from his gunshot wound to rejoin his troops. He returned to Fort Bliss on February 11 but remained on "sick" status at the post through March and April. In early March, his company departed Fort Bliss on escort duty with the U.S. and Texas Boundary Survey. He remained behind until April 26, when he left Fort Bliss to join his company on the Rio Pecos.

In July 1859, Lazelle and his troops made a reconnaissance from Anton Chico eastward to the Pecos River and southward along its right bank as far as Fort Lancaster, Texas. The command, which was accompanied by a train of 22 wagons, carrying 57,000 pounds of freight, was back in camp July 8. The expedition had been on the march for 21 days, covering a distance of 279 miles. "Lazelle found the route along the Pecos excellent, being plentifully supplied with water and good grass. By using this road, Lazelle pointed out, about 200 miles would be saved between Santa Fe and Fort Lancaster."[44]

Still suffering the effects of his wounds from Dog Canyon, Lazelle was back on leave status in November for two months, although Du Bois ran into him at Fort Craig, New Mexico, in late December. In May 1860, Lazelle and ten men from Company I were detached from Fort Bliss to Fort Fillmore, New Mexico, to form part of the garrison there. While at Fort Fillmore, still the junior-most officer, he was also appointed Acting Assistant Quartermaster and Acting Assistant Chief of Staff. In September 1860, he was "Commanding Post" at Fort Fillmore, and on October 15, he and his detachment of men from Company I departed the post, returning to Fort Bliss on October 20.[45]

TROUBLES BREWING

While Lazelle and his fellow officers and men were chasing Indians around the countryside in Texas and New Mexico, the Union was rapidly coming apart back east. On November 6, 1860, Abraham Lincoln was elected President. Six weeks later, South Carolina seceded from the

Union, and by Lincoln's inauguration on March 4, 1861, seven states had passed secession ordinances. Texas was among them, having declared its secession February 1, 1861, and joined the Confederacy March 2. By then, the seceded states had held a convention in Montgomery, Alabama, adopted a Constitution, and elected Jefferson Davis president.

There was strong pro-Southern sentiment among wealthy white landholders in New Mexico Territory, which then included much of Arizona. And since the Gadsden Purchase of 1853, there had been strong Southern interest in creating a slave state or two out of New Mexico Territory. The future of New Mexico's status was still being debated when Texas joined the Confederacy, and New Mexico remained "contested" territory throughout the war, garrisoned by Union Army troops who defended Albuquerque and Santa Fe against Confederate forays out of Texas.

In February 1861 at Fort Union, New Mexico, Lazelle's West Point classmate John Du Bois recorded in his diary that "nothing but secession talked of at the post," noting that only he and two other officers were "thoroughly loyal." With a sense of irony, he reported that the soldiers were "loyal" to the Union, and that most of the officers who opted to join the Confederacy themselves and "all of the West Pointers except [Major James] Longstreet" urged their soldiers to "remain true [to the Union]."[46]

In a twist of fate that would have a significant impact on Henry Lazelle's future assignments, Fort Bliss was shifted from the Army's Department of New Mexco to the Department of Texas in December 1860. Had Lazelle remained at Fort Fillmore, in the Department of New Mexico, instead of returning to Fort Bliss, in October 1860, his career might have taken a very different track than that which lay immediately ahead and which, in turn, shaped his next 35 years as an Army officer.

Chapter 3

From Prisoner of War to Prisoner Exchange Agent

During the Bonneville Campaign in 1857, Lazelle had foreseen conflict between North and South over the issue of slavery. Like most New Englanders, he found slavery morally repugnant, writing in his journal in May 1857 that it exposed Americans to "the scorn and ridicule of enlightened Europe, and the pity of a civilized world." Moreover, he had little, if any, respect for those who would fight over it: "Shame be on Northern fanatics and Southern madmen, those political fools who stand disputing, and endangering the happiness of millions for the possession of a curse!"[1]

Before the war, Lazelle had written articles about New Mexico for the St. Louis *Missouri Republican* newspaper and the *Merchants Scientific Magazine* in New York City emphasizing "the futility of the doctrine of devoting its territory to Slave labor."[2] Most of all, however, he rued the notion that he, himself, might have to fight over this issue, writing in his journal:

> I sank back in deep disgust as I thought what part I was playing in this mighty but fearful drama;—I for once, wished for that period to come, when swords should be beaten into plough shares and spears into pruning hooks, and when men should learn war no more.

While Lazelle abhorred slavery in the abstract, he still held and expressed views, typical of his times, which today would be considered extremely racist. He saw no redeeming qualities in either native American Indians or in the Mexicans he encountered, referring to the latter at one point in his journal as "dirty, wretched blanketed thieves" and "the most miserable portion of all the lowest most degraded and ignorant races of mankind."

Although he didn't explicitly reveal his opinion of blacks in his journal, he undoubtedly lumped them in with the Indians and Mexicans with whom he came into contact in the Southwest, considering all to be inferior races. He also probably shared the prevalent view of white Northerners that blacks could not and should not be assimilated into white society, and he may well have agreed with those who favored "resettlement" in Africa.

SURRENDER AT SAN LUCAS SPRINGS

In February 1861, with the secession of Texas from the Union, Gen. David E. Twiggs, Commanding General of the Department of Texas and a southern sympathizer, surrendered all Federal posts in Texas to officials of the state Secession Convention. According to the terms of agreement signed by General Twiggs, all troops garrisoned in West Texas, including much of the 8th Infantry, were to march to the Texas coast, where they would be allowed safe passage to the North. On February 18, 1861, Twiggs issued General Order No. 5, implementing this agreement:

> The State of Texas having demanded through its Commissioners, the delivery of military posts and public property within the limits of this command; and the Commanding General desiring to avoid

> even the possibility of a collision between the Federal and State troops; the posts will be evacuated by their garrisons, and these will take up, as soon as the necessary preparations can be made, their line of march out of Texas by way of the coast—marching out with their arms (the light batteries with their guns,) clothing, camp and garrison equipage, quartermaster's stores, subsistence, medical hospital stores, and such means of transportation of every kind, as may be necessary for an efficient and orderly movement of the troops, prepared for attack or defence against aggressions from any source. The troops will carry with them provisions as far as the coast.[3]

On March 31, Bvt. Lt. Col. Isaac V. D. Reeve, post commander, lowered the U.S. flag at Fort Bliss, and he, Lazelle and 134 men marched toward San Antonio. Along the way, troops from Fort Quitman and Fort Davis joined them. Reeve and Lazelle were said to be the only officers at Fort Bliss who remained loyal to the Union.[4]

After the various and scattered garrisons had united and were heading toward San Antonio, with those officers who had not resigned their Federal commissions and joined the Confederate Army, news of the April 12 firing on Fort Sumter in South Carolina reached Texas. State officials abruptly retracted the earlier safe-passage agreement, and nearly 400 officers and men under Reeve's command were forced to surrender to a much larger Texas force near San Lucas Spring, a few miles west of San Antonio.

In a dispatch back to Washington from San Antonio on May 12, Reeve reported that he was encamped near the head of the San Antonio River, awaiting the orders of President Davis, to whom a messenger had been dispatched by the commander of the Texas forces to whom he had surrendered. The officers on duty with the command were Captain Blake, Lieutenants Bliss, Lazelle, Peck, Frank, Van Horn, and W. G. Jones, 8th Infantry; Lieutenant Freedley, 3rd Infantry; and Assistant Surgeon Peters, Medical Department.[5]

According to the 8th Infantry's Lt. Zenas R. Bliss, when the combined command camped along the road to San Antonio near Castroville the evening of May 8, he and a lieutenant from the 3rd Infantry had gone into town. At a beer hall they were told that General Van Dorn, commanding Texas forces, "was on the road from San Antonio with two thousand men and would if possible surprise and attack us that night."[6]

Concerned about the possible attack, the Federal troops, at Bliss's suggestion, lit large camp fires as a ruse and left under the cover of darkness, aiming to reach Adams Hill "where there was a large stone ranch with corral walls, and a fine spring of water, and where we could make a better fight than at any other place on the road." Marching all night, they reached Adams Hill without being discovered. The next morning, however, they were confronted by a large Rebel force of 800 to 1,000 infantry along with cavalry and a battery of six-pounder guns.[7]

After consulting with his fellow officers, Colonel Reeve agreed to surrender and march his troops to the head of the San Pedro, camping there until further arrangements could be made. Upon meeting with General Van Dorn the next morning, the officers learned that the other U.S. troops had "all left the other posts long before we came down. Fort Clark and Fort Duncan had been turned over to the Rebels by orders from the Department Commander, Gen. Twiggs, and all had left the state. ... all troops near San Antonio were ordered to take transportation to the North. Some of them went unmolested by the Rebels."[8]

On Parole

According to Bliss, it was decided that the enlisted men would be placed under Confederate guard at a camp on the Salado River, about six miles east of San Antonio and that the officers would sign a parole but have general supervision of the men. This situation lasted for about a week, until all government property was turned over to an officer of Van Dorn's command. Bliss remained in San Antonio in hotel quarters for several weeks until he signed his parole. He stayed in Texas until he was exchanged in April 1862.

While Bliss, Lazelle, and the other officers were free on parole, Van Dorn had other intentions for the enlisted men being held in San Antonio. Formerly a major with the 2nd U.S. Cavalry, Van Dorn had resigned his commission and accepted appointment as a colonel in the Confederate Army. Charged with establishing a cavalry regiment in Texas, Van Dorn's primary motivation in dealing with the enlisted men of the 8th was to recruit as many of them as possible for service in the Confederate Army. To this end, his subordinate, Lt. Edward Ingraham, formerly of the 1st U.S. Cavalry, offered the men of the 8th and other units "bounties and officers' commissions," as well as their "choice of service branch." Companies were promised that, if they enlisted en masse, they could "keep their officers, or elect new ones."[9]

Ingraham had limited success with the men of the 8th and native-born northerners. Of the 68 recruits listed on his first muster roll at the end of June 1861, 51 were former Federals, but only eight were from the 8th Infantry. Fifteen were southerners. Of the 53 who were not southerners, only 13, including Ingraham, had been born in the North. The rest were natives of Ireland, Germany, England and Scotland.[10]

In his memoir, Bliss noted that a few weeks after they were captured, Lieutenant Lazelle, along with Lieutenant Peters and his wife, "left for Richmond after having signed the parole, and succeeded in getting through the lines and getting North," where they remained on parole, "til long after we were exchanged."[11] Lazelle would later note in a January 1862 request to be "exchanged" for a Confederate prisoner that he had accepted a "much more restricted parole" so he could leave the Confederate States.

In the early months of the Civil War, there was no formal system for the parole or exchange of prisoners (either officers or enlisted men), although the concept and practice of paroling captives on their honor not to fight had been around since before medieval times.[12] Once a "paroled" officer or enlisted man was officially "exchanged" with a prisoner or parolee of the opposing side, he was then free to return to military duty.

During the American Revolution, officers were routinely granted paroles, and both sides granted paroles during the War of 1812. During the Civil War, however, a formal parole and prisoner exchange system was not established until July 1862, with the so-called Dix-Hill Cartel. In the meantime, as with the officers of the 8th Infantry in Texas, commanders in the field both exchanged and paroled captured prisoners under flags of truce.

Reflecting the more rapid promotions common to armies building up in wartime and the abrupt thinning of the ranks as officers left to join the Confederacy, Henry M. Lazelle had been promoted to 1st Lieutenant on April 27, 1861, shortly before the events at San Lucas Spring. Less than two months later, while still on parole, he was promoted to Captain, effective June 11, 1861. Both commissions were signed by President Lincoln.

After the debacle in San Antonio, the 8th Infantry Regiment eventually was reconstituted. By September 1861, it was headquartered at Fort Hamilton, New York Harbor, with elements at Washington, D.C. Six of its company captains and lieutenants were still on parole as "prisoners of war." Lazelle had slowly made his way northward as far as Richmond, Virginia, where he arrived in July. He remained there, stuck by the terms of his parole, ill and in increasingly dire financial straits, for a month.

In a July 30 request to L.P. Walker, the Confederate Secretary of War, Lazelle asked for an extension of his parole to "the limits of the original United States" so he could leave Richmond and travel north, citing his health and personal hardship:

> In this application I beg to call your attention to the fact that I was made a prisoner of war by the simple accident of my position, having been an officer of the regular army stationed in Texas at the time of the stipulations between its Government and General Twiggs; and that a similar parole to that which I now ask has been granted to other officers made prisoners in Texas under similar

> circumstances. For more than five years past, with the exception of the three months I have been held a prisoner, I have been on active duty in that country. My health has been injured from the effects of a wound received in an Indian engagement there, and my present position is rendered more embarrassing by my pecuniary means of support having been exhausted without the possibility of my supplying myself with more.[13]

Washington City

His appeal was successful, and on August 1, 1861, he signed a new and very restrictive parole under which he swore an oath not to "bear arms against the Confederated States, nor exercise any of the functions of my office, under my Commission from the President of the United States, to the prejudice of the Confederated States," until he was released or exchanged. He further vowed that he would not "disclose or make known any information that I may have acquired to the injury of the Confederated States, or of the cause in which they are engaged." In return he was free to go "at large" wherever he saw fit, subject to recall or revocation by the Confederate Secretary of War.[14]

Upon his release, Lazelle made his way first to New York City, where his regiment was headquartered. At the end of the month, he was staying at the Metropolitan Hotel with another Army officer.[15] He remained there through early November. While in New York, Lazelle received orders to serve on a Court Martial, from which he requested relief on the grounds that the terms of his parole prohibited him from performing any military duty.

Sometime in mid- to late-November, while waiting for his exchange and release from parole, and still suffering the ill effects of his battle injuries and trek north from San Antonio, Lazelle left New York to live in Hagerstown, Maryland, with his sister Priscilla. She had divorced Calvin Brooks in June 1860,[16] and later met a Hagerstown banker, Peter Negley. They were married October 9, 1861, in Cambridge, Massachusetts, and settled immediately in Hagerstown, where he was cashier at the Hagerstown Savings Bank. Henry arrived by the end of November and reported his address to the Adjutant General's office December 4, apologizing for a delayed report due to "ill health."

On December 9, Lazelle penned an appeal directly to the Adjutant General asking if, indeed, there might be some civilian position to which he could be appointed, until his formal exchange was completed, so that he could go back to work. Noting that under the terms of his parole he was unable to perform even "minor military duties not directly opposing the enemy" that would place him in the position of a "military substitute" to the enemy's prejudice, he concluded:

> I am exceedingly anxious, Sir, to do something that I need not be longer useless, in the present struggle of the country. And I earnestly ask that I may have your recommendation to be placed in some position where I may perform some duty in a civil capacity, not under my Commission, if, in your opinion, there is no military service not conflicting with my parole to which I may be better assigned.[17]

Apparently, the request for civilian duty fell on deaf ears. In early January 1862, he requested expedited consideration of his exchange with an appropriate Confederate officer on parole. In making his case for early action, he emphasized "in this whole matter I have acted with the sole desire of doing my duty in the best manner, and it is a source of extreme mortification to me that the Department do not consider that this has been accomplished, for I have never turned my face from either duty, or danger, and in this case, have erred on the side of an active desire to perform what I conceived to be demanded."[18]

LAZELLE IN LOVE

As of January 21, 1862, Captain Lazelle, along with fellow 8th Infantry officers Zenas Bliss and J. J. Van Horn, both still waiting in Texas, was on the list of proposed exchanges submitted by Maj. Gen. John Wool at Fort Monroe to the Army's Adjutant General in Washington.[19] In the meantime, however, Lazelle's earnest desires for duty were distracted somewhat by his introduction to Ann Rebecca Gooding Hollingsworth, the twenty-five-year-old daughter of a prominent Hagerstown banking family. She was a descendent of Zebulon Hollingsworth, who accompanied William Penn to the "new world," and her grandfather, Colonel Samuel Hollingsworth, was a founder and original director of the Baltimore Equitable Society, Maryland's first fire insurance company.

Henry was introduced to Rebecca, as she was called, through his brother-in-law Peter Negley's banking and society connections. By this time, the lady to whom his journal had been dedicated was but a distant memory, and Rebecca seemed a good catch. She came from a prominent family, with social status and wealth that must have impressed the former orphan from a farming family of limited means. With long, flowing brown hair, a pleasant face, tiny waist and hourglass figure, she was attractive enough that Henry at first wondered why she had not already been taken. And most importantly, she had inherited enough from her mother's side of the family that she was independent financially.

For Miss Hollingsworth, the twenty-nine-year-old Army captain cut a dashing figure in his crisp dress uniform, despite the lingering effects of his wounds. Indeed, his stories of tracking and fighting Apaches and of his arduous travel north from Texas, only enhanced the image and stature of this tall, handsome man with steel blue eyes. And so, the two began seeing each other regularly.

Each month from February through May, Henry dutifully reported his Hagerstown address to the Adjutant General's office and continued to press for duty. Writing the Adjutant General in April, he asked to be exchanged with a Confederate officer whose capture had come to his attention: Capt. Thomas K. Jackson, West Point Class of 1844, former first lieutenant of Company I, 8th Infantry, and Henry's best friend at Fort Bliss. At the time of his capture at Fort Donelson, Tennessee, Jackson was serving as Chief Commissary Officer on Confederate General Buckner's division staff. If an exchange was not possible, could he be put on duty with the Coast Survey[20] or "in some capacity elsewhere not conflicting with my parole." Neither option was to be obtained.

As the spring of 1862 turned to early summer, the war ground on across both the eastern and western theaters—New Orleans, Front Royal, Winchester, Memphis, and "The Seven Days" in southern Virginia—and still there was no call to duty for Henry Lazelle. On June 11, he again wrote the Adjutant General: "I have the honor respectfully to apply for permission to go on duty with the paroled troops taken in Texas and New Mexico, or to be placed on duty with the Coastal Survey, or such other duty as in the opinion of the Department may be proposed assigned me under my parole, until such time as I may be exchanged."[21]

This time there was good news. On June 13, 1862, Lazelle was appointed Assistant Commissary General of Prisoners of War and ordered to report for duty in New York City.[22] Apparently, the Adjutant General's office had decided that this assignment would not be a violation of his parole. Despite his long struggle north and persistent pleas for speedy action, his exchange was not formalized until October, five months after Bliss, who had remained passively in Texas.

Commissary General of Prisoners of War

The War Department had selected Lt. Col. William Hoffman, an 1829 West Point graduate, as Commissary General of Prisoners, headquartered in New York City, in October 1861. Operating under the Quartermaster General, he initially had responsibility for overseeing the handling and treatment of Confederate prisoners of war. In July 1862, the War Department established the Office of the Commissary General of Prisoners as an independent agency, with Hoffman reporting directly to Secretary of War Edwin Stanton.

Hoffman and Lazelle had close connections. Hoffman had been appointed lieutenant colonel (second in command) of the 8th Infantry Regiment in October 1860 and was among those surrendered and paroled at San Antonio in May 1861. Whether Hoffman used this connection to obtain Lazelle's services, or Lazelle used his past connection with Hoffman to finally obtain an assignment, is not known. Whichever was the case, Lazelle departed Hagerstown in June and reported for duty in New York City.

The principal functions of the Office of the Commissary General of Prisoners included conducting business with Confederate authorities concerning U.S. prisoners of war, maintaining parole camps in which Federal (enlisted) prisoners of war released by the Confederacy were confined pending a prisoner-of-war exchange, and supervising Confederate prisoners of war and civilians interned in U.S. prisons and prison camps.[23]

As an Assistant Commissary General, Lazelle inspected military prisons and parole camps, including a camp for paroled Union enlisted men in Annapolis, Maryland, and acted as Federal Agent for the exchange in Vicksburg, Mississippi, of some 15,000 Confederate troops held in "western" prisons for Union troops held in the South.[24] His inspection trips to the parole camp at Annapolis in March and April 1863, enabled him to make brief visits to Hagerstown to see Rebecca, to whom he was now engaged.

Lazelle's official reports to Hoffman included detailed assessments of the facilities and living conditions in existing prison camps as well as the suitability of other Union camps to serve as prison compounds. For example, his report dated June 25, 1862, on a visit to permanent camps at Albany, Utica, Rochester and Elmira, New York, and to Army barracks at Buffalo, to "ascertain their capacity for quartering troops," included detailed descriptions and drawings of the camps and their facilities. His tutoring in drawing by James Whistler undoubtedly enhanced the precision and clarity of the graphics in his reports.

Camp Chase

In another report, dated July 13, 1862, from Columbus, Ohio, Lazelle expressed concern regarding some of the "political" and other prisoners being held at Camp Chase, just outside the city: "I have the official records of a number of prisoners sent here by him [Maj. Darr, Provost Marshal of the Mountain Department], seven of which state that the prisoner is charged with 'doing nothing.' One was taken from the almshouse where he had been nine years; another was a lunatic when arrested and is charged with being a lunatic. Many others have been sent here under equally slight charges. ... I believe it cannot be your desire that this camp should be filled to overflowing with political prisoners (made by half depopulating a section of the country where inhabitants are often compelled to expressions of apparent sympathy) arrested on frivolous charges."

Camp Chase, originally constructed as a recruitment and training center for the Union Army, would turn out to become one of the more notorious Union prison camps. During 1861 and early 1862, most of the prisoners were from Kentucky and western Virginia, having been arrested for their disloyal political sentiments. At one point during 1863, more than 8,000 men were housed there. Living conditions for prisoners were harsh, and the large number of men in close quarters led to outbreaks of disease. During the winter of 1863-1864, for example, hundreds of prisoners died of smallpox.[25]

After he returned to Camp Chase in early August 1862, Lazelle detailed a number of serious charges against Capt. Benjamin P. Walker, the Assistant Commissary of Subsistence at the camp, including "continued absence without leave from his post, inefficiency or unfaithfulness in receiving from the contractors and issuing to the troops inferior provisions, charging to the Department the expense of issuing the rations and the wastage which occurred, and in unnecessarily keeping on hand large quantities of provisions at the risk of the government." These charges were sufficient to have Walker cashiered from the Army by order of the President.[26]

Lazelle's report and charges were controversial. Walker appealed his dismissal, and on December 1, the Army Judge Advocate General (JAG) decided in his favor. In his ruling, the JAG largely condemned—and refuted point-by-point—Lazelle's charges, noting in passing that he seemed to have based them on "a very cursory and superficial examination." The report went on to conclude that it was "but charitable to infer from the mistakes he [Lazelle] made that he accepted as true complaints and hearsay, which reached him, without giving himself the trouble of scrutinizing them and ascertaining whether they were true or false."[27]

Beyond his initial report and the JAG's decision, Lazelle's side of the story was not published. It is reasonable to assume, however, that relations between the two captains were cold from the start. Walker, from Indiana, was not a West Point graduate but rather had volunteered for service. He was appointed a Commissary of Subsistence, essentially a camp procurement officer, with the rank of captain, in September 1861.[28] Lazelle likely held him in contempt—a volunteer rather than a Regular Army officer, of the same grade and drawing the same pay, but with no real military experience, and living in rather comfortable circumstances. Little wonder that he jumped on anything negative, both observed and alleged.

Lazelle also had to deal with more mundane matters, including economizing measures. In a late July 1862 memorandum to Capt. H. W. Freedley, 3rd Infantry, at Camp Butler in Springfield, Illinois, Lazelle ordered him, among other things, to purchase "six Farmer's boilers, barrel sizes (40 gallons), of the new pattern. These are completely enveloped by the fire and set down into the heat as far as the upper flange in a similar manner that the heater of a common glue pot receives the inner vessel of fluid." By using these, Captain Feedley was told, Colonel Hoffman expected him to achieve an "economy of fuel."

VICKSBURG

By far, Lazelle's most significant and challenging mission during his tour of duty with Hoffman was orchestrating the delivery and exchange of thousands of Confederate prisoners at Vicksburg, Mississippi.

On July 22, 1862, Maj. Gen. John A. Dix, commander of the Union Army's Department of Virginia, and Confederate Maj. Gen. D. H. Hill concluded an agreement for the general exchange of prisoners between the Union and Confederate armies. This agreement, which became known as the Dix-Hill Cartel, established a scale of equivalents to manage the exchange of military officers and enlisted personnel. For example, a colonel would exchange for 15 privates and a major for eight, while personnel of equal ranks would transfer man for man. It also designated two locations for the exchanges to occur, one at A. M. Aiken's Landing below Dutch Gap on the James River south of Richmond, Virginia, and the other at Vicksburg. Each government would appoint an agent to handle the exchange and parole of prisoners. The agreement also allowed the exchange or parole of captives between the commanders of two opposing forces.[29]

In the first week of August, the cartel's newly appointed agents, Confederate Col. Robert Ould and Union Brig. Gen. Lorenzo Thomas, conducted the first official prisoner exchange under the agreement's terms with a transfer of 3,021 Union personnel for 3,000 Confederates at Aiken's Landing.

On August 21, Lazelle, then on inspection duty in Indianapolis, Indiana, was appointed "Agent for the Exchange of Prisoners of War at or near Vicksburg, Mississippi," subject to future exchange.[30] In his instructions to Lazelle, Colonel Hoffman ordered the transfer of 12,000 Confederate prisoners from prison camps at Camp Chase, Sandusky Depot, Camp Douglas, Camp Butler and the Military Prison at Allen, Illinois. They would first be moved to Cairo, Illinois, then turned over to Lazelle and transported down the Mississippi River "under flag of truce" by a convoy of steamboats, and with an escort of guards, to Vicksburg.[31]

This transfer was fraught with challenges—mostly logistical—at the very outset. In a telegram to the Adjutant General dated August 26, for example, Lazelle reported that there was only one gunboat available in Cairo to escort three transports from there to Helena, Arkansas, where he would pick up a second gunboat. He estimated it would take eighteen days before he could return to Cairo with the gunboats to pick up and escort the remaining prisoner transports. Moreover, the local commander, Brigadier General Tuttle, estimated an expense of $250 to house and care for the prisoners awaiting transport.

Lazelle was instructed by Washington the following day to continue as ordered: "The movement of the Prisoners cannot be stopped. Proceed with those you have with the Gunboat Eastport. Ask the Naval Commander to immediately send other gunboats to Cairo to convoy the other transports. You need not go back to Cairo for the others."[32]

On August 28, Lazelle and Commodore C.H. Davis, Commanding Naval Forces in Western Waters, agreed on a set of instructions for the boats making up the transport convoy and its escorts. The vessels would keep together, with the gunboat *Eastport* in the lead and the armed ram *Queen of the West* bringing up the rear. Underway from Cairo on different boats, Lazelle and Davis communicated via written messages.[33]

On August 29, Lazelle informed Davis that the transports had only enough coal to reach Memphis and that he assumed Davis would authorize them to take on more at Memphis. Four days later in Memphis, Davis informed Lazelle there was less coal than anticipated and the transports would have to supplement it with wood from piles along the river. On September 3, he informed Lazelle that Gen. William T. Sherman had agreed that it would be unwise to further deplete Navy coal stocks.

On September 12, Lazelle reported to the Adjutant General that he had arrived near Vicksburg on September 10, with four transports and

3,200 prisoners on board, "except for a number not exceeding 20 privates who escaped at Memphis through the gross negligence of the guard of one of the boats while the boat was receiving coal." Four days later, he queried the Adjutant General regarding the disposition of weapons (side arms, swords and knives) taken from prisoners at Camp Morton in Indianapolis. Apparently they had been told that the weapons would be returned to them when they were exchanged. Lazelle had a list of weapons that included names of their owners, but the weapons had not been sent from Camp Morton.

That same day, Lazelle exchanged letters with Lt. Col. A. Bakley on board the steamer *Morton* (one of the additional transports coming from Cairo), in essence about who was "in charge" of the operation:

> My orders from the War Department are that prisoners will be forwarded to Vicksburg, and reported to me, and that when I think proper to dispense with the services of the Guards (to which you belong) I shall order them to their respective stations. I still expect you, Colonel, to report to me officially, your arrival with the prisoners of war of the transports: if you deem that your rank forbids you to do so in person you can, of course, do so by letter. And it would be quite as agreeable to me that you should adopt the latter course. When done, I will give to you the necessary instructions, as I am required to do, relative to your return and the Guards.

Apparently the two officers resolved their "command" issues. On September 18, Lazelle informed Bakley that he had released the guards to return to their stations and directed one of the transports to remain with him (he was on the gunboat *Lexington*) without either prisoners or guards, to await the arrival of additional prisoners for exchange.

This was not to be the only time a question of command authority would arise. It would recur several times later in Lazelle's career, not always to his benefit. Indeed, it would, one day, force his departure from West Point, as Commandant of Cadets, a year short of tour.

After the prisoner exchange was completed, Lazelle returned to Cairo. On October 6, he reported in a letter to the Adjutant General that he had delivered for exchange in Vicksburg a total of 15,260 Confederate prisoners, including 1,159 commissioned officers. In return, he received and transported to Cairo, 586 Union prisoners, including 36 officers. It is not clear why there was such a large difference in the numbers exchanged, although later exchanges suggest that balance sheets were kept. An article in *The Baltimore Sun* in November 1862, covering an exchange that month, indicated that it resulted in a "balance due" to the Union of some 6,000 privates.[34]

Seeking a Volunteer Command

Almost from his first day in Union territory, hoping that his exchange would be quickly affected, Captain Lazelle had been seeking a volunteer command or duty on the Adjutant General's staff. Sometime in January or February 1862, he had reconnected with Col. John T. Sprague, a fellow 8th Infantry officer who also had been caught up in the "Twiggs surrender" but became New York State's Adjutant General after he was paroled.

In January 1861, after an extended leave of absence from the 8th, Sprague had been ordered back to Texas. Upon his arrival in San Antonio in March, he was prevented from rejoining his regiment at Fort Bliss and was arrested by a Committee of Public Safety. On April 23, Sprague was paroled by Confederate authorities and left Texas for New York. There, he became a mustering and disbursing officer in Albany and soon thereafter Adjutant General of the state, with a rank of brigadier general. He held this post until 1865.[35]

In an early February 1862 letter to Sprague, Lazelle had recounted "a very satisfactory interview" with a Lieutenant Colonel Hall at Fort Marcy regarding a potential assignment in command of a regiment. At the time, Sprague was organizing volunteer units in New York, including what would come to be known as Sprague's Light Cavalry and ultimately consolidated with several other partially completed regiments into the 16th New York Cavalry. Lazelle reported that Hall was looking for a Regular Army officer to command this particular regiment, because it would "give it a tone and standing, and enable it to procure facilities, and to be provided for in a manner, not so often witnessed in regiments with volunteer commanders." In this case, Lieutenant Colonel Hall was expressing a view, held correctly by many during the Civil War, that units commanded by experienced career officers were much more effective than those led by volunteers.[36]

Covering His Bets

While he was being considered for regimental command in the New York volunteers, Lazelle also had been working his Washington connections to secure a staff position as an Assistant Adjutant General (AG) of the Army. Indeed, while considering him for regimental commander, his old friend Sprague also wrote on his behalf to Secretary of War Stanton, noting that "I have been associated with him professionally some years, and can bear testimony to his ability and zeal in all his duties, and most respectfully ask, that he may be appointed if a vacancy exists, or should one exist."[37]

Other proponents of his request for consideration for a staff position included Henry Wilson, U.S. Senator from Massachusetts; Governor John A. Andrews of Massachusetts; Maj. Gen. George Sykes, requesting that Lazelle be appointed Assistant Inspector General of the Fifth Army Corps which he commanded; and Maj. Gen. Gordon Granger, Commander of the Army of Kentucky. Both Sykes and Granger had served with Lazelle on the frontier prior to the war.

Granger, an 1845 West Point graduate and New Yorker who fought with Winfield Scott during the Mexican-American War and served in the West before the Civil War, endorsed Lazelle's request in a May 1863 letter to Senator Wilson. Characterizing Lazelle as "one of the most accomplished & energetic officers in the service," Granger assured Wilson that Lazelle, who had "already distinguished himself in the service of our country and was severely wounded," could be counted on to "strike heavy blows against the Cursed Rebellion."[38]

General Sykes, then commanding the Fifth Army Corps and in camp at Beverly Ford near Brandy Station in northern Virginia, wrote Lazelle on August 13 that he had written to the Secretary of War requesting Lazelle's assignment, not in the Adjutant General's Office, but rather as Assistant Inspector General of the Corps. However he reminded Lazelle that since he was only "temporarily" in command of the Corps, his wish was "not law," and that Lazelle should "back the appointment by any influence you can bring to bear."[39]

Lazelle quickly forwarded the Sykes letter to a friend in the Adjutant General's office asking him to do what he could to move it along. The request made its way through the system to General Meade, Commanding the Army of the Potomac, who sent it to the Inspector General for an opinion.

The Inspector General recommended against Lazelle's appointment on the grounds that he had no proven qualifications or experience as a staff inspector and that there were other officers on the Fifth Corps staff who did. Thus, he suggested, "that the officer herein nominated be first called to act, and when he shall have given evidence of fitness for the position, then to be placed here." General Sykes was duly informed, and Lazelle's bid for that particular job came to an abrupt end.[40]

Lt. Col. Isaac Reeve, his former 8th Infantry commander, then stationed in New York City where he headed up the Army's Mustering Office, also offered his support to Lazelle's quest for a staff position, writing in May that their "long and intimate service" together in the far west "enables me to state that I know of no one better fitted for the position, or any one who better deserves such advancement."[41] Alas, it was not in the cards.

SEEKING PROMOTION

At the same time he was lobbying for a staff position, Lazelle also was attempting to use his political contacts, including Charles Sumner, senator from Massachusetts and chairman of the Foreign Relations Committee, to obtain a promotion to major. His principle concern was that the period during which he was a prisoner and on parole was not being counted as "service time." Thus, there were a number of officers ahead of him on the captains' list who were actually junior to him in terms of date of commissioning. This situation had placed him at a significant disadvantage, since seniority, rather than formal performance evaluations—which didn't exist in those days—drove promotions. His appeal to his home state senator raised this issue, maintaining that:

> at present, my name appears on the roll of Infantry Captains of the Regular Army, seventy files [his emphasis] below where I have every reason to believe it would have been, had I not at the time been a prisoner of war in Texas. It is true, Sir, this is an accident of war; but an honorable accident, and unavoidable on the part of an officer who is and has been devoted to his profession, should not in my opinion debar him from just promotion, not divert that promotion to others.[42]

Unfortunately, whatever support his pleas received from Senator Sumner and others was to no avail. Lazelle would remain a Regular Army captain, still officially assigned to the 8th Infantry, while serving as a Volunteer colonel in 1863 and 1864, and then back with his regiment for reconstruction duties in the South and well into the early 1870s back out West and in the Dakotas. His promotion to major would not come until late in 1874, nearly 14 years after being promoted to captain.

It was not unusual that Lazelle would use his military and political connections in seeking both a position on the promotion list and favorable assignments. Indeed, in an era when there was no formal officer evaluation system, and when promotions were based largely on seniority, it was common practice to use whatever connections one had, both military mentors and political figures. Even Zenas Bliss, who wrote at the end of the Civil War that he had refused to "seek advancement over my comrades through outside or political influence," ended up engaging in the very practice he claimed to detest. By 1893, Bliss was actively lobbying both old military friends and politicians for promotion to brigadier general, and again in 1897 for promotion to major general.[43]

Chapter 4

Defending Washington

On September 17, 1863, Lazelle wrote to Lieutenant Colonel Sprague, still New York State Adjutant General, accepting his appointment as colonel of the 16th New York Cavalry, noting that he assumed command "with hesitancy and a want of confidence—the Cavalry is not my forte—even if I have one." Nonetheless, he assured Sprague that, as long as he was in command, he would do his duty "so far as I know and can learn it to the extent of my capacity—and I hope you will not have occasion to feel that your confidence in me has been misplaced even though you ask me to manage men, and horses" (his emphasis).

Lazelle was not necessarily displaying a false sense of modesty. He had ranked near the bottom of his class in cavalry tactics and horsemanship when he graduated from West Point, and his name had been absent on the list of graduates "especially recommended for promotion in the mounted corps." With somewhat limited "combat experience," mostly chasing Indians, and little direct familiarity with the complexities of managing and leading a regiment, much less a newly formed one with raw recruits and inexperienced company officers, he must have known he faced some major leadership challenges.

At the same time, it was clear he was more than pleased to be leaving Colonel Hoffman and the Office of the Commissary General of Prisoners, as he wrote to Sprague:

> I cannot say how glad I am to be removed from the command of an officer, who is selfish and ungenerous in the extreme; and who has never failed to absorb my individuality whenever it suited his interest, so to put me forward as the scapegoat of his own official blunders. Such a man is, and has been, Col. Hoffman. But he cannot say that I have not ever been faithful and attentive notwithstanding this.[1]

In his journal while in Texas, Lazelle had penned many disparaging words regarding a number of his peers and superiors, but those were private thoughts. His letter to Sprague, on the other hand, was formal correspondence that could find its way into the official record. At the least, he was risking embarrassment; at the worst, formal rebuke. Such was his dislike of Hoffman.

By the fall of 1863, Lazelle and Ann Rebecca Hollingsworth had set a wedding date, and on September 23, while in Hagerstown visiting his fiancée's family, he again wrote to Sprague, requesting a delay in reporting to his regiment. Citing official Army policy that he could not be officially mustered in as Colonel, or receive a colonel's pay, until the regiment was filled to its minimum required strength, he also pleaded on a more personal basis[2]:

> Again, I have a confidential reason to offer. I am engaged to be married. The lady resides here. For the last year and a half I have been here but a very few days before this visit and I very much desire dear Col that I may be permitted [a delay of] a couple of months or so. Of course, I make this request on the supposition that I would be of but little service to the Regt until I could be "mustered in" and exercise full command of it; and I do so knowing and desiring that your official considerations should be first—for I am ready and anxious, as I ever shall be, to do my whole duty to the State of New York as well as to the Whole Country.

> But I have spoken fully and freely to you, as a friend, and as my Comdg Officer, both, knowing that you will fully appreciate my position at present, and the position in which I would be placed if ordered now to duty. I have not accepted to be an ornamental officer, but a useful one. But yet for the present for reasons stated, unless you deem my services indispensable I would rather have my orders postponed.[3]

Lazelle was given a month's reprieve and was officially mustered in on October 23, 1863.

Sprague's Light Cavalry

What began as Sprague's Light Cavalry and eventually emerged as the 16th New York Cavalry—an amalgamation of three partially filled regiments—was a troubled organization from the start. Plagued by early desertions, criminal behavior, and weak officers, it would quickly gain a reputation among senior officers as the least reliable and capable of the three cavalry regiments charged with supporting the defenses of Washington in northern Virginia.

In January 1863, prior to Lazelle's appointment, Spencer H. Olmstead had received authority to recruit the Sprague Cavalry in New York State, named in honor of New York's Adjutant General. During the spring and summer of 1863, recruiting broadsides for the regiment were printed in New York City, showing a body of uniformed Union cavalry with drawn sabers attacking a battery of Confederate cannon. The posters proclaimed in large letters, "Now is the Time to Join the Best Corps in the Field," a slogan that was certainly questionable.

Companies for the regiment were recruited primarily in Plattsburgh, but it eventually drew volunteers from Syracuse, Massena, Mooers, Champlain, Troy, Buffalo, and New York City as well. Advertisements placed in local papers offered "extraordinary inducements" for recruits to take part in a "great national drama," including a state bounty of $75 and a U. S. bounty (enlistment bonus) of $25, along with one month's pay in advance. If potential volunteers needed further inducements, recruiting broadsides suggested they should enlist:

> Because you are at once into the service, with pay, rations, and relief for your families. Because you will have the best Horse and Arms, and wear the Handsomest Dress in the Army. Because, upon being discharged, you receive another Bounty of $75. Because you would like to see Richmond and the Elephant,[4] and be commanded by tried and capable officers. Because there is no use hanging around home ignobly, when Capt. McPherson is ready to take you to see the "Great Show" on the banks of the Rappahannock and Rio Grande [*sic*] Rivers. Now is your chance to change this Check for $175 and Clothing at the Show Tent in front of the Court House, Rochester, N.Y. [5]

Despite assurances of "Highest Bounties paid Promptly" and barracks that were the "finest and most comfortable in the State" with "neat rooms, well warmed, properly lighted, and good clean beds furnished to all Recruits immediately upon their arrival," the process of filling out the regiment was not without difficulties and controversy, which were duly reported in local newspapers.

Under the headline, "Important Military Arrest," in May 1863, the *New York Times* reported that John Abendorff, one of the new regiment's captains, had been arrested for conspiring to form a "band of guerrillas" who, once armed and equipped, aimed to embark upon a "career of robbery and bloodshed indiscriminately on friend or foe." Abendorff had been discovered communicating in cypher with his co-conspirator, Sergeant Buckler, at the regimental camp in Plattsburgh. Both were arrested and sent to Fort Lafayette, and those about to join them were under house arrest in Plattsburgh.[6]

A month later, the press was again reporting troubles with the cavalry, this time a near mutiny at the Plattsburgh camp. According to the report, some 400 to 500 new recruits had been ordered to prepare to move to

Harrisburg, but "a portion of the battalion refused to obey orders until they received their full bounty." Given Plattsburgh's close proximity to Canada and the temptation for men to desert as soon as the bonuses were handed out, regimental officers decided it was prudent to delay the payments and move the men to Harrisburg, well away from the Canadian border. "A flat refusal to march was the result." As a pre-emptive move, New York Governor Seymour ordered 150 men from the 34th New York Infantry, stationed in New York City, to proceed to Plattsburgh "to compel obedience." When the men from the 34th reached Plattsburgh, they "took possession of the cannon on the ground and of all the available arms, and were prepared to make prisoners of all the disaffected before they knew what was going on." Disarmed and faced with troops of the 34th, the new recruits "blustered a little, but finally quietly succumbed; agreed to behave themselves, came down with the detachment, and are now on their way to the seat of war."[7]

The 16th New York Cavalry Emerges

At the same time that Olmstead was recruiting for Sprague's Light Cavalry, Col. W. W. Hammill received authority, on July 27, 1863, to recruit the Washington Light Cavalry; and on July 29, Col. E. Schnepf received authority to reorganize the 20th New York Volunteer Infantry, which had been "discharged by reason of the expiration of its term of service." Neither unit was able to recruit enough men to fill out the required number and strength of companies.[8] As a result, on October 14, 1863, these two were formally consolidated with Sprague's Light Cavalry and renamed the 16th Regiment of Cavalry, with Lazelle as colonel. The regiment's companies were mustered in for three years at Plattsburgh and Staten Island.

From June to October 1863, as the regiment's companies deployed to Washington, D.C., they were assigned to the Independent Cavalry Brigade of Maj. Gen. S. P. Heintzelman's Twenty-second Corps. Command soon passed from Heintzelman to Maj. Gen. Christopher C. Augur, an 1843 graduate of West Point. When Lazelle reported for duty, the Corps was organized into two districts (Washington and Alexandria), each with assigned regiments; a reserve brigade of Pennsylvania infantry; a light artillery command; and the independent cavalry brigade. Throughout its existence, however, the organization, assigned units, and troop strength were constantly changing, as units were pulled off to reinforce other commands in the field.

During the Civil War, the organization and strength of individual units varied greatly in both the Union and Confederate armies. In general, however, Union brigades were made up of two or more regiments. Infantry and cavalry regiments were organized into ten companies and a headquarters. Companies were supposed to have 100 men, but most were rarely at full strength. In the field, ad hoc groupings of several companies often were referred to as "battalions" and commanded by the regiment's lieutenant colonel, major, or sometimes the senior-most captain.

LAZELLE JOINS HIS REGIMENT

Col. H. M. Lazelle, U.S. Volunteers, remained in Hagerstown while the companies of his new regiment completed the mustering-in process. He joined the regiment October 23, 1863, after the last company, Company L, was mustered into Federal service.

During the year and a half that Lazelle had served on staff duty with Colonel Hoffman, Union and Confederate forces had clashed at the Second Battle of Bull Run, at Antietam, and in costly Union defeats at Fredericksburg and Chancellorsville. The tide of war seemed to have turned at Gettysburg and Vicksburg in July 1863, but the South had again prevailed in September at Chickamauga on the Georgia-Tennessee border. Closer to Washington, John Singleton Mosby, a former Virginia lawyer with no military training, and his band of guerrillas, known officially as the 43rd Battalion of Virginia Cavalry, had been harassing Union forces, almost at will, throughout northern Virginia.

Map 3. Northern Virginia: 1863–1864

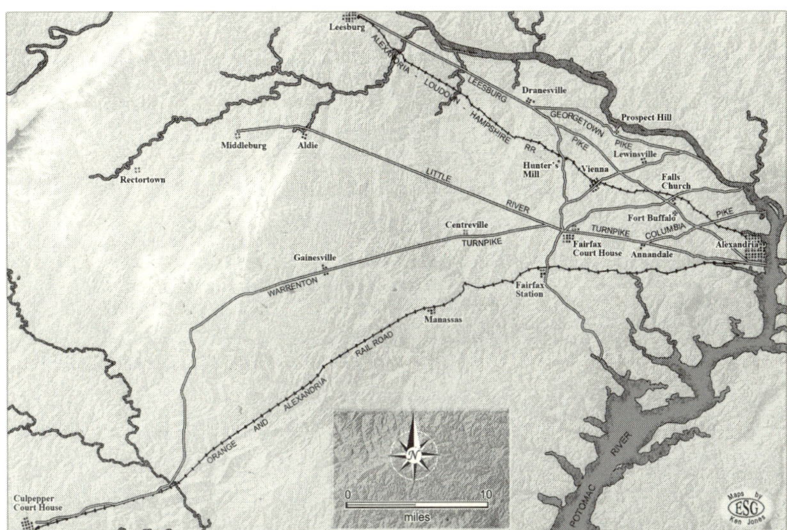

Individual companies of the 16th had already been engaged in action. Several served on patrol duty in the rear of the Army of the Potomac during the Gettysburg Campaign; Company B (mustered into service on June 19, 1863) had been involved in a skirmish at Lewinsville, Virginia in early October, with two enlisted men killed, another two wounded and ten missing; and other elements of the regiment had seen action at Bristow Station, Virginia (no casualties), on October 14. The only other recorded action of elements of the regiment in 1863 was a skirmish near the Blue Ridge Mountains, on November 18.[9]

Destined to Fail?

The circumstances and outcome of the Lewinsville skirmish should have been a red flag for the new regimental commander, particularly regarding the quality and leadership abilities of his cadre of volunteer junior officers. The story of William Jeremiah Keays, the officer in charge on that day in Lewinsville, underscores the operational impact of the lack of training and experience of many of the regiment's lieutenants and captains.

Keays, a Canadian, had moved with his wife and young child to Buffalo, New York, in 1861. Within a year, his wife and two-year-old son had died, and he had been forced by circumstances to place a newborn daughter in the care of a sister in Canada. In June 1863, he joined the 16th N.Y. Cavalry. Although he had no experience or training, he was "a natural leader of men and he was well educated."[10] He was immediately made a lieutenant and an acting captain. This was a recipe for disaster.

On Oct. 2, 1863, Keays, in command of his company, was bivouacked at an outpost at Lewinsville, Virginia, now known as McLean. During the night they were attacked by Confederate soldiers. Twenty men were killed, wounded, or captured. Four of those captured died at the infamous Andersonville prison in Georgia. According to an after-action report, Keays had placed his sentries "so close to his camp that there was insufficient time for them to warn of the attack. He was found responsible for the fiasco ... and was dismissed from the Army on Oct. 13, 1863."[11]

Shortly afterwards, Keays's commanding officer, Major Hazzard, recommended that he be reinstated, noting that his "connection with my Battalion has been flattering to himself and beneficial to his Company. He always has been prompt, thorough and effective, strictly temperate and considered a competent officer and good soldier." On Dec. 31, 1863, Keays was reinstated. [12]

In an ironic twist, Major Hazzard himself would be dismissed "by order of the President" in November 1863, for "habitual intemperance and neglect of duty." Keays, however, remained with the 16th—and was promoted to captain—until it was disbanded at the end of the war.

William Keays exemplified a problem that plagued many volunteer units. In the 16th, few of the company officers had training or experience. Only Lazelle, Col. Nelson Sweitzer, Lazelle's replacement in 1864, and

Lt. Col. George Hollister, who was dismissed for conduct unbecoming an officer and a gentleman in 1864, were West Pointers.

The individual companies of the 16th selected their officers either by popular vote or because of their social status. Most were sent to the line almost immediately after being appointed and had little time or opportunity for training. Instead, expertise and experience were gained on the ground. Many of those who did have experience had served previously as sergeants or enlisted men. A number of the companies were essentially manned and led by amateurs.

As an amalgamation of three partially formed regiments, the 16th also lacked the unit cohesion and personal loyalty (officers to men and men to officers) that was the major strength of most volunteer units recruited from specific geographic areas. With diverse companies, recruited from throughout the state of New York—major cities and smaller towns and villages—the regiment had no real common geographic identity beyond the state of New York.

Lazelle, himself a newly promoted captain in the Regular Army with no experience above the company level, faced the immediate challenge of commanding a regiment that lacked strong company leadership and that was inadequately prepared for the mission given to it. He had not participated in the officer selection process and had no time to observe basic unit training and weed out weak performers. With additional time for training and vetting—particularly at company level, since many of its operations were company-size actions—the regiment might have avoided the problems that would plague it over the next year and a half.

Cavalry Camp at Vienna, Virginia

When Lazelle joined his regiment, it was encamped in Vienna, the terminus of a key rail line from Alexandria. [13] In addition to the 16th New York, the Cavalry Brigade was composed of the 2nd Massachusetts Volunteer Cavalry, commanded by Col. Charles R. Lowell, and the 13th

New York Volunteer Cavalry under Col. Henry S. Gansevoort. Lowell also was formally in command of the brigade, but that responsibility fell to Lazelle when Lowell was with his regiment in the field. In July 1864, Lowell's regiment was transferred to General Sheridan's army in the Shenandoah Valley, and Lazelle took command of the brigade.

According to the 16th's muster rolls and individual returns, the regimental headquarters (and brigade headquarters when Colonel Lazelle was in command) remained at Vienna through at least March 1864. The Alexandria, Loudoun & Hampshire Railroad supplied the brigade with its horses, ammunition, and provisions. The railroad was known by both Union General McDowell and Confederate General Lee to be one of only two strategic routes (the C&O Canal being the other) for any large-scale movement of personnel and supplies westward out of Washington.

Knowing he couldn't hold onto the area at the start of the war, Robert E. Lee, Commander of Virginia Operations, had ordered the destruction of all bridges on the railroad on May 24, 1861, just one day after Virginians voted to secede from the Union. On June 10, Lee had further ordered that all rolling stock be transferred to Confederate rail lines and the road rendered "unserviceable to the enemy." Both the Confederates in the area and neighbors sympathetic to the southern cause had acted quickly on those orders.

Hence, Vienna became a railhead (terminating point) for supplies and munitions from Alexandria through the rest of the war. It not only supplied the encampment in Vienna, but also provided ammunition and provisions to soldiers encamped up and down Washington's outer defensive line, running from Prospect Hill, where today's Madeira School is located off Georgetown Pike, and roughly following Chain Bridge Road through Fairfax Courthouse and down to Fairfax Station.[14]

Several entries in the Brigade's logbook reflect a variety of mundane issues Lazelle had to deal with on a daily basis, in addition to the greater challenges involved in commanding a regiment and fighting a war. On November 22, 1863, he advised Headquarters that it had been reported to him that "Mr. Armstrong, Purveyor, has been selling an intoxicating cordial called 'Ginger Brandy' to enlisted men of the 16th N.Y. Cav." He also noted that beer had been sold to enlisted men at a house occupied by a son of Dr. Hendrick.

A month later, his request "to establish a Post Eating House at Vienna" was denied because private citizens had received permission to keep restaurants and there appeared to be no reason for increasing the number "as long as the prices are kept at a fair standard." So, even in 1863 there was debate over "contracting out" support services.

Photo 5. Cavalry Brigade Officers' Tents, Vienna, Virginia, Winter 1864

Col. and Mrs. Lazelle in front of tent, center

Photo 6. Sprague Cavalry Recruiting Poster

Courtesy of Collections of the Clinton County Historical Association

Photo 7. Cavalry Brigade Encampment, Vienna, Virginia

Photo 8. Cavalry Brigade Encampment, Vienna, Virginia

Photo 9. Freeman Store Hospital—Officers' Quarters, Vienna, Virginia

Courtesy of the Library of Congress

On January 15, 1864, John Mawxhurst, office of the U.S. District Tax Commission, wrote to the Brigade Headquarters at Vienna that an election of delegates to a State Constitutional Convention would be held in Fairfax County on the 21st. Lazelle was asked to provide facilities in Vienna "to bring out the loyal vote." [15]

A Wedding in Hagerstown

On January 19, 1864, Col. Henry M. Lazelle and Ann Rebecca Gooding Hollingsworth were married at St. Johns Episcopal Parish in Hagerstown, Maryland. [16] The Reverend Henry Edwards, who later baptized their eldest son Jacob, officiated, and the wedding was announced in the February 3, 1864, edition of the *Hagerstown Herald and Torch Light* newspaper. On January 26, while still in Hagerstown, the newly wed Lazelle requested permission to delay rejoining his regiment for four days "to attend to important business." A notation on the telegram reads "not granted."[17]

At some point that winter, Rebecca joined her husband in camp at Vienna. A notation on the back of a photo of the two of them standing outside an officer's tent reads "Winter '64 Vienna." According to Charles Humphreys, Chaplain of the 2nd Massachusetts, the chimneys in the officers' tents "were of necessity so shallow that on windy days the smoke would be forced in gusts down the flue into our tents, and I have often been driven out into the storm for self-preservation—though doubtless if I had stayed in I would have been preserved, but only as a smoked and dried specimen of suffering humanity."[18]

Into this rather bleak and basic camp environment the new Mrs. Lazelle arrived. However, she and the colonel apparently had some of the comforts and luxuries she had enjoyed in her parents' Hagerstown home. On December 15, Lazelle had requested "permission to occupy as quarters house in which Mr. Cummins [*sic*: Commins] lives. The house is within the limits of the camp." The request was granted.

In 1856, Moses A. Commins had purchased land west of the railroad line in Vienna, and built a foundry and plow factory near the intersection of today's Lawyers Road and Maple Avenue. As a strong Union supporter, he feared "rebel molestation" after the Battle of Bull Run, and vacated his property, moving first to New York and eventually opening a foundry in Washington, D.C. [19]

The 16th New York occupied the Commins property, cutting down timber to erect buildings and fortifications. In return for the use of the property, Lazelle signed a notice of "safeguard" on November 8, 1863, protecting the property and stating that "all officers and soldiers belonging to the Army of the United States are therefore commanded to respect this safeguard and to afford if necessary protection to the person, family or property of Moses A. Commins as the case may be." In March 1864, Commins signed an "Article of Agreement," that, in part, stated all of his claims for damages were cancelled "except that portion of hard wood timber that actually may have been cut by the 16th N.Y. Vol. Cav.

Regt.—the temporary buildings erected for use of the Regt. to be left on the premises of Commins for his benefit."[20]

Chasing Mosby

While the principal mission of the Independent Cavalry Brigade was to assist in manning the defenses of Washington "south of the Potomac," its regiments and their companies spent much of the time chasing the Confederate "guerrilla" John Singleton Mosby and his band of "rangers." Mosby was a lieutenant colonel in the Confederate Army, and his unit of partisans was subordinate to General J.E.B. Stuart's Cavalry Corps. Focusing much of his activity in 1863 and 1864 on Union forces and supply lines in northern Virginia, Mosby conducted an extended series of harassing attacks on patrols, encampments, and picket posts. In an October 1863 report, he told Stuart his objective was to "detain the troops that are occupying Fairfax, by annoying their communications and preventing them from operating in front." [21]

Following the Union Army's successes at Chattanooga and Knoxville in October and November 1863, both armies went into winter quarters, and neither saw major military action in either the eastern or western theaters. That does not mean, however, that the men defending Washington slept the winter away in camp. On the contrary, the Union cavalrymen in Vienna were almost constantly in the saddle, either reacting to Mosby's raids or scouting throughout northern Virginia.

On December 9, Mosby and 300 of his men attacked a "vedette" (mounted listening post) manned by a corporal and five privates. Two Union men and five horses were captured. Two weeks later, 20 to 30 guerrillas attacked a picket station near Hunter's Mill, wounding two. Shortly afterwards, an officer and escort on the road to Fairfax Court House were fired upon by 10 to 15 men.

On December 28, a detachment from the 13th New York, on a scout from Vienna to Hopewell Gap, skirmished with Mosby, losing one captured.

And in late January, Lowell was ordered to send a squadron of cavalry (two companies) to scour the country from Vienna, through Centreville, to Bull Run bridge in hopes of intercepting rebel cavalry reported to be in the neighborhood of Sangster's Station, near the current town of Clifton. None were found, as Mosby's men usually would slip away rather than fight when the odds were against them.

In early February 1864, General Stuart noted that Mosby's "sleepless vigilance and unceasing activity have done the enemy great damage. He keeps a large force of the enemy's cavalry continually employed in Fairfax in the vain effort to suppress his inroads."[22]

In one such operation, on February 22, according to Mosby's official report, his men ambushed a Union cavalry raiding party composed of troops from both the 2nd Massachusetts and 16th New York. Having received a report that Union cavalry were on a "raiding expedition" in the vicinity of Middleburg, Mosby took about 160 men to intercept them. Reaching Middleburg, he "learned they had come from Vienna and were headed toward Leesburg."

Discovering where they were camped, Mosby moved his troops "out to the pike about 2 miles from Dranesville, at a point offering fine natural advantages for surprising an enemy." Deploying his men so they could attack "their front, flank and rear simultaneously, we awaited the approach of the enemy." The Union cavalry troops were completely surprised, had no time to form a defense, and were "perfectly overwhelmed by the shock of the charge." Fleeing "in every direction in the wildest confusion," they lost, by Mosby's account, "at least 15 killed and a considerable number wounded, besides 70 prisoners in our hands, with all their horses, arms and equipments. Among their killed was a captain commanding. A captain and 2 lieutenants are among the prisoners who belong to the California Battalion [companies of the 2nd manned by California volunteers were known collectively as the California Battalion]. Many of them were also driven into the Potomac."[23]

Lazelle's report of this action confirmed that it, indeed, had been a major rout of Union forces, noting that "Captain Read's command fought well, but were finally driven toward the Potomac, in the vicinity of Muddy Branch [north of Herndon]. ... Our loss was 10 killed and 7 wounded. Among the former, I regret to say, was Captain Read, a brave and noble soldier. About 60 of the detachment are yet unaccounted for."[24]

In response to the attack on Read's troops, Lazelle ordered another large force out to Dranesville on February 25: a total of 525 men, with 200 each from the 2nd Massachusetts and 16th New York, and 125 from the 13th New York. The detachment commander, a major from the 2nd, reported that they "marched up the pike to Dranesville, where a large force of the enemy were said to have been the day before. On the way up one or two rebel cavalrymen were seen on the hills on the right of the pike at Dranesville," but no large party of rebels was found. The force moved on to Belmont, Middleburg, Aldie, Farmwell Station, Gum Spring, and Centreville, picking up various tidbits of information about Mosby's movements before returning to Vienna shortly after midnight. Based on the information they gathered along the way, the detachment commander judged "that Mosby had a force of 300 men, or even more, when he attacked Capt. Read. Many accounts put his force as high as 400 or 500 men." [25]

As emphasized by James Williamson, who served with Mosby, the rebel commander had the classic advantages of the insurgent over the regular military:

> While the enemy were compelled to guard their lines, Mosby had none. When a body of troops was sent in search of him it was a very easy matter to keep out of their way if in heavy force, or cut off and attack any detachments from the main body and harass them on their march; or, by ignoring their presence altogether, compel them to return to protect their own camps. It would have been folly for our little band to have met and fought every force sent against us. The enemy's resources being so much greater than ours, the contest would have been too unequal and it would have

simply been a question of time as to when we would be utterly destroyed or driven out of the country.[26]

As Lazelle wrote his official accounts of embarrassment after embarrassment at the hands of the rebel partisans, he must have thought back to his days on the trail chasing Mescalero Apaches, and his frustrations with Colonel Bonneville's largely feckless operation against them. The glaring reality was that the U.S. Army in 1863 and 1864 had learned few lessons from over a decade of fighting in the West. The operational structure and tactics of the Civil War-era Army were simply ineffective against enemy forces employing non-traditional, asymmetric methods of combat. Lazelle would soon recommend some changes to the defensive scheme in northern Virginia, but they too would turn out to be largely ineffective. He was no better prepared than any of his contemporaries to deal with guerrilla forces.

In March 1864, with his cavalrymen chasing Mosby—or reports of Mosby—throughout northern Virginia's countryside, a frustrated Lazelle sent a short memo to Brig. Gen. L. Thomas, Adjutant General of the Army, renewing his application for appointment as "Assistant Adjutant General in the Regular Army of the United States." It was not to be. Again, vacancies were filled by other officers, and Lazelle remained with the 16th.

The Ormsby Incident

A month earlier, on February 7, the troops of 16th New York and 2nd Massachusetts had been assembled in Vienna to witness the punishment of a Union deserter. On January 24, while on picket duty at Lewinsville, Private William E. Ormsby of Company E, 2nd Massachusetts, had deserted his post—taking with him two horses and six pistols—to join up with Mosby's Rangers. According to one account, Ormsby had "a relationship" with a woman in Aldie who had "close ties to the Confederacy." [27]

Determined to bring Orsmby back, Colonel Lowell sent 60 troops of the 2nd Massachusetts after him. They ran into him on February 5, as he and eight of Mosby's Rangers attacked them at Aldie Mill. Ormsby was the only one captured by the men of his old unit. Lowell quickly convened a court martial and found him guilty of treason the following day. He was sentenced to die by firing squad.

In part to discourage other desertions, Lowell ordered the members of both regiments in Vienna to witness Ormsby's execution. Therefore, at 11 a.m. on Sunday, February 7, the troops of the 16th New York and 2nd Massachusetts were assembled "some distance north of the railroad, behind the old Bowman property" on Ayr Hill, in a formation shaped like a hollow square, with Ormsby and the firing squad in the center.

Samuel J. Corbett, a soldier from the 2nd Massachusetts who witnessed the execution, wrote that "just before his eyes were bandaged, he stepped up before the firing party, placed his hand upon his heart, and said, 'Boys, I hope you will fire well.' He was then seated upon his coffin, his eyes bandaged; the word was given to the firing party, and William E. Ormsby was in eternity." Valorous Dearborn, a colorfully named soldier from the 2nd, noted that Ormsby "bore it bravely. He died at half past twelve with two bullets in his left breast." [28] He was buried on the spot of his execution. [29]

After the war, the federal government contracted a number of men to go out to Union encampments and battle sites and re-inter bodies into the newly established Arlington National Cemetery. As fate would have it, Ormsby's body was among them. His gravestone is located near the Confederate Memorial at grave number 12860. Private Ormsby may well be the only soldier convicted of desertion as well as treason—for firing on his former unit—resting in the nation's most hallowed ground.

While the Ormsby case was unique in its outcome, desertion plagued both armies during the Civil War. No unit, particularly of volunteers, was immune. Indeed, it was not uncommon for a soldier to "desert" for a while, return home to rest up and take care of family affairs, and then return to his old unit or volunteer for a new one. Neither the Union nor Confederate Army had well established, uniform leave policies.

According to unit roster data compiled by the New York State Adjutant General's Office, some 560 enlisted volunteers of the 16th New York had deserted by January 1, 1864. Of these, some 330 were listed as simply "deserted, as shown on descriptive list of deserters, dated January 1, 1864." For another 230, specific dates and, in many cases, locations of desertion were indicated. Many of these desertions—some 160—occurred between June and October 1863 as the regiment was forming and starting to engage in combat operations in northern Virginia. Some deserted more than once:

> COOPER, JAMES—Age, 21 years. Enlisted, May 12, 1863, at Buffalo, N.Y.; mustered in as private, Co. B, May 12, 1863, to serve three years; appointed sergeant, April 30, 1864; deserted, while on pass to Washington, October 24, 1864; returned, December 14, 1864; deserted again, August 12, 1865.

The number of desertions dropped off significantly in 1864 (64 men) and was down to a trickle in 1865 (45 through August).[30]

Officer Dismissals

The dismissal of officers for incompetence, inappropriate behavior, and in some cases cowardice also was relatively common throughout the Civil War, particularly among captains and lieutenants in the volunteer forces. The 16th New York was not necessarily unique among volunteer units. Of its 47 officers "in the field on the first day of Dec., 1863," over a third would be removed from their positions by the end of the war, including a lieutenant colonel, major, assistant surgeon, five captains, and ten lieutenants.

Officer dismissals in the 16th New York reflected problems that plagued units Army-wide, from character flaws and alcoholism to inexperience, cowardice, and dishonesty. In all likelihood, however, the problems that Lazelle faced, more than many regimental commanders, derived from poor discipline and insufficient training, from more senior officers down to green lieutenants.

The one exception was Lt. Col. George S. Hollister, Spencer Olmstead's early replacement as deputy regimental commander. Formerly a captain with the 7th U.S. Infantry, Hollister was dismissed October 7, 1864, for "conduct most disgraceful and unbecoming an officer and gentleman."[31] An 1860 graduate of West Point who had entered the Academy at the age of 16 years and 11 months, he had served in New Mexico prior to the war and was mustered in as Lieutenant Colonel of the 16th New York Cavalry on December 30, 1863. In a March 1866 letter to the Board of Adjudication Regarding Military Service History, Lazelle cited Hollister's "disgusting conduct" as one of the reasons he, Lazelle, resigned his volunteer commission in October 1864. In fact, Hollister "swung both ways," and his "disgusting" behavior included "not only groping women but also creeping into the beds of unwilling junior officers and sergeants." [32]

Other officer dismissals were based on behavior more commonly the result of inexperience, ineptness, or poor character. Major Morris Hazzard, who joined the regiment in June 1863, was dishonorably dismissed "by direction of the President," on November 27, 1863, for "habitual intemperance and neglect of duty." [33] Assistant Surgeon Nelson S. Drake, who was mustered in August 20, 1863, to serve three years, was dismissed May 11, 1864, for "conduct unbecoming an officer and gentleman—messing and drinking with enlisted men." [34]

Henry S. Larned was one of several lieutenants singled out by Lazelle for poor leadership during an action in September 1864 near Culpeper Courthouse. Recommended for summary dismissal by the 22nd Army Corps Chief of Staff, Larned and another lieutenant were sent packing for "leaving their companies while their commands were in front of the enemy, and neglect of duty in not controlling and giving proper orders to their men." [35]

Drunkenness on duty was another common reason for dismissal. 2nd Lt. Annesley B. Smith, who mustered in as a second lieutenant on May 31, 1864, to serve three years, was dishonorably dismissed in July 1864 for "drunkenness on duty, breach of arrest, and attempting to purloin from a Government stable a saddle and bridle" belonging to another officer.[36] Lt. F. A. Bardell was dishonorably dismissed in September 1864 "for contempt of authority in leaving his regiment, visiting Washington City without permission, and drunkenness."[37] Finally, 1st Lt. George H. Grosvenor was dishonorably dismissed September 27, 1864, "for conduct unbecoming an officer and a gentleman, breach of arrest, and obtaining the countersign by surreptitious means," most likely also under the influence. [38]

A Spy Among Us

It was common practice on both sides during the Civil War to employ sympathetic local civilians as spies or scouts to provide intelligence on enemy forces as well as take advantage of their knowledge of the local area, including its geography, people, and resources. One such person was Charles Binns, who had been a member of Mosby's command, but who, "while on a drunken frolic" had "committed some acts of rascality for which Mosby ordered his arrest. In order to escape the punishment he knew he deserved and which he feared Mosby would inflict, he deserted and fled to the Federal camp in Fairfax. Being familiar with the country in the vicinity of Middleburg, he carried the Federal cavalry around to places where he knew they were likely to find Confederate soldiers, particularly those houses where Mosby's men made their homes."[39]

Binns remained in the employ of the Cavalry Brigade for some time. In a report on operations in late November 1863, Colonel Lowell noted that on November 18 a detachment of the 2nd was sent out toward the Blue Ridge mountains to search for guerrillas, using as guides "Yankee Davis and the deserter Binns."[40] On Christmas Day in 1863, a detachment of the 13th New York, "piloted by Charley Binns," went out from Vienna to Leesburg to search houses. [41]

Eventually, the situation for Binns became too hot. Mosby put a price on his head, and in May 1864 he had to flee with a letter in hand from Lazelle, commending him for "arduous and dangerous service always at the peril of life" and giving him safe passage.[42]

During the Civil War, the terms "spy" and "scout" generally were used interchangeably. As a result, it is difficult in reading the record to distinguish between espionage agents, informants, and reconnaissance—the work of such observers as cavalry scouts. By custom and practice in this era, however, "if you were caught in your army's uniform, you were a prisoner of war; if you were in disguise, you were a spy and could be hanged."[43]

The closest to a formal military intelligence organization on the Union side was the "Bureau of Military Information," established in early 1863 by Col. George H. Sharpe, Provost Marshal for General Hooker's Army of the Potomac. Over time, Sharpe developed a comprehensive order-of-battle (listing of organization, location, and strength of units) of the Confederate Army of Northern Virginia. It was so accurate that he boasted he knew the strength of Confederate forces better than Lee.[44]

There also was no centrally directed national civilian intelligence agency during the war, although two detectives—Lafayette C. Baker, who performed counter-intelligence and security missions for Union General Winfield Scott, and Allan Pinkerton, who gathered intelligence for Union General George McClellan—both claimed broader roles. In the months following the end of the war, Pinkerton and Lazelle would briefly cross paths in New Orleans, where Lazelle would serve as an Assistant Provost Marshal.[45]

OPERATIONS INTENSIFY

In late May 1864, Rebecca Lazelle's nephew, George F. French, joined the 16th New York, no doubt through the intervention of his "Uncle Henry." George, the twenty-two-year-old son of Rebecca's older sister Elizabeth and Judge George French of Hagerstown, had enlisted as a private in the 1st Maryland Cavalry in September 1861. In all likelihood, his parents, fearing for his safety as a mere enlisted man, prevailed upon Lazelle to have him transferred. This was accomplished through the Provost Marshal of the Eighth Army Corps, headquartered in Baltimore, and on May 30, young George was mustered in with the 16th New York as a second lieutenant with Company E.

Throughout the summer and fall, Mosby's troops continued to harass Union forces in northern Virginia. Time and again, Union units were outwitted and out-maneuvered by Mosby, largely due to lax operational discipline and poor leadership on the part of the volunteer junior officers. For example, on June 24, Lazelle sent out a party of 40 men, under command of Lieutenant Tuck of the 16th New York, in search of a party of rebels that had attacked a patrol of the 16th the evening before, capturing two men. According to Williamson's account, three of Mosby's companies came across Tuck's patrol "feeding their horses in a field near by. A portion of Mosby's force was detached, and charged in among the Union troops, killing and wounding six and capturing thirty-one prisoners and thirty-eight horses. Mosby sustained no loss whatsoever."[46]

In a letter written from Falls Church on June 27, 1864, 1st Lt. William W. Parker, Company H of the 2nd Massachusetts, made note of the fight and expressed the kind of frustration that Lazelle certainly felt: "Mosby has a great advantage. If he is hard put his men scatter all over the country & collect next day if they please. We can't play that game. ... This guerilla warfare is the meanest imaginable. ... Won't fight fair and square ... it would be better to fight Indians for then one takes no prisoners. Now we catch a notorious character, he goes to the old capital [the former brick capitol building in Washington from 1815–1819 that was used as a prison during the Civil War] for a few months & then takes the oath [of allegiance to the Union] or is exchanged & goes at it again. ..." [47]

The official report from Colonel Lowell, in command of the Brigade, pulled no punches:

> Our party made no stand, and Lieutenant Tuck reports his men as appearing demoralized and panic-stricken, scattering in all directions. ... Citizens report that the horses were unbitted [their bridles and bits removed], some of the men in cherry trees on the other side of the road, some asleep; there was one man on picket sitting on the fence, but in a very poorly chosen position.
>
> Mosby, learning about Mr. Tuck in Centreville, sent part of his men rapidly on, who dashed into the field, shooting the man on post and making such a panic that no resistance was attempted. It is said that a couple of men who had gone to a neighboring house for breakfast and saw Mosby's men going past did the only firing that was done on our part. Three wounded men (two dangerously) were brought in by Major Forbes [who had led a mission to pick up stragglers and wounded] and five men are reported to have returned to camp on foot. All the horses and the rest of the men and arms are believed to have been captured.[48]

Firming Up Northern Virginia Defenses

In July 1864, his concern growing over the threat posed by Confederate General Jubal Early's movements in the Shenandoah Valley toward Maryland and Washington, General Ulysses S. Grant pulled Lowell's 2nd Massachusetts from the cavalry brigade and assigned it to Union forces facing Early in Maryland. In August, Lowell and his regiment would again be reassigned, this time to General Sheridan's Army of the Shenandoah. With the brigade now reduced to two regiments, Lazelle took command in Vienna.

Recognizing that the departure of Lowell's regiment would hamper his ability to maintain the defensive scheme originally established in

1863, Lazelle began to rethink the organization of the cavalry screen. He was concerned about Mosby's continuing ability to penetrate Union defenses and move, seemingly at will, through portions of northern Virginia close to Washington. He was particularly bothered that Union forces always were reacting to Mosby's attacks, rather than proactively denying opportunity to Mosby. Most of all, he was worried about his ability to continue both to man static defense positions and to mount scouting operations with a greatly diminished force.

Instead of sending out "search-and-capture missions," he recommended that three stockades be built "to concentrate our strength" and occupy "a defensible position." And he proposed that his two regiments, then camped on hills near Fort Buffalo[49] in Falls Church, build them: one at the Falls Church headquarters, another four miles north at Lewinsville, and a third four miles south in Annandale. Continuous patrols would be mounted to cover the territory between the three stockades.

Drawing on his experience in fighting the Apaches in Texas and New Mexico, he also recommended creating an ambush line of five-man posts to intercept Mosby's raiders, two to five miles forward of the stockade line and extending from the Potomac River on the north, 11 miles to Braddock Road south of Annandale. Twenty ambush posts were to be concealed in the woods day and night—with two days' rations—to ambush any rebel forces attempting to approach the stockade line.

Submitting his recommendations on July 19, 1864, to Lt. Col. J. H. Taylor, General Augur's Chief of Staff, Lazelle argued that there were only two ways of successfully dealing with this "wily and almost intangible" enemy:

> One is the occupation of his whole country by a commanding force in every district, which in the present emergency of the country could not, of course, be spared for an enemy so insignificant in numbers, and whose whole controllable force does not exceed 600 men, and whose immediate strength is not over 300. The

> other way is to fight him after his own manner with the force which we have. [50]

In order to fight Mosby on his own terms, Lazelle was proposing to use scouts, local supporters, and guides to gather intelligence and to send mounted troops out using "desirable forest covers, always moving by night," in hopes of achieving surprise and ambushing Mosby's men attempting to penetrate Union lines.

Lazelle's detailed recommendations were accepted, and in late July he reported that preparations were complete. However, he continued to be concerned about the limited manpower available to him. On July 31, he again emphasized to his superiors the tenuous nature of these defenses, particularly in responding to almost daily requests to mount scouting parties beyond the defensive line.

His pleas fell on deaf ears. Throughout early August, Lazelle's troops, in addition to manning their defensive lines, mounted scouting patrols out as far as Thoroughfare Gap in the Blue Ridge, the Catoctin Mountains west of Leesburg, and along the Rappahannock River. Closer in, Mosby continued to harass the Union scouts. In his memoirs, Mosby explained his objective: "The troops belonging to the defences of Washington and guarding the line of the Potomac were a portion of Sheridan's command [in the Shenandoah Valley]. To prevent his being reinforced from this source, I made frequent attacks on the outposts in Fairfax and demonstrations along the Potomac."[51]

On August 8, for example, eight of Mosby's men scouting toward Annandale from Centreville surprised a picket post from the 16th New York—a corporal and three men—stationed on the "Old Braddock Road" near Burke's Station. According to Williamson's account and the official Union report, the three enlisted men and four horses were captured. The corporal had gone to a nearby spring for water and escaped capture. [52]

"DISASTER" AT FAIRFAX STATION

Shortly after the Union pickets were captured at Burke's Station, there was a larger skirmish at Fairfax Station between Mosby's men and 60 Federal troops. As Williamson remembered, Mosby and 38 of his men were fired upon by troops of the 13th New York while "riding along the pines" near Braddock Road. The Federals, after firing, "fled in the direction of Fairfax Station" where they met up with a patrol from the 16th New York at St. Mary's Church on the Ox Road. Thinking themselves "more than a match for Mosby," the combined group of 60 Federals was ordered to "fire with their carbines and then charge with sabers."

Mosby chose not to wait for the Federal charge and "immediately gave the order to charge, and our men, drawing their pistols, dashed on with a yell. The Federals fired a volley and then fled" and were "completely routed."[53] In his official report on the incident, Lazelle minced no words: "I have nothing to report except disgraceful mismanagement and consequent complete rout of our men, and a second Aldie disaster," probably referring to Mosby's rout of 2nd Massachusetts and 13th New York troops in July at Mt. Zion Church. Preliminary losses were one officer, Captain J. H. Fleming of the 16th, missing and reported dead, and 33 men and 39 horses missing.

Probably in reaction to the Fairfax Station incident, as well as attacks on other scouting parties, Colonel Lazelle, on August 12, emphasized to higher command that he had "resorted to the expedient (in the entire absence of single scouts conversant with the country) of sending small parties of from 25 to 40 men each to obtain the information desired. These parties have always been instructed to move at night as rapidly as possible in the desired direction, resting by day, and concealing themselves from any force unless they were confident of success in attacking it. I have also set aside a number of men most conversant with the country as scouts, to relieve as much as possible the brigade from heavy details for parties of observation." [54]

Success in the Defense

On Wednesday, August 24, Mosby and 300 men, having moved across the Bull Run mountains to Annandale Tuesday night, attacked the Cavalry Brigade's stockade there. Early that morning, the Union pickets were "captured or driven in," Mosby's guns were placed in position, and at daylight "Capt. Montjoy [commanding Mosby's Company D] was sent to demand a surrender."[55]

When Capt. Joseph Schneider of the 16th New York, commanding the detachment at Annandale, refused to surrender, Mosby's guns opened fire, "one piece throwing shell, the other one grape," canisters filled with shot, like shotgun shells. After a dozen more shots, Mosby sent two more flags of truce, one on the northwest side, where Captain Mickles had charge of the defenses, and the other on the eastern side to Schneider. Both Mickles and Schneider told them "not to come with any more flags of truce, as he would not respect them."

At this point, probably "warned of the approach of reinforcements," Mosby moved his field pieces up Fairfax Courthouse Road and slowly withdrew. According to Schneider, the attack lasted nearly an hour and a half, and Mosby's men fired thirty to forty cannon shots in addition to "some small-arm practice."[56]

Later that day, Lazelle reported that the attack at Annandale had ceased and the rebels had withdrawn, "perhaps with the intention of attacking some other part of my picket line. The attacking party is said to have consisted of from less than 200 to 300, even to 500 men, with two pieces of artillery, all under Mosby."[57]

Mosby Wounded

Sometime on September 14, troops from the 13th New York were returning from a scout to Aldie in search of Mosby. Colonel Gansevoort, "learning that Mosby was in the vicinity, endeavored to intercept him on his way homeward." [58] Mosby and two of his men encountered five Union troops, and all fired at the same time. Mosby was wounded in the groin but able to stay on his horse and escape.

Lazelle reported September 22 that he considered it "certain that Mosby was really wounded in this fight in the groin and cheek, and I deem it just that the Thirteenth Regiment should have credit attached to the affair. Private Henry Smith, of Company H, Thirteenth New York Cavalry, is the man who wounded him. It was a bold deed and Smith deserves credit for it."[59]

In his memoirs Mosby refuted Lazelle's account and characterized the event as more of a chance encounter than a "bold deed."

> As the Federal dispatches said, I was wounded on September 14, four days before the battle of Winchester. But it was hardly the bold deed Lazelle described. Two of my men, Tom Love and Guy Broadwater, and myself met five of the enemy's cavalry in Fairfax. As we were within a few yards of each other, we all fired at the same time. Two of the enemy's horses fell dead, and I was seriously wounded. The other three cavalry then fled full speed with Love and Broadwater after them until I called them back to my assistance. We then left the other men under the dead horses, and I was carried, for safety, to my father's home near Lynchburg. Captain William Chapman commanded my battalion during my absence.[60]

Success at Rapidan—Almost

In a rare case of media coverage of the Brigade's operations, two newspaper accounts reported on a major operation, led by Lazelle, to interdict one of Confederate General Jubal Early's major supply routes between Richmond and Culpeper, and its associated facilities on the Rapidan River, south of Culpeper Courthouse. On September 16, Lazelle left camp in Falls Church with 325 men, 275 from the 16th New York and 50 from the 13th New York. By his own accounting of the operation, it was a tactical success that was marred when his troops were ambushed on the way back from the Rapidan.

Going by way of Kelly's Ford, on the Rappahannock near Remington, and Raccoon's Ford, on the Rapidan south of Culpeper, Lazelle's troops arrived on the south side of the Rapidan opposite the station before daylight after a three-day march. At daylight they crossed the river and captured 200 horses and mules, together with 20 men and two officers, a portion of a company of 70 men guarding Confederate supplies. Having secured the site, Lazelle's men:

> destroyed, by fire and cutting away the supports, the railroad bridge over the Rapidan, a structure 200 feet long and 40 feet high on trestle-work, burned the railroad station house, telegraph office, three cars, and a very large flour mill, running six sets of stones. In the building were 300 barrels of flour and a large quantity of corn and wheat. We pulled down the telegraph and destroyed a part of the railroad track. As I wished to destroy the train of cars, which was above me toward Culpeper, I then moved up the railroad, burning the station house at Mitchell's Station. [61]

Having completed its work at the Rapidan, Lazelle's command, along with their captured prisoners and stock, began the return march toward Culpeper Court House, intending to destroy Confederate stores there. They had encountered very light resistance on the way out from Falls Church, and Lazelle did not expect to meet much on the return trip. He was mistaken. Reaching the junction of the Culpeper and Stevensburg roads, a few miles southeast of Culpeper Courthouse, he ran up against a large force of Confederate General Kershaw's men: about 200 men and four pieces of artillery on the hillside overlooking the road, and some 100 cavalry and 300 infantry blocking the road.

Lazelle immediately moved his force away from the road to the base of a long, high hill on the opposite side, with forest above it, "intending to avoid the artillery and infantry, at the same time throwing out a line of skirmishers." As the Confederate fire intensified, Lazelle ordered his men to move toward the enemy flank. The flanking maneuver quickly turned into chaos. Many of the men rushed helter-skelter, ahead of their officers and the command's advanced guard, and kept on running toward Stevensburg.

During all of the confusion, a small group of about 60 men attempted to rally and charge the advancing Confederates. This action slowed the enemy advance long enough for Lazelle to partially restore order, form up the remaining men into a line, and escape through the woods, chased by Confederate cavalry.[62]

At this point, with his command scattered, Lazelle had to abandon his plan to return by way of Culpeper Courthouse, and instead headed with the remnants of his force toward Kelly's Ford on the Rappahannock, between Stevensburg and Fredericksburg, "skirmishing all the way." They bivouacked overnight near the ford. The following day they were harassed by some 40 enemy cavalry until they reached Bristersburg, about 16 miles northeast of Kelly's Ford. Lazelle reported his total loss in killed and missing as one officer and 27 men, along with 11 wounded.[63]

The missing officer was Lazelle's nephew, 2nd Lt. George F. French, who had been captured in the midst of the fighting. French was immediately sent south and would be held in Danville, Virginia, southwest of Richmond on the North Carolina border, until he was paroled at James River on February 22, 1865. Upon his release, he would return to the 16th New York, and rejoin E Company as a first lieutenant.

Although Lazelle gave credit to several of his junior officers for attempting to turn around a bad situation, he reiterated his disappointment with the behavior of his enlisted troops in a post-war letter to the Board of Adjudication: "My men behaved badly, nearly 150 of them breaking and going at once to camp 85 miles distance with the remainder, about 175, having a series of running fights with about 150 of the enemy's cavalry for 30 miles."[64]

In a report to Twenty-second Army Corps Headquarters on September 24, 1864, Lazelle hesitated to offer names "for censures," noting that "all have a multiplicity of excuses, some circumstances which are partially confirmed by reports of others." Nonetheless, he went on to single out Maj. George B. Bosworth of the 16th, in command of the advance guard, for failing to follow orders, along with second lieutenants Henry S. Larned (Company B) and Henry P. Fields (Company H) who joined their men in the headlong rush to Stevensburg. In Lazelle's opinion, moreover, the conduct of more than half the officers with the command was "deserving of the severest censure in not controlling and giving orders to their men."[65]

In late September, the Twenty-second Army Corps Chief of Staff informed Lazelle that "Lieutenants Larned and Field, who behaved badly during your recent expedition to the Rapidan, have been recommended for summary dismissal. Major Bosworth should be brought at first opportunity which offers before a general court-martial."[66]

A Promotion and More Scouting Missions

In recognition of his performance during the operation, Lazelle was brevetted to major in the Regular Army for "gallant and meritorious service." During the remainder of September 1864, he regularly dispatched elements of the Cavalry Brigade in response to requests from the Twenty-second Army Corps Headquarters in Washington to scout the countryside for Confederate forces, as he endeavored to maintain sufficient numbers on his defensive lines.

On September 23, he demurred on a request to provide an escort for a party of engineers who were to examine the Manassas Gap Railroad, arguing that "in my opinion it would be extremely hazardous to send a force of 350 men farther than the vicinity of Piedmont [the engineers wanted to go as far as Strasburg], and that a greater force than that cannot be spared from here with present dispositions. Even under these circumstances a portion of the picket-line would have to be removed."

In this case, he was overruled by Major General Augur, Twenty-second Corps commander, who promised to cover the men pulled for the mission by returning companies previously pulled from the line at "either Ethan Allen, Fort Reno, or at Alexandria." Lazelle responded that he would send a 600-man escort and requested at least 200 men—a company of infantry as well as three companies of cavalry from Forts Reno, Ethan Allen, and Alexandria. Again, he was overruled and told that a 500-man escort would be sufficient, "inasmuch as General Sheridan has driven, by his complete and decisive victory near Strasburg, the enemy entirely south of the Manassas Gap Railroad." A party of 500 men from the 13th New York Cavalry departed on September 24.[67]

That party, commanded by Colonel Gansevoort of the 13th New York, moved through Centreville and into Thoroughfare Gap, following the line of the Manassas Gap Railroad through Rectortown, about 10 miles southwest of Middleburg, to Piedmont. Near Piedmont, they searched and burned the house of Joseph Blackwell, along with its barns and outbuildings. According to Gansevoort, "a large quantity of ammunition, artillery harness, and equipments [*sic*] was destroyed, including a large quantity of pistols and carbines, which were concealed from search in the house, and whose destruction was only known by their reports." Gansevoort opined that this was Mosby's arsenal and headquarters, "as was shown by some articles of clothing and equipments."[68] Indeed, it was. Blackwell was a dedicated supporter of the Confederate cause, and his house had become one of two Mosby headquarters, the other located at the Turner house in Upperville.[69]

On September 26, Lazelle ordered Captain Schneider, commanding the stockade at Annandale, to dispatch a dismounted party of a few men at night to the house of Mrs. Dickens, "living on the Ravensworth Road next Mrs. Fitzhugh's place," to have her house searched. "She is reported as having frequent visitors from Mosby's gang and Kincheloe's [Capt.

James C. Kincheloe, commander of the "Chinquapin Rangers"] and that they are entertained there. Do the same thing to the house of an Irishman who lives on and takes care of Mr. Moran's place; also the same thing to the house of Mr. Seaton, who lives on the Fairfax road. Take away the passes from all these people if they have them. I wish you to send at night parties to search for guerrillas and examine houses at any time when you think it should be done."[70]

At 3 a.m. September 30, Lazelle left Fort Buffalo with 400 men, turning over command of the brigade to Gansevoort. In his report to Twenty-second Army Corps after he returned on October 5, he provided a detailed account of the party's observations, along with information he had picked up from local observers, including the condition of Confederate Maj. Gen. James Longstreet (his former 8th Infantry company commander at Fort Bliss) and Mosby, both of whom had been reported wounded. According to Lazelle:

> There is some doubt about Longstreet having left Richmond at all for active service, so the Hon. Mr. Botts informed me; and he further said that it was extremely doubtful, in the opinion of surgeons attending him, whether Longstreet would ever be able to resume active field service again, as his wound had been through the neck as well as shoulder, and had deranged some nervous center, so that it was found necessary to keep him more under the influence of morphine.[71]

Longstreet indeed had been wounded, accidentally by his own men, in May 1864, at the Battle of the Wilderness. As it turned out, however, Mr. Botts and the surgeons were wrong. Longstreet was initially treated for his wounds in Lynchburg, Virginia, and eventually recuperated in Augusta, Georgia, attended by his niece, Emma Eve Longstreet Sibley. He rejoined Lee in October 1864, commanding the defenses of Richmond during the siege of Petersburg, and the First and Third Corps, after Confederate General A. P. Hill's death, during the Appomattox Campaign.

As for Mosby, Lazelle reported that he had been seen in Culpepper by a son of Mr. Botts. "He walks with a cane with difficulty, and was on his way up the country to join his band with a few of his men." Lazelle then went on to describe the Orange and Alexandria Railroad as "in good order beyond Rappahannock Station to Culpepper, though trains do not now run beyond Orange Court-House."[72]

Mosby Strikes Again

In late September, Grant had ordered Federal forces to repair the railroad line supplying Sheridan's forces in the Shenandoah Valley, and on September 28, Colonel Gansevoort, commanding a reconnaissance party, reported that the line east of Piedmont was "passable except for grass growing on the tracks." A few days later a work party, made up of Pennsylvania infantry and a company from the 13th New York Cavalry, moved through Fauquier, checking the road bed. [73]

On October 5, south of Salem, on top of Stephenson's Hill, and about a mile from the tracks and railroad station, Mosby's forces opened fire on the Federal work party with two mountain howitzers, while "some 200 of his cavalry charged 'the British,' Sam Alexander's pet name for the Federals." [74] Mosby Ranger Williamson later remembered:

> Our guns no sooner opened fire than the Federals left their camp and fled towards Rectortown, leaving behind their tents and camp equipage. In possession of the camp, our men took what they wished and set fire to and destroyed the remainder. Men were put to work tearing up the railroad and undoing the labors of the construction party. Our First Squadron, about 80 men, was ordered to follow on after the retreating Federals. Their trail was easily followed, for as they fled they threw away everything likely to impede their flight—clothing, arms and ammunition, and equipments. In the pursuit 40 prisoners, including 2 lieutenants, were captured. Coming to a turn in the road near Rectortown, we found the infantry drawn up in line. They opened a brisk fire as we dashed forward, but Mosby called out: "Come back, men; come

> back!" ... When the Federals found they had checked Mosby's advance, they again started at a double quick and never halted until they joined their forces with those at Rectortown.[75]

On October 6, in response to Mosby's raid, Augur ordered Lazelle to "collect all your available forces (leaving a sufficient guard for your post and to patrol your front), and march with it to Alexandria, to take [railroad] cars there for the front. Take 200 rounds of ammunition with you. Subsistence and forage will be taken from Alexandria. I leave for Rectortown tonight, and hope to see you there tomorrow."

On October 7, Lazelle reported back that Gansevoort had left Alexandria that morning with 625 men from the 13th and 16th New York regiments. That same day, Augur reported to General Halleck that the telegraph lines had been completed as far as Rectortown, that Mosby had occupied Salem for awhile, and that Mosby reportedly had destroyed "a good deal of the track there." Augur went on to report that the rail construction train had reached Rectortown, protected by 5th Pennsylvania Heavy Artillery. Having no evidence of further activity by Mosby's troops, he then sent five companies to Salem and requested the construction train to return there and repair the road. "There is a large and heavy train off the track at Thoroughfare Gap, which will not be cleared away before this afternoon so that trains can pass. As soon as the cavalry [the 13th and 16th New York commanded by Lazelle] arrives, all will be well here." [76]

The following day, Augur reported that the railroad was open to Rectortown and the telegraph completed two miles beyond. Logistics were hampering further action: "It [the telegraph] can go no farther for want of wire, which is expected by train this morning. The railroad construction train is also here awaiting material and for wood and water." Two locomotives also had derailed the previous night, "which delayed the return trains until this morning. The cavalry from Falls Church are at Manassas Junction delayed by the return trains." Augur also expressed concern that the track was not in as good condition as it had seemed initially. "Heavy trains passing over it have shown that many of the ties are so much decayed as to be unable to hold the spikes, the track consequently spreads and the trains go off." By this time, Lazelle's troops, which had arrived the evening of the seventh, had left "to find Mosby."[77]

DISASTER AT FALLS CHURCH

As recounted by Mosby Ranger James Williamson, Mosby split his forces on October 16, leaving three companies to "operate along the railroad," and taking his other three companies to "attack a large wagon train between Burke's Station and Fairfax." They missed their chance, however, and moved on toward Centreville, where they camped overnight. On October 17, Mosby and his men moved to Annandale. Notified of Mosby's presence in Fairfax, Augur ordered Lazelle's cavalry out in pursuit, but Mosby was already "quietly marching back to Loudoun."

That night, however, a company-sized group of Mosby's men moved off toward Falls Church and prepared to attack the camp. According to Ranger Williamson, the pickets were captured, and "some of our men were leading horses out of the stables, when the camp was aroused. The blowing of a horn, which at first was thought by our men to denote the assembling of a party of coon hunters, was discovered to be a signal given by a citizen named Reed [*sic*] to alarm the camp. Reed was shot by one of our [Mosby's] men. The enemy, now thoroughly aroused, opened fire, which in the darkness did no damage. Three or four negro infantry were killed; 6 prisoners and 7 horses were brought out." [78]

The Reverend John D. Read, pastor of Columbia Baptist Church in Falls Church, was an abolitionist who "was aware he had access to important military information gained from wounded Confederate soldiers he visited in hospitals, and from the 'grapevine' of the black people living throughout Fairfax County." [79]

Mosby's men were well aware of Read's activities, in part through an intercepted Federal dispatch identifying him as an informant in August 1863. Read also had played a key role "in establishing a Home Guard to protect Falls Church from guerilla raids, integrating local black men into the organization," and developing "a system of horn signals to alert Home Guard members and a nearby Federal picket post of any surprise attacks."[80]

The official report of the incident at Falls Church and Read's death, prepared by the second in command of the brigade, portrayed an event much more horrific than Williamson's brief account.

> A negro named Frank Brooks, belonging to the citizens home guard of the village, was shot dead while attempting to assist the picket in making a defense. Mr. J. B. Reed [*sic*], a citizen and a member of the same guard, with one of his negro employees, were taken prisoners at the same time. Mr. Reed was afterward brutally murdered by the party who captured him in a dense pine wood near Hunter's Mill, and his body has been found and brought into his house. An attempt to kill the negro taken with Mr. Reed was also made, and the rebels, supposing him dead, left him in the woods. He escaped afterward, however, and has but a slight wound in the head, with the loss of an ear, blown off by a pistol shot.[81]

The report concluded that there was no doubt that Read had been murdered by the Rebels. The Union surgeon examining his body found that the skull at the base of the brain had been "blown to atoms, and the flesh about the wound is filled with powder, as if the pistol had been placed close to the head." Read was executed at a spot near the current mile marker 13.5 on the W&OD Trail in Oakton.

Colonel Lazelle Resigns

Later in the day on October 18, in a letter to the Chief of Staff of the Twenty-second Army Corps, Lazelle formally resigned his commission as colonel of the 16th New York Cavalry. It is not clear whether his resignation was precipitated directly by the disaster at Falls Church and murder of Reverend Read, or was simply the culmination of growing frustration with the lackluster performance of his troops and concern about his own leadership abilities. In a March 1866 letter to the Board of Adjudication Regarding Military Service History, however, he identified two factors: "the disgusting conduct of Lieut. Col. of Regiment [Hollister]" and his own inability, as commander, to make recommendations or otherwise influence the selection of the regiment's officers and their appointment by New York's governor, Horatio Seymour. This latter factor must have been particularly frustrating, given Lazelle's friendship with State Adjutant General Sprague. [82]

While his own leadership capabilities clearly were very much on his mind, Lazelle went to great length in his letter of resignation to blame officers and men alike, as well as factors he considered beyond his own control, for the poor performance of his regiment and his inability to turn it around:

> a year since I accepted the Command, with the resolution to do all in my power to achieve the interests of the regiment and that of the service—I believe I have zealously endeavored to accomplish this, but the results are not, nor can I make them, what I hoped and desired; and I believe that the fault is not mine.
>
> The great mass of the enlisted portion of the regiment contains much of extreme youth in age; and much that causes ranks to swell because of high bounties. But all this could have been corrected, had proper officers directed originally; but the regiment to a considerable extent, the result of consolidation of other regiments, partially completed, contained very many officers without pride, or courage, or honor. Fifteen have been dishonorably dismissed, and their places have in the most important instances been filled by executive appointments; in some cases, as bad as those dismissed.
>
> Bad officers, by long continued worthlessness, have destroyed the spirit of vigor and good which should have been evoked from the men; and one of them has given the regiment an unenviable ordure. So I have not been supported, I cannot make the regiment progressive; and my position as Colonel becomes little more than one of pay; and since I took the command to advance the service,

> interest, that of the regiment, and my own, I had rather resign it and do the duties of my legitimate grade, than fail, and have the failure known as my own.[83]

Although Lazelle ended his association with the 16th New York Cavalry on October 18, the regiment would continue to serve in northern Virginia through the end of the war. In November, the Independent Cavalry Brigade was discontinued and the 16th was re-subordinated to Gamble's 1st Separate Brigade of the Twenty-second Army Corps until June 1865.

In December 1864, a patrol of men from the 13th and 16th Regiments, led by Major Frazar of the 13th, succeeded in wounding Mosby yet again near Lakeland, and the 16th was still operating in the Vienna area in March and April 1865. In June 1865, the regiment was consolidated with the 13th, the new organization receiving the designation of 3rd Provisional Regiment, New York Volunteer Cavalry. It was disbanded in September.

The regiment completed its service with a total of 140 casualties: one officer and 20 enlisted men were killed in action; 119 enlisted men died of wounds or disease, 44 as prisoners. Although the 16th would have had an authorized strength of some 900 officers and men, its actual strength at any point in time would have been much lower. However, even had it maintained full strength, a casualty rate of 15.5 percent for the regiment's total term of service would have been at the high end of the spectrum. Losses of 10 to 13 percent were more common. If one assumes the regiment was normally at less than full strength, then its casualty rate was very high—another reflection of its overall ineffectiveness.[84]

Absent for a Historic Moment

Fate, particularly during war years, can relegate one person to obscurity and another to legacy. On Good Friday, April 14, 1865, an assassin's bullet took the life of President Abraham Lincoln at Ford's Theater. On April 24, while the nation mourned and Lincoln's funeral train was in

New York City, Lt. Edward P. Doherty and 26 troops from the 16th New York were dispatched in pursuit of John Wilkes Booth. The detachment, which became known as the Garrett's Farm Patrol, returned two days later with his body.

One can only conjecture about the impact on his Army career had Lazelle continued with the 16th for six more months instead of resigning his commission. As it was, however, he returned to the Regular Army as an 8th Infantry captain, and was succeeded by Col. Nelson B. Sweitzer, who had previously commanded the 1st U.S. Cavalry, Army of the Potomac.[85]

In his final act as Commander of the Cavalry Brigade at Vienna, Colonel Lazelle signed an affidavit recommending the release of Dr. James Hunter, a member of one of Vienna's founding families and owner of Hunter's Mill, from prison. Hunter, according to Lazelle, had been wrongly accused of harboring Mosby when, in fact, Mosby was "not an invited guest, but a self imposed one," and the hospitality was "rather obligatory on the part of Dr. Hunter, and was protested against by Mrs. Hunter."[86]

As he departed Vienna and the 16th New York, Lazelle might have thought back to his letter of September 1863 when he expressed "hesitancy and a want of confidence" in taking on command of the regiment. The regiment's performance over the past year had been mixed at best. There had been some minor achievements to be sure. But even those few successes of which he rightly could be proud, such as destroying the Confederate supply center, mill, and bridge on the Rapidan River, were less than complete.

Mustering the lessons that his limited command experience in Texas and New Mexico had taught him, Lazelle had struggled to find an operational concept that would offer better results against Mosby and his partisan rangers. His scheme approved by Augur, in all likelihood, could have been successful if his troops had not constantly been pulled away for scouting and escort missions. In the end, too much was being asked of too small a force with too limited a tactical capability.

Even his superiors recognized that the New York cavalrymen were simply not up to the task. In early October 1864, General Ulysses S. Grant requested permission to pull forces from the Shenandoah Valley in support of his so-called "Siege of Petersburg." In responding, General Halleck, chief of staff in Washington, expressed concern about the impact this would have on the security of the countryside between Washington and the valley. He was particularly concerned about Mosby, warning Grant that it would be necessary to "completely clean out Mosby's gang of robbers who have so long infested that district of country."

In Halleck's opinion, General Sheridan's cavalry, commanded by Lowell, would be needed to deal with Mosby before being sent out of the valley. He came to this conclusion, he wrote to Grant, because the "the two small regiments [the 13th and 16th New York] under General Augur have been so often cut up by Mosby's band that they are cowed and useless for that purpose."[87]

That, unfortunately, was the legacy of Lazelle's New York cavalry as 1864 drew to a close.

Chapter 5

The Pride of Mecklenburg County

With his resignation from the New York volunteers, Lazelle once again was a captain of the 8th Infantry, awaiting orders to his next assignment. He and Rebecca were about to begin a nomadic life. On October 20, 1864, he reported to the Assistant Adjutant General of the Army that his temporary address would be at the Office of the Commissary General of Prisoners, in care of Col. W. Hoffman. He was pleased to be back in the relative peace and calm of staff duty but had no intention of making his stay with Hoffman a lengthy one. Hoffman had been "breveted" to the rank of Brigadier General, but Lazelle chose to use Hoffman's regular rank in his correspondence, perhaps a reflection of his lack of respect for his former senior officer.

Hoffman, on the other hand, apparently had no legacy of issues with Lazelle, either from their early days together in the 8th Infantry or from Lazelle's inspector duty. He requested that Lazelle be permanently detailed to his staff, noting that his previous experience made him particularly fit for the service.[1] Hoffman's request was denied, much to Lazelle's relief, with the notation that "Capt. Lazelle will be ordered to join his regiment," then located at Hancock Barracks in Baltimore, Maryland.[2]

Sometime in October or early November, Lazelle suffered a flare-up of a rheumatic condition that had struck him early in 1862 and would plague him for the rest of his life. On November 23, he wrote the Adjutant General to explain that he was unable to rejoin his regiment because he was bed-ridden in Washington and under the care of an Army surgeon for severe rheumatism "contracted in the field during the past year." The doctor confirmed Lazelle's medical condition in a separate memorandum and endorsed his request for a duty assignment in the Department of the Gulf, where the warm weather would be more conducive to his recovery.

Provost Marshal Duty

As he prepared to leave Washington, however, he made yet one more attempt to secure a staff job, again presenting his name to Brigadier General Thomas, Assistant Adjutant General, as "an applicant for the appointment of Assistant Adjutant General in the Regular organization of the United States Army."[3] It was not to be. On December 1, Lazelle was ordered to report "in person, without delay" to the Commanding General, Military Division of West Mississippi, at New Orleans, Louisiana, which had been occupied by Federal troops since May 1862.[4]

Under the command of General Edward R. S. Canby, the Division—also known as the Army of West Mississippi—covered "all of the coast of the Gulf of Mexico west of Pensacola Harbor," and "so much of Gulf States as may be occupied by U.S. forces." The Division included 31 regiments of the United States Colored Troops, manned by free blacks and freed slaves who served during the last two years of the Civil War.[5]

Upon reporting for duty in New Orleans on January 6, 1865, Lazelle was further assigned on temporary duty as Acting Assistant Inspector General of "the troops now being collected at Kennerville, La.," (now Kenner, a suburb of New Orleans) and was ordered to report to Maj. Gen.

Frederick Steele "without delay."[6] He served in that capacity only slightly over a month. On February 12, he was appointed Assistant Provost-Marshal General of the Division.[7] Soon after Lazelle took up his new assignment under Canby, Rebecca joined him in New Orleans, sailing from New York harbor March 4 on the steamship *Evening Star*.[8]

The Office of the Provost Marshal General, established as part of the War Department in March 1863, was charged with arresting deserters, enrolling men for the draft, enlisting volunteers, and compiling statistics on the physical condition of recruits and on army casualties. Beginning in 1861, however, regimental provost marshals had been formed in the Army of the Potomac, and the position was later extended to division and corps levels. By the fall of 1862, provost marshals were operating in all Northern states, charged primarily with capturing deserters. A similar system existed in the Confederate Army; provost marshals were appointed to enforce conscription and other laws.[9]

When General McClellan assumed command of forces in the East and created the position of provost marshal, the duties he assigned were quite broad, much more akin to today's Provost Marshal and Military Police. Under McClellan, they included:

> the suppression of marauding and the depredations on private property, the preservation of good order, the prevention of straggling, the suppression of gambling houses or other establishments prejudicial to good order and discipline, and the supervision of hotels, saloons, and places of resort and amusement generally. To this officer was also entrusted the duty of making searches, seizures, and arrests, the custody of deserters from the opposing forces and of prisoners of war, the issuance of passes to citizens, and the bearing of complaints of citizens. [10]

For an army on occupation duty in the South in early 1865, the specific elements and limits of martial law governing civilians in occupied territory were not covered in federal statutes or Army regulations. Thus, for practical purposes, martial law was "anything the commander said it was, unless higher authority overruled him." [11]

It is not clear which of McClellan's long list of duties and powers Lazelle exercised as Assistant Provost Marshal of the Division of West Mississippi.[12] However, the records available in the National Archives include a report dated March 20, 1865, providing the statement of "Thomas Ballantine, late a member of the 3rd Company of Washington Artillery; a deserter from the Rebel Service; who has been escamined [*sic*] at this office." The statement taken by Lazelle included detailed information on Confederate forces. It was submitted and countersigned by Allan Pinkerton, founder and director of the Pinkerton Detective Agency, who had created and run General McClellan's intelligence organization. [13] At the time, Pinkerton was still working for the government investigating cotton claims in the Department of the Mississippi, under General Canby. In 1865, Pinkerton severed his connection with the "Secret Service of the United States" and returned to Chicago, but apparently not before assisting Lazelle with the interrogation of the Rebel deserter Ballantine. [14]

BACK TO THE 8TH INFANTRY

Three months after General Lee's surrender at Appomattox Court House in April 1865, Lazelle was ordered back to his original regiment as Captain of Company H, but on "General Recruiting Service" in New York City. He remained there through February 1866. Rebecca returned home to Hagerstown while her husband was on temporary duty in New York. In the meantime, Federal forces began to transition from combat and occupation duty—martial law—to the administration of law and order, governance, and social and public services. As Volunteer forces were mustered out of service, Regular Army units were reassigned and relocated to the former Confederate states.

In March 1866, six companies of the 8th Infantry received orders to proceed to the Department of North Carolina under Lt. Col. John R. Edie.

Lazelle's Company H was assigned to Charlotte. Still on recruiting service in New York City, he was ordered to rejoin his regiment in Baltimore and assume command of his company, which he did on March 22. [15] Rebecca, newly pregnant with their first child, remained at her parents' home in Hagerstown.

Reconstruction

Between the cessation of hostilities in 1865 and Congressional passage of the Reconstruction Act in March 1867, the Army carried out a variety of civil and military duties in the former Confederate states. Due in large part to policy disagreements in Washington over the process through which the former Confederate states would rejoin the Union, commanders in the field operated with only general guidance from the War Department. Most field generals "issued detailed instructions to their troops setting forth their conception of the proper relation of the military power to state and local governments and to individual citizens," but individual commanders were essentially on their own in setting policy and making decisions based on local conditions.[16]

Although the principal mission of the Army was the maintenance of civil order, individual units and commanders, in reality, took on many of the functions—de facto and de jure—of local government. One important responsibility was providing direct support to the Freedmen's Bureau—part of the War Department and run by military officers—as it provided services, aid, and other support to freed blacks and the destitute. This included providing local security as well as logistical, quartermaster, medical, and other support.

In many areas, Army troops also operated and maintained railroad and telegraph lines until they could be turned over to civilian control. For example, in North Carolina, the military controlled rail and telegraph lines between Raleigh and Goldsboro, and Wilmington and Morehead

City; and telegraph lines connecting Raleigh, Fayetteville, Weldon, and Greensboro.[17]

Probably the most unique function for Army officers was serving in place of local government officials and the judiciary, both running local government and dealing with criminal cases through the military justice system. In North Carolina between 1865 and 1868, for example, "military courts replaced civil courts that were non-existent or refused to act on behalf of freedmen or Republicans."[18]

With the passage of the Reconstruction Act in 1867, Congress divided the "rebel States" into military districts "subject to the military authority of the United States." The Army was charged to "protect all persons in their rights of person and property, to suppress insurrection, disorder, and violence, and to punish or cause to be punished, all disturbers of the peace and criminals." Local commanders were empowered to organize military commissions or tribunals in place of local civil courts. The Act also established the process for electing delegates to State Constitutional Conventions, the first step in the political process of re-joining the Union, and the Army played a key role in overseeing the registration of voters and monitoring elections.[19]

Company H Arrives in Charlotte

On April 2, 1866, six companies of the 8th Infantry Regiment, under command of Lt. Col. J. R. Edie, Bvt. Col., USA, left Baltimore for the Department of North Carolina. Company H, commanded by Lazelle, was to be stationed in Charlotte. Two of the other five were stationed in Raleigh, another two at Salisbury, and one at Morgantown.[20]

Charlotte, the county seat of Mecklenburg County, had first been occupied by Federal troops on May 7, 1865, when Company G of the 9th New Jersey, commanded by Capt. Morris C. Runyan, arrived from Greensboro. According to his own accounts, Runyan "found the town in a state of chaos." Bands of lawless Confederates roamed the streets terrorizing citizens. "Drunkeness and disorder" were "the order of the day," Runyan reported. Assuming command of the Post of Charlotte, he immediately "placed guards at the powder magazine and warehouses, formed around-the-clock patrols, issued provisions to starving soldiers and civilians, and banned the sale of alcohol. By this means, the Union soldiers soon restored order." [21]

In June 1865, Brig. Gen. Thomas H. Ruger, commander of the Department and District of North Carolina, noted: "I have been issuing such orders and regulations as I have thought proper for the maintenance of order. I find the citizens generally disposed to accept the new situation without complaint, and apparently desirous of resuming a condition of peace and observance of law. This region of country is strongly rebel, however." [22]

In July, he announced that as soon as town mayors and commissioners appointed by provisional Governor Holden, who had been appointed by President Andrew Johnson, indicated they were ready to govern, Federal troops would be withdrawn, although small detachments would remain to "guard public property and inspect trains." [23]

When Lazelle and his company arrived in Charlotte, Congress and President Johnson were still arguing over reconstruction policy, elections for a state constitutional convention were still 18 months in the future, and Ruger believed Charlotte still required a Federal presence. Lazelle's main focus was maintaining law and order.

In his first Post Return from Charlotte, a semi-monthly report dated April 15, 1866, Lazelle recorded a unit strength of 60 enlisted men, 59 muskets with 2,500 rounds of ammunition in reserve, 141 days' rations on hand, four days of forage, and one wagon, three mules, and one horse. [24] His next report, dated May 15, 1866, showed similar strengths, but also indicated that since his company's 1st and 2nd lieutenant positions were vacant, he wore multiple hats: Acting Post Quartermaster, Commissary of Subsistence and Ordnance Officer for the Post of Charlotte, and Captain of his Company. [25]

In October and again in early November, a frustrated Lazelle pleaded in letters to the Adjutant General that the Army fill the vacant officer positions. The difficulty of this situation, he argued, was compounded by several other factors:

> with raw and ignorant recruits as clerks; and with my storehouses of these Departments [quartermaster and commissary] in the center of the town, and unavoidably removed nearly a mile from my camp; I think it quite obvious, not that my duties have been excessive, but that many details, and the necessity of attending to their performance personally, demand more time than can be devoted to them; and that my property is more or less unsafe; and the exactions [*sic*] of the service imperfectly fulfilled, where so much is necessarily left to irresponsible non-commissioned officers, not always reliable. [26]

Despite the frustrations of too few junior officers and a still rather chaotic situation on the ground, Lazelle and his troops made a favorable impression on the local citizenry, nearly from the start. A newspaper article, probably published in December 1866, commended Lazelle, his troops, and their efforts to ease the burdens of martial law. The writer noted, particularly, that since his arrival in Charlotte, Lazelle had "evinced every desire to miligate [*sic*] the somewhat harsh rules of the general government as they seem to us, and has in every way he could, simply and conscientiously confined himself to the strict line of his duty." The Federal troops were so effective, he continued, that "a stranger would hardly know that we had Federal forces quartered here, except that, perhaps, now and then the blue uniform can be seen on the street. This is quite a compliment to this gentleman for, to his thorough management of his command, must be attributed, greatly, their good behavior." The reporter went on to note that recently "one of our prominent Confederate Generals" with whom Lazelle had served for five years in the 8th Infantry, most likely Longstreet, had called upon Lazelle, "as an old Lang Syne companion." [27]

In another article, probably about six months later, Lazelle again was commended for keeping the best interests of the local citizenry uppermost in his mind. According to this report, instructions restricting the sale of "distilled spirits," issued by General Daniel Sickles, commander of the Department of the Carolinas, had generated confusion and consternation among the local dispensing and imbibing communities. To his great credit, according to the reporter, Lazelle "deferred executing the order (at the request of city authorities) until more explicit instruction could be received from Gen. Sickles, and when those instructions were received it became his duty to promptly close the 'shops.' So far as we can learn, the citizens of this community do not complain of Capt. Lazelle's course in any respect, but on the contrary, are well satisfied with his administration."[28]

Throughout the latter half of 1866 as he was organizing military governance in Charlotte, Lazelle also was coping with a growing family crisis back home in Hagerstown. The last months of Rebecca's pregnancy were increasingly difficult. In mid-December, concerned about her health, he requested and received a twenty-day leave of absence, with an option to extend it for another ten days, and returned to Hagerstown. On January 4, 1867, four days after Jacob Hollingsworth Gaines Lazelle was born, Henry, still gravely concerned for his wife's recovery, requested a further extension, explaining that her condition was "still very critical" and her recovery "doubtful." He further feared that separation from his family would "greatly aggravate" her illness. [29]

His request was approved January 9, and he remained in Hagerstown with his wife and newborn son. Rebecca recovered quickly, however, at least well enough to travel, and they left, as a family, for Charlotte in mid-February.

Despite favorable reviews in the local press, Lazelle's tour of duty in Charlotte was not without controversy, once again born of challenging higher authority. In December 1866, while dealing emotionally with his wife's illness and the impending birth of their first child, Lazelle received an order from a first lieutenant of the 5th Cavalry, acting as Judge

Advocate General in Raleigh, to send prisoners under Lazelle's control to Raleigh for trial. Lazelle refused on the grounds that the lieutenant had not provided sufficient proof of his authority to direct the transfer. Lazelle was rebuked by Maj. Gen. J. C. Robinson, Commander of the Department of the South, who considered his refusal to obey the request to be "unwarranted," and ordered him again to dispatch the prisoners.

Lazelle complied with the second order but appealed the case to the Army Judge Advocate General in Washington. Armed with a judgment by the Judge Advocate General's office that his initial refusal was technically proper, Lazelle formally requested that General Robinson withdraw his rebuke. Robinson refused, telling Lazelle that he still believed Lazelle's refusal to be "captious and uncalled for." Lazelle then appealed to the Adjutant General of the Army, requesting that Robinson be ordered to withdraw his rebuke. Expressing half-hearted "regret" if his conduct had "generated on the part of the Major General Commanding a jealous fear of infringement upon his authority, to the extent that personal feeling should seemingly color his official language," Lazelle ended his letter impertinently, asking:

> Am I to accept the opinion of the Brevet Major General Comdg. this Department that the clearly defined enunciations of the learned Judge Advocate General are without force, and as held by the former officer "no reason to change his opinion"?
>
> Shall I accept the declaration of the Brevet Major General Commanding that if the views of the distinguished Judge Advocate General, stated in his letter to me, are enforced, they would be prejudicial to the aims of military justice; and trials retarded, or attended with great difficulties? [30]

Lazelle's appeal was forwarded through channels in Washington, eventually landing on the desk of General of the Army Ulysses S. Grant. On March 27, Lazelle lost his case. Grant instructed the Adjutant General to inform the upstart captain that "while strictly speaking Capt. Lazelle has right on his side, there is evidence of a captious spirit on his part which the General [Grant] does not approve. Unless he knew there was something wrong in this case, he could have furthered the interests of the service, and a simple representation to the proper authorities that he had done so notwithstanding irregularities to which he objected, should have satisfied all reasonable scruples on the subject." [31]

In the end, Lazelle's tour of duty in Charlotte was a complete success in the eyes of the local citizenry, if not in General Grant's. In June 1867, he autographed a pamphlet that he had authored and published ("A Review of the Situation, Addressed to the Citizens of Mecklenburg County, North Carolina"): "Mrs. H. M. Lazelle, with the love and esteem of her husband, presented June 8th, 1867 (written for the benefit of both) elevated and purified by her thoughts."

This wide-ranging essay, addressing, in passing, the impact of war on civilians in both the North and the South and the relationship between military forces and local civilians, received rave reviews in the Charlotte *Western Democrat*, which noted in particular that Lazelle had "handled the subject in the kindliest spirit, and in tracing our troubles and the mode of extrication, has given due weight to the sincerity of our people, the gallantry of our 'boys,' and the loyalty and good faith with which the inevitable result has been accepted."[32]

Lazelle, then a brevet major, undoubtedly was moved to pen this pamphlet after a variety of experiences and interactions with the citizens of Charlotte and Mecklenburg County as his company went about its duties. In one incident, Lazelle had ordered the local sheriff to arrest "a negro man" who had been seen carrying concealed weapons and "drilling the negroes in military companies." When the sheriff attempted to make the arrest, a "mob of blacks and whites" released the prisoner by force. Lazelle promptly sent a detachment of soldiers to arrest the group for interfering with the sheriff.

As reported in a local paper, the "gang" included pro-Union members of the Red Strings (a nickname for the pro-Union Heroes of America) and other anti-Confederate groups, led by a Confederate Army deserter, who, along with the armed negro, were holding a "mass meeting" near Grassy Branch east of Charlotte. After the war, these pro-Union groups apparently attracted a host of unsavory characters. A local paper commended Lazelle for his handling of the affair, noting that "The Commandant of this Post knows no political party in the administration of his duties, but to evil doers of every party he is determined to make his rule terrible. It is the only way to preserve peace and quiet." [33]

From both his actions reported in the local press and his lengthy observations in the June pamphlet, it is clear that Lazelle had two objectives in Charlotte. First and foremost was the maintenance of law and order, for which he drew substantial praise from the white community. Secondly, he sought, again successfully, to secure the cooperation of the white leadership, largely by sympathizing with their plight as they faced the political, economic, and social demands of reconstruction. In particular, Lazelle went on at length to affirm the views of his southern audience that, while black and white were now "equal before the law," the two races were not truly equal and might never be.

> If then, the status of the colored race is, by the unchangeable regulations of Nature inseparably fixed, and defined to be inferior to that of the white, with which it is in juxtaposition, and with which it is Equal only before the law of citizenship, what incentive has it to self-exertion, and what encouragement that its efforts, however well directed, will elevate it to any approximate true equality?

These words, and Lazelle's contention that as long as "inequality of race is substantial," the white race must "exercise a predominating power in all that pertains to government," would have been music the ears of Charlotte's white leadership.

On December 19, 1867, Company H left Charlotte, reassigned to Columbia, South Carolina. Before his departure, Lazelle was recognized and honored by the Board of Aldermen with a "Resolution" dated December 9, expressing regret that he was leaving his post and commending the "uniform courtesy and the justice which characterized his actions" and the "faithful manner" in which he performed the functions of his office. The special citation and his letter of thanks in response were reported in the Charlotte *Western Democrat*, which noted among other things that the only sentiment expressed by the people of Charlotte was one of "regret," and that as long as they were under military authority, they would "prefer a fair-minded gentleman like Capt. Lazelle as their commander." [34]

Columbia, South Carolina

When Lazelle and Company H arrived at the post of Columbia, located on the city's outskirts, on December 20, 1867, the people of South Carolina were preparing for the state constitutional convention scheduled to be held in January. In March 1868, Lazelle was granted a leave of absence for twenty days. Rebecca's father, Jacob Hollingsworth, had died on March 19, deeply in debt—including to his daughter—with numerous creditors waiting in the wings. On April 3, Lazelle requested an extension of his leave "my presence here being very desirable (to attend to unsettled business matters of a private nature)." The extra time was granted, and he rejoined his company on April 14.

Almost immediately upon his return from leave, Lazelle and his company were ordered back to Charlotte on temporary duty by General Canby. Canby was responding to a letter from the Reverend W. L. Miller, a local Presbyterian minister, who complained that "a Unionist was threatened and insulted during a Conservative torchlight procession through town and a riot had erupted during a Republican rally in Union County." According to official accounts, Lazelle reported that the incidents had been blown out of proportion. During the parade, "some mischievous and unprincipled" outsiders, not connected with the political procession, had "dressed themselves fantastically and insulted by rude actions the family of a local Republican politician." As for the riot in Union County, Lazelle reported that "one man was stabbed and several [were] more or less injured. The fight was not general, serious, or of long duration." He assured his superiors that when the Congressional election was over, there would be no more excitement "to alarm the proverbial timidity of any reverend gentlemen."[35]

In late May 1868, Lazelle was again dispatched outside of Columbia, this time, with two lieutenants and 57 enlisted men, to Anderson in the northwestern corner of South Carolina and the foothills of the Blue Ridge. On May 23, Canby had issued an order postponing the election of municipal officers, due in part to heated political maneuvering between the Republican and Democratic parties. He also had invalidated a local election, replacing a newly elected all-white Board of Aldermen with six blacks and seven "congenial" whites.

The June 3 edition of the *Anderson Intelligencer* noted the arrival of the Federal troops on May 27, speculating that "the troops will remain for the season [election period]. Some suppose that the pending election has induced the authorities to garrison our town again, but we have no doubt that Radical [a faction of the Republican party favoring harsher measures against ex-Confederates] lying and misrepresentation about the former election brought about this result."[36]

The newspaper was correct. Lazelle and his troops were there to serve charges of election fraud on two local politicians and order them to Charleston. The April South Carolina gubernatorial election, held simultaneously with the vote on the South Carolina Constitution, had been won by Robert Kingston Scott, largely due to the support of newly enfranchised black voters. Canby was responding to allegations of fraud against H. O. Herrick and Z.T. Taylor, local precinct managers and opponents of Scott.[37]

Herrick and Taylor were given several days to collect evidence for their defense and then left for Charleston on June 8. Lazelle and his men departed for Columbia on June 4, the *Intelligencer* noting after their departure that they were "orderly and well behaved during their stay in our midst. The officer in command, Maj. Lazelle, is an old Army officer, and doubtless a good disciplinarian. We were much pleased in an interview with him, and are satisfied that he is disposed to act fairly and justly with all parties."[38]

Henry, Rebecca, and Jacob remained in Columbia through the fall of 1870, and their second son, Horace Gibbs Lazelle, was born there September 10. As the senior captain (and brevet major) on post, he assumed the position of Post Commander whenever Colonel Edie was absent. In this temporary capacity, he commanded the post from August to December 1868 and again in late January and early February 1870.

Return to New York City

On September 21, 1870, Company H left Columbia for New York City via Charleston, along with the rest of the regiment. Departing Charleston aboard the steamer *Clyde* on September 24, they arrived in New York on September 27 and proceeded to David's Island the next morning.[39]

David's Island, off the coast of New Rochelle, New York, in Long Island Sound, had been rented by the U.S. Government in April 1862 to house wounded prisoners. At the end of the war, Congress authorized its purchase for military purposes, and it was conveyed to the United States in 1867. Used initially as a recruiting depot, it was later converted to a coastal artillery defense post and named Fort Slocum after Maj. Gen. Henry W. Slocum, U.S. Volunteers.

Ensconced in New York and apparently unhappy at his prospects for permanent promotion to major in the infantry, Lazelle penned a letter to General Terry, under whom he had served in the South, requesting support for his transfer into the Artillery branch where he felt he stood a better chance. By his own calculation, because his time as a parolee was not counted toward his time in grade, there were 15 infantry captains ahead of him on the promotion list who were actually junior to him in total service time. Additionally, he counted seven infantry officers already promoted to major who also had served less total time. Nineteen of the 22 had been commissioned in 1861, six years after Lazelle received his commission.

On a transmittal slip, dated December 20, 1870, General Terry forwarded Lazelle's request to Army General Sherman recommending this officer "of great ability and of the highest character" for the transfer. Lazelle's request fell of deaf ears. He was neither transferred to the Artillery Corps nor advanced on the Infantry promotion list.[40]

PUBLISHED AUTHOR

Unable to secure a transfer or promotion, Lazelle left New York in July 1872 with his regiment for duty in the West. In his "spare time," however, he had been busy at the very non-military pursuit of physics and philosophy. And 1872 also was the year that Henry M. Lazelle published his first book, *One Law in Nature: A New Corpuscular Theory, Comprehending Unity of Force, Identity of Matter & Its Multiple Atom Constitution: Applied to The Physical Affections or Modes of Energy*, printed by D. Van Nostrand of New York, with a retail price of $1.50.

In this tome, Lazelle was grappling with metaphysical questions that have mystified men for thousands of years and which still are a matter of debate among physicists today: What is matter made of and why does it behave as it does? One of the more elusive goals of physics, into the twenty-first century, has been defining a "unified field theory," which would explain the relationship between the four observed forces in the universe: electromagnetism, gravity, and strong and weak forces "which operate on the subatomic level." [41] Lazelle appears to have been chasing, some 140 years ago, that same so-called "God particle," now recognized as the "Higgs Boson."

In *One Law in Nature*, Lazelle introduces and explores the basic hypothesis that a single primary force, what he calls a "single origin of all physical phenomena," drives all observable phenomena, down to the atomic level. After a lengthy introductory discussion of the then-accepted laws of motion pertaining to light, heat, electricity, magnetism, and chemical action, he argues that there is not a specific and unique force driving each. Rather, there must be a single "primary attractive force" driving all forms of motion:

> It is not disputed that there are a great variety of motions; and that they are persistent for matter conditioned in a particular manner, as motion of units in heat, motion or the same units in gravitation, and in organic movement. But—given invariable conditions of restraint—it is as rational and conceivable that motion in all the physical affections of matter should continue under the influence of one primary force, as that the heterogeneous forms of motion in a large manufactory should be derived from a single mechanical power.

Subsequent chapters of the book address in detail the nature of matter, including its elasticity and thus its capacity to change form under different amounts of force, and the notion that the forces which formed the planetary system also apply to all systems of matter. He describes the nature and characteristics of heat, light, electricity, and magnetism as simple manifestations of different degrees of "dynamic energy" or "planetary motion." Similarly, he argues that chemical energy can be explained as deriving from a single primary force. Acknowledging that chemistry involves much more complex organic compounds, with atoms of many different elements, he nonetheless maintains that chemical action, like all other forces of matter, essentially involves an interchange of primary force and motion: the "differential attraction between multiple atoms—a consequence of inequality of motion and primary energy."

In his final chapter, Lazelle expands his theory of a unified primal driving force from basic chemical compounds and reactions to complex organisms—both fauna and flora—and ultimately to humans. Here he focuses on what he calls the "organizing force" driving the development of an organism from "germ to maturity." In a nod to "creationists," he argues that the existence of a primal physical force driving evolution is completely consistent with the notion of a supreme being who provides "directive supervision consistent with eternal law." Therefore, he concludes, "seen from the harmony of nature, we may perceive a presiding Intelligence expressing his processes with simplicity and governing by the unity of law, through which elemental matter becomes animated vitality."

Throughout the book, Lazelle reflects a solid basic understanding of extant scientific theory based on extensive reading of past and then-current scientific literature. In addition to classical theorists, he cites numerous contemporary scientists. Among them: British mathematician and astronomer, Sir John Herschel; August Arthur del la Rive, who studied electric discharge in rarified gasses and developed a new theory of the aurora borealis; Michael Faraday who discovered electromagnetic induction and electrolysis; Herve Faye, an astronomer at the Paris Observatory who developed theories on the nature and form of comets; Andre-Marie Ampere, the father of electrodynamics; evolution theorist Herbert Spencer; and Italian physicist and neurophysiologist Carlo Matteucci. His deep understanding of modern scientific theory was not something he would have picked up at West Point, except for the very basics. Much of his discourse, rather, seems to have been based on extensive reading and independent thought after he left the Academy.

Lazelle dedicated a copy of the book to his wife, signing it: "Omaha Barracks, Omaha Nebraska, January 9th, 1873. This volume is presented to a loving wife, whose affectionate devotion, faithful courage and hope, sustained her husband through years of repatious [*sic*] toil and doubt to its final completion. H. M. Lazelle." A month later, Lazelle received a letter from General Sherman, commenting on the tome:

> I received some time ago from Van Nostrand a copy of your volume entitled "One Law in Nature." I am glad to learn that it comes from you for it will add additional interest to the volume. The subject is one of intense interest, a little ahead of the time, yet toward which we are shifting. I hardly feel equal to the subject, but will commend it to some friends whose tastes lay in that direction. It

> surely is commendable that one of our officers can find the time to pursue such subjects. [42]

The book received mixed reviews in the press. *The Nation* judged that, while the book did not "betray the dense ignorance which many pretentious theories of the universe do," it had no value as a "contribution to natural philosophy." Challenging Lazelle's notion of a single driving force as particularly flawed, the reviewer concluded "while we doubtless are ignorant of the precise form of the fundamental principles of nature, we at least are not mistaken as to their number."[43]

On the other hand, *The Journal of Applied Sciences* concluded that Lazelle had given "close attention to the recent investigations into the properties of matter, the doctrine of the correlation of forces, heat as a mode of motion, and the analogies existing between heat, light and sound, and out of it all has constructed a theory reducing all to one grand uniting force." The *Journal's* reviewer suggested that "to any one fond of discussions of this character the book will afford pleasant reading, as the author presents his views in a modest and candid manner, ensuring respect even if he does not convert every one to his way of thinking."

Commenting that the notion that "a single primary principle underlies all the variety of phenomenal manifestation has been assumed by thinkers from the early days of the Greek philosophers down to Mr. Herbert Spencer," *The New York Evening Post*, nonetheless credited Lazelle with developing a theory that was "ingenious as well as original, is closely reasoned out, supported by strong analogies; and so far as we see, and in defect of a better, is quite as satisfactory as any other scheme of metaphysical physics that has been suggested."[44]

Chapter 6

Indian Territory

On July 5, 1872, Capt. Lazelle and his company, along with the regimental headquarters and five other companies, departed David's Island, en route by rail to Sioux City, Iowa, arriving on July 9. From Sioux City, the regimental headquarters and band left for Omaha Barracks (Fort Omaha) on July 11. Lazelle and the six companies—now a "battalion" commanded by Lt. Col. Henry D. Wallen—boarded the steamer *Mary McDonald* for a 630-mile trip up the Missouri River to Fort Rice, located south of Bismarck, arriving there on July 21.

Although ranked as a brevet major at the time, Lazelle was still serving as Captain of Company H. Lazelle family records give no indication of where Rebecca and the young boys were from July 1872 to July 1874 when he was operating in the field. However, the regiment's Monthly Return from July 1872 indicates that the "officers' wives" of the regiment accompanied the headquarters element to Omaha Barracks. It is quite possible that this included Lazelle's family, as there were sufficient quarters for officers' families on post.[1]

The United States Army of 1872 was a mere shadow of its Civil War strength, with fewer than 30,000 officers and men organized into 25 infantry, ten cavalry, and five artillery regiments, supported by drastically reduced engineer, ordnance, commissary, quartermaster and medical departments. Freed of its post-war reconstruction duties, the Army had turned its attention to the challenges posed by westward expansion and an increasingly restless and combative native Indian population, especially in the northern territories where a second transcontinental railroad was being constructed across traditional Indian hunting grounds.

In 1862 Congress had authorized the Pacific Railroad to construct the first transcontinental line from Council Bluffs, Iowa, to San Francisco. The route selected, the so-called "central route," avoided the most challenging portions of the Rockies by following the Platte River through Nebraska, across the South Pass in Wyoming, and along much of the Oregon Trail. In 1864, Congress had authorized the Northern Pacific Railway to survey and build another route across the northern territories from Minnesota to the Pacific Coast and gave the railroad nearly 40 million acres in land grants. Construction had begun in 1870. [2]

THE ARMY, THE NORTHERN PACIFIC AND THE SIOUX

With the completion of the Pacific Railroad line in 1869 settlers had surged west in ever-increasing numbers. As clashes with still-nomadic Indian bands intensified, especially on the plains and in the Southwest, the Army was increasingly called upon to support the political leadership's efforts to rein in the Indians and place them on reservations.

Potential routes for the Northern Pacific ran through the hunting grounds of the nomadic northern tribes, including the Sioux and Cheyenne. Three Sioux chiefs—Oglala Lakota Red Cloud, Brule Lakota Spotted Tail, and Hunkpapa Lakota Sitting Bull—would have a major impact on Washington's efforts to secure the northern route.

Red Cloud and his Oglala Sioux had been living near whites since they had migrated into the Platte River country in the 1830s. Contact with whites at first had been limited, although settlers felt the incidental impact of Indian "raiding, fighting, and competing for dwindling buffalo herds." [3] By the 1850s, however, clashes between whites and Indians had become more common and Red Cloud had mounted his first major operation against whites in July 1856.

Spotted Tail, like Red Cloud, had initially earned his spurs fighting neighboring tribes, but he also had played a leading role in the Lakota Sioux's first major confrontations with the Army in 1854 and again in September 1855. For the next nine years he and his fellow Brule had largely stayed away from the whites in their tribal hunting grounds. Their quiescence ended, however, in November 1864, after an unprovoked attack by the 3rd Colorado Cavalry against a Cheyenne and Arapaho village in west-central Colorado. Now a "war chief," Spotted Tail had responded to the call for vengeance and joined in attacks on a stagecoach stop at Julesburg on the Platte River and close to Fort Rankin in early January 1865. [4]

Meanwhile, political opinion in Washington had been growing that perhaps "peace with the Indians could be achieved without resorting to violence." [5] The first attempt, in the spring of 1866 to obtain Indian acquiescence to strengthening and better protecting the Bozeman Trail —an overland route connecting the gold rush territory in Montana near Virginia City to the Oregon Trail in Wyoming—and to securing potential routes for a northern rail line had failed. Both Red Cloud and Spotted Tail—then seen as the "two most important Sioux leaders"—attended. While some chiefs signed the treaty, Red Cloud had stormed out as soon as he discerned that Army troops would be protecting the trail, "vowing to fight any white who tried to use the route." [6]

In mid-June, Col. Henry B. Carrington, charged with establishing a more permanent military presence along the trail and expecting little or no resistance, left Fort Laramie with a battalion of his 18th Infantry Regiment and marched up the Bozeman, dropping off a company at Fort Reno. On July 13, he camped at the forks of Piney Creek, some 65 miles northwest of Fort Reno, and his troops began building a stockade that would become Fort Phil Kearny. In early August, Carrington sent another two companies further north to establish a third post, to become Fort C.F. Smith, some 90 miles from Kearny. [7]

Carrington's expectations for Indian acquiescence were short-lived. Less than a week after his arrival in Piney Creek, Red Cloud's warriors, bolstered by Oglalas, Miniconjous, Sans Arcs, Brules, as well as some Cheyennes and Arapahoes, struck nearly every white man, military or civilian, who ventured up the trail and closed in on Fort Phil Kearny. Lacking the manpower to mount effective counter-offensives against the Indian harassment, Carrington focused instead on finishing construction of the forts. It was not until early December, after receiving direct orders from department commander General Philip St. George Cooke to attack the Indians in their winter camps, that he authorized offensive action. [8]

On December 6, responding to an attack on a wood train a few miles from Fort Kearny, Carrington mounted a two-pronged response but was soon surrounded and rescued in the nick of time by Capt. William J. Fetterman, leading a detachment of cavalry and mounted infantry. Sobered by this experience, Carrington intensified training and doubled the guard on wood trains, but remained largely in a reactive stance.

His next opportunity came on December 19, when Indians again attacked a wood train. This time a relief column, under orders not to pursue beyond a ridge some two miles north of the fort, mounted a successful rescue mission. On December 21, however, Red Cloud decided to mount a major operation, using an attack against a wood train in hopes of drawing Federal troops out of the fort. Carrington again dispatched a relief party, commanded by Captain Fetterman, again with orders not to pursue beyond the nearby ridge. The attack on the wood train, however, was merely a deception, and Fetterman's troops soon were struck and massacred by a much larger force of Lakota, Cheyenne, and Arapaho warriors. There were no survivors. A second relief column from the fort found the bodies of Fetterman and 80 men stripped naked and mutilated. [9]

In the aftermath of the Fetterman disaster, General Cooke almost immediately replaced Colonel Carrington as commander of Fort Kearny. A few weeks later, Army Commanding General Grant, apparently not convinced that Carrington was solely to blame, issued orders replacing Cooke with Bvt. Maj. Gen. Christopher C. Augur. In the end, after two investigations, Carrington essentially was exonerated, and General Sherman authorized aggressive operations against the Indians in both the Department of the Platte's Powder River country and the Department of the Missouri south of the Arkansas River. [10]

Operations in both the Platte and Missouri were largely ineffective in altering Indian behavior, and in July 1867, Congress authorized a new peace commission. Spotted Tail was persuaded to attend a conference at Fort Laramie in November, but he had insisted the Bozeman Trail must be closed. Red Cloud had refused to attend, sending word that he would not make peace until Fort Phil Kearny and Fort Smith were closed. The Commission gave up and returned to Washington. [11]

In March 1868, Washington had ordered the closure of Bozeman Trail Forts Kearny, Reno, and Smith, and a new Commission had been sent to Fort Laramie to negotiate a new treaty. This time, Washington had offered to set aside land for the Sioux covering basically the western half of present-day South Dakota. They also would be offered hunting rights along the Republican River on the Nebraska-Kansas border and on land above the North Platte, as well as rations and annuities for 30 years.

Red Cloud initially had again refused to attend until the Bozeman Trail forts were closed as promised. In November, after the closures were completed, he had agreed to make peace but would not sign a treaty confining his people to a reservation. Sitting Bull also had refused to sign, and his Hunkpapa band continued hit-and-run attacks on settlers and forts along the upper Missouri throughout the late 1860s and early 1870s. Spotted Tail, on the other hand, acting as chief of all the Brules, did sign and had moved his people to the White River, about 100 miles from Fort Randall.[12]

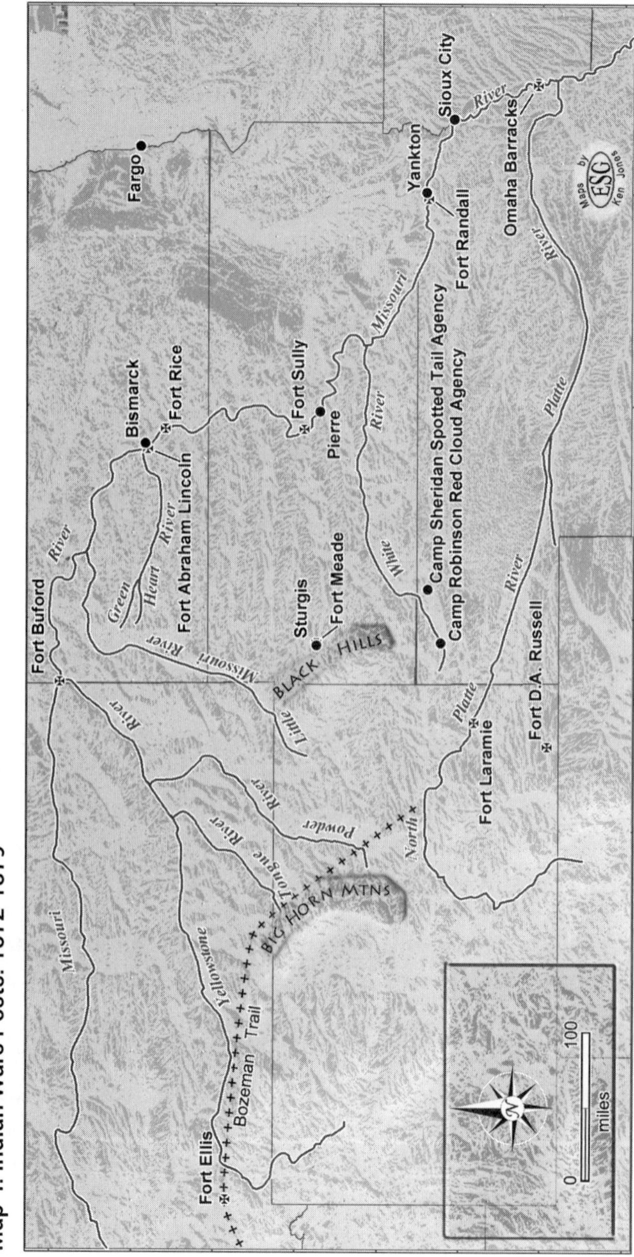

Map 4. Indian Wars Posts: 1872-1879

Red Cloud would continue to obfuscate for the next several years. However, by the time Lazelle and his company arrived in the territory in July 1872, Red Cloud had finally agreed to move his Oglala Sioux to the vicinity of a new "agency"—an area set aside and run by agents of the Office of Indian Affairs—on the White River near the present-day town of Crawford, Nebraska. [13] He back-peddled one more time in September but did move with a group of followers to winter along the White River. He and his people did not formally occupy the new agency on the White River until the next summer.

The Northern Pacific's Yellowstone Expeditions

As Lazelle and Company H pulled into Sioux City on their way to Fort Rice in July 1872, work was progressing on construction of the eastern (Dakota) and western (Washington) ends of the Northern Pacific Railroad, while survey missions diligently scouted for the best possible route through western Dakota and Montana. By early 1872, the line in the east had been extended 255 miles across Minnesota from Duluth on Lake Superior to Fargo on the Red River; the "Dakota division," some 200 miles west from Fargo to Bismarck on the Missouri River, was under construction. Further west, 65 miles of track were being laid between the Columbia River and Puget Sound. The Northern Pacific, however, faced a "600-mile information and engineering gap" in western Dakota and eastern Montana. [14]

A new Northern Pacific surveying expedition into the Yellowstone Valley was organized the summer of 1872, comprised of teams from Fort Ellis, near present-day Bozeman in the west, and Fort Rice on the Missouri in the east. They were to meet at the convergence of the Yellowstone and Powder rivers. Captain Lazelle and Company H, newly arrived at Fort Rice, were to participate in the escort for the eastern group. The six-company battalion of the 8th Infantry took several days to prepare for departure. Comprising about half of the military escort, which was under the overall command of Colonel David S. Stanley, 22nd Infantry, they left on July 26. [15]

Stanley, extra-cautious because of Indian threats, assigned a full company of infantry each day to accompany the surveyors. A portion of the rest of the escort was sent out as pickets (scouts in front and on the flanks of the main body), and the remainder "marched in formation around the wagons and beef herd." The command was supported with multi-barrel, rapid-fire Gatling guns "front and rear" and a 12-pound cannon and Gatling gun "in the center." [16]

The first two weeks for the Fort Rice group were quiet. However, on the morning of August 15, "before daylight, a party of Indians (numbers unknown) charged through camp yelling and firing." [17] According to Stanley, the attack was mounted by "a party of probably 20 Indians [who] rushed out of one of the clumps of wood, yelled, fired a volley into camp ... and ran away just as fast as their ponies could go." [18]

There were no casualties, and 8th Infantry companies A and C reached the Yellowstone, eight miles north of the Powder River on August 17. On August 22, however, there was a more serious attack, this time including Sitting Bull and some 150-200 Indians, that forced the main body of troops to pull back to the accompanying wagon train "while the skirmish line was thrown out to drive them back." The two 8th Infantry companies were "deployed as skirmishers but, the attack being confined to the right flank of the column, did not participate in the skirmish." Two days later, the two companies were detached to escort a train of empty supply wagons back to Fort Rice for resupply. Leaving Fort Rice again on September 9, they rejoined Stanley's main group, now on its way back to Fort Rice, at the Little Missouri on September 22. They returned to Fort Rice October 15.[19]

Meanwhile Lazelle's company and three others saw no recorded action, reporting only that they had left "Camp No. 6" (not further identified but possibly near Heart Butte) on August 1, arrived at the Little Missouri on the 9th, the Yellowstone on the 17th, Powder River on the 18th, and at Cottonwood Creek on the 31st. On September 26, Companies F and H left "Camp 47" escorting a wagon train back to Fort Rice, arriving at Camp No. 5, 43 miles from Fort Rice, on September 30. They remained there until October 7 when they rejoined the main Expedition at "Camp No. 60" and returned to Fort Rice October 15. Leaving Fort Rice on the steamer *Esperanza* on October 17, Lazelle and his men returned to Omaha on October 27. They had traveled 1,208 miles in one month. [20]

Having been granted leave for most of November, Lazelle remained at Omaha Barracks with his company through April 1873. The following month, along with three other companies, they left Omaha Barracks "to form part of the Command" of the 1873 Yellowstone Expedition.[21]

This expedition was intended to complete mapping out a northern rail line. Ten companies from the 7th Cavalry along with 19 infantry companies from five different regiments, an artillery company, 75 Indian scouts and some 275 wagons, again commanded by Colonel Stanley, now a brevet major general, provided the railroad surveyors with a heavily reinforced military escort. The expedition's cavalry troops were commanded by Lt. Col. George Armstrong Custer, who would lead his 7th Cavalry into annihilation three years later at Little Big Horn.[22]

Lazelle and the soldiers of Company H were part of the infantry contingent. They left Omaha Barracks May 24 on the steamer *Western* and returned in October.[23] During the expedition, probably at Fort Rice, Lazelle obtained a photo of Sioux Chief Red Cloud and sent it to his sons, signing it: "Red Cloud War Chief of the Sioux Camp near Fort Rice, June 16th '73, for darling Jacob and Horace, with Papa's Love." In fact, Red Cloud was far from Fort Rice that June, meeting yet again with Indian commissioners at the agency near Fort Laramie, this time to finally agree to move to the White River. [24]

The main goals of this third Northern Pacific expedition were to complete the line to Bismarck and "once and for all finish the Yellowstone mapping to have a 'line of survey' from Lake Superior to Puget Sound." Secondary objectives were "to find a shortcut west of Bismarck, thus avoiding potentially expensive construction along the east half of the Heart River, and to complete the Musselshell [River] surveying." [25]

General Sheridan also saw this expedition as an opportunity to "awe" and possibly punish the Sioux, and he planned to establish one or two new forts along the railroad line between the "crossing of the Missouri and the mouth of the Powder River." The escort plan involved over 1,500 men leaving from Fort Rice and Fort Buford. Once they reached the Yellowstone at Glendive, northeast of O'Fallon Creek, they would "march upriver to Pompeys Pillar, cross to the Musselshell, loop back east to the Yellowstone and return, selecting the site for a new fort along the way." [26]

The four companies of the 8th arrived at Fort Rice by rail and steamer in late May. There, Lazelle and Company H were assigned to escort the expedition's "Scientific Corps," which included a Harvard zoologist and mineralogist, a Harvard artist, a geologist, and a photographer. Lazelle and his charges left Fort Rice June 14 and arrived at Muddy Creek on the 30th. The main group covered 69 miles in the first six days, crossing the Heart River on June 25. "Rain, humidity ... the custom of marching 50 minutes and resting 10, with a 30-minute lunch, and [the threat of] Indians dictated the daily pace." [27]

Arriving at the convergence of the Heart and Green Rivers on July 5, the military group met survey party leader Thomas Rosser who announced that he had found a better route from Bismarck that would save "dozens of miles of difficult construction along the Heart River." [28] When the command reached the Yellowstone on July 15, they established a supply depot at its junction with Glendive Creek, called Camp Canby.

Lazelle and his company crossed the Yellowstone on July 25, marched up its western bank for 68 miles and camped once more on the 31st, about seven miles southwest of the mouth of the Powder River. Leaving camp on August 2, they reached the Musselshell near Swimming Woman's Creek on the 19th, having marched some 220 miles. Along the way, Colonel Stanley and the military command found an Indian camp, recently abandoned by Sitting Bull, at the confluence of the Rosebud and

Yellowstone. Lt. Col. George Custer, leading the advance scouting group, found another large abandoned village the next day, and was harassed by Indians on August 11. Lazelle and the Scientific Corps, however, escaped any contact with Indians, marching along the Musselshell for 68 miles and then cross-country back to the Yellowstone, arriving at the mouth of the Little Porcupine River on August 31. All told, in August they had traveled 376 miles. [29]

On September 1, Lazelle and Company H left Camp No. 59 on the Yellowstone, at the mouth of the Little Porcupine, marching 126 miles down the Yellowstone along its banks and reaching the stockade at Glendive on September 9. There they, along with Colonel Stanley, the Scientific Corps and the other infantry companies, boarded the steamer *Josephine*, destination Omaha, where they arrived October 8. Rejoining the regimental headquarters at Fort Russell on October 12, the company had traveled another 1,218 miles in less than two weeks.[30]

One of the newspaper correspondents traveling with the 1873 expedition was Samuel June Barrows, working for *The New York Tribune.* "Brilliant but sickly," Barrows had served as Secretary of State Seward's personal secretary and wrote for the *Tribune* during the summer to help pay his way through Harvard Divinity School. [31] Lazelle and Barrows developed a friendship during the expedition, one that would last for the rest of Lazelle's life.

Fort Russell and Spotted Tail's Agency

During the fall and early winter months at Fort Russell, Lazelle and his company were largely engaged in routine garrison duties. In February 1874, however, the garrison was called upon to furnish troops for an expedition, organized by General Edward Ord, commander of the Department of the Platte, to Red Cloud's and Spotted Tail's agencies. Ord was responding to a January request from J. J. Saville, the Indian Agent at Red Cloud Agency, that a military post be established there to provide security. He also was reacting to hostile northern Indian activity at the agency and near Laramie Peak on February 9.[32]

In all, eight companies of infantry and eight of cavalry were sent out. Three companies of the 8th, commanded by Lazelle, left Fort Russell on February 22, reaching Fort Laramie and camping "near post" on February 26. It was "bitter cold," and the temperature the day before had been twelve degrees below zero. Another two companies left the following day, reaching Fort Laramie on the 28th. [33]

On March 3, Lazelle, now commanding a battalion with companies B, C, H, and K of the 8th, and a company of the 3rd Cavalry, left Fort Laramie for Spotted Tail's Agency, 120 miles away on the White River, arriving on the 11th. Company F left Fort Laramie for the Red Cloud Agency and Camp Robinson about 90 miles away, arriving there on March 7. [34]

In April 1874, a *New York Herald* reporter noted that the Indians had been generally "well disposed and quiet" at the two agencies until they learned the Federal troops were coming, which had "greatly changed their pacific disposition and exasperated them." The reporter worried that the "reoccupation" of this territory by Federal troops could lead to a "long war, and of no small magnitude, not only with the northern bands [bands under various chiefs who had refused to be confined to their reservations] ... but with the greater portion of Spotted Tail's and Red Cloud's bands."

The solution, in the reporter's eyes, was to relocate the two agencies to the Missouri River, "where all the other agencies of the Sioux nation are located," a recommendation, he noted, already made by General Sherman. He also noted one major advantage of the Missouri River agencies, that they were "far removed" from any white settlement, while the present locations of the Spotted Tail and Red Cloud agencies were within a three-day ride of many cattle ranches and small settlements. [35]

This view was shared by a group of Indian Commissioners sent out from Washington. The Commission had been appointed in late February

1874 to visit Red Cloud's and Spotted Tail's agencies in an attempt to get the Indians to "abandon their nomadic habits and accept a permanent home within the Sioux reservation or elsewhere," and to establish a permanent agency where they agreed to be settled. The Commission was also to get the Indians to agree to abrogate key provisions of the 1868 treaty. One gave them the right to hunt on lands north of the North Platte River and Republican Fork of the Smoky Hill River as long as buffalo were there. The other declared the country north of the North Platte and east of the Big Horn Mountains "un-ceded Indian country" that was closed to whites. [36]

The commissioners' first visit to the two agencies in March achieved none of their objectives. Red Cloud resisted all of their entreaties. While the tribal chiefs at Spotted Tail seemed willing to give up their hunting rights after the next winter hunt in return for compensation, they rejected the proposal to relocate and establish a permanent agency.

Having attended the meeting with Spotted Tail, Lazelle reported that the Chief, who was the only speaker for the Indians, began by saying that this was the last council with the commissioners they would hold, that they would not move, and that, if the whites moved them they would have to send more soldiers here than they had now. He went on to argue that the soldiers sent to the agency were no longer needed because the northern Indians who had caused the trouble were now gone and "we are now at peace."

Despite this setback, Lazelle believed that the commissioners were "resolved to carry out their intention of changing this agency location," and would return with enough troops to scout the country, select a site for the agency, "put the buildings there, and grub and annuities, then tell the Indians to come or stay away." He went on to express grave concern that:

> The buzz of these Commissioners will end in smoke, also their plans unless the Agency is moved to the Missouri. ... These Indians had better by far be left alone at their Agency than to be forced into hostility by being forced to accept civilization, and a religion

> they can't understand and don't want to understand. The peace Commissioners have simply made mischief here by irritating these people and insisting upon impracticable measures and those which the Government will not (at present at least) second them in. [37]

The Commissioners returned in August 1874, escorted by two companies of the 32rd Cavalry and the Spotted Tail Indian Agent. After a lengthy survey of the countryside, they selected a location along West Beaver Creek, just ten miles south of Spotted Tail's "Brule" encampment. In justifying the new location, the Commissioners pointed out that Beaver Creek would "support the agency and post, and Spotted Tail can remain in Brule, and the whites and mixed-bloods find good land for farming on White Clay, both locations being sufficiently near Beaver on either side to come to that place for supplies and rations."

They also were successful in convincing Spotted Tail to give up his hunting rights on the Republican River in Kansas and Nebraska, in return for $25,000 in compensation, which he would take in the form of "American horses and a few light wagons." Red Cloud, however, refused to budge on hunting rights even though some of his younger chiefs accepted the terms. The Commission never did raise with either Red Cloud or Spotted Tail the issue of relinquishing their rights to the unceded territory east of the summit of the Big Horn mountains, in part because "the temper of the Indians was such as to make it apparent that an effort to accomplish too much would end in accomplishing nothing." [38]

In May 1875, Red Cloud, Spotted Tail, and other chiefs travelled to Washington, and met with President Ulysses S. Grant, pleading that he honor the Indian treaties and stop the surge of white miners. Grant urged them instead to sell the Black Hills and settle down in Indian territory. The chiefs refused and returned with no agreement.

Neither Red Cloud nor Spotted Tail participated in the so-called "Great Sioux War" of 1876-77, led by Crazy Horse and Sitting Bull, when Custer and his 7th Cavalry troops were decimated at Little Big Horn. Both kept their people on their agencies. Spotted Tail participated in the final negotiations leading to the sale of the Black Hills, and both helped orchestrate Crazy Horse's surrender.

Onward to California and Fort Yuma

In April 1874, as the Commissioners were meeting with Spotted Tail, Lazelle, apparently having had his fill of "field duty," again applied for staff duty, using the good offices of a friend in Washington to deliver his request. While undoubtedly anxious to move with his family back to "civilization," Lazelle also may have been motivated by the difference in pay received by staff and line officers. As Wilhelm noted in his reporting, a major with 20 years' service as a staff officer in a city received about $100 a month more in pay and allowances than his counterpart serving in the field with a regiment. Thus, the officer in the field would received some $3,500 annually, while his city-dwelling counterpart would earn $4,700, which also was $200 per year more than was paid to a full colonel in the field.

Lazelle's request either was never forwarded or ultimately refused, and he returned to Fort Russell from Spotted Tail's Agency in mid-May, conducting a group of prisoners, and stayed there in leave status through the month of June.[39]

In July 1874, the 8th Infantry was ordered to relocate to Arizona Territory. Lazelle—reunited with his family—and his company left for San Francisco on July 29, arriving there on August 2. The company was quartered on Yerba Buena Island in San Francisco Bay until September 5, when it departed for Arizona.

Leaving Yerba Buena on the steamer *Montana*, Lazelle, his family, and his troops sailed south along the coast of California and Baja California, arriving at the mouth of the Colorado River in the Gulf of California on September 11. There, they transferred to a flat-bottom steamer for the trip up the Colorado to Fort Yuma. The company reached the fort on September 24.

Yuma served as the major supply depot for Federal forces operating in the Arizona Territory. It received and forwarded supplies to forces north of the Gila River and served as a "supply reserve" for the entire territory. It also served as a "quartering place for Army mules, and often had as many as 900 animals in readiness." [40]

In her memoir, Martha Summerhayes, wife of 1st Lt. John W. Summerhayes of the 8th Infantry, described a brutal voyage from San Francisco to Port Isabel at the mouth of the Colorado. During the trip, with the supply of ice nearly exhausted, the meat "turned green" and an "indescribable odor" emanated from the refrigerator below decks. "It followed us to the table, and when we tasted the food we tasted the odor." [41]

After 13 days marked by wild seas, stifling heat below decks, and debilitating sea sickness, the officers and their families transferred to a river boat, towing a barge filled with enlisted men, for the trip up the Colorado to Fort Yuma. During the final few days sailing up the Colorado, Summerhayes and her fellow passengers "resigned ourselves to the dreadful heat, and at the end of two more days the river had begun to narrow, and we arrived at Fort Yuma ... which was said to be the very hottest place that ever existed."

Many years later, Lazelle's younger son Horace also remembered Fort Yuma as being very hot, even in the winter. He was four years old at the time, and they often slept on the roof of their flat adobe house at night. He also remembered watching cattle being shipped by boat. The ranchers would swim the cattle out into the Colorado, as there was no dock to which the boat could tie up alongside their ranches. A rope hoist would be lowered from the boat and put around the horns of the cattle that were lifted individually to the boat, "bellowing heartily." Horace remembered his father asking one of the men supervising the job, "Isn't that rather painful for those animals?" The man replied "Oh no, they get used to it." [42]

A Promotion and a Transfer

After less than three months at Fort Yuma, on December 15, 1874, Captain Lazelle was promoted to major and assigned to the 1st Infantry Regiment at Fort Sully, South Dakota, on the Missouri River about 100 miles north of Yankton, and not far from Pierre. His reporting date was initially delayed to March 1, 1875, and eventually to April 1. Until then, he remained on the 8th Infantry rolls. However, he and his family began the slow trip back to Omaha Barracks after Christmas.

On the return voyage, they again took a flat stern-wheeler, the *Cocopaw*, down the Colorado River to the Gulf of California where they were picked up by an old ocean-going side-wheeler that took them to San Francisco. The *Cocopaw* was named for the Cocopaw Indians that were in this part of the country. Horace remembered seeing them down at the river's edge putting mud on their heads to get rid of lice. After a few weeks in San Francisco, they left for Omaha on a train "with a wood-driven locomotive with a large smoke stack," a trip that took four or five days.

As Horace recollected, the trip from Omaha to Fort Sully required them to take the train to Yankton, on the Missouri River, northwest of Sioux City, and then a river boat up the Missouri. The boat, a stern-wheeler, drew only about eighteen inches and got stuck for two or three days on a sand bar en route. The currents in the river changed so frequently that the crew didn't know where these bars were and kept running up onto them.

Major Lazelle reported for duty at Fort Sully and assumed command of the post on June 9, 1875. At that time, the regiment was headquartered, along with five of its companies, at Fort Randall on the Missouri River about 100 miles southwest of Sioux Falls; four companies were at Fort Sully; and one was stationed at the Lower Brule Agency, about 50 miles southeast of Pierre.[43]

Photo 10. Red Cloud

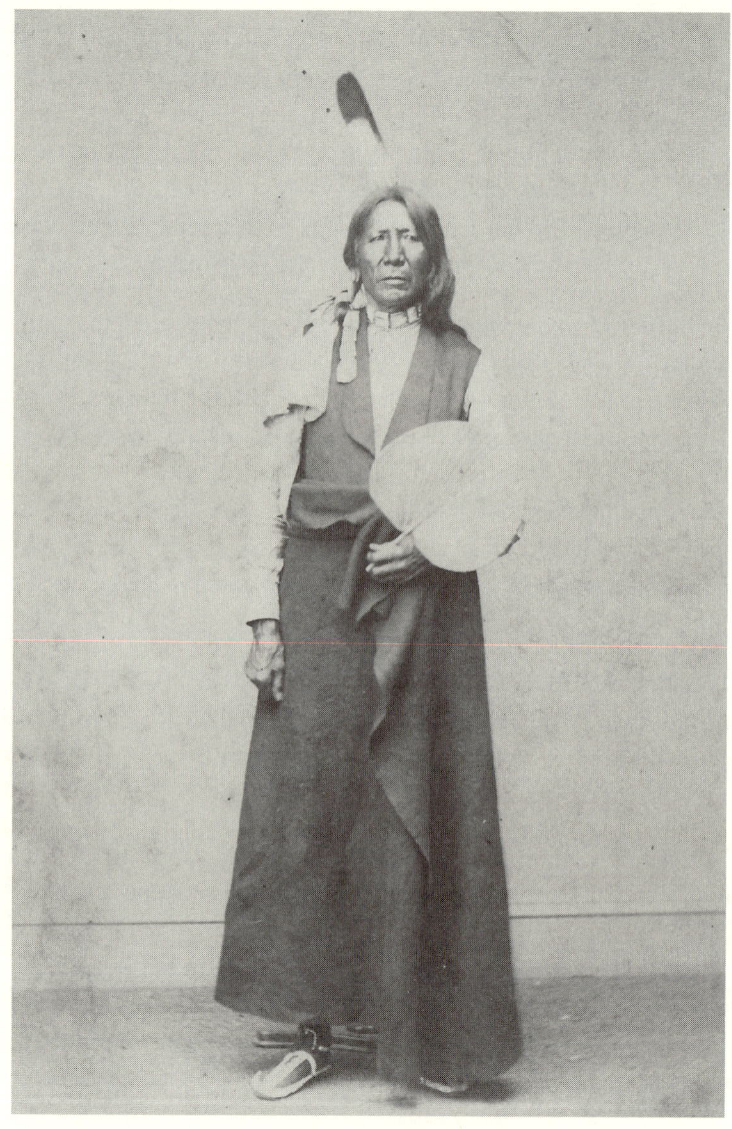

Photo 11. Fort Sully—Guard Mounting and Enlisted Quarters, 1875

Photo 12. Fort Sully—Officers' Quarters, 1875

Photo 13. Maj. Lazelle, Jacob, Horace, Their Pony and Dog Nick at Fort Sully, 1875

At Fort Sully, Lazelle commanded about 200 men; with wives and families, a total of about 300 people lived on post. Among the costs listed in various post accountings were one interpreter at $50 a month and a blacksmith at $60 a month. Horace remembered Pierre as nothing more than a "swamp on the Missouri River" and Fort Sully as "very isolated," but an "important post" against the Indians along the Missouri River, with stockades built using 16-foot-long planks.

Known as "Fort Sully II"—the original post was abandoned in 1866—the fort was located on a mile-long plateau just east of the Missouri River and below a range of bluffs, about ten miles southeast of the Cheyenne River Agency. One of a string of forts along the Missouri, it was described as a "good defensive position easily protected by cannon ... situated on grassland with numerous trees, including cottonwood, willow, elm, cedar, and dogwood."[44]

A BOY'S VIEW OF INDIAN COUNTRY

Horace recalled the winters as "so very cold and long," but he had many fond memories of Fort Sully—a "beautiful prairie country where we could look miles and miles in each direction with nothing but flat grassland—no hills or mountains." As he recalled many years later:

> There were no large cities there in any part where we lived but there were some few white people whom we would go to visit. When we did do so, we would always go in an army wagon driven by a soldier with four mules. It had three seats in it: the front seat on which the driver sat and then inside the wagon were two more seats facing each other, one right back of the driver's seat and one in the rear facing forward—how we would go racing over the country when we would go for a drive, and the driver, a soldier, would crack his whip over the four mules and away we would go.
>
> The Indians came to the fort to confab with Major Lazelle, the commanding officer, about their petty problems. The arrived in full regalia and sat around on the porch and in the living room

smoking their awful pipes. Father would speak to them and they'd say "Humph" and then he'd say "Humph" back to them. Some of the important ones included Yellow Horse and Black Eagle. They were Cheyenne Indians and were friendly to the government, helping scout against savage Indians on the warpath. They were good fighters and reliable. They once came to get an old cow that had died on the post and they wanted to eat it. They were not allowed on post unless on legitimate business.

One winter, the family took a trip down to the Riggs Indian School, about 12 miles south of Sully, for either Christmas or Thanksgiving. It was a great treat. The missionaries there, Mr. and Mrs. Riggs and his sister, were devoting themselves to the care (medical and religious) and education of the Indians. We traveled in an "ambulance"—later called a doughty wagon—which sat a driver and one passenger in front and four inside facing each other. The two seats inside could be flattened out to accommodate stretchers. There was a boot in back for baggage. Either I or Jacob rode on our pony, depending on whose turn it was to ride, and the other rode in the wagon with Mother.

At Fort Sully we used Missouri River water that was the color of coffee with cream. Wagons with water tanks pulled by eight mules went down to the river daily. Each house had three to five large heavy wooden barrels that were charred inside. These were filled with water and left to stand for 24–48 hours. It would then be clear and could be drunk. When the water got close to the bottom of the barrel, the mud was poured out and the barrel cleaned.

There were vegetable gardens for the troops and private gardens for the families. Vegetables were stored in root cellars over winter. A herd of cattle supplied meat to the commissary store where everyone got their food. Supplies were also brought in by boat, but they never knew when they would arrive, because the boats got stuck on sand bars.

Our family had its own cow, milked by a soldier and sort of "striker" named Madill, who also was paid to do other chores. We also had two Norwegian girls—Martha and Mary—one a cook

> the other a maid. Laundresses were wives of common soldiers. Not many soldiers had wives with them—it was discouraged. The laundresses lived in small quarters of their own. Through them the "bad" element could get in to the soldiers. Otherwise there was no place on post for hangers-on and women. The soldiers might be able to contact some of the Indian women. There was not much chance for philandering around, but also no weekly inspection for disease.
>
> There also were sutler stores [or trading posts] near the post, but not in the garrisoned part. They were run by civilians, sort of concessions granted by the government to sell things that weren't available in the commissary. No liquor was allowed at first. Later, when beer was allowed in the canteen, it was available in the sutler's store. Similarly, no firearms were allowed until legislation permitted the sale of firearms; later the Indians were better armed than the soldiers. They could buy Winchester rifles.
>
> Father liked to play games with us and take us fishing. One day while fishing, we took Nick, our old Newfoundland dog along. We used raw meat as bait and laid down one of the baited hooks for a minute. Nick swallowed it, hook and all. We couldn't get the hook out, and so we just cut off a section of the line. The next day we took Nick to the post hospital to see if anything could be done, but they couldn't. Nick never seemed to be any worse for wear and the hook never bothered him. The post doctor, Dr. King, who looked Nick over, had a daughter, Nita, about my age who was my "sweetie," and an older son who played with Jacob. [45]

During the first six months of their stay at Fort Sully, Lazelle's troops were largely occupied with garrison duty, while he dealt with the day-to-day challenges of a post commander, including desertions by enlisted men in July, September, and October 1875. In May, 1876, one of Lazelle's companies was dispatched to Fort Rice for the summer months and replaced by another company from Fort Randall. In June, a second company was dispatched to the field, this time to "prevent immigration to the Black Hills," setting up camp "near old Fort Pierre," Dakota Territory. [46] A surge in interest by settlers and speculators had been stimulated by persistent rumors of Black Hills gold reserves, government efforts to purchase the Black Hills from the Sioux, and a geological expedition to the area during the summer of 1875.[47]

Lazelle's men returned from the Black Hills in August reporting that they had found "no pure water" for the first 120 miles of their 420-mile trek back to Fort Sully. That fall and winter, the troops of Fort Sully remained largely on garrison duty, punctuated by short forays, including small parties to repair telegraph lines and a three-company operation in October a few miles up the Missouri "to the camp of Tall Mandan, to assist in disarming the Indians."[48]

The regiment was not always focused solely on protecting white settlers. At times, the troops simply were policing thievery and disputes among the Indian tribes. For example, in September 1876, Lazelle wrote to the Department's Adjutant that he had received information that "thieves" who had stolen horses from Two Kettle's band of Sioux in August were located near Fort Rice, south of Bismarck. He sent out a party of troops and "captured three of the thieves and five of the stolen horses. The horses were given to the Two Kettle's Band, and the thieves are now at this post [Sully], awaiting transportation to Yankton, D.T., where they will be turned over to the civil authorities as previously directed by you."[49]

Horace remembered that while his father was away from Fort Sully on one foray, an illustrator from one of the New York newspapers went along with the scouting party. He made a sketch of the first house in Fargo, North Dakota, and gave it to Lazelle, who later had it framed and presented it to the city of Fargo. They put it in the courthouse and sent him a testimonial of appreciation.[50]

Lazelle, Miles, and the "Great Sioux War"

While Lazelle and his soldiers were largely inactive at Fort Sully in 1876 and early 1877, the same could not be said for other troops in the

Department of Dakota, commanded by Gen. Alfred H. Terry, or the Department of the Platte, under Gen. George R. Crook. Both commanders were dealing with the aftermath of the Battle of the Little Bighorn in June 1876, in eastern Montana, where five of Lt. Col. George Custer's 7th Cavalry companies from Fort Abraham Lincoln in Dakota Territory had been annihilated by a combined force of Lakota, Northern Cheyenne, and Arapaho Indians, led by Sitting Bull, Crazy Horse, Chief Gall, and other notable chiefs.

Almost immediately, Congress authorized two new forts for the Yellowstone region, and General Sheridan dispatched reinforcements for both General Crook and General Terry. Among them was the 5th Infantry Regiment, commanded by Colonel Nelson A. Miles, a veteran of Antietam, Fredericksburg, and Chancellorsville, who had been brevetted to major general in the Regular Army and had taken command of the 5th in 1869.[51]

Initially operating under separate command structures, much to the consternation of Colonel Miles who "found it ridiculous that Terry and Crook acted with so little coordination" against the Indians, the two generals decided to mount a joint operation in August 1876. Miles, dubious that a 3,200-man force would have much success against a wary opponent, volunteered to "guard the fords of the Yellowstone between the Powder and Tongue Rivers" and block any attempt by Sitting Bull and his followers to escape to Canada. General Terry agreed:

> During the campaign of 1876 it became evident that to contend successfully with the hostile Sioux it was necessary to obtain a firm foothold on the Yellowstone River, to establish posts which would serve as bases of supply for troops operating in the field and from which the winter camps of the Indians could be reached.[52]

The regiment reached its "cantonment" at the Tongue River by the end of September and engaged in its first fight with Sitting Bull's warriors near Cedar Creek, Montana, north of the Yellowstone in October. The bulk of the Indian force and five chiefs surrendered, but Sitting Bill and a small band of warriors escaped. In November, Miles split his regiment into two battalions. Commanding one of the two, Miles had running encounters with Sitting Bull well into December, but the Sioux chief would elude capture. [53]

In late December 1876, Miles turned his attention to Sioux and Cheyenne bands led by Crazy Horse up along the Tongue River valley, eventually engaging in a major fight in the Wolf Mountains and returning to his Tongue River post with captives. According to Lt. Gen. P. H. Sheridan, commanding the Division of the Missouri, this action and the "constant pounding and sleepless activity upon the part of our troops" began to take effect. In February 1877, over 200 lodges of Minneconjous and Sans Arcs surrendered at Cheyenne Agency. In March, more than 2,200 Indians surrendered at Camp Sheridan and Camp Robinson in the Department of the Platte, and in April, 300 Cheyennes surrendered at Miles's Tongue River cantonment. Finally, on May 6, Crazy Horse and nearly 900 of his people arrived at Camp Robinson and surrendered to General Crook. [54]

With the so-called "Great Sioux War" nearly over, there was one more immediate task: tracking down and subduing the Minneconjou chief, Lame Deer, and his small band of holdouts. On May 1, with four companies of the 2nd Cavalry from Fort Ellis, two of his own infantry companies and four from the 22nd Infantry, Miles set out after Lame Deer who had been reported to be in the vicinity of the Rosebud. After six days, Miles found the Indians' camp and attacked in the early morning darkness. Fourteen Indians, including Lame Deer, were killed.

According to General Terry, the actions of Miles and his troops to date had "substantially clear [ed] the country west of the Missouri River, south of the British line [Canadian border], and north of the Black Hills, of hostile bands." Crazy Horse had been compelled to surrender, Lame Deer's remaining followers had been forced south and east and eventually surrendered, and Sitting Bull had been forced to flee across the border into Canada. [55]

With Sitting Bull still at large and reportedly ready to resume fighting, General Terry's command was reinforced once again in June. Six companies of the 11th Infantry were sent to the convergence of the Bighorn and Little Big Horn rivers to establish a fort, and eleven companies of the 7th Cavalry, under Col. S. D. Sturgis, and four companies of the 1st Infantry, under Maj. H. M. Lazelle were "held for service in the field." [56]

Lazelle and his battalion of four companies left Fort Sully April 24, 1877, on the steamer *C. K. Peck* and reached Miles's cantonment on the Tongue River May 23, having changed steamers at Fort Abraham Lincoln. One company was immediately dispatched to provide security for Camp Sherman at Cedar Creek, which served as a supply base for the 7th Cavalry.[57]

That summer, having determined that he should "hold strongly the line of the Yellowstone" to prevent any Indians breaking away from their agencies from joining up with Sitting Bull, Miles maintained the bulk of his force along the river. However, he also sent out periodic scouting parties "for the purpose of patrolling the country and keeping it clear of small parties that might otherwise stray into it." According to General Terry, the "most important of these movements" through the country between the Yellowstone, Tongue, Powder, and Little Missouri rivers and the Black Hills, were made by Lazelle, commanding detachments of the 1st and 22nd Infantry and 7th Cavalry, and Maj. J. S. Brisbin, commanding a battalion of the 2nd Cavalry. [58]

In their first foray into the field, Lazelle was ordered on June 7 to take his three Tongue River companies, along with three others from the 22nd Infantry and one from the 2nd Cavalry, and try to establish a road along the south side of the Yellowstone to the Rosebud. Horace remembered that his father was mounted on horseback, as were most officers, while the enlisted men marched or rode in covered wagons pulled by six mules each. The Indians called the infantry "walka-heaps." They returned five days later, "the attempt to establish the road having proven unsuccessful." [59]

Less than a week later, Lazelle, with his three companies, and six from the 22nd Infantry, left the Tongue River Cantonment for the mouth of the Powder River on the steamer *Ashland*, "equipped for the field and to operate against hostile Indians." Lazelle's orders were to scout the country east and west of the Little Missouri and east of the Powder and investigate the possibility of opening a wagon road to the Black Hills. [60]

Joined by a company from the 7th Cavalry and accompanied by scouts, a Napoleon gun (12-pound cannon), and a wagon train with 40 days of rations, Lazelle's command left the Powder River on June 16. Marching upstream to the southeast, they reached their initial destination—the "point at which Custer's trail from Fort Lincoln to Black Hills intersects the headwaters of the Little Missouri"—on June 27 and found Custer's trail a half mile from the river.

Along the way, Lazelle's troops found two small Indian trails, and on June 24 his scouts and cavalry troops found an abandoned village of about 200 Indians on the Little Missouri with a trail "apparently seven days old" leading northward down the Little Missouri. For the next ten days, Lazelle followed the trail, which eventually left the river "for a mountainous ridge running parallel to it." On July 4, near the "big bend of the Little Missouri," his scouts and cavalry engaged about 15 Indians. Learning from friendly Cheyennes that the Indians were Sioux and their camp was at Sentinel Buttes, Lazelle pushed ahead the night of July 7. Arriving at the camp early the next morning, they found it hastily abandoned. Examining what the Indians had left behind, Lazelle was convinced they were "a remnant of Lame Deer's band" with "little to subsist on" and with "a considerable number of women and children." [61]

Finding evidence of more Indians, Lazelle followed the trail to a second camp, also deserted, but at this point decided to end his pursuit. Releasing the companies of the 22nd Infantry and 7th Cavalry, Lazelle and his battalion returned to Cedar Creek on the Yellowstone to resupply on July 21.

Three days later, Lazelle received orders to escort a large wagon train that was heading out to resupply Maj. James Brisbin's battalion of the 2nd Cavalry that had taken up the pursuit of Lame Deer's holdouts. Joining Brisbin near Slim Buttes, Lazelle turned over the supplies and on August 12 started back to the headwaters of the Little Missouri to construct a stockade that would be guarded by a company of the 5th Infantry. Completing that task on August 19, Lazelle and his battalion returned to the Tongue River Cantonment September 1, having covered a total of just over 1,000 miles. [62]

BLACK "GOLD"

During the summer 1877 operation, Lazelle discovered an "exceedingly valuable and practically inexhaustible" deposit of lignite coal along the Yellowstone River, about 100 miles from its mouth. In a memorandum that was widely reported in the local press, he described the deposit, a few feet under the surface, as "solid, pure and massive." At the landing where he discovered the coal, a steamer could run up to the bank and "put a plank on the bed where nearly 2,000 tons lay almost uncovered." He also believed that, "with very little labor," some 4,000 to 5,000 tons could be uncovered and "taken out immediately."

In concluding his report, Lazelle noted the potential savings to the government if the coal deposits were exploited to provide fuel for Army posts in the region along the river:

> Boats going down the Yellowstone empty could take on two hundred tons in a few hours, and the barges more, and as the expense of transportation would be small, in my judgment, there may be made a large saving to the Government in its use as fuel. Barges towed up empty and left to be filled with coal could be taken down by return steamers which will almost invariably come down without a load. [63]

An article in the *Bismarck Tribune* stressed the significance of the find, since steamers running up and down the Upper Missouri and Yellowstone rivers were "dependent entirely for fuel upon the scanty fringe of timber found along the banks of the rivers, and only at rare intervals at that." The newspaper, in a second article, went on to opine that the coal and easy access to it would "eventually furnish the fuel for generating the motive power for all the boats, engines, and may I not say for claiming this vast and beautiful grazing and farming country." [64]

While the local press waxed eloquently over this important new discovery and its potential benefits to the territory, Lazelle's report made its way up through channels from the Department of Dakota to General of the Army Sherman and Secretary of War, George Washington McCrary. McCrary forwarded it to Carl Schurz, the Secretary of the Interior, endorsing Sherman's recommendation that "the Land Office extend its surveys so that private parties may purchase these mines."

With a degree of political finesse not uncommon today, Secretary Schurz responded in late November, forwarding to McCrary a memo from J. A. Williamson, Commissioner of the General Land Office, who professed that there were no funds available in the budget for such a survey. However, Williamson also objected on more fundamental legal grounds: the area in question appeared to "fall within Indian Reservations." [65]

Today, Montana is the fifth-largest coal producing state in the country, with substantial reserves of lignite in the area first discovered by Lazelle.

During the fall of 1877, Lazelle and his troops continued scouting. From October 1 through 29, Companies G and K, under his command, lay at "Lazelle's Crossing" on the Yellowstone River near the mouth of O'Fallon's Creek, where they constructed a ferry across the Yellowstone, five miles below O'Fallon's Creek. They also escorted wagon trains hauling government freight between Glendive Cantonment on the Yellowstone north of O'Fallon's Creek and the Tongue River to the south. In early November, Lazelle and his men returned to Lazelle's Crossing to form part of an escort taking Nez Perce Indians (prisoners) to Fort Buford. They returned to Fort Sully in December. [66]

FORT MEADE

In mid-August 1878, Lazelle was ordered on detached service to oversee construction of a new post in the Black Hills near Bear Butte, Dakota Territory. He departed Fort Sully on August 18 and was joined soon thereafter by companies F and K. He remained at the new post, eventually named Fort Meade, as Commanding Officer, along with his family, through May 1879.

The establishment of Fort Meade was driven, in part, by the discovery of gold in the Black Hills, which had led to the signing of the Black Hills Agreement with the Sioux in late 1876 and its Congressional ratification in February 1877. Among other provisions, the agreement ceded the Black Hills back to the United States, removing the territory from the Sioux Reservation and permitting the construction of three wagon roads across the reservation to the Black Hills. Nonetheless, many Sioux continued to attack the settlers, who lobbied for a Black Hills fort after attacks in June 1877 along the valleys of Bear Butte and False Bottom creeks. Congress authorized construction of a post in April 1878, and General Sheridan dispatched his brother, Bvt. Lt. Col. Michael Sheridan, to the Bear Butte area to scout a proper location. [67]

Photo 14. Fort Meade—1878

Courtesy of the Old Fort Meade Museum

Lazelle and 1st Lt. George Ruhlen of the 17th Infantry, an experienced engineer who would design the layout of the fort and undertake its construction, were preceded to the area by eight cavalry and six infantry companies from Forts Sully, Laramie, and Abraham Lincoln, including three companies of the 1st Infantry. They arrived in July 1878 and pitched their tents at the base of Bear Butte close by a rudimentary cavalry encampment named Camp J. G. Sturgis, after the son of 7th Cavalry commander Col. Samuel D. Sturgis. The site also would be known as Camp Ruhlen. [68]

In September, Lazelle returned to Fort Sully to move his family, who at some point had relocated to Fort Sully from Omaha, to Camp Sturgis, even as construction of a permanent fort continued. The family's household goods were loaded onto large six-mule wagons, while Rebecca, the boys, and their personal effects rode in a four-mule ambulance. Jacob and Horace shared riding a small Indian pony.

Accompanied by an infantry escort of some 50 or 60 men, their route was through "wild prairie country, no towns or villages," stopping each night near water. Usually they would go about 15 to 20 miles a day, stopping around 4:00 p.m. Before supper, the two young lieutenants with the party would drill the troops on mounting arms and gun inspection and drill. After taps was sounded at night, usually 9 o'clock, all lights were put out and the camp was dead quiet.

One night, Horace remembered, they were abruptly awoken by a rifle shot, and Major Lazelle was "up and out in a second." It turned out to be one of the sentries on post, who thought he saw something, which he took to be an Indian. It proved to be a false alarm, and though most of the camp was disturbed for the rest of the night, "we kids went right off to sleep again." [69]

After about two weeks, the wagon train arrived at the Bear Butte camp. While the post was being built in the fall and winter of 1878, most officers, their families, and the enlisted men lived in tents—well into the winter months with the temperature often dipping below minus 30 degrees. Lazelle's family was lucky. They had a small, four-room log cabin, one room deep with three bedrooms and a parlor. As there were limited cooking facilities, they took most of their meals in the village of Sturgis, just off the camp about a quarter mile away, which had a restaurant, saloons, and a grocery store.

The establishment of Camp Ruhlen, renamed Fort Meade in December, was not without its frustrations, particularly in dealing with the Washington bureaucracy. On September 13, 1878, in his capacity as commander of Camp Ruhlen, Lazelle wrote to the U.S. Postmaster-General, via the Headquarters of the Department of Dakota, requesting the establishment of a money-order Post Office and "brass-lock" office at Camp Ruhlen.

In making his case, Lazelle emphasized that a money order office would be "obviously advantageous to officers and soldiers who as is well known transmit in the aggregate great sums of money." Brass-lock offices were permitted to handle registered mail transmitted in secure pouches with brass locks and keys, and Lazelle argued it was equally important that Camp Ruhlen's post office "should be a 'brass lock office' to insure greater security in remitting money."

Lazelle's request for a brass-lock office apparently was approved quickly; however getting approval for a money-order office faced tougher bureaucratic challenges. Again, in November, he wrote to the Assistant Adjutant General of the Department of Dakota, noting that the post office at Camp Ruhlen had been made "brass lock office," which "to a certain extent, insures the passage safely of money and money orders, though from general distributing Post Offices." However, he argued, there were still concerns about the overall security of the process.

Again, Major Lazelle's request was forwarded to the Postmaster-General, this time with written endorsements from the Commanding General of the Department of Dakota, the Adjutant General of the Army, the Commanding General of the Army, and the Secretary of War, who penned a personal note.

The Postmaster-General's response to a request that had seen the attention of the modern-day equivalents of a two-star, three-star, and four-star general and the Secretary of Defense, was an example of Washington bureaucracy at its finest. Claiming that it was far too late in the current year's planning process, he promised that Lazelle's request would be considered in 1879. He reminded all concerned that "additions to the number of money order offices in operation are made, customarily, once, and but once, in each year, usually at the commencement of the fiscal year."[70]

Major Lazelle and his family moved into their permanent quarters on post in February 1879. In addition to the closest town of Sturgis, two mushrooming mining towns, Leed and Deadwood, 15 or 20 miles away, offered even greater temptations to the lonely soldiers at isolated Fort Meade. Horace remembered that occasionally a soldier, lured by gold or the vices available in town, would desert or go AWOL. After too much drinking, card playing, or quarreling, he would end up in jail. Troops would go over, round him up, and bring him back.

These cases were not always benign. In February 1879, three soldiers charged with desertion escaped from post and were found at the Big Bonanza Saloon in Sturgis City by a detail lead by Lieutenant Starr. They attempted to flee, and Starr fired at them, wounding one and capturing the other two. The wounded man, a private, died later on post. [71]

Horace also remembered some trying times, including terrible winds and prairie fires. One particularly terrifying fire first appeared on the horizon one day "as we went to dinner at noon time—just a tiny column of smoke way off." By 3:00 or 4:00 p.m., however, it was headed right their way, threatening the wooden buildings on post as well as the troops who were still quartered in tents. "All kinds of game were chased down ahead of the fire trying to escape it, deer, rabbits, squirrels, and coyotes. The smoke was so thick you could see only 50 yards."

He also remembered that several times the stagecoaches bringing the mail were robbed between Bismarck and Deadwood. "Lots of money was traveling over that road in those days." Whenever the paymaster came, however, he had an escort of soldiers and was never bothered. "The privates got $13 a month, and on pay day there was a lot of boozing."

In April 1879, Lazelle was appointed Commandant of Cadets at West Point. He remained at Fort Meade until his replacement, Maj. Marcus A. Reno, arrived in May. Reno, an 1857 graduate of West Point, had fought at Antietam and Gettysburg during the Civil War and was one of the surviving officers from the Little Big Horn. He had been accused of cowardice and drunkenness during that battle, but was acquitted by a Court of Inquiry. In 1880, he would be court-martialed again for drunkenness, brawling, and conduct unbecoming an officer—peeking in the sitting-room window of the post commander's house late at night. This time, he was found guilty and dismissed from the service. [72]

Lazelle's orders from the Adjutant General's Office directed him to report to West Point by June 1, 1879, "preparatory to entering his duty as Commandant of the Corps of Cadets at the U.S. Military Academy." There is no indication, either in Lazelle's official files or in family records, of how he managed to secure this plum assignment. He did not have a personal relationship with Commanding General Sherman, nor had he served with then-Superintendent Gen. John Schofield, who had graduated from West Point two years ahead of Lazelle. In any case, he was relieved of command at Fort Meade by Reno on May 15 and departed post on May 27. [73]

As Horace remembered, his father first took the family to Chicago and then went on to West Point to arrange quarters. They went to Chicago by train, first through Sioux City where they changed cars, and where old Nick, their dog, escaped from the baggage car. They thought they had lost Nick, but he apparently found the car they had traveled in to Sioux City and crawled under the seat where they had been sitting. The railway people found him there and shipped him to Chicago free of charge.

Instead of biding their time in Chicago, the boys and their mother went on down to Hagerstown for a visit with her family. They stayed there until quite late in the summer when they joined their father at West Point. Both of Rebecca's parents had died (her father in 1869 and her mother, who suffered from severe dementia, in 1872), as had several of her siblings. However she still had a married sister living in Hagerstown along with Hollingsworth relatives in the area.

Reconnecting with Whistler

In December 1878, well before his appointment as Commandant of Cadets, Lazelle had penned a nostalgia-filled letter to his old West Point roommate, James Whistler. The days that he and Whistler had roomed together—and misbehaved together—clearly were the fondest of Lazelle's memories of the Academy. Writing to Whistler that "you have lived in my memory as freshly and as much admired as when we parted," and telling Whistler that he would "always sacredly keep the little sketch you made for me," Lazelle evidenced the softly humorous and nostalgic side to his personality rarely seen in his official correspondence.

> How I should love to be boys again at West Point with the experience of a life in my head. I wonder if we would enjoy it? Do you remember "Mammy" Thompson's [the widow of a West Point colonel known for her cooking and with whom Whistler had been allowed to take his meals for a time]? All Dead. None of the old professors are left at West Point.

Lazelle clearly had kept up with Whistler's successes and travails in Europe—including occasional financial difficulties as well as his highly publicized libel suit against art critic John Ruskin—confessing his one wish would be to meet again and hear Whistler "explain and discourse upon" his creative work. "But that can never be my happiness. We are too far apart and I am too poor to go to you."

Lazelle told Whistler little of his own life and career, save that he was married with two children, had "passed through the war and several Indian campaigns with but one wound," and was grey haired and getting old but "as young in feeling as ever." Ending his letter, he assured Whistler that while they probably would never meet again, he would "always live in my memory." There is no record that Whistler responded. [74]

Lazelle had now been away from West Point and serving as an officer for over 20 years. In today's Army, he could easily have reached the rank of lieutenant colonel, retired with benefits, and gone on to a second and, most likely lucrative, civilian career. In the Army of the late nineteenth century, however, he still had many years of service ahead before he would be eligible to retire, had perhaps only faint hope of making it to full colonel's rank, and had watched several of his classmates advance much more rapidly.

Having reached his mid-40s in a decade during which the average life expectancy wasn't much greater than 50, it was not unusual that Lazelle was feeling nostalgic for the good old days of his youth with Whistler at the Academy. However, as he sat writing in his drafty log cabin, watching a rough-hewn military post slowly emerge from the frozen grasslands of the Dakotas, he may also have felt a bit jealous of Whistler. After all, Whistler's paintings were hanging at the Grosvenor Gallery in London, he had recently been featured in a London weekly's "celebrities at home" interview, and he was locked in a widely publicized court battle with the world's most highly regarded art critic. [75]

Chapter 7

West Point—A New Battleground

Lazelle arrived at West Point in mid-June 1879, "assigned to duty as Commandant of Corps of Cadets, to take effect July 1, 1879," and brevetted to the rank of lieutenant colonel. He would not be promoted to lieutenant colonel (23rd Infantry) permanently until a year later. As had his predecessors, he also served as Instructor of Artillery, Cavalry, and Infantry Tactics, and was in charge of the Tactics Department.

When Lazelle's family joined him from Hagerstown, the cadets were still "in camp," sleeping in tents on the Academy grounds, just north of the library. Horace, then almost nine, remembered that they had their own house, still the Commandant's Quarters today, and an Irishman and his wife as servants, Patrick and Mary. Mary was the cook, and Patrick did the gardening, milked the cow, and did general chores.[1]

The boys were quite impressed with their life at West Point. As the commandant's wife, their mother was one of the "leading ladies" of the post, which made for an active social life. She had two "tailor-made" dresses for special occasions—one a deep green and the other garnet.

They also went to a real school for the first time. The West Point School, a private school on post conducted by Major Braden, a retired officer, for the officers' children, was only a three- to four-minute walk from their house.

Photo 15. Commandant's Quarters, West Point

Courtesy of Stockbridge Collection, U.S. Military Academy Archives

Lazelle's superior at the time of his arrival, Maj. Gen. John M. Schofield, had been serving as Superintendent since September 1876. Schofield, the first general appointed to the position (Robert E. Lee, for example, was a captain when he was appointed in 1852), was an 1853 graduate of West Point, had held major command positions during the Civil War, and eventually would succeed Philip Sheridan as Commanding General of the Army.

Schofield, like Lazelle, had achieved some notoriety for antics as a cadet, and, in all likelihood had participated in hazing Lazelle during the latter's plebe year. In one notable incident of deviltry, Schofield succeeded in sneaking off campus, making his way down to New York City, and returning undetected between the morning and evening roll calls. As he later remembered:

> A discussion arose as to the possibility of going to New York and back without danger of being caught, and I explained the plan I had worked out by which it could be done. ... I cared nothing for a brief visit to New York, and had only five dollars in money which Jerome N. Bonaparte [2] loaned me to pay my way. But I went to the city and back, in perfect safety, between the two roll-calls I had to attend that day. Old Benny Havens of blessed memory rowed me across the river to Garrison's, and the Cold Spring ferryman back to the Point a few minutes before evening parade. I walked across the plain in full view of the crowd of officers and ladies, and appeared in ranks at roll-call, as innocent as anybody. It is true my up-train did not stop at Garrison's or Cold Spring, but the conductor, upon a hint as to the necessity of the case, kindly slacked the speed of the express so that I could jump off from the rear platform. [3]

Schofield also shared Lazelle's youthful disdain for higher authority, noting that the "hardest lesson I had to learn was to submit my will and opinions to those of an accidental superior in rank who, I imagined, was my inferior in other things." [4] In his final year, his willingness to challenge his superiors probably saved his Army career. After being accused of allowing some fellow cadets to interrupt and bother a class of candidates he was preparing for the entrance examination in arithmetic, Cadet Schofield was summarily dismissed from the Academy. A complaint by one of the candidates who failed the exam had made its way to the War Department. Schofield professed his "innocence of all that had been done, except my neglect of duty in tolerating such a proceeding," but the Secretary of War ordered his dismissal "without trial."

Undaunted, Schofield enlisted the support of his classmates in a letter-writing campaign to their congressmen and senators, and traveled to Washington, where he appealed to his home-state Senator Stephen A. Douglas. Douglas took pity on the young cadet, and Schofield was granted a court of inquiry and court martial. After "some five or six months, diligently attending to my military and academic duties, and trying hard to obey all the regulations (except as to smoking)," he was reinstated with his class. [5]

HAZING AND HELL-RAISING

Schofield and Lazelle quickly established a "harmonious" working relationship, due in part to their mutual interest and focus on the professional training of the cadets but also as a result of their cadet experiences at the Academy. Indeed, an academy archivist once told the author that Lazelle was viewed by some as one of the most effective to hold the position of Commandant, in large part because he, as a cadet, had committed just about every disciplinary offense that one of his charges could contemplate.

The Superintendent and Commandant also shared a strong conviction that the practice of hazing must be brought under control and that discipline needed to be tightened. By 1880, hazing had become virtually institutionalized, starting with the period when new "candidates" were prepared for the entrance examinations and following the exams during what by then was called "Beast Barracks," when upperclassmen supposedly taught plebes "the rudiments of drilling, barracks life and other aspects of soldiering," but which in reality "became an ordeal by torture."[6]

In August 1878, Schofield had directed that newly nominated candidates would henceforth be treated as "civilians" while in camp preparing for entrance examinations, "under constant care and protection" of a staff officer and cadet officers, but not "placed under military discipline and instruction." Officers could set limits and rules "required to observe good order," but the candidates must be protected against "any annoyance or distraction which might interfere with their success at their examinations."

Schofield noted in his directives that there had been "frequent complaints that unaccustomed subjection to drill, discipline, and, perhaps, 'hazing,' have prevented the candidates from doing themselves justice at the examinations. This must be prevented in the future." [7] He must have been thinking back to his own experience as a cadet when his days at West Point almost ended for allowing such interference.

In July the following year, about the time that Lazelle reported for duty, a case of large-scale hazing of new cadets by six third-classmen was sufficiently serious that Schofield recommended to the Army Adjutant General that all six be summarily dismissed. After a second case of brutal hazing against the plebes who had complained, the third classmen refused to identify or testify against the perpetrators. Schofield characterized the third class as "in mutiny" and argued against the President's suggestion that the original six be reduced back to the fourth class. In the end, two of the six were sent back a year and the other four dismissed. The four dismissed cadets would be reinstated a year later into the third class. [8]

By the end of 1879, Schofield and Lazelle apparently felt they had made some progress. In his October "Annual Report," Schofield described the state of "discipline" in the Corps of Cadets as "all that could be desired," but admitted that "the chronic vice of hazing" was still a problem, albeit "gradually yielding before the more enlightened and refined sentiments which govern the relations between young gentlemen of the present day." He concluded optimistically that "this cause of reproach will soon disappear forever from the Military Academy." [9]

A year later, in his October 1880 "Annual Report," Schofield declared confidently that the hazing had been "so far suppressed that no case worthy of notice has occurred in more than a year," and that "continual diligence and discretion on the part of the officers of the Academy for a few years will make these reforms permanent, without in any wise marring the perfection of drill or discipline of the Corps of Cadets." [10] Schofield was not the last Superintendent to declare hazing no longer a significant issue. It was proclaimed abolished "at least a dozen times by various authorities," but it actually continued "with unabated intensity through the turn of the century." [11]

Lazelle's first disciplinary trial by fire as Commandant erupted, literally, in the early morning hours of January 1, 1880. In a New Year's Eve celebration that was "remembered for a generation," six members of the first class, who had smuggled fireworks onto the campus, orchestrated a massive display. After sentries posted at the barracks had departed for the night, the outside doors to the barracks were locked and cadet duty officers were locked in their rooms. Fireworks were "distributed to all those who volunteered to participate," and other cadets were dispatched to fire off the "reveille gun" and "as many guns as possible in the siege battery." [12]

The cadets executed their plan perfectly. With the firing of the cannons, tactical officers rushed to the barracks, "only to be met by an incredible barrage of rockets, cherry bombs and strings of sputtering firecrackers." By the time the tactical officers ordered the corps to assemble "every culprit was on hand to be present and accounted for." [13]

The Commandant of Cadets reacted to this horrific display of ill-discipline as expected, offering the guilty a chance to confess their sins in hopes of leniency under the honor code. When only a few, professing innocence, came forward, Lazelle placed the entire Corps of Cadets on indefinite confinement within the cadet area. Two days later, however, he had collected enough evidence to charge four first classmen—Cadet Captain Sidney E. Stuart and Cadet Lieutenants Charles J. Bailey, David J. Rumbaugh, and James S. Rogers—with "willful neglect of duty in tacitly consenting to and encouraging riot and mutiny," and a fifth, Cadet George R. Burnett, with "having nine pieces of fire-works in his possession." All five were placed in "close arrest." [14]

The five miscreants would go on to graduate the following June, with Sidney Stuart ranked third in his class of 53. Ironically, Stuart, then a captain of ordnance, would perish at the Dupont Powder Works near Wilmington, Delaware, in June 1894, "killed by the bursting of a shell while compressing gun cotton into shells." [15]

In March, still reeling from the refusal of the first class to cooperate, Lazelle recommended a change in the regulations governing visits between cadets in the barracks area. Noting that permission to visit in the barracks on Saturday evening was being "taken advantage of to go elsewhere by evading the sentinel in various ways," he proposed a new set of rules that he believed would "at least prevent the abuse of a general permit."

Writing to General of the Army William T. Sherman the following April, Schofield expressed some reluctance to holding "public graduation exercises" in June, in part due to "the affair of last January which gave the Commandant so much trouble and in respect to which the conduct of the first class has not yet been satisfactory." [16]

While both hazing and occasional serious lapses in discipline remained core problems at the Academy, the disciplinary issues with which Lazelle, as Commandant, dealt on an almost daily basis were mostly less serious escapades, attributable largely to youthful high spirits. In February 1880, for example, Lazelle reported disciplinary action he had taken after a plebe prank in the gym:

> [W]hile the Fourth Class were in attendance at the Gymnasium and Fencing Academy, a disturbance occurred at the Gymnasium during the absence of the instructor and during the temporary absence of the Officer in Charge, Captain E. S. Godfrey, 7th Cavalry. This was caused by some Cadet detaching the chain from the climbing post and wrapping it firmly around the knobs of the double doors opening into the fencing academy, then locking that door; then rolling balls of the ten-pin alley toward the door, so that they would strike in the vicinity. This door of the Fencing

> Academy is the only entrance, and the Cadet in locking it locked in the instructor and the sections under instruction.
>
> There is direct and positive testimony that Cadet Primm of the Class rolled the balls referred to, and he has acknowledged having done this. Each Cadet without exception, except Cadet Primm, then in the Gymnasium, has unequivocally and fully declared that he had nothing to do with fastening or locking the door, and no participation in that act. Cadet Waters, J. F. has besides informed me that Cadet Primm consulted him as to fastening the door before it was done, and that he, Waters, advised against it. In consideration of these facts, there can be no doubt but that Cadet Primm alone was the author of all the trouble. He has been given the opportunity but declines to make any statement. I have placed him under arrest and reported him for both offenses, i.e. rolling the balls against the doors, and locking the same and fastening them with a chain.

Other issues with which he dealt ranged from the mundane—members of the band acting inappropriately during ceremonies, cadets writing letters to newspaper editors in violation of academy rules, and drummers failing to show up for the "calls" [17]—to the absurd. In early September 1880, for example, the Academy doctor recommended changing over to winter uniforms earlier than usual, out of concern over the onset of cold weather and its impact on the cadets' health. In a lengthy rebuttal, Lazelle noted that the current practice had served the cadets well for some 25 years and argued against allowing the daily vagaries of the weather to determine the uniform of the day. It would be a simple matter, he maintained, for a cadet to "increase in quality, or quantity, of his under-clothing if desired." Moreover, he noted, there were not enough winter pants in stock for the plebes, "the class perhaps most requiring them." [18]

African American Cadets: Dispute and Disgrace

An even greater challenge than hazing and "deviltry," for both the Superintendent and Commandant, was posed by the racism, prejudice, and ostracism that accompanied the presence of West Point's first African American cadets. Dealing with those challenges and the controversy surrounding an incident involving one particular black cadet would eventually hasten the departures from West Point of both Schofield and Lazelle.

In the decades following the Civil War, the enrollment of African American cadets at West Point was fraught with controversy. With the passage of the 13th, 14th and 15th Amendments to the Constitution, and the election of African Americans to Congress in the southern states, the first African Americans were nominated to the Academy. Black cadets, however, were treated miserably by their white counterparts, far in excess of routine hazing by upperclassmen. Disciplinary issues often exploded in the press.

When Major Lazelle arrived at West Point, the Academy already had amassed a dismal record in handling its first African American cadets. Between 1870 and 1877, more than two dozen blacks had been nominated to the Academy. Most failed to pass the entrance examinations. Some of those who did pass and were admitted were lucky enough to have black roommates on whom they could depend for support and comfort. Others suffered alone, as the Academy's leadership refused to force white cadets to room with black cadets. Only one, Henry O. Flipper, had graduated, in 1877. [19]

In June of 1879, there again was only one African American in the Corps of Cadets, Johnson Chestnut Whittaker. He already had endured three years of hazing, racist remarks, and ostracism, two of them alone. In his 1880 "Annual Report," General Schofield attempted to both explain and justify the poor track record of African American cadets and their less-than-hospitable reception and treatment by white cadets. Schofield's report displayed the prejudice and racism that was common to most of white society and the officer corps and that was certainly shared by his Commandant of Cadets. Contending that "every lawful right" of the black cadets had been fully protected and that their official treatment had been "not only just but very kind and indulgent," he nonetheless argued that military discipline was not an appropriate vehicle for "promoting social intercourse or of overcoming social prejudice."

Opining that it was "an act of doubtful kindness" to expect "young men of a race so recently emerged from a state of slavery" to compete successfully with their white counterparts, he concluded that only the "education and moral elevation of the race" would enable African Americans to achieve intellectual and moral equality. And this would take time:

> To send to West Point for a four years competition a young man who was born in slavery, is to assume that half a generation has been sufficient to raise a colored man to the social, moral and intellectual level which the average white man has reached in several hundred years! As well might the common farm horse be entered in a four mile race against the best blood inherited from a long line of English racers. [20]

This was the prevailing attitude and atmosphere in which thus far only Henry Flipper had survived, but one in which Henry Lazelle, like John M. Schofield, seemed comfortable. Lazelle also was fully aware of the issues and challenges related to the treatment of black cadets, having sat on a court-martial panel at the Academy in 1871 for Cadet James Webster Smith, West Point's first black cadet. Based on that experience, his contact and correspondence with fellow graduates, and the attention given in the press to the plight of black cadets, he undoubtedly had formed his own opinions on how to deal with them. He could not have anticipated, however, that the case of Cadet Whittaker would thrust him into the national limelight.

JAMES WEBSTER SMITH

The first two African Americans nominated to the Military Academy, James Webster Smith of South Carolina and Michael Howard of Mississippi, took their entrance examinations in June 1870. Howard failed and returned home. Smith's score, however, was so high "it was impossible for the examiners to legitimize a failing grade." [21]

Smith grew up a slave in Columbia, South Carolina, and after the Civil War attended its Freedmen's School, whose benefactor, philanthropist and former Union Army officer David Clark, recognizing his academic potential, took James back to Hartford, Connecticut, where he enrolled in Hartford High School. Smith, who had just entered Howard University in May 1870, was appointed to West Point by South Carolina Congressman Solomon L. Hoge, a native of Ohio, and a Union Army officer during the Civil War. [22]

Facing strong resistance to the presence of a black man in the Corps of Cadets from fellow cadets and faculty members as well, Cadet Smith almost immediately became a center of controversy within the Academy and in the public media. In a late June 1870 letter to Clark, complaining about the harassment he was facing on a daily basis, Smith expressed concern that "these fellows appear to be trying their utmost to run me off." Maintaining that he had borne "insult upon insult" until he was worn out, Smith admitted he was not sure at all that he should stay and "take all the abuses and insults that are heaped upon me." Moreover, if he complained to the Commandant, he had to find someone to testify on his behalf to "prove the charge" or nothing would be done about it. Still, he maintained, he didn't want to resign if he could "get along at all." In the end, he made the decision to stay and challenge a system that wanted him to leave. [23]

And challenge the system he did. After his mentor Clark gave Smith's June letter to the *Hartford Courant*, the public controversy generated by its publication escalated to a Court of Inquiry in July that found his allegations either "unfounded or exaggerated." At the direction of the Secretary of War, William W. Belknap, he was reprimanded but not court martialed as the Court of Inquiry had recommended. [24]

Two additional incidents in August, 1870—a charge that he filed a false statement after he was accused of being disrespectful during drill, and two days later, an altercation with a white cadet over getting water from a water tank—led to a Court Martial in October. The presiding officer was Lazelle's former plebe-year roommate Brig. Gen. Oliver O. Howard, a founder of Howard University and former director of the Freedmen's Bureau. While required by regulation to be impartial, Howard certainly must have been sympathetic to the plight of the Academy's only black cadet. Nonetheless, the panel found Smith "guilty of conduct prejudicial to good order and military discipline" in the water tank incident but "not guilty of conduct unbecoming an officer and gentleman," nor of filing a false report, in the drill incident. He was sentenced to "walk post under charge of a Cadet sentinel" from two in the afternoon until retreat for six consecutive Saturdays. [25]

In reviewing the October case for the Secretary of War, the Army Judge Advocate General (JAG) was much less sanguine about the water tank incident—which involved an alleged assault by Smith against the white cadet—than was General Howard's court martial panel. In a blistering critique of its results, the JAG expressed his opinion that the assault was "deserving of severe rebuke and punishment" and that the sentence of the court was so inadequate that its "approval or enforcement cannot be recommended as a step at all calculated to maintain the discipline of the service or advance the interest of the Academy." He therefore recommended that the Secretary overturn the decision rather than sanction "a punishment so utterly insufficient as that proposed to be inflicted." The Secretary allowed the decision to stand. [26]

Then-Captain Henry M. Lazelle stepped into this highly charged racial and disciplinary quagmire on January 6, 1871, as a member of Cadet Smith's next court-martial panel. [27] The incident precipitating this court martial—a report of "inattention in ranks"—was extremely minor and certainly not uncommon among West Point cadets. However, the charge against Smith of conduct unbecoming a cadet and gentleman for making false statements with the intent "to deceive the Commandant and cause the erasure of the report," was serious, especially given his recent track record and the prevailing atmosphere at the Academy. The *New York Times* was blunt in its criticism of what Smith had to endure:

> With one or two honorable exceptions, the entire cadet corps cherish the most bitter hatred against the color of Smith, and have been eagerly waylaying for the first little possibility in his conduct to cook up a charge, and, to use the language of one, "kick the d____d nigger out!" The fault of the accused simply consisted in an inadvertent sidelong glance while marching in from parade. There is no question that the officers of the post at least wink at the cadets' conduct, and more or less share their prejudices. [28]

The *Times* went on to observe that Smith had conducted himself "most manfully under all his trials and throughout these bitter persecutions," concluding that Smith's persecution was "decidedly 'conduct unbecoming military gentlemen.'" [29]

Six of the seven members of the court, including Lazelle, were West Point graduates. Although West Point did not have a formal "Honor Code" until the early 1900s, the members of the court were well familiar with "the importance of honor as an essential component of the character development of an officer and gentleman," a concept drilled into each cadet from his first day at the Academy. [30] Indeed, during his summation, the Judge Advocate of the court emphasized that "the Cadets being upon honor, their word is deemed sacred, and any false statement made with intent to deceive is deemed proportionally scandalous." [31]

Photo 16. Court Martial of James W. Smith

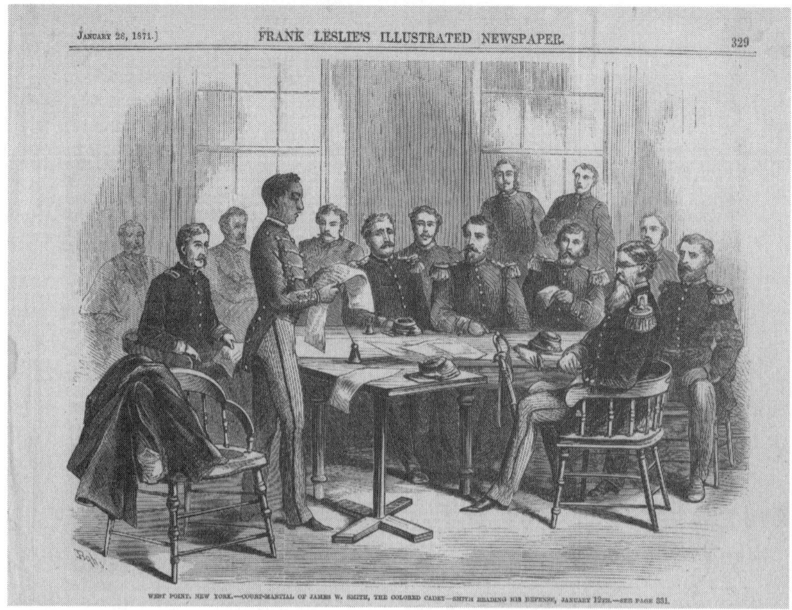

From *Frank Leslie's Illustrated*, January 28, 1872. Courtesy of the New York Public Library.

While the deliberations of the panel members, like any jury, were unrecorded and held in secret, Lazelle and his fellow officers would have found it unthinkable that any of the cadets and officers who testified as to the circumstances, sequence of events, and inter-actions between Smith and the white cadets would tell anything but the complete truth. The court found Smith guilty and sentenced him to dismissal. The findings were sent to Washington where they sat for six months under review by the Army's Judge Advocate General, Secretary of War William Belknap, and President Ulysses S. Grant. It was not until June 1871 that Belknap announced the final decision: a reduced sentence, pushing Smith back to the incoming Class of 1875. [32]

Meanwhile, Smith had passed his first-year examinations, placing high in his class. He struggled, however, over the next three years. Following his year-end examinations in 1874, Smith, along with another cadet, was found "deficient," having failed philosophy. The other cadet—white—was allowed to stay at the Academy and graduated in 1875. Smith was expelled.[33] In 1996, at the urging of Senator Strom Thurmond, President Clinton approved the posthumous commissioning of James W. Smith to the rank of 2nd Lieutenant, US Army. [34]

During the trial, Lazelle was exposed to a different kind of black man than he had met during the early days of Reconstruction in the Carolinas. Choosing to be his own counsel, Smith was smart, confident, and aggressive in defending himself. Although he was found guilty as charged, Smith acquitted himself well during the proceedings, sticking to his story and challenging his accusers and their witnesses. Thinking back on that court martial, Lazelle should not have been surprised at all in the summer of 1879 when he first met Johnson Chestnut Whittaker, who was equally self-assured, confident, and willing to challenge the system.

The Whittaker Affair

Johnson Chestnut Whittaker, born a slave in South Carolina and later a scholarship student at the University of South Carolina, was appointed to West Point in 1876, also by Congressman Hoge. He was only 17 but had excelled in his studies at South Carolina under the tutelage of Professor Richard T. Greener, the first African American to graduate from Harvard College. [35]

Unlike Smith, Whittaker had a fellow African American upperclassman as a roommate and mentor during his plebe year, Henry O. Flipper. The next year, after Flipper graduated, the first to survive four years at West Point, Whittaker found companionship with another black cadet, Charles August Minnie. However, Minnie was discharged mid-year for academic deficiency in mathematics, and from January 1878 until he left

West Point, Cadet Whittaker suffered alone the prejudice and hostility of his fellow cadets.

In January 1879, the Academic Board recommended he be dismissed after failing the semi-annual examination in philosophy. Schofield, however, noting that Whittaker was "the only one of his race now at the Academy and has won the sympathy of all by his manly deportment and earnest efforts to succeed," recommended that he be turned back to join the next lower class. The Secretary of War agreed, and Whittaker got a second chance. [36]

On April 6, 1880, however, Whittaker burst forth onto the pages of the national media under sensational headlines: "Villainy at West Point—The Colored Cadet, Whittaker, Outrageously Treated" (*New York Times*), "Criminal News—Atrocious" (*Chicago Daily Tribune*), "Outrage on a Colored Cadet" (*San Francisco Chronicle*), and "Shameful Affair" (*Fort Scott* [Kansas] *Daily Monitor*), among many. In the most detailed account, the *New York Times* provided a lurid description of what it labeled a "brutal outrage"—a middle-of-the night attack on Whittaker in his barracks room by masked assailants, who seized him by the throat, tied him up, beat him on the head and nose, and then, one of them growling "let's mark him like they do hogs down South," cut off the tip of one ear lobe and slit the other. [37]

According to Whittaker's account, when he started bleeding, one of the men took a handkerchief to clean off some of the blood. They then tied his hands, secured his feet to the iron bedstead, and, at his request, put a pillow under his head. After they left, he tried to untie his hands, using his teeth on the knots without success. He cried for help and then lay on the floor for three hours until reveille sounded.

When Whittaker was discovered absent from the morning formation, the Cadet Officer of the Day went to his room, found him bound and bleeding on the floor, and immediately notified the Post Surgeon and Commandant, who hastened to his room. Whittaker ended his initial account by noting that about a year prior he had received "a note on which was written 'Look out.' I don't know where it came from. Last Sunday I found a sealed envelope in my room, and opening it, found a note inside which read as follows: 'Look out; keep awake; you will be fixed. A Friend.'" [38]

The *Times* reported that the members of the Corps of Cadets openly expressed "the greatest indignation" over the matter, that several had sought interviews with General Schofield, and that each cadet was being summoned before Commandant Lazelle to be "questioned sharply." The story also noted that Schofield had advised the Secretary of War about the situation. [39]

The War Department took the incident seriously enough to dispatch Colonel Thomas F. Barr from the Judge Advocate General's office to confer with Schofield on steps the Department should take to assist the Academy's investigation of the incident and then report back to Secretary Alexander Ramsey. [40]

Meanwhile, Lazelle, who had rushed to Whittaker's room upon hearing a report that he had been gravely injured, completed his initial investigation and questioned every cadet in the Corps, all of whom "frankly and unhesitatingly disavowed any knowledge whatever of the affair." He reported his findings on April 7, providing a detailed account of what he and the Post Surgeon had found upon entering Whittaker's room, Whittaker's account of the incident, his physical condition, and various articles of evidence related to the actions of the alleged perpetrators.

Since all cadets had expressed their innocence, and believing it "utterly improbable" that "citizens" (civilians) would have attacked Whittaker "without apparent motive," Lazelle was driven to conclude that Whittaker, himself, had "inflicted or consented to the infliction of all his apparent injuries; and himself arranged all the striking surroundings of his position" when he was found. Noting that Whittaker's treatment by his fellow cadets had been "uniformly tolerant" and that there was "no cause for change now," Lazelle professed his belief that it was impossible that three cadets would perpetrate the "outrage," even as an act of "mere mischief," and then lie by denying any knowledge of it. He, therefore, recommended that Whittaker be given the choice of resigning or requesting a Court of Inquiry or Court Martial. [41]

In his report, Lazelle covered a number of details, questions, and conclusions that would figure prominently in the deliberations of both a Court of Inquiry at West Point and a later Court-Martial in New York City. All of them supported Lazelle's belief that Whittaker was at least complicit in the attack but that it more likely was self-inflicted. Bolstered by the Post Surgeon's conclusion that Whittaker, when first found, was "not as insensible as he appeared" and was initially feigning unconsciousness, [42] Lazelle noted in quick order that:

- There was no physical evidence of his claims that he was struck in the face seriously enough that he lost "partial consciousness" and his nose "bled freely," that he was struck on the forehead with his looking glass causing it to break, or that he was injured in the side seriously enough that he could not get up from the floor without "great pain and effort."
- The Post Surgeon believed his wounds, which were still bleeding when he was first examined, were superficial enough that the bleeding would have stopped within a half hour of the alleged attack, well before he was found.
- The bindings on his hands and feet were so flimsy that he could easily have removed them himself.
- He was not gagged, could have called for help, and, since the transom above his room door was open, his cries would have been heard.
- The knife used to cut him and the scissors used to chop his hair both belonged to Whittaker, and, in Lazelle's opinion, the cutting of his hair appeared to be self-inflicted.
- The handkerchief with its owner's name cut out, used to staunch his bleeding was identical to others in Whittaker's room all marked in the same location as the cut-up handkerchief.

- One piece of several burned scraps of paper found at Whittaker's feet, of which he disavowed any knowledge, had been torn from his Bible.
- Finally, the handwriting on the note Whittaker claimed to have received bore a "very marked resemblance in general to his own."

After reviewing Lazelle's report, Schofield called Whittaker to his office and informed him of the results, "it being his right to know promptly any fact that seemed to be prejudicial to him." As Schofield later testified, the manner in which Whittaker "dismissed the truth of that report, as far as it affected him, and quickly demanded a Court of Inquiry" led him to conclude that Whittaker was innocent of any "criminal connection" with the incident. Since the investigation also failed to uncover any guilty parties among the Corps of Cadets or others under his command, Schofield could only conclude that the incident "had its origin beyond the limits of West Point," which made it imperative to turn the investigation over to civil authorities. In the meantime, he reasoned, it would be unfair to Whittaker to remain in limbo—essentially accused of fabricating the incident—for an indeterminate amount of time. Thus, Schofield, decided, it was also imperative to proceed with a formal Court of Inquiry. [43]

Court of Inquiry

The Court of Inquiry was convened the morning of April 9, charged with investigating "the facts and circumstances connected with the recent assault made upon Cadet Whittaker and the imputation cast upon his character in relation thereto." At Whittaker's request, he was represented by 1st Lt. John G. D. Knight, an Assistant Professors of Mathematics and 1864 graduate of the Academy. With discussion of the case beginning to whirl in the press, Whittaker's interests also were represented, indirectly, by Martin I. Townsend, U.S. District Attorney for the Northern District of New York, who was dispatched at the last minute by the Justice Department—at the request of President Rutherford B. Hayes—to render assistance through his "professional skill and experience." Given the political sensitivity surrounding the case, Townsend was also instructed to report back to the President. [44]

Photo 17. Official Investigation into the Alleged Outrage on Cadet Whittaker

From *Frank Leslie's Illustrated*, May 1, 1880. Courtesy of the New York Public Library

Somewhat similar to a grand jury in a civil criminal case, the court of inquiry was charged, essentially, with determining the facts and rendering an opinion as to whether "the imputation upon the character of Cadet Whittaker" in the initial reports of the Post Surgeon and Commandant of Cadets was sustained by the evidence it examined. Lazelle was called to testify on April 16 and 17.

In his testimony, Lazelle reviewed the sequence of events and the evidence he found in Whittaker's room, generally following the lines of his official report, and emphasizing at the outset that, in questioning

Whittaker's fellow cadets, he determined that none had "any knowledge" of either the attack or the notes of warning. Expressing skepticism of Whittaker's account, Lazelle reviewed his doubts about the amount of blood loss; the ease with which Whittaker could have called for help and freed himself; his suspicions about the handkerchief, knife, and scissors; and the similarity of Whittaker's handwriting to that on the final warning note. He also described at length his belief that there was no reason for the "apparent stupor and difficulty of rousing Cadet Whittaker."

> There did not seem to be loss of blood, or wounds, or sufficient fright, and I think it was Wednesday evening [April 7] that he was at my office, and I asked him something to this effect: "Mr. Whittaker, there is no apparent cause, or not sufficient cause, for your having been insensible or without knowledge of what transpired generally in your room." He said, "I know it, sir,"—or something to that effect—"I did know generally what went on in the room, but there are many little things that I don't remember in my fright, and in my excitement." ... Now as he admitted that, it goes to confirm my own opinion that there was not evidence of the exhaustion and of apparent stupor, and I may say, insensibility—for I don't know what else to call it—that appeared when I went there. His quick recovery from that extreme condition is a reason that presented itself to my mind. [45]

In the end, however, for Lazelle, the issue of whether Whittaker was attacked or staged the attack himself came down to two fundamental questions: on the one hand, was there any motive or reason for a group of civilians to wantonly attack Whittaker and, on the other, was it conceivable that fellow cadets would attack him, again unprovoked, and then lie about it. In Lazelle's mind, the answer to both questions was a very certain "no." He could not conceive of a motive that would "sufficiently activate citizens [civilians] to make that attack. ... and therefore that it must be placed at the door of cadets—that the parties guilty must be cadets: that was the only inference, unless he did it himself."

Honor code aside, however, Lazelle saw absolutely no reason why cadets would have been motivated to attack Whittaker. He noted that Whittaker's treatment by his fellow cadets had been "uniformly quiet, that is to say tolerant, and extended to letting him alone so far as I know in everything, never molesting him." He took the argument one step further, however, contending that if it could be argued that cadets "committed this assault because they did not want him here," it could equally be argued that Whittaker, himself, who was slipping in his academic rankings, "committed this assault because he wanted to stay."

During a short cross-examination, District Attorney Martin Townsend leapt upon Lazelle's "either—or" judgment, asking pointedly, "Do you know of any reason in the world why the oath of Whittaker is not as credible as the oath of any other man?" Lazelle responded with a "no." Townsend continued: "Do you think that a man who would perpetrate such an act as Whittaker alleges was perpetrated upon him deliberately would hesitate to deny it afterwards?" Lazelle again said "no," but qualified his answer expressing his opinion that it was "rather improbable" that one cadet would commit the act and then lie about it, but even more improbable that two or three would conspire to do it and then lie about it. Townsend pressed him harder, however, and in the end Lazelle had to admit that "if a man should do so base an act," then he would "most likely tell a lie about it."[46] Nonetheless, the die was cast. Indeed it had been cast with Lazelle's initial report.

While Lazelle clearly had convinced himself that Whittaker was the guilty party, Schofield, at least during the Court of Inquiry, was still torn, testifying that, in his mind, there was "very strong evidence of his innocence, and the bearing of the Corps of Cadets has manifested to me a very strong evidence of their innocence." Noting that it was generally recognized within the Corps of Cadets that Whittaker was under the "special protection of the military authorities," and that he was the one cadet who was "not to be abused or treated harshly in any way because of his isolated position," Schofield concluded that Whittaker was the one cadet "exempt from possible indignity or abuse of any kind." [47]

With the Court of Inquiry underway, Schofield, convinced of the innocence of the cadets and still mulling over his theory that an outside conspiracy was at the core, issued General Orders No. 14, in which he assured the cadets of his "unshaken faith in their honor and integrity" and commended them for their "manly bearing under the grievous wrong and injustice which they have recently suffered." Describing the attack on Whittaker as "no less an outrage upon the Corps," even if perpetrated by one of their own, he commended them for enduring the crisis "with becoming dignity and confidence that justice would be done to all," and rescinded all restrictions he had placed on the usual privileges of cadets. [48]

The court wrapped up its deliberations on May 29 after additional testimony that focused, particularly, on the question of the similarity, or lack thereof, of the handwriting on the note of warning and Whittaker's own handwriting. Five experts had examined the note and handwriting samples from all cadets, and in the end, they all identified Whittaker as the writer of the note of warning. One of the experts also proved to the satisfaction of both the court and Whittaker's counsel that the paper used for the note of warning had been "torn from a sheet upon which Cadet Whittaker has written the first part of a letter to his mother, dated April 5, 1880." [49]

Based on a "strong array of circumstantial evidence," the testimony of the handwriting experts, "conflicting statements" made by Whittaker, and his "lack of veracity" during the investigation, the court concluded that the "imputation upon the character of Cadet Whittaker, referred to in the order convening the Court, and contained in the official reports of the Commandant of Cadets and the Post Surgeon, is fully sustained."

General Schofield approved the report and opinion, placed Whittaker under arrest in his quarters, and forwarded the package to the Adjutant General of the Army, "for action of the proper authority," on June 4. In a cover letter, he recommended that Whittaker be "promptly" separated from the Academy. Acknowledging that he found it impossible to believe Whittaker's statements, he concluded his letter noting that "many thousands of the colored race, to which he belongs in a small degree [he was light-skinned with freckles], have displayed commendable courage in circumstances far more trying than those in which he claims to have been placed."

Schofield also included a copy of additional charges that had been filed against Whittaker on May 25 by Lazelle for "making a false official statement" regarding civilian clothing in his room while the Court of Inquiry was under way. He recommended that, if it was decided to proceed with a Court Martial, it should be appointed by a higher authority and not include officers stationed at West Point. And he assured the Adjutant General that the proceedings had not interfered with Whittaker's "academic exercises," nor would his arrest hamper his preparations for the June examinations. [50]

As Washington considered the conclusions of the Court of Inquiry, debate in the press and in Congress over whether Whittaker had been treated fairly, and more broadly on the plight on black cadets at West Point, continued. In defense of West Point, Academy Professor Peter S. Michie argued that the problem of prejudice there was driven less by hatred of blacks in general than it was by the intellectual and academic inferiority of the black cadets who had entered the Academy. Noting that only one had succeeded in graduating, Michie opined that while they all had excellent memories, they generally "displayed a marked deficiency in deductive reasoning, and have taken very low rank in mathematical subjects." In his view, one most likely shared by Lazelle and Schofield, not until the Academy received "some young colored men who in ability are at least equal to the average white cadet, and possessed of manly qualities," would the question of race be settled "on the basis of human intelligence and human sympathy." [51]

A few days after the court finished its work, the June examinations began. Cadet Whittaker passed all of his except for philosophy, which—

along with a drop in grades in his other courses—meant he was deficient and subject to dismissal. On June 25, the *New York Times* reported that "as he was found to be deficient in his studies, and having been two years in the same class, he can be discharged. The report [of examinations] has not yet been received by Secretary Ramsey. If he concurs in the recommendation the dismissal of Whittaker will finally dispose of his case as far as the Government is concerned." [52]

But this was not to be the "final disposition" of the Whittaker case. On June 25, the Adjutant General approved all recommendations of the Academic Board except for Whittaker's discharge. Rather, he suspended action on Whittaker "not with a view to his restitution," but rather "to preserve his military status for trial by court martial," should it be determined that a court martial was necessary to "enable him to vindicate his character." The Secretary of War concurred. [53]

In July, the Secretary of War also received a report on the court of inquiry from the Army Judge Advocate General. The July 17 edition of the *Times* noted that the document was "very long and reviews critically the evidence and findings of the West Point court of inquiry. Nearly an hour was occupied in reading it. The Secretary will not pass upon it for some days, and, in the interim, declines to make public its recommendations." [54]

On August 17, Schofield was called to Washington to meet with President Rutherford B. Hayes, concurrent with a visit to the Secretary of War by Whittaker's Harvard mentor, Professor Greener, who urged that Whittaker's request for a formal Court Martial be honored. According to the *Times*, Greener argued that the West Point inquiry was biased, that Whittaker had been the victim of a conspiracy, and that only a court martial would afford him a "more impartial hearing and more systematic defense than he had before the preliminary court." [55]

In his meeting with the President, Schofield was informed "that a decision had been made to change the command at West Point to insure fair treatment of black cadets." By the end of their discussion, the President had agreed to delay Schofield's departure until the end of the year, and he had accepted Schofield's recommendation that Whittaker's request for a court martial be granted and that the cadet be placed on leave until the trial commenced. [56]

In a bitter letter to General Sherman, Schofield, now convinced there was an outside conspiracy, attributed his imminent dismissal to a politically motivated attack on the institution of West Point itself, all because of Whittaker:

> The young colored man who became the willing instrument of an infamous attack upon the Military Academy and (doubtless unwittingly to him) of a like attack on me, who had for more than three years been his best friend, is to be discharged only because [he is] deficient in studies, while the Superintendent [is] to be removed for alleged wrongs done to him, whom they had only treated with greater kindness, indulgence, and protection than is ever shown to any white cadet! And all this is to be done in confessed obedience to a low partisan demand for social equality which no where in the United States is voluntarily practiced even to so great an extent as it is enforced at West Point, a fact which the great mass of the public now well understand. [57]

While the Secretary of War and President pondered the Whittaker question, the situation must have weighed heavily on Lazelle's mind. On August 29, in a memo to Schofield, he proposed reconsidering a more elaborate and strict plan for patrolling the barracks at night, a plan he had first suggested after the New Years Eve fireworks antics. Noting that "night is the only time when cadets are not under surveillance," and that "whatever lawlessness has been committed has been at night," Lazelle proposed establishing a system of Cadet Officers of the Guard and sentinels with guard stations to control cadet activity: "With the view of stopping all this so far as is possible by guards, there could be posted at 10 P.M. a night Cadet guard of three posts to be kept up until 6 A.M. After which time the Officer of the Day and Officer in Charge will be required to remain at the Area building."

Lazelle went on to detail the number of cadets in each class and how often, under the proposed scheme, each cadet would have to stand guard duty. The Cadet Officer of the Guard on duty would be responsible for assuring that there were no unauthorized lights after taps and for the "preservation of perfect quiet and order." The sentinels would be required to demand the name and identification of all cadets leaving the barracks and to search for them if they didn't return within ten minutes. The guards also would be responsible for preventing any visiting between divisions of barracks and for insuring that the "area" doors were open and the front doors "constantly shut and locked." [58]

Schofield agreed to the new scheme and, under the cloud of the Whittaker affair, ended his tour as Superintendent in January 1881. He would be succeeded by Brig. Gen. Oliver O. Howard, Lazelle's plebe-year roommate. Howard came to the Superintendent's position with a completely different outlook on African American cadets. An ardent abolitionist before the war, he was a key post-war proponent of higher education for freed blacks, serving as Howard University's president from 1869 to 1874. Howard supported Whittaker's December 1880 petition to the President for a court martial.

Court Martial

The court was carefully selected to avoid any suggestion of pro-West Point or anti-black bias. The President of the Court was Brig. Gen. Nelson A. Miles, with whom Lazelle had fought against the Indians in Dakota Territory. The prosecuting officer, Judge-Advocate Maj. A. B. Gardner, had served as counsel to General Sheridan. Cadet Whittaker's civilian counsels were former Governor of South Carolina, Daniel H. Chamberlain, a well-known lawyer and abolitionist, and Professor Greener, Whittaker's teacher at the University of South Carolina and dean of the Howard University School of Law from 1878 to 1880. Of the ten military members of the court, only three were West Point graduates. Neither Miles nor Gardner was an Academy graduate. [59]

In a short, initial session in New York City on January 20, 1881, both the prosecution and defense requested a delay to better prepare their cases. The court reconvened two weeks later to hear testimony on two basic charges: "conduct unbecoming an officer and a gentleman" (the alleged fabrication of the attack in his quarters and the warning letter found in his room) and "false swearing" (related to his testimony during the court of inquiry). The trial was essentially a rehash of the court of inquiry, although this time Whittaker had competent legal counsel, and "much counterevidence was introduced in opposition to the various accusations against him." In the end, however, as in the Court of Inquiry, the driving issues behind the panel's verdict would be the handwriting on the warning note and Whittaker's physical condition the morning after the alleged attack. [60]

Both Lazelle and Schofield were called to testify. Since his testimony at the Court of Inquiry, Lazelle had not shared his views publicly. Schofield, on the other hand, had discussed the case and the question of black cadets extensively in his official 1880 Annual Report and in his regular correspondence with General Sherman. Lazelle most likely went into the Court Martial firm in his belief of Whittaker's guilt and that his initial report and prior testimony would stand on their own merits.

Schofield, on the other hand, would approach the panel convinced that Whittaker, while not innocent of the charges, was merely an "instrument in the hands of malice used to strike a blow at the Academy and doubtless at me personally." Writing to General Sherman in late July 1880, Schofield had been adamant in his belief that Whittaker had been "acting under orders from some authority which he believed perfectly competent to protect him from any possible harm." This was the view he carried into, and articulated at, the New York court-martial proceedings. [61]

Schofield was called first, on February 4, and his initial testimony, under questioning by Major Gardner, the Judge Advocate, was straightforward: covering the sequence of events, Lazelle's report and Whittaker's denial of its allegations, and his own actions and efforts to assure a complete investigation. Gardner also used his questioning to make the point that the Academy leadership had bent over backwards in helping Whittaker through his academic difficulties, particularly in setting him back a year rather than dismissing him. [62]

Under cross-examination by Daniel Chamberlain, Schofield admitted Whittaker had been of good character before the incident and that his deportment had generally been "very good," about as good as the top twenty in his class. What threw him, he confessed, was Whittaker's "perfect confidence, perfect composure and perfect readiness" to request the Court of Inquiry after being told of Lazelle's conclusions. In Schofield's mind, this could only mean he was "confident of the support of those who had originated the whole affair, whoever they may be." [63]

Chamberlain was incredulous and pursued Schofield's conspiracy theory at length but to little satisfaction, as Schofield was unable to provide any real basis for his suspicions. In the end, after Chamberlain challenged him to provide evidence, Schofield could only reply that he had felt it his duty make his suspicions known but that he could not "see, in my conscience anything which I know now that would be of any benefit to the cadet on trial." [64]

On February 15, following a "severe" cross-examination of West Point's surgeon regarding his medical evaluation of Whittaker, the question of whether he was shamming unconsciousness, and whether his wounds could have been self-inflicted, Lazelle "was next examined, and testified in corroboration of what has already been published concerning the occurrences of the morning of April 6." [65]

Lazelle's early questioning was largely perfunctory, describing the sequence of events, how he found the scene and Whittaker's condition when first arriving in his room, and Schofield's instructions to make "an examination and investigation so far as I could of the facts." This was followed by an extended series of questions on what evidence had been given to Lazelle, when he had received it and from whom, and what he had done with it. Of particular interest was the bloody handkerchief and the scorched pieces of paper that had figured prominently in the Court of Inquiry. [66]

During a lengthy cross-examination, Chamberlain probed Lazelle's assessment of Whittaker's demeanor and attitude during the investigation. Describing the cadet's manner during various interviews as "very frank and straightforward," Lazelle conceded that he had never observed any "inclination to conceal anything" and that Whittaker had never resisted handing over everything requested. Nor did he observe anything that would indicate Whittaker was "making up the story to suit the occasion." When Chamberlain asked about Lazelle's impression of the cadet's character as far as he had observed it up to the time of the incident, Lazelle responded that he regarded him as "a very manly boy." "In point of conduct, exemplary?" asked Chamberlain. "Quite so," Lazelle responded.

Referring back to the Court of Inquiry, Chamberlain attempted to challenge Lazelle's statements that, in his opinion, Whittaker could fairly easily have kicked off the bindings on his feet, but Lazelle stuck by his original statement, albeit admitting that his view was based on general supposition rather than first-hand knowledge of the nature or tightness of the bindings, since they had been removed by the time he entered Whittaker's room. On the question of his belief that Whittaker could have cut his own hair, however, he demurred, having already conceded that the Post barber found it unlikely, and acknowledged there was no reason why his hair could not have been cut by a third party.

During further cross-examination on the 16th, Professor Greener attempted to establish a case that Lazelle was biased in his reporting to Schofield and had quickly convinced himself that Whittaker had fabricated the incident. Greener pointedly asked Lazelle whether his initial report to Schofield was "to the actual facts" or more of an "argument in support of the theory that Whittaker did it himself or knew who did it." Lazelle responded angrily that he had "stated what I understood to be the facts." When Greener persisted and asked Lazelle to read the report, Lazelle responded more angrily that he considered his report to be "a statement of facts and an expression of my opinion necessarily from my official position. The report contains ... facts as I observed them from my own personal knowledge, and as they were presented to me and as I observed them; and my expression of opinion was based upon those facts; and I have never changed it."

Greener pressed harder, and Lazelle admitted that his initial impression was that Whittaker had been attacked by someone and "was not a consenting party to it," but that by the time he issued his report he had ruled out an attack by civilians. "That idea I had been disabused of, at least in my own mind, by the facts and by my own thoughts on the subject." In later questioning, Lazelle conceded that he did become suspicious that Whittaker had fabricated the story and faked the attack, based on the evidence he developed in his investigation and other facts that were reported officially to him, as well as on the surgeon's observations during Whittaker's physical examination at the Post Hospital.

Greener then shifted gears, asking bluntly whether Lazelle had made any remark "which would have been apt to have influenced this case among outsiders during the course of inquiry." Challenged by both Lazelle and the Judge Advocate as to the reason for this line of questioning, Greener admitted his intent was to show not only that Lazelle's initial report was "based entirely upon the supposition that Cadet Whittaker was guilty," but also that he had "communicated to the papers his suspicion as to the person who wrote a certain portion of the note of warning before that was communicated to the public, thus prejudicing this case."[67]

Lazelle responded categorically that he had not had any unauthorized discussions with the press, and he vehemently denied Greener's assertion that he had told a reporter from the *New York Evening Post* that one of the handwriting experts had identified the writing on the note of warning as Whittaker's, before that information became public.

On re-direct, Judge Advocate Gardner again asked Lazelle if he had any direct knowledge of Whittaker's treatment as a cadet, and Lazelle responded that it was "just the same as that of the other cadets, as far as

I was concerned. And so far as I know by others in command." As to his personal views, Lazelle asserted, he "never had any other than very kind feelings towards him up to the time when I supposed him to be concerned with this affair." Also on redirect, Lazelle again asserted that his mind had "never been made up upon the subject" of who committed the offense against Whittaker, but that his initial impression that Whittaker had "no connection with his mutilation" had changed during his investigation. [68]

The trial continued into early June. Chamberlain took three days to complete his summation. Major Gardner presented his closing arguments on June 6 and 7. The court then went into conference, rendering its verdict on June 10: guilty as charged, with some modifications to the original charges. It recommended Whittaker be dishonorably discharged, fined one dollar, and confined to hard labor for one year. In forwarding the court's findings and recommendations to the Judge Advocate General for review, however, General Miles recommended clemency, with the fine and prison sentence dropped. [69]

Because the decision of the court was not released publicly, and the members of the court were bound to secrecy, the press was left to speculate while the Judge Advocate General and Secretary of War reviewed the report and prepared a final recommendation to the President. On June 17, 1881, the *Times* only could report that the record had "not yet been received at the War Department, and is still in the possession of the Recorder of the Court, who will forward it to the Judge-Advocate-General as soon as completed." [70]

On December 8, 1881, the *Times* reported that Army Judge Advocate General D. E. Swain had completed his review and would soon submit his report to the Secretary of War. In its December 15 edition, the *Times* speculated that the President ultimately would overturn the conviction. And on January 4, 1882, the *Times* reported "on high authority" that the Judge Advocate General's report had concluded that the court had been illegally constituted in the first place.

Indeed, Swain did argue that the court had been illegally constituted, because the President had no legal authority to convene a court martial in this case, "either by virtue of any statute or by the common law." However, he went much further and questioned the validity of the verdict as well. He declared the first charge of "conduct unbecoming an officer and a gentleman" in violation of Academy regulations "void," because a criminal charge could not be legally sanctioned by a "mere regulation of the Academy." He further argued that the comparison of handwriting was "contrary to the rules of the common law," and, moreover, the evidence and testimony on handwriting was "insufficient to establish that Whittaker wrote the note of warning." Rather, he argued, the "legal evidence of record" regarding the note was "conclusive that Whittaker is neither the writer nor author of it." Therefore, it was his conclusion that "the prosecution has fallen short of sustaining the charges and specifications by adequate legal proof, or such as would be sufficient in law to justify a jury in uniting in a conviction, and that the proceedings, findings and sentence should be, therefore, disapproved." [71]

Swain's discussion of Lazelle's role in the case was straightforward and reportorial. However, he castigated Schofield, both for the "prejudice which existed in the mind of the Superintendent," and for meddling when he should have "kept aloof from the investigation until completed by the court" of inquiry. Beyond mere meddling, however, he essentially accused Schofield of attempting to influence its outcome, particularly in issuing his April 21 general order "exonerating the cadets from suspicion," which Swain asserted "substantially foreshadows the conclusions of the court of inquiry" over a month later. [72]

Swain's report was forwarded to the Secretary of War, Robert T. Lincoln. On March 6, 1882, Lincoln, in turn, sought an opinion from Attorney General Benjamin Harris Brewster, on the admissibility of the handwriting evidence, which Swain had questioned, expressing his own "grave doubts" about the "legality of the action of the court." Brewster responded on the 17th, concluding, based on his review of the case and extant common law, that "the sentence should in my opinion be set aside. Justice forbids the enforcement of a sentence which is founded upon a conviction illegally obtained."[73]

On March 21, the Cabinet and President Chester A. Arthur took up the case, the President ruling that, because of "error in the proceedings of the Court in relation to a material issue, the foregoing proceedings and sentence are disapproved, and it is ordered that Cadet Whittaker be released from arrest."[74]

On that same day, Cadet Johnson Chestnut Whittaker was separated from the Academy because of his deficiency in the June 1880 examinations and disappeared from public view. On July 24, 1995, however, again partly due to efforts by Senator Strom Thurmond, President Clinton, in the presence of Whittaker's great-grandson—a Harvard Law School graduate—and other relatives, posthumously commissioned him a 2nd lieutenant and presented his lieutenant's bars to the family.

Thus ended a difficult chapter in the early history of African-American cadets at the United States Military Academy. For Lt. Col. Henry M. Lazelle, however, the final resolution of Whittaker case was but a mere distraction in what had become a tumultuous relationship with the newly appointed Superintendent, Oliver Otis Howard.

Chapter 8

A New Challenge—General Howard Takes Command

General Howard arrived at West Point in January 1881, as the Whittaker court martial was getting under way. Although roommates their plebe year, he and Lazelle had had no contact during their respective Army careers. Nonetheless, Lazelle undoubtedly knew a good deal about his former classmate, given Howard's reputedly poor performance as a corps commander at the battles of Chancellorsville and Gettysburg, and his high-profile post-war assignment as commissioner of the Freedmen's Bureau.[1]

In March 1881, Howard told his good friend Gen. Irvin McDowell that things were "working in nicely" at the Academy, but he later characterized his tour as Superintendent as "the hardest office to fill that I ever had." While to the outside viewer everything was neat and orderly, there was a "social undercurrent that was not so pleasant," and resistance against his attempts to "relieve the overpressure of 'the West Point system,' particularly of the demerit part."[2]

In an analysis published shortly before his arrival at the Academy, the *New York Times* speculated that one of Howard's principal concerns was the strictly military relationship maintained between instructors and cadets, the latter treated primarily as privates rather than students. While this "hardens the lads and makes them self-reliant," the *Times* contended, "its most marked result, has been to make the corps of Cadets maintain their own code of unwritten law and social discipline. Its most severe weapon, and the one used most mercilessly, is that of ostracism." General Howard, according to the *Times*, believed that it was time to "cultivate a closer relation" between the cadets and the officers instructing them. Another of his goals was to eliminate the practice of ostracism and "the caste spirit," fostered by "pro-slavery influences," which tended to encourage it.[3]

General Howard himself, while a cadet, had been ostracized for well over a year by members of his class, both for associating with his guardian's son, then a sergeant in the corps of sappers and engineers stationed at West Point, as well as for being an outspoken abolitionist. Eventually, he returned to good graces, and by his final year was popular enough within his class to be elected president of the Dialectic Society, West Point's literary club.[4]

HOWARD AND LAZELLE

In his autobiography, Howard never mentions the issues that divided him and Lazelle, but it is clear from the record that theirs was a conflicted relationship, probably from the start. For one, Howard had advanced to the rank of major general during the Civil War and remained a general in the regular Army despite his questionable record as a corps commander. Lazelle had made it only to lieutenant colonel. Moreover, even before taking command as Superintendent, Howard had urged the President to take the Whittaker case "away from West Point, where the social prejudice was strong against a negro cadet," and suggested "yielding to his desire to have a regular court-martial and to locate the court in New York."[5]

While Howard's advice to the President and his broader views on the plight of black cadets may have colored his attitude and dealings with Lazelle, the record suggests that other fundamental issues divided the two officers as well. Two in particular—changing the overall "culture" of the cadet corps and making adjustments to the system of discipline—were at the root of disagreements on policy that would shortly develop between the new Superintendent and the Commandant.

Howard and Lazelle first came to loggerheads over Howard's proposal to alleviate some of the harsher elements of cadet life, particularly the guard posts that had been recommended by Lazelle and approved by Schofield after the Whittaker affair. According to Howard, his intention was to "relieve them of the stringency that had been put upon them" after a number of incidents prior to his arrival, one of which involved sneaking a cannon and live cow up into the tower of one of the Academy buildings.

In addition to posting cadet guards in the barracks all night, Lazelle, with Schofield's concurrence, had ordered tactical officers to live in the barracks "so that every division should have at least one army officer constantly on the watch to supervise and report delinquencies." As a result of this "sudden severity," Howard often observed cadets "who happened to be seen off limits running to cover, skulking, and hiding behind logs. It seemed to be just the thing to do to avoid an officer and deceive him, and break the regulations without scruple." [6]

On January 26, 1881, the Commandant wrote a lengthy defense of the system that he and General Schofield had established, emphasizing the importance it played in the cadets' military education. Offering a strong case that the extra guard duty did not pose an undue hardship, Lazelle maintained that it helped cadets to understand and appreciate "the dignity and severity" of military life and "to look duty, trial, hardship and all other discomforts in the face, and regard them as nothing." Contending that there also had been no detrimental impact on the cadets' academics thus far, he suggested that his system was by far the best defense against both hazing and incidents like the attack on Whittaker:

> When the new Cadets come nothing could more effectively prevent hazing than the present system. And should there be, as there doubtless will be, more colored boys, no system can be devised which will so thoroughly prevent injustice to them, in the hours of the night, most favorable to mischief. I can but think that under rigid discipline, we would never have had a cause of complaint against the colored discrimination. General Schofield was so much pleased with the advantage of the present system that he called particular attention to its good results in his Report to the Secretary of War.[7]

Lazelle's defense fell on deaf ears. Howard implemented the change, noting in his autobiography that he "never had cause to regret this method of effecting the change." Eliminating Lazelle's 24-hour guard and taking other steps to "relieve them of the stringency that had been put upon them," all he asked of them, in exchange, was that they uphold the honor system with "courage and manliness." Howard's broader hope was to relieve the "overpressure of the West Point system," especially the severity of demerits, but in his memoirs he admitted that he met with little success: "there is no relief from its severity except in the kindness of the officers who are in charge." [8]

While Howard grappled with achieving the proper balance between the need for discipline and its negative impact on morale and behavior by too great a rigidity, the Academy's Board of Visitors unequivocally defended both the need for and value of the system that Lazelle and Schofield favored. In its June 1881 "Annual Report" to the Secretary of War, the Board championed a system which had "brought the Military Academy to great perfection and usefulness," and castigated previous efforts to "propitiate the cadets by indulgences and by relaxation of the traditional requirements of duty," all of which it contended had "uniformly been singular failures, filling the barrack yard with extra-duty men and crowding the demerit reports."[9]

Chaired by Gen. George S. Greene, who had distinguished himself at the Battle of Gettysburg, the Board was charged with submitting a report to the Secretary of War "for the information of Congress" on the administration, discipline, instruction, fiscal affairs, and any other concerns of the Academy. Traditionally, the Board visited the Academy during the June examinations. The 12-member Board in 1881 included two senators, three congressmen, and four generals and three senior political figures appointed by the President.

Among the officers on the board was Gen. Don Carlos Buell of Kentucky, a controversial Union commander who believed he had saved General Grant's hide at the Battle of Shiloh in April 1862, and who had been relieved of command of the Army of the Ohio in October 1862 for failing to pursue the forces of Confederate General Braxton Bragg after the Battle of Perryville. Buell was known popularly as "the General who never laughed."

In accordance with his responsibilities as the Academy's senior tactical officer, the Commandant of Cadets was charged with assisting the Board in its examination of the military training and discipline of the Corps. Thus, one morning that June, Lieutenant Colonel Lazelle escorted General Buell as he made a perfunctory inspection of the cadet barracks. Unfortunately, however, two cadets who were not sitting for exams that morning happened to be loitering in their quarters. Having found the 90-degree heat and stuffiness of their room unbearable, they had stripped to their underwear and moved their mattresses under the windows to take advantage of what little air might blow in.

They had just lit their pipes—the use of tobacco in any form by cadets had just been prohibited—when there was a "clink of a sword" in the hallway, the door burst open, and in walked Lieutenant Colonel Lazelle and General Buell. The two cadets immediately sprang to attention. One dropped his pipe, the hot ashes landing on his foot, and yelled out in pain. Lazelle reportedly turned purple with rage, while Buell "leaned back against a table and roared" with laughter. Solemnly, the Commandant of Cadets assured the inspecting general that the miscreants would be reported for "three flagrant violations of the rules," but Buell, still laughing, pushed Lazelle out of the room and down into the courtyard below.

It is said the two cadets could still hear Buell's laughs and chuckles as he and Lazelle made their way across the barracks courtyard. Fully expecting several months's confinement to quarters and many extra tours of guard duty, they were shocked to discover that evening that neither of their names was posted on the list of delinquents. General Buell had asked Lazelle to "spare the offenders." [10]

Howard-Lazelle Relationship Sours Further

As time passed, Lazelle and Howard were increasingly at odds on numerous issues, including the members of their staffs. A key element of dispute was Lazelle's refusal to acknowledge that requests or orders passed to him by Howard's adjutants carried the same authority as coming directly from Howard. He also was annoyed by Howard's habit of having his adjutant sign correspondence for him.

Since these officers were lieutenants, very much junior to Lazelle, he simply refused to accept the validity of any instructions, orders, or requests he received from them. In Howard's view, however, communications from him to Lazelle via his adjutants were the same as face-to-face. The lieutenants, in essence he believed, were exercising legitimate authority on his behalf.

In a May 1881 memo to Lazelle, Howard noted that his senior aide, Lt. C. E. S. Wood, felt "hurt that you reproved him in severe tones for doing what he declares I ordered him to do."[11] However, while Lazelle had issues with Wood, he saved most of his vitriol for 1st Lt. Joseph A. Sladen, Howard's other aide, who in August while Howard was away on leave, questioned Lazelle's decision to grant permission to a Tactics Department lieutenant to leave the post, "without obtaining the authority of the Commanding General in the manner provided by orders and regulation." Sladen apparently believed he could exercise the general's authority in Howard's absence. In his response, Lazelle politely but acerbically informed Sladen that he had acted in accordance with Academy regulations and that it was Sladen who was out of order.

Although the lieutenant's leave was a minor issue, the next one was more serious. On August 30, Sladen formally accused Lazelle of disobeying orders he had signed, on behalf of Howard, related to lighting gas street lamps at night. Lazelle, for various reasons, had chosen to ignore Sladen's orders, and Sladen preferred charges against Lazelle for disobeying a direct order. Three days later, Lazelle returned all of the original orders from Sladen along with a lengthy rebuttal, and asked that both Sladen's charges and a follow-on rebuke from Howard be withdrawn. The censure was not "recalled," and relations between Lazelle and Howard and his aides continued to fester. They would erupt again—this time with finality for Lazelle—in the spring of 1882. [12]

Proposed Revision of Tactics

In the midst of his ever-intensifying rhetorical battle with Howard, Lazelle continued to take his assignment as the senior tactical officer and instructor of tactics for the Army seriously. In his capacity as Commandant and head of the Department of Tactics at West Point, Lazelle had the time, resources, and motivation to give a good deal of thought to the impact of improvements in weaponry on battlefield formations and tactics. In September 1881 he offered General Sherman "some observations concerning our present tactical system and some suggestions looking to its modification."[13]

Citing vast improvements in infantry and artillery firepower, Lazelle suggested that the then-present system of tactics being taught at the Academy must be adapted to fit the new realities of weaponry: particularly the greater range and accuracy of breech-loading rifles and artillery.

Certainly this was an appropriate suggestion for the Commandant to make, but in suggesting that Army doctrine, codified in "Upton's System of Tactics," was in need of revision, Lazelle was treading on hallowed ground.

Brevet Maj. Gen. Emory Upton had first earned his spurs as a tactician commanding the 121st New York Volunteer Infantry, known as "Upton's Regulars," during the Civil War. At Salem Church in May 1863, he "learned to appreciate and thus fear the power of nineteenth-century weaponry" and recognized the need move away from the prevailing dependence on long, thin lines of infantry in linear attacks against troops armed with longer-range, more accurate, and faster-loading rifled muskets.[14]

Advocating, instead, "an attack in column" charging close to the defenders to "force a breach in the enemy's lines," Upton proved the effectiveness of this approach a year later commanding a brigade at the Battle of Spotsylvania. There he showed that, "if a charge were properly handled, closely mounted, and made in column rather than a line, a strong trench position could be carried." [15]

Following the war, Upton worked on perfecting his ideas and developing a new tactical system, which, at his urging, was examined by a board of officers meeting at West Point. Using the cadets as his tactical laboratory, Upton demonstrated the fundamental aspects of his scheme. Essentially, he replaced the French system of three ranks with a single rank of companies, each company divided into groups of four men. Each group of four was a distinct maneuver unit, similar in concept to today's infantry fire team or squad.

Under this scheme, a company commander could quickly and easily form a line in the direction required by "ordering the 'fours' forward, left, or right." More importantly, however, a unit could advance "either in column or in two or three ranks, then through a simple command expand or deploy into a single rank," facilitating, especially, the use of skirmishers to create break-through points in an enemy line that could be exploited by companies held in reserve. [16]

Upton's system had been adopted for use in the Army in August 1867, and in 1870 he returned to West Point as Commandant of Cadets and as head of a new board, charged with synchronizing cavalry and artillery tactics with those of the infantry. His revised *Infantry Tactics* was published in 1873, followed by *Cavalry Tactics* in 1874 and *Artillery Tactics* in 1875. Before his death by suicide in 1881, Upton also focused his efforts and writings on structural reform, particularly on the role of citizen soldiers and the need to insure they were "prepared to fight when called into service." [17]

While Lazelle did not necessarily propose that the Army discard Upton's system, he warned that "the necessities imposed by modern weapons," including the machine gun, "seem to demand further change." In particular, he argued that, given the "destructive intensity" of infantry and artillery fire, "our present tactical depth or rank must yield, as others have done before it, to improved fire-arms, in order that we shall not present live targets, easily decimated to an enemy. Our double rank must yield to the single rank, and the latter become the rule and the former the exception, in our formations." In particular, he suggested, it was time to abandon close-order formations and substitute thin lines, similar to those used by skirmishers.

The double rank—two lines of soldiers, one behind the other—was critical to maintaining a high volume of continuous fire when the muzzle-loaded musket was the most common weapon. The first rank would fire en masse, drop to its knees and reload while the second rank fired, thus keeping up a more or less continuous rate of fire. With the greater range and accuracy of new breech-loading and rifled-bore weapons, the massed double-ranks became more vulnerable to enemy fire. Lazelle was arguing for a single rank, more spread out like a skirmishing line, that would reduce this vulnerability while still maintaining the same volume of firepower.

In a characterization that would have led Upton, who died in 1881, to turn over in his grave, Lazelle acknowledged that his system of fours was "very pretty for drills," but warned that it had not been "exclusively tested in the field," and that exposure to severe or even moderate fire could "destroy all symmetry and order of fours in any single rank formation; and probably would greatly cut up that of a double rank."

Lazelle also criticized the reliance of Upton's skirmish method on the unit of fours, arguing instead that skirmishers should be deployed "by entire ranks on the right, left, or centre files in double or quick time." He concluded by urging that any modification of Army tactics "tend to greater simplicity," but offered no comprehensive approach of his own. Instead, he "most respectfully but urgently," recommended that the present system be modified by a Board of Officers.

Lazelle's letter to Sherman—a major stakeholder and proponent of Upton's system—was picked up and published by the *Army and Navy Journal*. It is not known whether Sherman took the letter as a personal insult, but in his curt reply—also picked up by the press—the General of the Army rejected the proposal that a Board of Officers be convened, noting that "the work of preparing tactics is better accomplished by the spontaneous effort of one individual [e.g. Upton] than by a board or even a single individual appointed to it." And he dismissed Lazelle's suggested changes, concluding that until a "complete system is offered for judgment and trial, the partial application of remedies to the system now used is not worth the time and labor."[18]

Lazelle apparently was not alone in his view that changes were required. In November 1878, the editors of the *Army and Navy Journal* had urged the development and adoption of a "new method of leading infantry troops into action and of handling them during the fight." Reviewing the infantry tactics of other "civilized nations, " the *Journal* asked rhetorically "have we studied or adopted any such formation, or do we exhibit the slightest interest in this most important matter to military men of all armies, who are entrusted with the lives of their men and the honor of their flag?" The *Journal* concluded:

> The time has passed, as the standard has changed, for us to continue drilling troops in close order over and over again, without developing a single tactical idea. We must place our men in positions similar to those they would occupy on the field of battle, and teach them so to act as if they were in the immediate presence of the enemy from the moment they leave the barrack-yard ... thus they will be forced to think, and not follow blindly the reiterated commands of their drill master. [19]

This article may well have started a prolonged debate within the officer corps and on the pages of the *Journal* over Upton's system of tactics, one in which it would have been natural for the Commandant to participate. Indeed, in an opinion piece accompanying the printing of the Lazelle letter and General Sherman's response, the editors noted that the two letters would "probably re-open for general discussion a question started by some officers last winter in the *Journal*, after the death of General Upton." The editorial went on to conclude:

> Our officers well remember when they were drilled under Scott, when Scott gave way to Hardee, when Hardee gave way to Casey, and when Casey gave way to Upton; and they expect to see the time when Upton gives way to some other tactician. And there are two special reasons why the change in the case of Upton should be more prompt that it might otherwise have been. In the first place, the improvements in modern weapons of all arms, and the additions of new weapons are such, that any system of maneuvers founded on an existing system, is likely to become superannuated, without any reflection being thereby cast on the skill or foresight of its author. Modern armies in Germany and France have perceived this necessity, and have acted accordingly, ever since Upton became authority for us, and the same work is still going on, so that Upton's unknown successor may be superseded in turn within the experience of soldiers now living. [20]

While he may have been in the vanguard of those advocating change, Lazelle was but one of a number of military theorists who, concerned about the continued dominance of ever more powerful defenses, had come to appreciate that "frontal assaults by close-ordered lines moving at cadence must give way to more flexible tactics." [21] They also worried that too much emphasis was being given to the rote drill in published manuals, a concern shared even by Upton who wrote to General Sherman a year before his death, "Tactics in all arms of the service have been simply a collection of rules for passing from one formation to another. How to fight has been left to actual experience in war." [22]

PRIZE-WINNING ESSAY

The Military Service Institution [23] also contributed to the debate over tactics, and its annual essay contest would have been another motivating factor for Lazelle and others advocating reform. Among the prizes awarded each year were the Gold and Silver Medals for the best two essays on topics of current military interest selected by the Institute's Executive Council. At its June 1881 meeting, the Council had voted "that the prize essay for the current year [1881] be omitted, and that the subject selected at the last meeting of the Council for this year be adopted as the subject for the prize essay for the ensuing year [1882], viz: 'The Important Improvements in the Art of War during the past twenty years and their probable effect on future military operations.'"

In January 1882, the Council selected Generals George McClellan, Irwin McDowell, and James Fry to review the 1882 submissions and select the winning essay. The names of the authors of each essay were not revealed to the members of the Board until they had finished their review and selected the winners. [24]

Lazelle was one of five officers submitting essays for the competition. The first half of his essay focused broadly on changes in artillery and small arms, including such factors as sights and rangefinders, with detailed charts and data. He also discussed important advances on the "support" side, including shelter trenches and entrenching tools, the use of armored defenses, field telegraphy, and railroads. In Part II, Lazelle analyzed the "probable effect" of these advances on future military operations. Among his conclusions:

- With the greatly increased range and accuracy of the breech-loading rifle, the dimensions and lines of defense could be increased, limited only to the distance of fairly accurate fire. The advantages gained for defensive works: larger lines of defense at less cost and greater unity of artillery and infantry fire.
- The questionable value of permanent fortifications, covering frontiers, for example. "The defence is forced to seal up a large force in such works, where they are consigned to inactivity, or disconnected effort. ... Real defense is in armies, with defensive lines of field works if required."
- The increased importance of "shelter trenches," given the growth in firepower, accuracy and range of artillery and infantry weapons. However, he warned, there also was a danger of "too much intrenching [*sic*], as it often seriously threatens to destroy the confidence and audacity of the best troops. The shelter trench best serves its purpose, when the soldier is convinced that it is only a resort of a weak line for desperate defense; and merely takes the place of natural cover."
- The cavalry would be the most greatly affected, with the "shock" of massed cavalry charges "rarely seen again." Rather, he argued, cavalry would become the "antennae of an army," and would best be employed as a combined-arm force with infantry in the offense or defense. He suggested that rather than large, separate cavalry divisions, the best organizational arrangement would be to assign a cavalry brigade to each infantry division and corps.
- One distinctive feature of cavalry would be its use as a raiding element. "The more dispersed order of battle, as well as its more extended front will contribute to this use of cavalry; and its success would be quite probable against a gap in the enemy's line, or in its weak extension. Or he may be taken in flank, or reverse, while sharply attacked in front by infantry."

- Infantry and artillery must be much more closely coordinated and would become more mutually reinforcing. "On the field, artillery should now prepare the way for infantry, and must support and cover it; and as the companion of infantry, the intimacy of relation of fire will guide its action. ... A front attack by infantry alone upon a defensive line has little chance of success; obstacles and defensive strength should first be crushed by artillery, posted if possible for oblique or enfilade fire."
- The breech-loader "enables troops to safely assume the open order, since its aimed fire is five times faster, and five times as effective as that of a muzzle-loader. Hence one man is now in all respects the equal or superior of four formerly, in the power of fire and may therefore take the space of four."
- Major changes in Upton's system of organization and maneuver are required. "Napoleon said that a nation should change its tactics every ten years. They certainly should be modified to suit the development of the power of arms, and as often as necessary. They are now greatly encumbered by movements for massing belonging to shock tactics; and by flank movements along an enemy's front."
- Finally, command relationships must change: "fighting is more individualized, from the lowest to the highest unit of command. More is left to the judgment of the commanding officer of each, from the company to the corps commander, and more is required of each. The fate of battles depends more on the courage and capacity of individuals; and the difficulty is greater of holding men in hand, and maintaining a close directing power. The General may order the attack, but the careful disposition of troops on the ground, and their forcible use to a common purpose, must be left to the company, to field, and to subordinate general officers." [25]

When the Board of Award completed its review, it concluded that of the five essays reviewed, three were especially meritorious, but the paper written by "Aleph" (the identity given to Lazelle) was the "most thoroughly worked out in detail" and thus "entitled to the prize." [26] The awarding of the prize in December 1882 was covered both by the military journals and the popular press. *The Army and Navy Journal* published a straightforward summary of the essay, concluding "we have not attempted to more than indicate Col. Lazelle's line of argument. So important an essay, densely written and closely argued, needs to be carefully read as a whole to be appreciated."[27]

The *New York Times* also published a lengthy review and summary of the essay judging (probably tongue in cheek) that it would be "read with great interest not only by military men but by everybody who cares to keep abreast of the world's progress in the art of killing men rapidly and in large masses." The *Times* judged it "satisfactorily thorough, though necessarily brief" in its treatment of "all that pertains to field operations, including arms, equipment defenses, and maneuvers," although it said "scarcely anything" about organization. The article concluded: "In short, army tactics have undergone material changes at every point to meet the advance in the art of throwing projectiles, for it is a rule of warfare that the defensive and offensive must march side by side. If some competent authority would attempt to trace out the effect of all these wonderful changes upon the morale of the common soldier, the result would be of interest. Their tendency would seem to reduce the rank and file to a mass of machines set to work certain other machines." [28]

Howard Requests Lazelle's Relief

In the spring of 1882, General Howard's imminent departure on leave once again surfaced the question of the authority of the Commandant and Howard's adjutant while Howard was away. This time, however, Lazelle went straight to the top, requesting a ruling from the Adjutant General of the Army in Washington. Noting that "by law I am Superintendent of the Academy and commanding the Post of West Point during the absence from the Post of General Howard," Lazelle cited numerous instances during Howard's absences when he received peremptory orders on matters he believed were "within my exclusive control," including granting cadets leave and directing him to send a cadet to New York City.

Wrapping up his request for Washington's intervention, Lazelle concluded that he was "not of the opinion that discretionary command and authority can be left with Lieutenant Sladen, the Acting Assistant Adjutant General, to issue orders in the absence of the Department Commander, as heretofore and as now exercised, leaving the former to judge in the matter."[29]

Lazelle won. On May 5, 1882, the Adjutant General informed Howard that, in the view of the Secretary of War, "in the absence of the Superintendent, the next in rank shall have the immediate government and military command of the Academy and shall be commandant of the Military Post of West Point." [30]

According to media reports, Howard and Lazelle presented a civil front as they presided over the June 1882 graduation ceremonies, with Lazelle delivering a short lecture to the graduating class at noon on June 9 on "The Customs of the Service," and their wives assisting the "Reception Committee" for the graduation ball.[31] However, issues between Howard and his Commandant soon came to a head.

On June 16, after discovering that Howard's aides had been requesting information from his tactical officers, and "disturbed by what he considered an improper disregard of his prerogatives," [32] Lazelle fired off a letter requesting that all inquiries be addressed directly to him. Howard's adjutant returned Lazelle's letter asking for "specific allegations," which Lazelle provided the following day. Lazelle's response was returned with a notation from Howard that "officers who complained of the Superintendent could be influenced by no good motives." [33]

Lazelle was outraged, and returned the entire package to Howard asking if his remarks were "intended as a reflection upon my motives." Howard, in turn, replied by letter on June 27, "declining to make any explanation in regard to the matter or to return the original letter with its indorsements [*sic*], or to furnish a copy of the same." At this point, the two belligerents were no longer on speaking terms, and Howard was unwilling to continue the battle in writing. Lazelle bundled up the entire package and sent it off to the Adjutant General of the Army, requesting his intervention:

> My original letter was based on the requirements of Paragraph 648, Army Regulations, there having been many instances of its non-observance, in instructions and inquiries conveyed to my subordinate officers in the tactical department, which I have known nothing of except through them; and which they have reported to me as official matters; and which I have considered as official up to the present time.
>
> I do not understand that it is the right or privilege of any higher officer to freely impute to me any improper motive in writing the letter; and I respectfully request that General Howard be requested to withdraw the indorsement [*sic*] conveyed officially to me; or that he disclaim its application to my communication. [34]

Once again, providence was on Lazelle's side. On July 15, General Sherman penned his judgment, ruling that he considered the Corps of Cadets to be a "military body under the immediate command of Lt. Col. Lazelle, Commandant of Cadets," but subordinate to the Superintendent. That said, however, Sherman went on to inform Howard he would "maintain better discipline, surely preserve a higher tone and better feeling, if he will administer his command of the Corps of Cadets by and through the Commandant. I am strengthened in this conclusion by observing the effect, on board of a man of war, having a Captain and an Admiral on board at the same time." [35]

While Howard apparently had had enough and submitted his resignation, effective the end of August, Lazelle's victory was pyrrhic. By late July, it was being reported in the press that he was about to be relieved as Commandant of Cadets, one year short of the usual four-year term. In a letter dated July 20, Lazelle expressed his concerns over the rumors to the Adjutant General of the Army. On an attached transmittal slip, the Adjutant General wrote: "Inform him no order has come on the subject," and a response was dispatched from Washington stating simply: "I have the honor to acknowledge the receipt of your letter of the 20th instant, and in reply, to inform you that your relief from duty at the Military Academy has not been ordered." [36]

Two days later, Lazelle wrote a second missive to the Adjutant General again expressing concern over the "prominence given in the press of my proposed removal from here, for assorted censurable conduct, and repeated semi-officially in the Army and Navy Journal of today's date," and asking that his situation be brought to General Sherman's attention. Assuring the Adjutant General that he was not "begging to stay at West Point for the sake of the place or the duty," and that he would "cheerfully go" when his four-year term was up, he maintained that he had "no fear of duty" anywhere the Army might send him, but he did fear "a bad name." Lazelle concluded his plea: "If it shall be found on investigation that my failure or misconduct here merits termination at once of my duties, I shall not ask delay." [37]

There was no response to Lazelle's second letter, but in a curiously worded item in its July 27 edition, the *New York Times* reported that "It is been decided not to relieve Lieut.-Col. Lazelle as Commandant at the West Point Military Academy." In fact, on July 31, in a letter to the Adjutant General of the Army, Howard requested officially that Lazelle be relieved of duty:

> I do not ask this as a punishment but in the interest of peace and order. In the correspondence forwarded by Col. Lazelle during my absence, I am made to appear at a disadvantage. My course, all the time, was intended to avoid a quarrel which this officer evidently sought with me. Why he has done so I cannot tell, but certainly, taking everything into account in the best interests of the Military Academy, as I conceive it, I most decidedly and earnestly recommend a change of Commandant. [38]

The response came two days later. Special Order No. 178, dated August 2, 1882, Paragraph 7, relieved Lt. Col. H. M. Lazelle from duty at the U.S. Military Academy, effective August 5, 1882, per Special Order 91,

Department of West Point.[39] The August 11, 1882, edition of the *New York Times* reported that Lazelle had been granted a leave of absence for four months to take effect from the date of his relief from duty, and prior to rejoining his regiment (the 23rd Infantry).

General Sherman had supported Lazelle's arguments against the manner in which Howard administered the Superintendent's responsibilities, and the Board of Visitors had supported him on maintaining the West Point System. Nonetheless, Howard had succeeded in having Lazelle removed before he, too, departed after less than two years as Superintendent.

Lazelle's son Horace recollected that the family remained at West Point until the fall of 1882, when they left for Fort Craig in New Mexico, where his father was reassigned as lieutenant colonel of the 23rd Infantry Regiment. Just before leaving for the West, however, the family traveled to Lake Memphremagog in Canada where they stayed at the Georgeville Hotel. Horace remembered that the Barrows family was there. His father had met Samuel Barrows out in Dakota Territory, and this was the first of many visits to the Barrowses and their summer cottage on the lake. After retiring from the Army, Lazelle would purchase a portion of the Barrows family's property and build a summer cabin.

Chapter 9

First to Purgatory, Then to India

Reassigned as lieutenant colonel of the 23rd Infantry Regiment, effective June 26, 1882,[1] Lazelle remained at West Point until August 4. After spending time on leave, including the visit with the Barrows family in Canada, the family traveled to Fort Craig in December. Lazelle assumed command of the post on December 18. They remained there for just over a year.

Fort Craig

At Fort Craig, Lazelle was officially on "detached duty," as the headquarters of the regiment was located at Fort Union, northeast of Santa Fe. The post had a complement of some 13 officers and 145 enlisted men, with one company of the 23rd Infantry and two troops (companies) of the 4th Cavalry.

Established in 1854, the fort was located 35 miles south of the present town of Socorro, about halfway between Santa Fe and El Paso. At the time, it was one of the most desolate of eight forts along the main north-south road in the Rio Grande Valley, part of a 1,200-mile-long Spanish colonial trail—the El Camino Real—from Mexico City to Santa Fe.[2]

Following the Civil War, there were persistent rumors that Fort Craig would be closed, and, in August 1878, it was deactivated and abandoned. Continued raiding by local Apaches, however, gave it new life, and it was formally reestablished in November 1880. That same month, the post commander described the buildings as "very much dilapidated, the roofs and walls badly washed, and in some cases they had fallen entirely to the ground." He noted that doors and windows had nearly all been carried away (probably by locals), and the drain spouts were "gone or spoiled."[3]

Three years later, just a few months after the Lazelles arrived, a local journalist described the "antiquated fort" as "merely a Mexican plaza, surrounded by adobe buildings" and "almost deserted." Those who lived there "wished to make it as presentable as was possible," and the Army officers there expected it soon to be expanded to ten companies.[4]

Horace remembered Fort Craig as an open fortification surrounded by a moat and a dirt wall, with wicker baskets filled with dirt to hold up the sides for cannon openings. Their house was in one angle of the fortifications and was made of adobe. At one point, there were torrential rains, almost a flood. The rain filled the moat with water, which came through the walls of the house and "squirted like a hose into the rooms." He also remembered that butter from the sutler's (post trader's) store came in cans and, since there was no ice, was like soup in summertime, so they had to spoon it. Fort Craig definitely was not West Point!

Photo 18. Fort Craig, New Mexico

Courtesy of the William A. Keleher Collection, University of New Mexico

Photo 19. Fort Craig Officer's Quarters

Courtesy of Palace of the Governors Photo Archives (NMHM/DCA), Farnsworth Collection, Negative 014511

Photo 20. Captain Jack Crawford

Captain Jack Crawford ran the sutler's store. Known as the "Poet Scout," Crawford had made his name as a scout in the Black Hills, where he served as the first "Captain" of Custer City's Black Hills Rangers militia in 1875 and then joined Buffalo Bill Cody as a scout for General Merritt's 5th Cavalry the summer of 1876. Following the Battle of the Little Bighorn, Crawford was with General Crook's command at the Battle of Slim Buttes, the Army's first significant victory over the Sioux after Custer's last stand. Later that fall he left to join Buffalo Bill's Wild West show, known as the "Buffalo Bill Combination." [5]

The partnership with Cody ended in Virginia City, Nevada, in the summer of 1877, when, in a combat scene staged on horseback, Crawford allegedly shot himself accidentally in the groin. Later he blamed Cody, maintaining that Buffalo Bill had been drunk and slashed him twice during a knife fight scene. Crawford went on to establish his own show, the "Captain Jack Combination," but by late January 1878, it was disbanded in San Francisco for lack of funds.[6]

After a year of prospecting in the Cariboo Region of British Columbia, publishing his first book, and taking a play he had written on the road with his own theater troupe, Crawford ended up in Santa Fe, New Mexico, in May 1880, in the grips of yet another financial crisis. There he offered his services as scout to Col. Edward Hatch, commanding the Military District of New Mexico, whose troops had mounted a campaign against the Indian leader Victorio and his Warm Springs Apaches. Crawford resigned his position as Chief of Scouts after Victorio was killed, deciding to make New Mexico his permanent home and get back into prospecting and supplying forage and fuel to the Army. In June 1881, he was appointed post trader at Fort Craig, and his family joined him. The Crawford family would live close by the fort for nearly 20 years, "remaining as caretakers even after troops were withdrawn." [7]

A published author and journalist in his later years, Crawford traveled the country lecturing and reading his "frontier" poetry. Most of his stories and poems were nostalgic looks back at the good old days of frontier life and the larger-than-life men with whom he served. Years later, Crawford wrote to Horace, then a doctor in Seattle, reminiscing about their days at Fort Craig:

> I have just written your good father who was my commanding officer when you were a boy, at old Fort Craig when I was Chief of Scouts and I am sure you will be glad to hear from the old Bronco who used to entertain you when you were a boy. I am sending you some material [promotional fliers and poems] that will explain itself. With all good wishes, believe me, sincerely yours, J.W. Crawford (Capt. Jack). [8]

The Lazelles had some thirty cats at Fort Craig: Button Hook, Button Hook Jr., Gracie, etc. In the evening, the family would go out for a walk with all the cats trailing along behind. Horace and Jacob once killed and skinned a skunk. Horace remembered it was so smelly that their mother made them undress outside and bury their clothes. They trapped beaver and badgers here also, and even a wildcat. It was at Fort Craig that Horace first fired a shotgun, an old muzzle-loader whose kick knocked him flat on his back.

The area around Fort Craig was largely desert with mesquite and sage brush and cottonwoods in the valley near the water. Lazelle drilled a well so that the family could get clear, fresh water. But the water still had to be transported in barrels on wagons from the well to the post. Until the well was dug, they had to use muddy river water and let it settle as they had done at Fort Sully.

For most of Lazelle's tour at Fort Craig, the troops were in garrison or on escort duty. He remained at the post except for short tours of "detached service"—at Tucson, Arizona, for eleven days in October 1883 and during December 1883 and January 1884 at Fort Cummings, New Mexico, and Fort Leavenworth, Kansas.

In May 1883, still smarting over his dismissal from West Point and his banishment—as he undoubtedly viewed it—to Fort Craig, he wrote to Lieutenant Charles Braden, Secretary of the Association of Graduates and a teacher at the Academy's preparatory school in West Point that:

> ... I belong to the graduating class of 1855; that I cannot very well be present at the [annual alumni] dinner; that I cannot see the clothes taken off from poor Gen. Thayer [his statue was to be unveiled]; that I cannot listen to the eloquent [General] Cullum [who was to speak at the unveiling]; that I live at this place without any street and without any number; that I do not care a d_ _n for [General] Howard; and that I would not believe if anybody straight from Heaven should tell me that there is any use for him there. [9]

TRANSFERRED TO SAN FRANCISCO

According to Horace, the 3,000-foot altitude at Fort Craig bothered his father's heart, and early in 1884 he requested a transfer. On January 31, Maj. Gen. John Pope, commanding the Military Division of the Pacific, formally requested Lazelle's assignment to the Division as special inspector for the Department of California at the Presidio of San Francisco. He was transferred to the department, and the family left Fort Craig on February 21.

Horace remembered traveling to the Presidio of San Francisco by train but being stuck in Los Angeles because the tracks had washed out. The family had to wait to get passage on a side-wheel steamer with a "walking beam" (similar to those used on the Colorado River to get to Fort Yuma) to get to San Francisco. On February 29, Lazelle reported the delay to the Adjutant General in Washington.

The three-day trip to San Francisco on the steamer *Ancon* was very rough. Horace and his father were fine, but Jacob and his mother were seasick. The steamer stopped at Port Orford on the coast to "take on cheese from a Dutch colony near San Louis [*sic*] Obispo." The 500 "red cheeses" were brought to the coast on a small rail line, loaded onto lighters, and brought out to the steamer.

Having completed his penance at Fort Craig, Lazelle reported for "inspection duty" at the Presidio March 3, 1884, and the family was assigned quarters on post. Once again, they were back in civilization. Serving as General Pope's Inspector General, Lazelle was sent all over the Division, inspecting troops, posts, quarters, etc. in California, Nevada, and parts of Oregon.

While at the Presidio, Jacob attended high school on post, and Horace began preparing for high school at home. There were many families and children on post, so the Lazelles once again had an active social life. Horace remembered one particular dance held at the Post Exchange. He wore a new pair of trousers, and on the way to the dance, while tossing their house keys up in the air, they fell through a crack in the board walkway and were lost. On the way home from the dance, he fell getting off the wagon and tore the knees out of his new pants. He had to climb a porch post to get back into the house, fell through the window of his bedroom, catching his foot in the lace curtains and knocking over and breaking the water pitcher and bowl in his room. His parents were not amused.

On post, both Horace and Jacob joined the Presidio Minstrel Troupe. An undated news clipping, headlined "Entertainments at the Presidio," reported that: "The first appearance in public of the Presidio Minstrel Troupe ... proved to be a most successful and finished presentation of the melodies and comicalities of minstrelsy." The club was composed of members of the officers' families, and the audience was "entirely unprepared for the merit which was found in the performance. The songs were admirably rendered, the endmen's jokes were new and to the point, and the farcical sketches were brimful of fun." [10]

In April 1885, Lazelle was detailed as Inspector General for the Department of Columbia at Vancouver Barracks, Washington, and then assigned there on detached service through October 1885. He was one of four field officers serving on temporary detail to the Inspector General's Office. Congress had authorized and funded four fewer officers than required to fill all of the Army's inspector general positions. The family remained in San Francisco.

Lazelle's inspections at each post he visited in the department were all-encompassing, covering topics and issues such as financial accounting, purchasing and supplies, the sanitary conditions of the facilities and troops, and troop training. In his and other inspectors' reports, the latter topic often was singled out for criticism. In his 1885 annual report to the Secretary of War, the Army Inspector General noted that, at the majority of posts, there had been improvements in troop instruction. At some posts however, there still were serious deficiencies:

> There is neglect in carrying out the requirements of the Army regulations in respect to guard-mounting, parades, inspections, the superintending of the stated roll calls by company officers, the wearing of uniform by officers and men, and military bearing of officers in the presence of enlisted men. At the posts referred to, some officers do not appear to take sufficient interest in their duties and show want of adequate knowledge in their profession. It is believed that much of this unsatisfactory condition of things at some posts is due to the apathy and neglect of the post commander. [11]

The Inspector General did not single out specific posts by name in his report; however, he did provide specifics on issues related to contracting for horses and other supplies. On the procurement of horses, he noted reports from Lazelle on the inefficiency and cost of procuring animals "at ranches and other points of delivery convenient to the sellers." In one case, Lazelle noted, the horses were then sent to their destinations by rail, over 1,000 miles, at the cost to the Army of $235 per car-load. Upon arrival, "all were more or less emaciated," two had died, and 63 percent were found unfit and sold at auction at a loss. According to Lazelle, in another case where the seller was required to deliver the horses to the posts where they were needed, only 35 percent had been rejected, and none were lost to death or injury. [12]

Finally, in a nineteenth-century version of the modern-day military procurement issues, Lazelle and one of his fellow inspectors challenged the Army's requirement that all purchases of supplies be advertised and competed. In 1884, Congress had passed legislation requiring all purchases by the Army of "quartermaster's and subsistence supplies" be done by contract after public notice, except in emergencies, which would require approval by the Secretary of the Army.

In his report, Lt. Col. Roger Jones, Assistant Inspector-General for the Division of the Atlantic, noted one case in which the advertising costs ($30.75) were greater than the cost of the supplies procured ($23.50). While this may have been an extreme case, Lazelle also reported a case in which contracting costs were higher than the value of supplies procured:

> In the purchase by this method at the depot of the Presidio of San Francisco of various articles of small value, but which aggregated a little over $500, it was estimated that 8 percent above the ordinary market price of the articles was expended in printing, posting, and preparing the papers required. [13]

The Inspector General concluded his report by suggesting that the procurement requirement, if continued, would not be in the best interest of economy or "the good of the service."

Off to India

In its November 17, 1885, edition, under "Army and Navy News," the *New York Times* printed the short announcement that President Grover Cleveland had selected Col. H.M. Lazelle, Inspector-General of the Department of the Columbia, to represent the United States at British military maneuvers in India in January. In fact, he had been picked by General of the Army Philip H. Sheridan, who, in part, may have been rewarding Lazelle for his prize-winning essay of 1882, and perhaps compensating him for his shortened West Point tour and banishment to Fort Craig.

Lazelle departed Portland, Oregon, November 19 en route to Washington, where he received written authority from the Army Adjutant General "to make your personal report to this office, by telegraph in the fewest possible words at the end of each month, during your absence from the United States." His application for mileage in advance to Suez and return was approved by the Secretary of War. [14]

Lazelle was accompanied on the trip by Capt. Samuel M. Mills, 5th Artillery, his "line officer." In today's parlance, Mills was his "bag carrier." They sailed first to England, on the steamer *Oregon,* en route to Egypt where they were to be met by a British officer and joined by other representatives including French Colonel Descharme, former Military Attache in London, and Russian Col. Prince Odojewsky, an aide-de-camp to the Czar. [15]

Lazelle's trip and the British military exercises came at the height of strategic rivalry between Britain and Russia over Afghanistan, the so-called "Great Game." The British, threatened by Russian expansion into Central Asia, had sought to secure Afghanistan as a buffer state between Russia and Britain's South Asian empire. During the First Anglo-Afghan War in 1838, the British had attempted and failed to install a pro-British puppet regime in Kabul.

In 1872 the British and Russians had agreed to respect Afghanistan's northern border, but the accord disintegrated in 1878 when Russia sent an emissary to Kabul. The British demanded equal access to the Afghan government but were turned away. In response, they launched the so-called Second Anglo-Afghan War, forcing their way across the Khyber Pass. British forces withdrew in 1880, signing a peace treaty with the Afghan leader that formally demarked India's northern border with Afghanistan.

Another series of incidents in 1884 brought Russia and Britain to the brink of war, as Russian forces moved into areas of Turkmenistan controlled by Afghanistan, including two important oases, one on the road south toward the Afghan city of Herat. Afghan Army attempts to retake the territory failed. In the end, the British decided not to challenge the Russians and to accept Russian occupation of territory north of the Amu Darya River. In 1885, a Joint Anglo-Russian Boundary Commission began meeting to formally establish Afghanistan's northern border. The Afghans were not invited to participate.

Against this background, the British decided in early 1885 to increase the Army in India by an additional 11,000 British and 12,000 Indian troops, bringing their total force in India up to nearly 200,000. Then, in late 1885, London directed the command to mount the largest ever British-Indian Army exercises. According to Field Marshal Lord Frederick Sleigh Roberts, who commanded British forces and the exercises, London was particularly concerned that the Russians were now in an "infinitely more advantageous" position and were persisting in their attempts "to encroach on Afghan territory, in order that they might be in a position to control the approaches to Herat, a Russian occupation of which fortress we could not permit." [16]

After a series "semi-private" meetings that March between the British Viceroy, Lord Dufferin, and the Amir of Afghanistan, the Amir eventually declared his intention to side with the British and that he was ready "with my army and my people to render any services that may be required of me or of the Afghan nation." The boundary commission, however, continued its work, without Afghan participation, and preparations began in earnest that fall for the massive Anglo-Indian Army exercises. It was not by accident that the Russians were invited to join the group of international observers, nor that the Russian delegation included a close confidant of the Czar.

En route to Suez, Lazelle and Mills traveled through Europe and, in his account of the trip, Lazelle expressed "an utter lack of admiration of a Southern European winter; I rejoiced when at last the steamer hurried me away from Italy—a land fruitful of murky skies and freezing and musty hotels; swarming with beggars; abounding with cheese, dirty snow, macaroni, and shameless art—and [quoting Lord Byron] when at last we shot along 'o'er the glad waters of the dark blue sea' toward the shores of Africa."[17]

When their ship docked in Alexandria, Lazelle was immediately taken with the city, again quoting Byron: "Here Cleopatra once balanced her loves against the safety of the state, and Roman emperors, bewitched, became oblivious to their crowns ... here was the vast library which for ages was the repository of the learning of the world ... on these very shores the mighty Napoleon once marshaled his armies."

At the Alexandria docks, a man who, to Lazelle, "could have been Moses," approached slowly and in a dignified manner "raised one hand in respectful salaam and extended the other saying solemnly: 'Backsheesh!' [plea for tips] Vanish, shades of the past, for we are in modern Egypt, a land of beggars and corruption." But here, in the mysterious and intoxicating land of Arab princes, he was willing to forgive what he had criticized in Italy.

On his last day in Cairo, Lazelle was treated to an audience with (or "presentation to") the Khedive, Tewfik Pasha, at his palace: " [A]fter a tedious delay ... we were finally conducted through multiplied halls and corridors, into the very pleasing presence of the Khedive, the figurehead of Egypt, for he is nothing more—an attractive-faced, unpretentious gentleman who speaks English perfectly ... and who is striving to undo some of the riotous mischief of his dissolute father." Pasha, whose father had nearly bankrupted Egypt, was essentially a constitutional monarch with no authority, "ruling" under control of the British.

From Cairo, the group proceeded 600 miles up the Nile to Suez where they met Colonel Upperton of Her Majesty's Indian Army and officers from Russia, Germany, Austria, Hungary, Italy and France. There, they embarked on the voyage to Bombay, through the Red Sea and past the port of Jedda, and anchored in Aden. According to Lazelle, Aden, a naval and coaling station, was "so important to England that unlimited labor and expense has been devoted to rendering it immensely strong." He went on to describe it as:

> built literally on the solid rock, and its fortifications are hewn out of the mountains from base to summit, both on the sea and land side, the two sides being connected by tunnels through the mountain chain. The place is almost impregnable. The entrance to the Red Sea is through a ship channel of not over one and a half miles wide, fully commanded by fortifications on the black, dismal and barren island of Perrim [*sic*—Perim]. So long as England holds these two points, and maintains control of the Suez Isthmus, so long is her road to India free.

On the boat trip to India, Lazelle met a Parsee merchant from Bombay who later entertained the colonel at his house.[18] They kept up a correspondence for years, and the merchant sent many stamps to Horace for his collection. Describing the house as "richly and elegantly furnished in all that is costly and tasteful of Eastern devices," and the family as "easy in manner, composed and dignified in conversation," Lazelle felt everything about them "suggested luxurious ease and the delight of living."

The two American representatives arrived in Bombay December 29, 1885, where they and the other foreigners were hosted by Colonel Upperton before proceeding to Delhi. Their schedule in Bombay was less than rigorous: on Wednesday, an official visit to Government Horse Training School followed by an evening dinner and reception given by Sir Robert Fair; on Thursday, a morning sail to the "Elephantine Caves," lunch with the Lord-Chief-Justice and dinner at the Bombay Club; on Friday a morning visit to the "Towers of Silence," an afternoon inspection of the troop ships, and dinner with Lord Ray at Bombay Government House followed by a ball given by civilian authorities.

Leaving Bombay, the group made its way overland to Delhi, stopping at several of the "most important sites a considerable time," including Ajmer and Jaipur in Rajasthan, where they were "conducted through the royal palaces and shown many works indicative of the wealth, splendor and power of the former Rajahs."

According to Sir Edwin Arnold, the British poet, author, and journalist, as the foreign observers arrived Delhi was "astir, outside and inside her walls, with 'the pomp, pride, and circumstance of glorious war'" (from Shakespeare's *Othello*) as an army of forty thousand troops—"the flower of the Queen-Empress' forces in India" —gathered for "elaborate martial manoeuvres ... beyond a doubt, the finest military spectacle ever witnessed in Hindostan [*sic*]."[19]

Arriving in Delhi, Lazelle, Mills and the other foreign observers drove immediately to the camp of Field Marshal Roberts, beginning three weeks in the area lying between Delhi and Ambala, 100 miles to the north. The permanent camp they occupied for a few days before and after the maneuvers consisted of "vast double tents floored with rugs and divided by hangings into apartments, and in front of the tent of each foreign officer was displayed the flag of his nation; carriages and servants were always at hand, and each day was a fete day."

In the field's so-called "flying-camp," however, conditions were a bit different:

> ... [O]ur daily life was that of active service: small tents, limited personal baggage, pack animals and starlight breakfasts were the rule. Not so with dinner, however; an army of servants took the burden and care of the great mess tent and its stately outfit, and every evening at eight, a formal dinner of many courses was served, at which were usually seated forty or fifty officers and guests. After dinner, around an immense campfire, (for nights in the hill country are cold, although the days very hot) camp stories, and what are called "Army pegs," carried us usually into the early morning hours. [20]

In his memoir, Field Marshal Roberts admitted that earlier in the year when the crisis with Russia was coming to a head, "many weak points in the Commissariat and Transport Department" had arisen when mobilization of the two-corps force had been imminent. Thus, the exercise, in part, was intended to "test our readiness for war," in addition to impressing the foreign observers with the capabilities of the combined forces. In concluding his discussion of the exercise, Lord Roberts noted that the foreign officers were "somewhat surprised at the fine physique and efficiency of our Native soldiers, but they all remarked on the paucity of British officers with the Indian regiments, which I could not but acknowledge was, as it still is, a weak point in our military organization."

The final "grand review" was held January 19, with the Viceroy on the reviewing stand. Earlier, local Hindus had predicted there would be rain on the day of the review. When the day came, it started out gorgeous with no rain, and the officers all pooh-poohed the Hindus' predictions. Just as the review began, however, the heavens opened, and it poured for four hours straight, thoroughly soaking all the officers—and their dress uniforms.

Photo 21. Elephant Siege Battery in India

Photo 22. Foreign Officers in Camp Near Panipat

Lt. Col. Lazelle is standing on the far right.

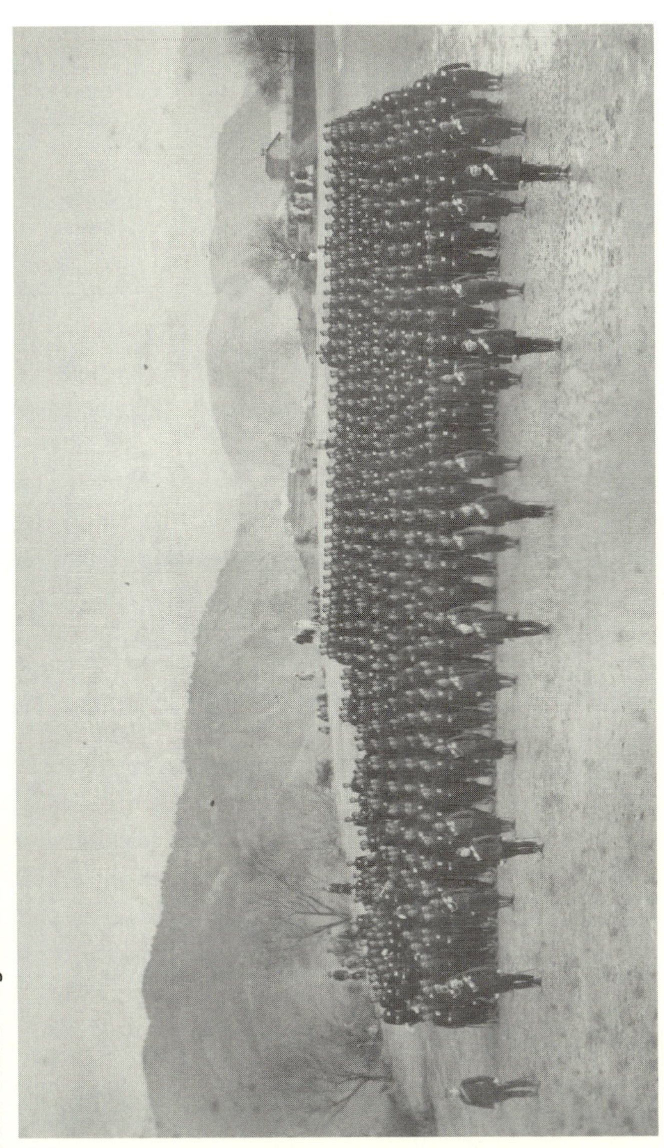

Photo 23. Gurkha Regiment in India

Lazelle later told his sons that the native troops wore sandals rather than boots, and kept losing them in the mud, nearly breaking ranks to retrieve them. One foreign officer wore gold-plated chest armor, and his fractious horse threw him into the mud. He was so angry he left for home early. Nonetheless, in his article for the *Journal*, Lazelle characterized the review a complete success: "the military formation was on a perfectly level, treeless plain, all the troops being constantly in view, and the whole effect very fine."

The review was widely covered in the British press. Hyperbole was much in evidence. According to *The Ipswich Journal*, the grand review was a "spectacle impossible to parallel in the world" and due to "the pluck and discipline of the troops," they presented to the Viceroy "a front as compact and well-drilled as if the affair had been a regimental barrack-yard parade." The *Glasgow Herald*, also noting weather that would make any Scotsman envious, reported that "the difficulties which the two armies had to contend with, the heavy rains, the strong wind, and the impassable mud, while they detracted from the outward brilliancy of the occasion, served to throw into relief the sterling qualities of pluck, perseverance, endurance, and discipline."[21]

Following the final review, there was one more day devoted to exhibits of some of the unique skills of the Indian troops. Lazelle was especially impressed with the horsemanship of the Sikhs of Northern India, who were "the most accomplished riders in the world; their feats at full speed, in sticking with the lance tent-pegs driven into the ground, in cutting lemons on the ground, in riding bareback, standing up, and even changing horses at full speed, were fine exhibitions of their complete training." [22] As the *Glasgow Herald* noted, these "games" were opened by Lord Roberts, "who took the first tent-peg in brilliant style."

Lazelle also was quite taken with "quoit throwing," describing the quoit as "a circular steel blade of about one foot in diameter, the outer edge of which is very sharp. It is thrown by first spinning it rapidly on the fingers, then hurling it by a circular motion of the arm; it flies whirling with great accuracy and swiftness for two or three hundred yards, and will terribly wound whomsoever it strikes."

After leaving Delhi, the delegation was taken to "the great cities of Kanpur, Lucknow, Agra and the Taj Mahal, Banares [Varanasi—one of India's holiest cities] and Allahabad, ending up in Calcutta for voyage home." According to Horace's remembrances of what his father told him, the Russians were very interested in the northern passes into India and asked to see the Khyber Pass. They were taken there. His father and other delegation members also were entertained by Maharajahs, one of whom traced his family back fifty generations.

In a second article written for the *Journal of the Military Service Institution of the United States* after his return, Lazelle warned about the long-term outlook for British military rule in India and the potential for conflict with Russia over Britain's Indian Empire. Noting that Russia already was "a colossal power among nations," he predicted that in 50 years the tsar would rule over a population of 150 million, "homogeneous and united under one will." England, he contended had already "reached the summit" of its strength in the East and could not "hope to extend her nationality in India one jot further than now." Thus, the power of Russia would steadily increase in the East, while that of England declined. Ultimately, he predicted, the two would clash:

> The battle-ground will be on the Helmund [Helmand] River, far beyond the Indus, for England can on no account afford to merely defend that line. This would be at once the surrender of all the sacrifices she has made to place Afghanistan in the breech as a buffer; and it would be to reveal to the natives of India her inability to protect their boundaries. ... On the ground in that region, therefore, are to be fought bloody battles, on the part of Russia, for supremacy on the Bosphorus; and, in the part of England, for the preservation of her Eastern Empire... [23]

Lazelle's comments on the role Afghanistan played as a buffer between the British Empire in Asia and Russian tsarist expansionism were prescient. The collision of British and Russian interests in the region already had precipitated the two Anglo-Afghan wars. By the time Lazelle arrived in the region, the British and Russians recognized official boundaries of what would become modern-day Afghanistan, and the British had substantial influence over the Afghan leader, Amir Abdur Rahman.

On January 31, 1886, Lazelle reported from the steamship *Mirzapore* in the Indian Ocean that he was en route to America, and on March 13 that he had arrived in New York City. En route home, he stopped in Washington and presented his formal report in person to President Cleveland, who later would award Jacob Lazelle a Presidential appointment to West Point. Lieutenant Colonel Lazelle returned to Vancouver Barracks on March 24 and resumed his duties as Acting Inspector General of the Department. [24]

Photo 24. Lazelle's House at Vancouver Barracks

Chapter 10

Back to Washington and Controversy

Lazelle's family joined him in Vancouver, Washington, in the fall of 1886, moving into a large, two-story house on post with a wrap-around porch. Perhaps in celebration or to show his family what his job entailed, Lazelle mounted an inspection of Vancouver Barracks, "quite unexpectedly to the troops."[1] Jacob and Horace went to high school in Portland, Oregon, across the Columbia River from Vancouver, at a new school (the only one in the city) that had just been completed. However, the family's stay in Vancouver was short, and their father soon headed to the other Washington on the Potomac River with a new assignment.

In May 1887, Lazelle received orders to oversee publication of the Official Records of the War of the Rebellion. This assignment was not without controversy and uncertainty, both in its origin and Lazelle's execution of his duties. As with other assignments, such as taking command of the 16th New York Cavalry, it also reflected the contradictory elements of bluster, on the one hand, often challenging authority, and humility—or, perhaps, insecurity—on the other, in expressing concern about his ability to tackle new and challenging responsibilities.

Compilation and preparation of the Civil War records for public use had begun under a Congressional Resolution in May 1864. Work in earnest, however, did not start until 1874, when Congress provided the funding. The effort had progressed slowly under various War Department officials until late 1877, by which time the Secretary of War G. W. McCrary had become "painfully aware that the war publications undertaking would take years to complete." Just the Confederate records thus far collected "filled a three-story building, and a single collection of Union telegrams amounted to more than two million entries." All in all, there were tons of records yet to be exploited.[2]

In December 1877, McCrary detailed Lt. Col. Robert N. Scott, 3rd U.S. Artillery, to "take charge of the bureau and devote himself exclusively to the work."[3] Scott, who had studied law before joining the Army as a second lieutenant in 1857, approached his task of collecting, selecting, and organizing the vast amount of material with "a legal concern for documentation and evidence." Scott's most significant contribution to the compilation of the records was to establish a set of criteria for selecting and authenticating records and documents to be included. First, the authenticity of any material obtained from private individuals must be certified in writing by the source. More importantly, each record must be "significant, official, and produced during the war," which meant that it had to have been originated by "a contending army or government." The set of procedures embodying these criteria, endorsed by the Secretary of War, became the rule of the road for the War Records Office.[4]

The first volume was issued in the fall of 1880, and Congress authorized the printing of 10,000 copies, all for Congress and the Executive Branch. A subsequent act in 1882 directed that 8,300 copies be sent to "such libraries, organizations and individuals as may be designated by the Senators, Representatives and Delegates of the 47th Congress." Scott proceeded to publish the next four volumes as well.

Scott died suddenly, however, on March 5, 1887, long before work on the records was completed. Within a week, the press was full of speculation on who would succeed him. According to the *Chicago Daily Tribune*, applications were "pouring in thick and fast." Speculating on potential candidates, the *Tribune* singled out Lt. Col. Henry M. Lazelle of the 23rd Infantry as having "acknowledged qualifications for the work, and, as he has many friends around the War Department who are anxious to have him here, it would not be surprising if he secured the detail." A week later, the *Tribune* again reported that a decision was expected within a day or two and identified Lazelle and Maj. Robert H. Hall, of the 22nd Infantry, as the top contenders.[5]

A decision was not forthcoming. On April 2, Washington's *Evening Star* reported an appointment was "daily expected" and that Lazelle and Assistant Adjutant General Thomas M. Vincent were the most prominently mentioned. Still, no decision was announced, but the *Evening Star* persisted, reporting on April 19 that Lazelle would be named.[6]

The *Evening Star's* story was picked up on April 20 by *The Philadelphia Inquirer*. In fact, however, Lazelle was not asked whether he would be interested in the war records position until April 22 in a telegram from the Adjutant General. Initially, he declined the assignment, and in a follow-up telegram, dated April 23, he explained that:

> while sensible of the high compliment conveyed, I was apprehensive that I could do the duty satisfactorily, and was unwilling to attempt it and fail. I knew that the work of the late Colonel Scott was admirably conceived and thoroughly done, and that for me to hope to continue it, even passably well, would require close study and unremitting effort; this I could give, but I thought that even then I might fall short in something and fail, and that I had no right to jeopardize anything, or stand in the way of others more capable.[7]

Somehow, the *Tribune* got wind of this and reported in its April 30 edition that "the Secretary of War is experiencing much difficulty in his efforts to secure an officer possessing the necessary qualifications" and noted that both Lazelle and Vincent had turned down offers.[8]

Once again the *Tribune* had it wrong. On May 1, Lazelle accepted the assignment, and a week later it became official in AGO Special Orders 105: "By direction of the Secretary of War, Lieutenant Colonel Henry M. Lazelle, 23d Infantry, is assigned to the charge of the publications of the Official Records of the War of the Rebellion, and will repair to this city and enter upon duty accordingly, with as little delay as practicable. The travel enjoined is necessary for the public service." [9]

The family remained in Vancouver until the boys finished school, which was especially important for Jacob, who was applying to West Point. Back in Vancouver, the Lazelles attended one last party "at the garrison hop-room, which was beautifully decorated with flags and banners for the occasion." They then traveled east on the Canadian Pacific Railroad, which had just opened a transcontinental route. Theirs was one of the first trains over it. They arrived in Washington on June 13.[10]

INTRODUCTION TO WASHINGTON POLITICS

When Lazelle arrived in June 1887, Grover Cleveland was two and a half years into his presidency. The first Democrat elected to the office since before the Civil War, Cleveland was known as a reformer who had won the support of the like-minded "Mugwump" wing of the Republican Party. After the scandals of the previous Republican administrations, the Mugwumps considered Cleveland, "party notwithstanding, the only man then before the public capable of initiating the new cleaner era in American politics that they believed to be their sacred cause."[11]

Determined to minimize political controversy, Cleveland had appointed a cabinet whose members were fellow Bourbon Democrats, "figures closely identified with big business and railroad interests, whose names could not arouse editorial displeasure and who could keep a low profile in their new posts." His appointees included Secretary of War William C. Endicott, a Massachusetts lawyer whose wife came from the wealthy Peabody family. [12]

Cleveland and his cabinet, however, faced a divided Congress: Republicans had a two-seat majority in the Senate, while Democrats controlled the House. The President had sparred with the 50th Congress (1887-1889) on a number of issues, and 1888 was to be a politically charged election year in which the Republicans hoped to regain the presidency, expand their slim lead in the Senate, and possibly take over the House. Thus, they were looking for issues that would excite the electorate.

Aware that he was entering a politically charged environment, Lazelle was committed to continuing the policies and procedures established by his predecessor. By October, he had clearly established who was in charge at the War Records Office, directing that "all matters of whatever nature relating to office duties, the affairs of the office, or the duties of those engaged therein," would be submitted directly to him.[13]

Had he picked up a copy of the *Cleveland Commercial Gazette* the day after Christmas in 1887, however, Lazelle might have realized that trouble was lurking in the wings. Owned and managed by an ardent Republican Party supporter, the *Gazette* regularly railed against the Democrats and the Cleveland administration. On December 26, reporting a story from its Washington correspondent, the paper warned with great hyperbole that the Secretary of War had ordered an examination of War Department records "with the view of destroying a portion of them," possibly including records of the Freedmen's Bureau, which, the *Gazette* alleged were viewed as mere "waste paper."

> It is in those records that may be found the original papers proving the awful extent of the massacres of colored citizens in the process of nullifying the Constitution of the United States for the benefit of the Democratic party. It was through the shedding of blood and a reign of terror that the South was made solid and the fraudulent Administration of Cleveland became a possibility.[14]

The article went on to predict that the next target of the reviled Democrats would be the War Records Office, in an effort to "pervert the whole story of the rebellion and its overthrow by force of arms" by destroying those portions of the war records viewed as "obnoxious to the regime of fraud," and that Secretary of War Endicott, "as a Mugwump, is the chosen instrument."

This should have been Lazelle's first warning that he was in the crosshairs of the *Gazette's* Washington correspondent, Henry V. Boynton. A graduate of Kentucky Military Institute, Boynton had been a major in the 35th Ohio Infantry, nicknamed the "Persimmon Regiment." He had fought at the Battle of Stones River in Tennessee, later commanded at the Battle of Chickamauga, and eventually received the Medal of Honor for action in the Battle of Missionary Ridge in November 1863. A virulent opponent of the Democrats, his dispatches from Washington were consistently inflammatory.

In fact, there was no plan to destroy either the Freedmen's Bureau records or any important war records. In late November, Lazelle simply had reported to Secretary Endicott that the War Records Office had "a great accumulation of useless papers of no value whatever ... except to the paper maker," and had requested authority to turn them over to the official in the Adjutant General's Office in charge of the accumulation of waste paper. In a follow-up letter, Lazelle estimated the total amount of waste paper to be "over a ton's weight."[15]

A week after Boynton's politically charged allegations, the *New York Times*, under the headline "Much Official Rubbish," published a much more benign report, noting that Senators Cockrell (Dem., Missouri) and Cullom (Rep., Illinois), in a bipartisan effort to reduce federal paperwork, were investigating the retention of millions of records in the Executive Branch, believing Congress should be able to authorize the departments to eliminate paper from time to time. The Army Adjutant General already had appointed a board of officers in November to determine "what papers and records might be disposed of as waste paper," should Congress pass enabling legislation. Cockrell was proposing that a bi-partisan committee of two senators and two representatives be established "to pass upon lists of paper proposed to be disposed of as waste." According to the *Times*,

Lazelle had already concluded that there were some papers that could be tossed "without impairing the historical value of the collection." [16]

While Lazelle successfully dealt with the first Republican skirmishes, newspaperman Boynton's friends in Congress were preparing a more serious barrage. In January 1888, spurred by "a rumor that the rules laid down by Congress" for producing the Official Records and "the plan and methods pursued by Col. Scott thereon were being departed from," [17] the House of Representatives passed a resolution targeting the War Records Office. The Secretary of War was to provide a "full statement of the plan and scope of the compilation of the official records," specifying any changes made or being contemplated, whether any restrictions had been placed on access to the records, and if so, upon whose authority they had been made. [18]

The resolution had been introduced in December 1887 by Congressman Charles H. Grosvenor, a Republican representing Ohio's 50th District and Chairman of the House Republican Conference. In addition to his partisan political motives, Grosvenor had a personal interest in the War Records Office. As a lawyer from Athens, Ohio, he had enlisted as a private in the 18th Ohio Volunteer Infantry at the outbreak of war. He had fought at the Battle of Stones River in Murfreesboro, Tennessee, in late 1862. Promoted through the ranks, he took command of his regiment in October 1864 and eventually was brevetted to brigadier general.

Within a month, Secretary of War Endicott responded to Grosvenor's resolution, enclosing a February 3 report from Lazelle stating categorically that no changes had been made in the plan and scope for the compilation of the Official Records that had originally been adopted in August 1880, and that the office had rigorously followed Congressional requirements laid down in the Appropriations Act of July 31, 1886. Providing documentation to back up his assurance that he had continued to follow both the letter and the spirit of the law, Lazelle concluded his report by noting that "all applications for information have been granted by myself, except in two cases, in each of which the applicant was referred to the Secretary of War."[19]

Lazelle, in all likelihood, considered the matter closed and resumed his efforts to get the next volumes of the Official Records into print. Work on Volume XX, covering Operations in Kentucky, Middle and East Tennessee, North Alabama, and Southwest Virginia from November 1, 1862, to January 20, 1863, had been completed in late 1887. When Lazelle arrived on duty, the bulk of the volume had been sent to the Government Printing Office and only its appendix remained unfinished. By mid-February, printing of the entire volume was nearing completion. Just as the bound volume was being finalized, however, the next act in the political drama opened.

THE ANDERSON CAVALRY DEBACLE

The seeds of Lazelle's main battle with the Republicans—this one much more serious and ultimately leading to his early departure from Washington and the War Records Office—were sown late in 1862 when Confederate General Braxton Bragg's Army of Tennessee clashed with the Union Army of the Cumberland under General William Rosecrans along the Stones River in Murfreesboro, Tennessee. Among the Union troops fighting from December 31 to January 2, 1863 were volunteers of the 15th Pennsylvania Cavalry (160th Volunteers), popularly known as the Anderson Cavalry, named in honor of the Army of the Ohio's first commander, Brig. Gen. Robert Anderson.

When the 15th was organized in the summer of 1862, its recruits were told they would be serving as the headquarters guard of the Army of the Ohio, then commanded by Maj. Gen. D. C. Buell. In October 1862, however, the Army of the Ohio was incorporated into the Army and Department of the Cumberland, commanded by Maj. Gen. William S. Rosecrans. When the 15th arrived in Nashville on December 8, the men were told they would be going "to the front," instead of serving as a guard force at Army headquarters. According to General Rosecrans, many of them refused to move. He took swift action and "put some in the penitentiary and some in jail and some in the yard and showed them that they were in a state of mutiny." [20]

On February 16, 1863, the *Philadelphia Inquirer* published an account of the battle at Stones River, including a "Roll of Honor" listing of the men of Anderson Cavalry who had fought at Murfreesboro instead of mutinying. The story of the so-called mutiny and who had actually fought at Stones River, however, was not the focus of the struggle between Lazelle's War Records Office and the United States Congress. Rather, the controversy swirled around accusations that unofficial information—the list published by the *Inquirer*—had been inserted into the Official Records, which would have been strictly against War Department policy and in violation of Congressional legislation. [21]

A Simple Story ...

Back in the fall of 1887, Henry C. Wood, a clerk in the Adjutant General's office, responsible for processing papers related to the U. S. Military Academy, came across the *Philadelphia Inquirer* article in the files of John G. Bourke, a candidate for admission to the Academy shortly after the war. Bourke had included the list with his Military Academy application as proof that he "went to the front" at Stones River.

Looking over the newspaper list, Wood came upon the name of John Tweedale, Chief Clerk of the War Department, who had been an enlisted member of the Anderson Cavalry. Knowing that Tweedale had served in the unit, Wood showed the list to him "as a mere matter of curiosity." However, because the War Department had thus far been unable to locate a complete list of names of the members of Anderson Cavalry who fought at Stones River, Tweedale sent the *Inquirer's* list to the Adjutant General's Office requesting that it be "verified." Under questioning by the House Committee on Military Affairs, Tweedale conceded that his primary motivation was to ensure that the list, if verified, would be placed in the Official Records so that members of his company would be given credit for "having been in the battle and not among those who refused to go to the front." [22]

In the Adjutant General's Office, the Chief Clerk gave the *Inquirer's* list to Henry Douglas, Chief of the "First Division of Volunteer Rolls." Douglas checked the newspaper's list against the official muster rolls on file, verified that the list was accurate, and sent it back to Chief Clerk Tweedale who forwarded it to the War Records Office with an endorsement signed by the Adjutant General, General Richard C. Drum:

> The inclosed [*sic*] roll [copied from the *Philadelphia Inquirer* of February 16, 1863], purporting to be a list of the members of the Fifteenth Pennsylvania Cavalry, who went to the front and were engaged in the Battle of Murfreesborough [*sic*], and made from the official report to General Rosecrans, has been carefully compared with and is confirmed by the official records of this office. [23]

When the "Roll of Honor" was received in the War Records Office, around October 20, 1887, Lazelle and his staff understood that it was "a compilation from official records in the Adjutant General's office," and did not question its authenticity. Indeed, Lazelle would later testify, the information was "precisely analogous to that contained in rolls of officers and men who received medals of honor," prepared and published by the Adjutant General's office. Thus it was "an official document, as far as known to the War Records office, and was received and published as official." [24]

... EXPLOITED BY POLITICAL PROTAGONISTS

The first sign of major trouble for Lazelle and the War Records Office came on March 1, 1888, in a lengthy dispatch from Henry Boynton splashed across four front-page columns of the *Cincinnati Commercial Gazette*, with blazing headlines: "Re-Writing War History. Disgraceful

Falsification of Rebellion Records. Compiler Lazelle Whitewashes the Anderson Cavalry Mutineers. A Lying Appendix that Flatly Contradicts the Text of the Twentieth Volume of the Records of the War, Ruining It for Historical Purposes and Mutilating a National Work—An Imposition Upon Congress and the Country." [25]

Describing what the *Gazette* editorial page decried as an attempt to rewrite war history and "whitewash two or three hundred mutineers who refused to fight at the battle of Mufreesboro," Boynton's article laid out in great detail his charge that "a most disgraceful chapter of dishonest dealing in the compilation of the official records of the war of the rebellion has now been added to the list of War Department blunders." At issue, Boynton contended, were two significant transgressions: the insertion of unofficial matter (the *Philadelphia Inquirer's* list of battle participants) into the records and what he viewed as a blatant attempt to fudge the numbers and include mutineers among the list of those who fought.

Providing a detailed account of the mutiny and battle and the confusion surrounding the question of which members of the unit fought and who and how many were among the mutineers, Boynton asserted that the *Inquirer's* "Roll of Honor" printed in the Appendix of Volume XX not only contained "from 150 to 200 names that do not belong to it," but also failed to include 31 members of the unit reported in the main text of the volume "as members of the troop who went to the front." In so doing, Boynton charged, "Colonel Lazelle's list whitewashes considerably over 150 mutineers and relieves them by name of the infamy which attached to their cowardly conduct." Moreover:

> If the injection of newspaper clippings into this official history, and falsely declaring them to be official, is not a change from "the subject-matter to be published," as contemplated in Colonel Scott's plan, it would be difficult to imagine what Secretary Endicott and Colonel Lazelle regard as a change. [26]

Boynton concluded his diatribe with a direct attack on Lazelle, charging that there was "no standard by which to measure the stupidity, as well as a certain kind of boldness" that would lead Lazelle to assume that he could "tamper with the official history of an event as notorious and widely understood as this and escape detection." In the end, he opined, it would be interesting to see how the matter would "strike the House of Representatives, which has been trifled with and imposed upon, and President Cleveland, under whose administration such mutilation of the war records is going on."

Lazelle and Secretary Endicott didn't need to wait for long. Congressman Grosvenor, who along with Boynton had fought at Stones River, joined forces with the newspaperman in a quest to discredit the Democratic administration in the name of preserving the integrity of the Official Records. Their main target: War Records Chief, Lt. Col. Henry M. Lazelle.

In what the *Boston Daily Globe* characterized as "another attempt to throw mud at the administration" by Republicans who believed in "drag-not [*sic*] investigation for the purpose of trying to make political capital," [27] Grosvenor introduced yet another resolution. This one, based on "good reason for the belief that unofficial matter" had been "inserted in Volume 20, part 2, of the Records of the Rebellion," directed the Committee on Military Affairs to determine whether, indeed, unofficial material had been used, "under what circumstances, and by whose authority it was done." [28]

In fact, Grosvenor, who had arranged to provide Boynton with an advance copy of the volume in question, was referring to the charges Boynton had made in the *Commercial Gazette*. Grosvenor would later maintain that he had wanted to "proceed cautiously" on the matter, having only "heard a rumor" that the volume contained unofficial matter, and that he had remained "wholly disconnected with any publication" about it, despite his close relationship with Boynton:

> He [Boynton] never said a word to me about the source of information whatever. I did a great deal more talking with others than I did with General Boynton. I talked about it as a matter of

> misfortune to us all that this work was likely to go astray; but I want to put it into the record, if the committee will let me, that I did not enter upon it with the slightest disposition of attacking anybody. I did not know Colonel Lazelle. [29]

The subcommittee of the Committee on Military Affairs, chaired by Levi Maish, a Democrat from Pennsylvania, along with Charles E. Hooker, a Democrat from Mississippi, and Byron M. Cutcheon, a Republican from Michigan, convened on March 24. Lazelle was their first witness, and in lengthy testimony he reviewed the sequence of events leading to the verification and inclusion of the Anderson Cavalry Roll of Honor in the Appendix of Volume XX.

As Lazelle explained it, in preparing the main body of the volume, his office had not been able to locate a definitive official accounting of the number and names of those members of the unit who had gone to the front and fought at Murfreesboro and those who had "mutinied" and remained behind. They could fix the total number of men assigned to the regiment, but the number who went to the front ranged in various reports from 200 to over 500. Because of these uncertainties, Lazelle decided to place the Roll of Honor published in the *Inquirer* into the Appendix, since it had been certified by the Adjutant General and being "made from the official report to Gen. Rosecrans" and "confirmed by the official records of the Adjutant General's office." [30]

Next up was General John C. Kelton, Assistant Adjutant General, filling in for his boss, General Drum, who was ill. Kelton essentially corroborated Lazelle's testimony on the origins and processing of the *Inquirer's* list at the War Department. He threw a monkey wrench into the proceedings, however, when he admitted that his office had been unable to find any official report to General Rosecrans regarding the men of the 15th Pennsylvania fighting at Stones River. General Drum, on the other hand, testifying later, contradicted Kelton, noting that the "official report made to General Rosecrans" could in fact have been a collection of reports to the general's adjutants, including company-level reports or "returns" as they were called in official parlance. In his testimony, several days later, Rosecrans confirmed that his personal reports did not contain a listing of the men of the Fifteenth who fought, but that he did give them "handsome credit."[31]

After lengthy testimony about document processing from several clerks in the Adjutant General's office, John Tweedale, Chief Clerk of the War Department, and a former private in Company B of the 15th Pennsylvania Cavalry, was called to the witness table. Tweedale confirmed prior testimony as to the sequence of events, adding that before the *Inquirer* list had been brought to his attention, he had written the governor of Pennsylvania to see if there were state records giving a complete list of the men who had fought at Stones River. After the governor had responded that there were none, and Tweedale became aware of the list in the *Inquirer* that "purported to give the names of all the men" he thought it should be "supplemented in an appendix [to Volume XX] giving the names of the men who really went to the front and did service." [32]

On April 5, Lazelle was offered the opportunity to question his antagonist, Congressman Grosvenor, about his role in the affair. Lazelle leapt at the chance. In what the *Washington* Post characterized as "some very irritating personal remarks" [33] between the two combatants, Lazelle attempted to establish that Grosvenor and Boynton had conspired to cast dispersions upon him personally, as well as more generally upon the War Records Office. He first asked whether Boynton had told Grosvenor "that the addenda or appendix was not Colonel Scott's work; that it was mine?" Grosvenor responded in the negative, maintaining that he did not know "who I was aiming at when I introduced this resolution." Lazelle then asked whether the Congressman knew "from what source General Boynton received this information about this matter?" Again, the answer was "no."

Lazelle went on to challenge Grosvenor's denials, harkening back to earlier testimony that he, Lazelle, had sent Lieutenant Knox from his office down to the Government Printing Office (then called the Public

Printer) after Boynton's newspaper article appeared, and that Knox had been told that the relevant material had been given to Grosvenor prior to its publication. Grosvenor categorically denied receiving anything, in essence calling Knox a liar. He later backed off slightly, suggesting that Knox may have misunderstood what the printer said. Grosvenor, in fact, had requested page proofs in mid-February but maintained he never received them.

Lazelle next tried to establish a connection between Grosvenor, Boynton, and John Moody, one of the civilian clerks in the War Records Office, but to little avail, so he quickly returned to the Grosvenor-Boynton relationship:

> Q: Did you ever hear anything concerning complaints from Mr. Moody against me, from him or General Boynton? A: No sir.
>
> Q: He never told you that when I first came to the office that I reprimanded Mr. Moody for intemperance and neglect of duty? A: I never got the impression he had any grievance at all. If I have entered into anybody's quarrels here, I did it as innocently as anybody or anything in the world. I thought I was being very careful in the manner in which I was proceeding with it, and I think I have been.
>
> Q: Did he [Boynton] tell you about the appendix, that it was wrong and he believed it to be wrong, and that he was examining it and asked you to attend to it? A: I do not think that General Boynton told me that he had ever seen it.
>
> Q: Did he tell you that or anything like that? A: He told me generally that he had information, or that he had knowledge or believed (I can not give you the conversation and I qualify that authority) that unofficial matter was being published in this work.
>
> Q: Did the general tell you what part of it? A: Not at all.

> Q: You discovered all that yourself by an examination of the volume? A: No, sir; I did not.
>
> Q: Will you tell me how you did get it? A: How I got the details?
>
> Q: How you got the idea; there is nothing in the volume to show it. A: When I got this volume General Boynton gave me points and specified wherein he thought the errors were, and I put (there is no secret about it), I put a memorandum into the volume and brought it here. There it is.
>
> Q: Did you know at the time that General Boynton has steadily vilified me in the press since I have been here? A: No, sir.
>
> Q: You have never read an article in the press concerning me and the office? A: Never until I read these articles in regard to this publication. That is to say, colonel, if I did, they made no impression on me. [34]

Once more Lazelle asked whether Boynton had ever told Grosvenor that he had received any information about the Anderson Cavalry issue "from or through" the War Records Office. Grosvenor again replied in the negative, stressing that he had "no information from General Boynton as to his source of information." Lazelle then wrapped up his questioning.

However, he took one final stab at Grosvenor on April 28, this time in a letter to the editor of the *Washington Post.* Returning to the Lieutenant Knox issue, Lazelle repeated that he had sent Knox to the Public Printing Office on March 1 to ascertain whether any portion of volume 20, part 2 had been distributed before it was sent to the War Department two days later. Knox learned that Grosvenor had twice requested portions of the document, which had been sent to him in mid-February.

Noting that Grosvenor in his sworn testimony had vehemently denied Knox's report, stating that there was "not a shadow of truth whatever in either the direct statement or imputation made by Colonel Lazelle," Lazelle then reproduced a letter and a telegram sent by Grosvenor to the printer on February 15 and 16 requesting page proofs of specific sections. Lazelle concluded his letter to the editor noting that the Public Printer had affirmed that "the requests contained in Mr. Grosvenor's letters were in each case complied with." [35]

Grosvenor returned fire two days later. Writing to the *Post's* editor that he had at first "hesitated to notice the absurd card of Col. Lazelle in your issue of Saturday," Grosvenor went on to vow once more that he had never received, "in compliance with any request or in any other way, any 'advance sheets' or any other sheets from the Government Printer or anybody else of part 2, volume 20." [36] Technically, Grosvenor was correct in his assertion. According to later testimony from Boynton, who had drafted the requests for Grosvenor to sign, Grosvenor had left town before receiving a response from the printer. Before Grosvenor returned from his home district, Boynton had managed to get the material he wanted through the chairman of the Senate Committee on Printing.[37]

Going into recess for extended periods, the Military Affairs Committee did not wrap up testimony until early October 1888. In the meantime, both Lazelle and Congressman Grosvenor had been busy. Just prior to their exchange of letters in the *Washington Post*, Grosvenor had submitted yet another resolution, this time directing the Committee on Military Affairs to examine the "feasibility and advisability" of completing publication of the Official Records "under the supervision and control of a joint committee of Congress." The resolution was referred to the committee on April 2, 1888.[38]

Early in June, Lazelle had reported to the Secretary of War that he could have sent an additional two books to the printer had more funds been available. He had requested $70,000 for printing and binding in the next fiscal year, which would give the War Records Office a "maximum working capacity" of about eight books a year. However, he feared that Congress would continue allocating only $36,000 as it had for the past six years. Reminding the Secretary that "one of the irritating arguments unceasingly brought forward against the War Records publication is the extreme slowness of its advancement," Lazelle recommended that Endicott make the case for an increased budget to both the House and Senate appropriations committees. The Secretary had forwarded Lazelle's letter to Congress on June 8. [39]

In early July 1888, the first sign that, perhaps, not all was well between the War Records Office chief Lazelle and the Secretary of War had appeared in the *New York Times.* Reporting that the War Department had emphatically denied rumors that Lazelle would be relieved from duty when he returned from a well-deserved two-month leave of absence, the *Times* quoted his friends as saying that Lazelle was "very much dissatisfied with the office" and "greatly annoyed by the attacks made upon his administration of its affairs." They speculated that he would probably ask to be relieved but that he could stay as long as he wished since there was "no disposition on the part of the War Department authorities to relieve him." The *Times* report bore an uncanny resemblance to those just prior to Lazelle's relief as Commandant of Cadets six years earlier. [40]

Waiting the outcome of the House hearing, Lazelle still had mundane matters to attend to. One of the substantive questions the War Records Office dealt with was fixing the exact date of the end of the Civil War. In a late September letter to the Army's Acting Judge Advocate General, Lazelle asked whether he was aware of any Supreme Court decision that established the official date, or whether there might be any authority other than "the proclamation of the President of the United States of August 20th, 1866, which does fix a date on which the war of the rebellion is recognized as ended." [41]

Upon his return from leave, Lazelle's next challenge from Representative Grosvenor and his fellow Republicans was the appropriation bill for continuing publication of the records during the 1888-89 fiscal year. This bill, which had been passed in August, contained a provision that from then on "the manuscript copy shall be submitted to the Secretary of War and revised by him, and shall not be published until he shall verify that it only contains the contemporaneous Official Records of the War of Rebellion as provided for by the Act June 30th, 1887." In a lengthy analysis of the bill for the Secretary of War, Lazelle maintained that the "examination imposed by the law upon the Secretary of War is simply an impossibility, and the very act of Congress making appropriation for publication, makes further publication practically impossible," since the Secretary, personally, would have to undertake a task which required the "united labor of more than one-half of the force" of the War Records Office.

Arguing that this was the work of a "well known newspaper correspondent" who had been "steadily active in every form of denunciation and persecution of the office," Lazelle urged the Secretary to request that the restrictive language be removed from the bill. Instead, he proposed alternative language that would require the Secretary to "cause such examination to be made of each volume before its publication as shall satisfy him that it contains no unofficial matter, and he shall so certify." [42]

In February 1889 the language, indeed, was altered, but in a manner that still presented major challenges for the War Department. The Senate Appropriations Committee Sundry Civil Appropriations Bill provided that:

> Hereafter, before publication of any volume of said records, the manuscript copy shall be submitted to the Secretary of War, and revised by him, or under his supervision, by a board of officers other than those attached to the War Records office, and shall not be published until he shall certify that it only contains the contemporaneous official records of the war of the rebellion. [43]

On February 14, 1889, Lazelle appeared before the Senate Appropriations Committee to make his case. Noting that since the legislation requiring the Secretary's personal certification had been passed in August 1888, "no new matter has been sent to the Printing Office," Lazelle then described the potential impact of the wording in the new language before the Senate, but not before being forced by Republican Senator Eugene

Hale of Maine to rehash all the old arguments and discussion related to the Anderson Cavalry affair.

Lazelle's basic argument against requiring a board of officers, "other than those attached to the War Records Office," to certify that the records contained only official material was that such a board would, in effect, have to duplicate or replicate all of the work done by the office in preparing each volume. Citing, as an example, the work involved in tabulating the strength and organization of General Sherman's three armies in the Atlanta campaign, Lazelle informed the committee that it took him ten weeks, working an average of five hours a day, to create tables based on the original reports held by the Adjutant General's office. In order for a board of officers to verify that work, Lazelle maintained:

> the board would have to go through the same work, and I say that in my judgment it could not be done anything like as rapidly as the ordinary annual work of the office goes on. It would practically suspend three-fourths of the labor of the office. [44]

In essence, Lazelle argued, the review board would have to be on duty working the same schedule and activity as his staff, and thus "you might just as well let them take charge of the office at once and supervise the publication ..." Instead, he suggested, as he had in his letter to Endicott, the Secretary could "cause such examination to be made of the record as shall satisfy him that it is original in character and matter and that he shall so certify." Responding to a query from Senator Hale, he agreed that a board of officers could perform that role on behalf of the Secretary: "I am sure that would not delay the work. That is all I want to guard against." [45]

The testimony quickly wrapped up after a short discussion of funding for the new fiscal year. Asked if the traditional $36,000 was sufficient, Lazelle replied it was not enough for what he could publish annually, especially if he was "not delayed by this proposed examination." Even Senator Hale seemed disposed to appropriate additional funds. [46]

Lazelle won. The final appropriation, enacted by Congress, provided the War Records Office $100,000 for the fiscal year ending June 30, 1890, and included a provision that hereafter the preparation and publication of the Records would be conducted, under the Secretary of War, by a board of three persons: an Army officer and two civilian experts. All three were to be selected by the Secretary and, importantly, "the whole work and publication shall be completed within five years." With all restrictive language gone from the bill, Lazelle quickly nominated two clerks "of high standing" in the Adjutant General's office to serve in the civilian positions.[47]

February 1889 indeed had been a good month for Henry M. Lazelle. Not only had he succeeded in obtaining appropriations language that would not unduly retard publication of the Records, but the House Committee on Military Affairs at last had issued its final report on February 14, finding that, in the Anderson Cavalry case, the War Records Office had been "misled by the official character given to the paper [*Inquirer* list] by the Adjutant-General's certificate," and that "Lieut. Col. H. M. Lazelle, in charge of the War Records Office, was responsible for its publication only as he adopted the official certificate of the Adjutant-General, and is fairly exonerated from blame."[48]

Lazelle's victory was pyrrhic, however. On May 4, 1889, Maj. George B. Davis of the Judge Advocate General's Office in Washington was ordered to report to Colonel Henry M. Lazelle for duty with the War Records Office.[49] According to the *Washington Post*, Davis had been selected "as the army officer at the head of the commission provided for in the Sundry Civil bill." The *Post* article noted that the two civilian experts had not yet been selected and that the new scheme would not be put into place until the start of the new fiscal year. Until then, Lazelle would remain in charge, but Davis would begin immediately "in order to be given an insight into the methods that have been heretofore pursued, and to devise plans for the future."[50]

Once again, Henry Lazelle had won the battle but lost the war. Going on leave for three months, he and the family left Washington soon after Major Davis's arrival at the War Records Office, first to Rebecca's family in Hagerstown and then on to New England. In June, he wrote to the Adjutant General asking whether the Secretary of War might consider recommending him for the Superintendent's position at West Point. That recommendation was not forthcoming.

In the end, the controversy in Washington over the Anderson Cavalry proved not to be all that "injurious" to Lazelle's reputation. He had been promoted to full Colonel in February and his next assignment was to take command of the 18th Infantry Regiment in Denver, Colorado.

Shortly after Lazelle had arrived in Washington, he had resumed his correspondence with Samuel Barrows, whom he had first met at Fort Sully and visited in Canada after leaving West Point. Theirs had become a lasting friendship and Lazelle's only friendship outside of the military that can be documented. In May, after learning of Major Davis's appointment, Lazelle wrote Barrows, expressing relief that his duty in Washington would soon be over:

> I am to be relieved from here on the first of July, and shall then be ordered to Colorado to take command of my new regiment. I am glad of it I assure you. It is a matter of my own seeking, for I am sick and tired of the debris of the Rebellion which I have been rolling in for so long. I shall take a leave of absence until about the 1st of October and shall then join the 18th foot [infantry].[51]

It must have been hard for Lazelle's family to leave the comforts and glamour of Washington for the West again. Rebecca's relatives were close by in Hagerstown, and Horace had just finished high school. The class yell was "Fine, fine, damn fine, eighty nine!" They also had had quite an active social life, with frequent receptions and teas, and an invitation to President Cleveland's New Year reception. Horace remembered that the President actually had three receptions: one for the diplomatic corps;

a second for senators, congressmen, and Supreme Court justices; and the third for army and naval officers.

According to Horace, during the summer of 1889 the family first went to West Point to visit Jacob, who had been appointed to the Academy by President Cleveland and was, by then, a corporal and in camp as a second-year cadet. He was doing all right in his academic work, except for calculus, which he found difficult. The family stayed on post at Craney's Hotel on the edge of the hill by Trophy Point. From there, for about a month, they went up to Barrows' Camp on Lake Memphremagog in Georgeville, Quebec. Writing to Barrows that June, Lazelle had warned him that he expected good fishing, noting that he was "passionately fond of that pastime—when there are fish," and that Barrows had "plainly intimated that there is fun in that direction" in a book he and his wife had published recently about their summers at the cottage in Georgeville —*Shaybacks in Camp: Ten Summers Under Canvas.* He then implored Barrows to "have the lake stocked as soon as you can" if "there really are no fish there."[52]

In October, he would write to Barrows' wife, Isabel, remembering the good times the family had "at camp" that summer: "Horace and I were so much improved by the trip and Horace had a truly charming summer thanks to Mabel [the Barrowses' daughter] and the delightful people of your camp. If we could all have gone there [Jacob had remained at West Point] it would to me have been what I should have most enjoyed, for I like camp life." [53]

A Final Move

After their summer stay in Quebec, the family expected their next journey would be out to Denver, Colorado. At the time of Lazelle's promotion to the 18th Infantry Regiment as its colonel, the unit had been headquartered at Fort Hays, Kansas, about 100 miles west of Salina and at one time home to Custer's 7th Cavalry. Now the regiment was due to move to Fort Logan, eight miles southwest of Denver.

In August 1889, however, Col. Henry C. Merriam, along with five companies of the 7th Infantry Regiment, took command at Fort Logan, and the 18th was redirected to Fort Clark, Texas. In September, the regimental staff and two companies of the 18th Infantry left Fort Hays for field duty and the entire regiment was formally transferred to Fort Clark. Fort Hays was abandoned in November 1889.

Based on Lazelle's original orders to Fort Logan, the family's furniture already had been shipped to Denver when his new orders arrived for Fort Clark. The family spent the month at Barrow's Camp while their furniture made its way from Denver to Texas.

In September, Lazelle again wrote to the Adjutant General, this time about his moving expenses:

> Just prior to going on my present leave of absence, I had the assurance of the Honorable Secretary of War, that my post would be Fort Logan, Colorado, whenever I joined my regiment. Upon that, some weeks since, I shipped all my effects to that point. Since the arrival there of my house-hold goods, the order changing the station to Fort Clark Texas of my regiment has been issued.
>
> I have now the honor to ask that the order issued, changing my station from this city to Fort Clark Texas may authorize the transportation of my official allowance of baggage to Fort Logan Colorado and thence to Fort Clark Texas. If this be not done, I will have to bear, personally, the whole charge from Washington to Fort Clark of my transportation and will be allowed no return whatever. [54]

Ironically, after Lazelle and his family had settled in at Fort Clark, someone working in the "record rooms of discontinued commands" at the War Department found the official list of names of members of the Anderson Cavalry who had fought at the Battle of Murfreesboro. The document, dated December 26, 1863, and signed by the regimental commander, had been prepared in accordance with instructions from General Rosecrans and was addressed to his adjutant general. The list was identical to the *Philadelphia Inquirer's* list that John Tweedale had sent the Adjutant General's Office for certification and that was subsequently published in the War Records.[55]

Writing to the Army Adjutant General from Fort Clark, Lazelle agonized that "yet for all this miserable error of another, in failing to properly search for and find this list, I have been hounded and abused and made to suffer both in reputation and in the eyes of the public, without one iota of real cause." His main concern, however, was that if it hadn't have been for the "assaults, slander and abuse of my official record from those in political power," he would not have been relieved of duty short of tour and "continually placed on the defensive as to my conduct of the War Records Office." In closing, he requested that the Adjutant General endorse his claim to the Secretary of War that "there has been administered to me a silent and severe rebuke, unmerited, yet none the less injurious to my reputation."

On October 23, 1889, the Adjutant General forwarded Lazelle's plea to the Secretary of War without comment. On December 19, Lazelle's letter was placed in the "seen" file "by order of the Secretary of War," again without comment. [56]

Chapter 11

Fort Clark, the 18th Infantry and Retirement

Colonel Lazelle and his family joined the 18th Infantry Regiment on October 24, 1889. When the Lazelles arrived at Fort Clark, the 3rd Cavalry was still headquartered there and its colonel was post commander. During October and November, the Headquarters and companies of the 18th Infantry made their way from the Department of Missouri to their new assignment. The Field Staff and Band, along with eight companies under the command of Maj. George K. Brady, arrived on post October 16. The last two companies arrived in November.

Fort Clark was established in June 1852 at Las Moras Spring, opposite the village of Brackettville, 17 miles from the Rio Grande, to protect travelers along the "Lower Road" from San Antonio to El Paso. The earliest quarters for enlisted men were tents along Las Moras Creek. An Inspector General report of November 1859 described the men's quarters: "The troops are in tents & the ground dispersion is of course very unfavorable to discipline."[1]

The fort was virtually abandoned during the Civil War, and permanent quarters for the troops were not completed until 1870. By 1872, the post quarters, built of locally quarried limestone, included barracks for two hundred men; seven officers' quarters—three of stone and four of wood with thatched roofs—and a variety of offices and storehouses. The only arable land around the post was bottomland subject to flooding. The post was supplied with water from Las Moras Spring, which Horace remembered was similar to springs in Florida: all limestone with very clear water. Horace also remembered going fishing at Devil's River, near Del Rio, and on the Nueces River. The climate was described as "mild, seasonably dry," and health conditions as "average." Indians in the vicinity were identified as "Lipans, Mescaleros, Apaches, and Kickapoos, who depredate on the herds of the stock raisers."[2]

The Commanding Officer's Quarters in which Colonel and Mrs. Lazelle set up house in the fall of 1889 was an imposing structure, built according to Army Plan No. 4, prepared by the Quartermaster General, Montgomery C. Meigs. Hoping to "control costs and to establish consistent construction standards," Meigs had developed a set of standardized plans for post construction. Plan No. 4, "Commanding Officer's Quarters," was published in the War Department's *Annual Quartermaster* Report in 1872.[3]

While Meig's model plans were "modified or even ignored" at many posts in the West, the quarters at Fort Clark followed Plan 4 "in every detail." Constructed of local limestone blocks, with a broad wooden front porch flanked by a large chinaberry tree and picket fence (intended to keep animals out, not in), the house had a total of some 4,000 square feet of living space with servants' quarters in the rear. On the first floor were two bedrooms on one side and a parlor, dining room, pantry, and kitchen on the other. Four additional bedrooms and servants' quarters were upstairs. The house had no indoor plumbing; water was drawn from the spring in barrels and brought to the house. [4]

With the parade field and bandstand directly in front of the house, the front porch afforded a broad view of troops conducting drills and ceremonies. According to local historians, Lazelle often would invite junior officers and their spouses to join him and Rebecca on the porch to observe reveille, retreat, or tattoo. At "reveille," the first troop formation of the day in the early morning, the national flag was raised. At "retreat," which signaled the end of the official workday, the flag was lowered. Both usually included the band playing the national anthem. "Tattoo" was a ceremonial drum performance, often at twilight, dating back to the British military practice of sending drummers into town to signal to troops in pubs that it was time to return to their tents.

Bachelor officers on post formed an "officers' mess," since they had to provide for their own meals. This is the origin of today's post officers' club. They would pool their money, usually with a married company-grade officer or two. The wives would do the cooking, and the bachelors would eat at the married officers' quarters.

Photo 25. Fort Clark—Parade Ground and Post Commander's Quarters

Photo 26. Colonel Lazelle and Family, Fort Clark, 1892

Photo 27. Colonel Lazelle, 1892

Photo 28. Rebecca Hollingsworth Lazelle, 1892

Photo 29. Family Photo Taken in Minneapolis. Horace on left, Jacob on right.

Photo 30. Fort Clark Post Commander's House Today

In late November, Lazelle, desiring to have his own horse—and not issued one for personal use—wrote to the Army Adjutant General requesting permission, under Paragraph 1164 of the 1889 Army Regulations, to purchase a horse from the Quartermaster's Department. Under this regulation, horses held by the Quartermaster "in the field, on the frontier, or in active service," for "issue, sale, or keeping" could be sold to "mounted officers." However, the sale could only be made with the approval of the Commanding General of the Army or "on the authority of the Secretary of War." [5]

Such was the degree of bureaucracy in the Army and limits on the fiscal authority of a colonel commanding an Army post, that Lazelle had to forward his request to purchase surplus Army property to the Commanding General of the Department of Texas, who, in turn, forwarded it to the Adjutant General. In this case, perhaps because Lazelle commanded an infantry unit, and thus was not formally a "mounted officer," his request was then forwarded by the Adjutant General to Major General Schofield, who approved it in his capacity as both Commanding General of the Army and Acting Secretary of War. The entire process took about two weeks. [6]

A December 1889 newspaper article updating events at Fort Clark noted that the 18th Infantry had completed its move onto the post. Along with two companies of the 3rd Cavalry, the two units made "a very pretty sight on parade. Both the Eighteenth and Third bands furnish excellent music." The writer maintained that the 18th did not like Fort Clark when it first arrived, but "as each day goes by they become more and more satisfied." [7]

In January 1890, the 3rd Cavalry Headquarters completed its departure from Fort Clark and Colonel Lazelle took over command of the post, although some 3rd Cavalry troops remained behind. Throughout 1890, both infantry and cavalry troops were regularly on field duty at Camps Del Rio, Langtry, and Eagle Pass, and on detached service at Fort Davis. They were supported by "Seminole Negro Indian Scouts." [8]

Troops remaining behind performed general garrison duties. In March and April 1890, an infantry company was sent out in the area near post to "collect telegraph poles," traveling a total of 27 miles in March and 60 miles in April. In June, five companies left post for "camp duty" on the Nueces River, 34 miles from the post. Another five went out in July to the same location, returning August 8. [9]

In June 1890, Lazelle was able to get back to West Point for the annual reunion and to see Jacob, who was just starting his third year at the Academy. Horace had his first real job at Fort Clark, serving as a census taker for the 1890 Federal Census and earning a little over $83. That summer, however, the nineteen-year-old had a bad attack of malarial fever and was sick in bed for three months. While he was convalescing, he came down with diphtheria, catching it from the daughter of another officer stationed at Fort Clark. Her mother had made chicken soup for him during his bout with malaria, and when he was feeling better he had gone to their house to thank her. The girl had a "sore throat" at the time, which they called tonsillitis but turned out to be diphtheria. Horace remembered he had a partial paralysis in the back of this throat; when he swallowed liquids, they came out his nose.

CHANGE AND CONTROVERSY

The period of Lazelle's command at Fort Clark was one of significant change in the Army, particularly for the officer corps, and was not without local controversy as well. In October 1890, an act of Congress authorized the President to establish a system of "physical and professional examinations" for all officers below the rank of major, to determine their fitness for promotion, and stipulated that if an officer failed to pass the examinations and was reported unfit for promotion, the officer next below him in seniority, having passed, would receive the promotion. [10]

Lazelle took the new promotion system seriously after several of his junior officers failed the initial set of exams that fall and were forced to retire. In December, the New Orleans *Times-Picayune* reported that Lazelle had announced that "none of his officers shall fail if he can help it." To that end, he established a special school on post:

> where daily instructions in military matters will be given, and has ordered his officers to attend. They do not like it particularly, but can't get around [it]; therefore, at Fort Clark, on five days out of the week, there is the novel spectacle of grizzled captains, lieutenants and others wending their way to school like village boys. The system of daily instructions has been established but a short time, but, it is asserted, is already bearing good fruit.[11]

While his lieutenants and captains grumbled over being sent back to school for remedial officer training, Lazelle's enlisted men raised a stink about new restrictions he placed on their drinking. In a January 1891 article, *The Kansas City Times* reported:

> Colonel Henry M. Lazelle, Eighteenth Infantry, commanding at Fort Clark, Tex., is determined that his name shall go down to history as the crankiest officer in the army of his time. His latest fad is the restriction of the sale of beer to the enlisted men of his post to five glasses per day. His plan, as started yesterday, is the keeping of a "roster of drinks" and as each man buys his glass of beer a hole is pegged and so on until five drinks have been obtained, when the sale to the individual soldier stops. The correspondent does not say whether each glass is a "schooner or a small" one, but it is presumed that small glasses are used. If this proceeding is not a ridiculous one then it would be difficult to estimate what it is.[12]

Lazelle didn't budge. He had been singularly focused on cadet discipline at West Point. The training program had instilled a more serious sense of professionalism in his lieutenants and captains. He was not about to give in to the desire for more liquor among the enlisted men, especially after someone went crying to the press.

Indeed, Lazelle was simply attempting to deal with a perennial Army problem in his own, perhaps draconian, manner. "Drunken revelry," especially around payday, was an Army "constant" that commanders had attempted to control in various ways, including a blanket War Department prohibition on alcohol sales in enlisted canteens on all posts in 1888. [13] As could have been expected, under this prohibition the drinking simply moved off-post. A year later, the sale of some alcohol in canteens was again authorized. Army regulations, however, gave the post commander fairly wide discretion:

> The sale or use of ardent [distilled] spirits in canteens is strictly prohibited; but the commanding officer is authorized to permit wines and light beer to be sold therein by the drink, on week-days, and in a room used for no other purpose, whenever he is satisfied that the giving to the men the opportunity of obtaining such beverages within the post limits has the effect of preventing them

> from resorting for strong intoxicants to places without such limits, and tends to promote temperance and discipline among them. [14]

While Lazelle's efforts to curb the deleterious effects of alcohol on discipline may have seemed over the top to some, they might well have been viewed with favor by Secretary of War Proctor and Commanding General Schofield. Both had been endeavoring to improve the overall lot of the common soldier while also firming up discipline, and especially curbing a high desertion rate.

In addition to reducing enlisted terms of service by giving soldiers early release options, improving living conditions somewhat, increasing rations and re-opening beer and wine sales on post as incentives, Proctor and Schofield also had convinced Congress to authorize two deterrents to desertion: holding back a portion of each man's monthly pay, to be returned upon discharge, and permitting civil authorities to arrest deserters. [15] Undoubtedly, they also recognized that permitting alcohol consumption in the post canteen, as long as it was tightly controlled, was much more conducive to good discipline than driving the men off post for their spirits.

In the spring of 1891, Horace was sent to live in the colder climate of Minneapolis to facilitate his recovery from malaria. He got a job with the Soo Line railroad through the owner of the West Hotel, Mr. Gray, whose wife was a family friend.[16] That summer, Horace stayed at Lake Gogebic in northern Michigan about 275 miles northeast of Minneapolis with mutual friends of the Lazelles and Grays. Mr. Gray came up and fished with him, and they caught "razorback" bass.

Meanwhile, Colonel Lazelle also suffered from recurring bouts of fever, which, along with an enlarged heart, would eventually lead to his disability retirement. He was "sick in quarters" from January 16 to 31, 1891, and on "light duty" status the entire month of February. He was on leave and away from post for a month from July 21 to August 20, and may have gone east to visit Horace and Jacob.

Increasingly concerned about his health and the continuing physical stress of Army duty, Lazelle formally requested a ruling by the Army Adjutant General in early October as to whether his four years as a cadet at West Point would count toward the 40 years of service required for retirement. In November, the Secretary of War, based on recommendations of the Adjutant General and Judge Advocate General, ruled that time spent as a cadet would count toward total service time for retirement. [17]

Throughout the fall and early winter of 1891, the 18th Infantry was engaged primarily in garrison duty, practice marches into the field, and instruction in field duties. However, on the morning of December 22, a detachment of infantry and cavalry troops "met and engaged in action with a band of Mexican revolutionists, presumably a portion of Catarino Garza's command." Garza was a Mexican journalist living in Texas who organized and led an abortive "revolt" against the Mexican regime of Porfirio Díaz, after Garza's friend and fellow Díaz opponent Ignacio Martínez was killed by Díaz agents in Laredo. [18]

In September 1891, Garza had led a group of 26 armed men across the Rio Grande, returning nine days later after a brief engagement with Mexican forces. Over the following months, the "Garcistas" made at least two more incursions into Mexico. In response, the Mexican government sent Gen. Lorenzo Garcia to the border. Garcia "so brutally suppressed anti-Díaz dissent that his cruelties caused a pro-Garza reaction in Texas. Fearing border war, influential Texans urged South Texans to remain neutral and petitioned the governor for special rangers to drive out Garcistas." [19]

The December engagement, a consequence of the Army's increased patrolling along the border, was reported as "brisk and lasting about 20 minutes, resulting in the killing of Corporal Easton, Troop C, 3rd Cavalry, and the killing and wounding of about 16-20 revolutionists." Lieutenant Hays, 18th Infantry, received several contusions and abrasions of the cheek, "due to his horse becoming unmanageable under him and finally falling with him." [20]

In the first several months of 1892, companies of the 18th again engaged in routine garrison duties and a series of training marches and encampments. Lazelle spent some of his free time that winter reading and writing a lengthy review of a new book by Theodore Ayrault Dodge, titled *Great Captains: Hannibal* for the February 25, 1892, edition of *The Christian Register.* Lazelle credited the author with having done his work "faithfully" and "completely" in providing a history of Hannibal and of the "means and methods of war-making of his period." However, he chastised the publisher—Houghton, Mifflin & Company—over the poor quality of the main military map of ancient Italy, noting that "to understand a campaign, a good military map is indispensable." [21]

In May 1892, Lazelle was granted four months' sick leave on the Post Surgeon's certificate of disability, which concluded, in part, that he suffered from an enlarged heart, arterial sclerosis, and urinary tract dysfunction, aggravated by both the heat and exertion:

> This officer has been suffering with this trouble for the last three years and is becoming more and more susceptible to the debilitating effect of heat, and from undue sense of fatigue from slight exertion. ... His disease cannot be satisfactorily treated in this Department, as the element of heat, which enters largely into causing the medical debility from which he is suffering, cannot be eliminated. The sea coast of the Northern and Middle Atlantic States is believed to be the most suitable locality for him. [22]

Despite his maladies, Lazelle was able to travel to New York for Jacob's graduation and the annual reunion of graduates at West Point, stopping off first in New York City. The *New York Times* covered the festivities at the Academy, noting that Lazelle was among the alumni in attendance (the only one from the class of 1855). The *Times* writer went on to observe "a strong brotherly feeling that classmates and comrades of the academy have for each other, and it is a genial army hospitality that warms the greeting between those here and those returning." Jacob was among a number of graduates who were sons of "eminent men and army officers." [23]

Jacob graduated 26th in a class of 62, a much higher academic position than that of his father (30th out of 34), and with considerably fewer demerits. Within the Cadet Battalion, he was one of 12 company lieutenants, ranked ninth of the 12. According to the annual report of the Academy for that year, the cadet officers were selected "from those Cadets who have been the most studious, soldier-like in the performance of their duties, and most exemplary in their general deportment." In that sense, he was among the elite since there were only eighteen cadet officer positions: four captains, an adjutant and quartermaster, and twelve lieutenants. His highest academic order of merit was in law, his lowest in Spanish. [24]

Jacob was commissioned a second lieutenant in the infantry, assigned to the 18th Infantry, and ordered to Fort Clark. It is unclear whether his father had any influence over his initial duty assignment, as graduates were assigned to vacant positions. At any rate, he was granted "graduating leave," and, in the August 1892 regimental monthly return, listed as 2nd Lieutenant of Company C, "absent with leave with permission to delay joining unit until September 30th."

That summer, while Colonel Lazelle was in Minneapolis on sick leave, Jacob joined him from graduation leave. Horace and his mother came from Fort Clark. The family stayed at the Lafayette Hotel on Lake Minnetonka's north shore. The 300-room hotel, built in 1882, hosted grand events, such as formal dances, concerts, and tennis tournaments. It burned down in 1897.[25] Today, the Lafayette Club stands on the site of the original hotel.

Lazelle returned to Fort Clark from sick leave on September 30, 1892, the same day that Jacob joined his company from graduation leave. Beyond normal garrison duties, the major event for the 18th that fall appears to have been Columbus Day celebrations. According to regimental and post monthly returns, the band and seven companies, under command of Maj. Thomas Rose, left Fort Clark October 20 and marched to Spofford Junction.

There, they boarded a train for Eagle Pass where they participated in festivities celebrating the 400th anniversary of Christopher Columbus's arrival in the New World. They returned October 22.

DEATH OF REBECCA

Colonel Lazelle's wife died unexpectedly at Fort Clark on January 24, 1893, at the age of 56 of complications from gall bladder disease. According to Horace, his mother had had gallstones and gall bladder attacks for years, but that winter got an intestinal obstruction that the doctors did not know how to treat in those days. Colonel Lazelle and Jacob both were granted ten days' leave. Joined by Horace, they departed post on January 29 to take her body back to Maryland by way of New Orleans. "Uncle Yellot" (related through Rebecca's mother's adoptive father, Samuel Yellot) and his daughter Francine, then living in Biloxi, Mississippi, came up to New Orleans to see the family. Rebecca was buried in the Hollingsworth family plot in Hagerstown, and Colonel Lazelle and Jacob returned to duty at Fort Clark on February 6.

On February 24, 1893, Lazelle again requested a medical examination and certificate for sick leave for one year, noting "recent family affliction [his wife's death] has intensified a heart trouble of long standing; and I feel myself steadily losing ground physically under the depressing influence of mental distress." He also requested "authority to go beyond the sea" (travel outside the country) while on medical leave. In a certificate accompanying his request the Post Surgeon found Lazelle to be suffering from "hypertrophy of the heart" (thickening of the heart wall), arteriosclerosis, and urinary blockages. His pulse was "abnormally rapid," rarely falling below ninety. [26]

In a second medical certificate, the Post Surgeon recommended an additional twelve months of medical leave, citing "marked nervous depression and insomnia" in addition to previous symptoms, and a year's leave with permission to go beyond the sea. Permission was granted by the Adjutant General on March 11, 1893.[27]

Lazelle left Fort Clark March 29, but not before requesting, in a letter to the Secretary of War, that his name be included on the list of officers to be considered by the President for promotion to Brigadier General. In an endorsement dated March 16, Army Commander Maj. Gen. J. M. Schofield, his former commander at West Point, wrote simply: "Respectfully submitted to the Secretary of War. Colonel Lazelle is a very meritorious and faithful officer."[28]

On his way east, Lazelle stopped in Charlotte, North Carolina, to renew local acquaintances. As reported in *The Charlotte Observer*, "a tall, distinguished looking man, with gray hair and beard" stepped off the train and slowly walked up the main street of town, "looking first on one side and then the other as if in search of familiar objects." Recognized as soon as he registered at the Central Hotel, Lazelle was soon joined by Col. William Johnston, Col. R. M. Oates, and Mr. S. A. Cohen. [29]

All three were prominent leaders in Charlotte. Johnston, a lawyer and financier who had served in the Confederate Army, had played a key role during Reconstruction in Charlotte, including rebuilding the Charlotte and South Carolina Railroad. He also had served twice as mayor, most recently in 1884 to 1887. Robert Oates had served as a brigade quartermaster in the Confederate Army. After the war he began a grocery and cotton business in the city, established the Charlotte Cotton Mill in 1880, and was appointed president of the First National Bank of Charlotte in 1891. Cohen was a member of the Chamber of Commerce when Lazelle visited.

Reminding its readers that Lazelle had been the first Federal commander in Charlotte after the war, *The Observer* noted that he had "ingratiated himself into the esteem of the people, treating all with courtesy and kindness." According to the reporter, Lazelle "was surprised beyond measure" to have "left the place a village" and "come back to find a beautiful city." [30]

Meanwhile, Jacob and the rest of the regiment were busy with routine garrison duties and field training. On April 18, 1893, Jacob's Company C, along with several other companies, left Fort Clark for a practice march and instruction in field duties, marching to camp at Eagle Pass. Leaving Eagle Pass on April 29, they went into camp at Thompson's Ranch the morning of the 30th, broke camp on May 1, and returned to Fort Clark the next day. [31]

Horace remembered that his father was very much a lost soul for months after Rebecca's death. During the summer months, he traveled to Massachusetts and then on to Chicago and the World's Fair—where Jacob joined him on leave. While staying in Onset on Buzzards Bay between Boston and Cape Cod, he wrote his good friend Samuel Barrows:

> Your lovely letter duly came, and like all, every line was freighted with the very spirit of true sympathy and affection. I am trying to recover from my selfish grief, which I know pains the loved one more perhaps than it pains me; for she not only has her own pain of separation to bear but a part of my sorrow.
>
> I don't know that I told you any of the particulars of her death, but if not, I will remove, until I see you, sorrowful memories. Your pleasing invitation, prompted by the best impulses, I cannot accept this summer. Possibly next summer I may. I hope very much to see you soon, as I shall go to either Minneapolis (or Chicago) by way of the Canadian Railroad from Boston; or to Lake Edmund (North of Quebec) by the same channel. In either case I will run down to our camp and see you. 'Till then I will say Goodbye. My love to all whom I know with you. [32]

From Chicago, Lazelle went on to Minneapolis, staying again at the West Hotel. After seven months, however, he returned to duty, relinquishing the rest of his leave, and was back in command of his regiment on November 19, 1893. In the meantime, however, the entire regiment had been relocated to the "New Fort Bliss," the site of modern-day Fort Bliss.

Fort Bliss

The notion of expanding the Army's post in El Paso had first been raised by Gen. Philip Sheridan, Commander of the Military District of Missouri, after an inspection tour of New Mexico and Texas in 1881 to identify a post "to enlarge while closing other frontier forts." Sheridan initially did not recommend Bliss for expansion because of its proximity to the border with Mexico. However, Army Commanding General Sherman, after visiting the area in 1882, reversed Sheridan's recommendation and proposed expanding the El Paso post to regimental size. Eventually, Army interest and lobbying by prominent locals were strong enough that Congress passed a resolution, signed into law in 1890, to sell the old Fort Bliss and construct a new, larger fort within ten miles of downtown El Paso. [33]

Legislation authorizing the new fort, however, provided funding only for its construction, so local citizens banded together—as the El Paso Progressive Association—to raise funds to purchase the land identified by the Army for the new post. The citizens' group ended up buying a total of 1,266 acres and, at the Army's urging, also drilled a well for the fort. [34]

Construction of the new post began in 1892 under the direction of Capt. George Ruhlen, the same George Ruhlen who had overseen construction of Fort Meade in the Dakotas in 1878 with then-Major Lazelle. By this time, Ruhlen was a 19-year veteran and "highly regarded construction engineer." He arrived in El Paso in March 1891. It took him over a year to complete and get approval of the post plans, and start construction. Initial construction was completed in June 1893, and the first elements of the 18th Infantry arrived in October. [35]

The main body of troops from Fort Clark—eight officers and 202 enlisted men—arrived in El Paso October 27, 1893, aboard the Galveston, Harrisburg and San Antonio Railroad. Commanded by Capt. William H. McLaughlin—since Colonel Lazelle was on sick leave and Major Rose, the next-most-senior officer, also was absent on leave—they comprised the regimental headquarters and four companies. Upon arriving on post, McLaughlin and his troops found a row of two-story brick officers' quarters on the west side of the parade field, facing an administration building with enlisted barracks on either side, and three large, two-story brick quarters for non-commissioned officers. [36] As the inaugural Post Commander, Lazelle would have occupied one of the officer's quarters, since the Commanding Officer's house (now known as The Pershing House) was not constructed until 1910.

Photo 31. New Fort Bliss from the East, 1890s

Courtesy of the Fort Bliss and Old Ironsides Museum

Photo 32. New Fort Bliss Officer's Row, 1890s

Courtesy of the Fort Bliss and Old Ironsides Museum

According to one description of life on post at Fort Bliss in late 1893 when both Lazelle and Jacob were stationed there, "the members of the garrison felt somewhat removed and isolated. During the day there was a line of misty smoke which obscured the city from view and at night a hazy string of lights was the only positive reminder of the sportive, bustling town." On the positive side, however, "the air was crisp and breezy while the supply of water was abundant and excellent. The health of the men was reported to be much better than at Fort Clark." [37]

Upon returning to his regiment in November, Lazelle immediately went on sick call, again diagnosed with hypertrophy of the heart and intermittent fever, and was "sick in quarters" until December 2, 1893. On November 27, he penned a personal note to Major General Schofield, indicating he was still very much interested in being on the list of officers considered for promotion to brigadier general. In all likelihood, Lazelle had in mind requesting disability retirement if a promotion did not appear to be in the cards. [38]

A promotion was not in the offing, and, although he was afflicted again with "remittent fever" in January and February 1894, Lazelle remained in command of the 18th Infantry and Fort Bliss until mid-July. In May, Fort Bliss underwent its first Inspector General inspection. Although the post made a creditable showing, the inspector noted a number of deficiencies: no post garden due to the lack of water, no fire engine, no post school, and no chaplain. He also noted that "low groggeries have sprung up on private land within a stone's throw of the officers' quarters," concluding that "it has been truly said of the site that its selection was an insult to the intelligence of the Army." [39]

On June 21, Lazelle applied for a leave of absence of four months "with the expressed understanding that at the expiration of that time he may be retired." The request noted that he had had 22 months of leave in 39 years of service, with the exception of the two periods of sick leave for disability in the line of duty. His leave was approved, and he departed post on July 18, 1894.[40]

Meanwhile, 2nd Lt. Jacob Lazelle continued to serve with his company at Fort Bliss. In April and May 1894, the company completed annual target practice; in June, he was transferred from Company C to Company B, which was stationed at Fort Sam Houston. He left Fort Bliss for Fort Sam Houston that month. In August, he was on detached service at Fort Clark for ten days "in connection with Department Rifle Competition."

Jacob remained with his company at Fort Sam Houston until June 1898, although for an extended period (December 1896–April 1898) he was on detached service at Fort Ringgold (the southernmost of the western tier of forts constructed at the end of the Mexican War on the Rio Grande near Rio Grande City), commanding a detachment of Seminole Indian Scouts. [41]

Retirement

After leaving Fort Bliss, Colonel Lazelle made his way back East and was in Boston at the United States Hotel from September through his official retirement in November 1894. In early September, he had penned a note to the Adjutant General of the Army noting that he had been "very much annoyed by a statement that the Army & Navy Journal has recently published my resignation from the Army. The statement if made is utterly without foundation; and if it has in any way reached your office I beg to discredit it, as I have and have had no such intention." [42]

Two months later, on November 10, 1894, Lazelle formally surrendered the remaining portion of his leave of absence to the Adjutant General of the Army and requested to go before a retirement board "with the view of retirement for disease contracted in the line of duty, evidence of which was admitted with letter to your office dated the 27th ulto. If the Board convened should not think it consistent to recommend me for retirement on account of disability, I shall in that event, at once apply for retirement *under the Statute* [about which he had inquired back in 1891]."[43]

The Army moved quickly. The Adjutant General's Office convened a board on November 15 in New York City, and the board rendered its opinion the same day that Lazelle was "suffering from hypertrophy of the heart accompanied with a very rapid pulse from the slightest exertion, that the resulting disability is permanent, that it originated in the line of duty, and that it was caused by long and arduous military Service." On the 16th, having returned to Boston from New York, Lazelle wrote again to the Adjutant General providing him a change of address from the United States Hotel to "care of Lee, Hammond, 14 Kneeland St., Boston," and requesting that all official correspondence be sent there.

On November 27, 1894, under Special Orders No. 279, Adjutant General's Office, Headquarters of the Army, Colonel Henry M. Lazelle, 18th Infantry, was retired from active service, per War Department order dated November 26, 1894. On December 3, he wrote from the West Hotel in Minneapolis, asking that he receive travel orders from Boston to Minneapolis, since the latter "is my home now." He request was granted December 8. [44]

Chapter 12

A Lost Soul

According to Horace, his father was very much at loose ends upon his retirement. Once ensconced at the West Hotel in Minneapolis, he could not stay put for long. In January 1895, he headed south, first to Thomasville, Georgia, just north of the Florida border near Tallahassee, and eventually on to Jamaica where he whiled away his time fishing.[1] In March, he was back in New York City. Eventually, he returned to Minneapolis to build a house.

During this unsettled period, Lazelle also became increasingly drawn into spiritualism, which he first began exploring after Rebecca's death. As Horace remembered, his father had long been fascinated with dreams, kept a dream book, and would interpret all of his dreams. Both he and Rebecca were quite superstitious. For example, she would never go out on Fridays. In exploring spiritualism after Rebecca's death, Horace believed, his father was driven partly by guilt that he had given her too hard a life, and wanted to reach her after her death to say he was sorry. As he had written to his friend, Barrows, shortly after her death, he also believed that she, too, felt "a part" of his sorrow. He longed to share these feelings with her.

At the time, there was a good deal of controversy over spiritualism and the legitimacy of "mediums" who claimed to be able to contact, and act as a communications link with, the dead. While acknowledging that there were "rational, law-abiding men and women among spiritualists and sympathetic investigators," one book published in 1892 went to great lengths—and detail—to expose the frauds perpetrated by "vile creatures" in the Boston area who "under the mask of mediumship, have been coining money from the most sacred feelings of the heart" and who had "plied their wiles to victimize and demoralize heart-broken mourners seeking knowledge of their beloved dead." Among the charlatans "exposed" in the booklet were George T. Albro, who sponsored séances, and Dr. and Mrs. C. B. Bliss, mediums used by Henry Lazelle in his attempts to reach Rebecca in the afterlife. (These Blisses were not related to Lazelle's fellow 8th Infantry officer, Zenas Bliss.) [2]

The American press tended to treat spiritualism as a valid news story, but often focused on attempts to root out charlatans and fakers who made considerable profits taking advantage of naïve believers. The *Boston Herald,* for example, ran a story in March 1884, about an attempt—successful, as it turned out—by some prominent Bostonians to expose the very Mrs. Bliss and her husband in whom Lazelle had great faith. As reported by the *Herald,* Henry W. Holland, a Boston lawyer, along with a prominent State Street banker, a retired manufacturer from Natick, and "other persons of respectability" attended one of her séances. The *Herald* described what ensued:

> During Mrs. Bliss' séance there appeared what purported to be a "materialization" of the spirit of "Capt. Hodges," described as a soldierly dressed man, who came often and was said to be a very strong and interesting spirit and a remarkable evidence of the super-human, and there was also a materialization of "Little Billy" and "Blue Flower." The last mentioned appeared first, and a gentleman in the room arose and put his arms around the "spirit," which, according to Mr. Holland, muttered "Go away, you devil!" and fled back into the cabinet [closet]. Several persons, among

> them Mr. Holland, entered the cabinet, and there saw Mrs. Bliss crouched on the floor in one corner almost naked, nothing being about her but the muslin in which she had appeared outside as a "spirit." There was a pair of shoes inside which one of the visitors threw out, saying they were the spirit's shoes. Mr. Holland, without touching Mrs. Bliss, tried to induce her to get up, but she declined, saying that she was in a delicate condition and needed a physician. The intruders, however, were satisfied that her reason for not getting up was that she would expose to view "Capt. Hodge's" whiskers and make-up, upon which she was sitting. Mr. Holland produced a cheap piece of cotton on which tinsels were stuck to look like brass buttons, while on the other side was the imitation of a child's jacket, and this, with a thin, cheap cap which "Billy" wore, he said he got inside the cabinet, and they would be sworn to by the 10 persons who were present. It is claimed, therefore, that the exposé was complete.

The *Herald* article concluded by noting that Dr. Bliss and his wife allegedly also had been "exposed" in Chicago, that they had been doing a "very profitable business" in Boston, and that charges of "obtaining money under false pretenses" might be brought against them.[3]

Despite considerable controversy over spiritualism, and its condemnation by Protestant and Catholic clergy alike, spiritualists like Dr. and Mrs. Bliss attracted large numbers of interested Americans. Indeed, spiritualism's adherents were not limited just to easily duped common folk. Among the many famous people of the day who shared Lazelle's passionate belief was Sir Arthur Conan Doyle, creator of Sherlock Holmes, who, like Lazelle, found comfort in spiritualism after the death of his wife. The Irish poet William Butler Yeats also had a lifelong interest in spiritualism. Both he and Conan Doyle—as well as Charles Dickens and other notables—were members of the Ghost Club, a paranormal organization founded at Cambridge in 1862 and devoted to the scientific study of alleged paranormal activities. The Ghost Club still exists.

While Lazelle may have had many sympathetic fellow spiritualists, his close friend Barrows, a Unitarian minister and editor of *The Christian*

Register, was not among them. Responding in December 1894 to a "frank but narrow-minded" letter from Barrows, who apparently had pulled few punches on the subject, Lazelle likened "the beautiful truths of spirit-belief" to Christian beliefs that were "just as lofty and beautiful without the idea attached of his miracles, which probably never occurred."

Acknowledging that there were "many unmitigated villains" motivated solely by the quest for money, he nonetheless asked Barrows to explain how it was that in more than twelve visits to his spiritualist:

> the form of my darling came from the floor, never in the same place twice; how it was that once I was induced to look behind me, and there I saw within reach of my arm a shadowy indefinable appearance without form, take on a human shape and with outstretched arms clasp me around the neck; how it was that she did rise from the floor many times slowly steadily within reach of my arm wherever I chanced to take my seat.[4]

Lazelle went on at length to describe how Rebecca's spirit had talked to him "of matters known only to us," and had sent "divine messages" to Horace, Jacob, and his sisters, "whom she knew mentioning them by names never referred to or mentioned by me in that [the medium's] house." He described how her "figure and voice," and "slow deliberation of speech and language and refinement of thought" were "always precisely the same, from the first time that I went there 18 months since" and offered Barrows detailed descriptions of two particularly vivid encounters during private séances, concluding that until someone could explain all of these events "on natural or physical grounds," he would continue to believe that "materialization" was possible.

In the end he challenged Barrows to seek out a medium in whom Lazelle had complete confidence—"she is personally trustworthy"—and engage her in a private séance:

> in your house. Your library room or elsewhere. Make your own test conditions; exclude everybody, except your friends who will not absolutely antagonize her by prepared positive doubt and

> denial, but treat her as I know that you and dear Mrs. Barrows will with gentleness and kindness. Do this, I say, and I will pay half of all expenses; and if you do not get results, which you will concede to be demonstrations from the other side of the veil, I will pay all expenses.[5]

By early 1895, however, Lazelle had moved beyond pure spiritualism to a more sophisticated investigation of the hereafter and had published his second book, *Matter, Force and Spirit or Scientific Evidence of a Supreme Intelligence*, in which he attempted to establish a more fundamental, scientific basis for the existence of God than mere faith alone.[6]

As Horace remembered, when the family was in California his father had become acquainted with Katherine Tingley, a social worker and prominent Theosophist, who founded the Theosophical Society of Pasadena and led the Theosophical community Lomaland in San Diego. Theosophists essentially focused on the nature of God and the soul, incorporating aspects of Buddhism and Brahmanism, including a belief in reincarnation and spiritual evolution.

In *Matter, Force and Spirit,* Lazelle essentially applied a theosophist's approach to his study of the relationship between God, man, and universal scientific truths. In a way, he was moving beyond the spiritualists' realm in search of a connection to Rebecca in the afterlife. In February, he again wrote to Barrows, asking him to "give it a whirl in your review [in *The Christian Register*], to nothingness, if this is deserved; helpful, if otherwise." [7]

In June, Lazelle attended the 40th reunion of the Class of 1855 at West Point. According the press coverage, all surviving members were present. Of these, only three were still on active duty, including George D. Ruggles, Adjutant General of the Army. Five were in "civil life," including former Union Army Generals David Gregg, Alexander Webb, and John Turner; former governor and then-Chief Justice of Louisiana Francis Nichols; and president of the University of the South in Tennessee Francis Shoup. [8]

In all, of the 34 members of Lazelle's graduating class, 12 had been brevetted to general's rank during the Civil War. Only one of these, however, attained general officer rank in the regular Army. William B. Hazen retired as a Brigadier General and Chief Signal Officer of the Army. Two of the twelve others retired as colonels, and the rest resigned or retired at lower ranks.

Of the remaining 22 members of the class, only Lazelle reached the rank of colonel in the regular Army before retiring. So, despite his frustrations over the promotion system, his lost opportunities, and the controversies that, in retrospect, he might have believed held him back, Lazelle actually was one of the more successful careerists in his class.

ENTER THE WENTWORTH WOMEN

The Minneapolis house, in the section of town still known as Kenwood, was completed in September 1895. While Lazelle could hardly have afforded a large house on his colonel's pension, he had inherited Rebecca's money after her death. Through Samuel and Isabel Barrows, he arranged for the services of a housekeeper, Mary Perkins Wentworth, a divorcee, who had been employed in Salem, Massachusetts. Mrs. Wentworth had a 17-year-old daughter, Martha Kemble Wentworth, who was still in high school. Horace, 25 years old at the time and living with his father, was immediately taken with Martha when the Wentworths came to Minneapolis.

Photo 33. The Minneapolis House

Mary Perkins Wentworth was born in Salem, Massachusetts, July 22, 1855. Her father, Jonathan C. Perkins, a graduate of Amherst College who studied law at the Dane Law School in Cambridge, was an eminent lawyer, on Amherst's Board of Trustees, and a member of the State Constitutional Convention. Her mother was the daughter of Robert Brookhouse, a wealthy Salem merchant and ship owner.

Mary's former husband, William P. Wentworth, born in Boston February 22, 1849, and a Harvard graduate, also came from a distinguished New England family, tracing his lineage back to Benning Wentworth, the first royal governor of New Hampshire, and John Wentworth, royal governor at the outbreak of the Revolutionary War. William and Mary Perkins were married in October 1877, and their daughter was born in June 1878. William turned out to be "no good," and after he ran away with all of Mary's money, she divorced him and found employment in Salem.

Horace remembered the Minneapolis house as "very fancy" for its time, with walls that were stenciled in fancy designs, a drawing room, hall, library, den, dining room, kitchen, and pantry on the first floor; and four bedrooms and servants' quarters over the kitchen on the second. However, his father was cold all the time, wrapped the arms of chairs in flannel, and was always fussing over the weather—either too hot or too cold. There was an open arch with vertical spindles above the folding door between the drawing room and library. Colonel Lazelle was so cold that he had red and green flannel woven between the spindles to cut down on the draft.

Martha completed high school in Minneapolis and graduated in June 1896. That summer, Colonel Lazelle, Horace, and the Wentworths stayed in a cottage on Lake Minnetonka. Jacob came from Fort Bliss on leave that summer and again in the fall. Horace, hopelessly smitten with Martha, proposed to her that fall on a bridge over the lake. [9]

That same fall, Lazelle—too restless to stay in one place—sold the house in Minneapolis and went wandering off to Honolulu, Hawaii, eventually spending the winter on the island of Kauai. Horace, believing he wanted to be a farmer, went scouting for farm property as far south as Melbourne, Florida, but eventually purchased "the Coleman Place—Estranola—in Virginia," which appears to have been part of the Beaumont property originally owned by the Michaux family in Powhatan County on the James River. [10]

Horace put the Virginia house in order, and Martha and her mother joined him on the farm in March 1897. His father returned from Hawaii that summer and also built a house on the property. In the end, however, Horace found farming not to his liking, and in the fall of 1897 entered the University College of Medicine, now part of Virginia Commonwealth University, [11] commuting from the farm to Richmond. The next spring, Colonel Lazelle asked Barrows, then a Congressman from Massachusetts, if there were any diplomatic posting that might be available for him. Barrows wrote back in early May 1898 that all vacancies had been filled except for three, including one in Bermuda and another in Turk's Island in the West Indies, but that neither paid well enough to meet Lazelle's needs. So, he stayed on at the farm.

Another Tragedy

In 1898, with the outbreak of the Spanish-American War, Jacob, then a first lieutenant, resigned his position commanding the Seminole Scouts and requested to be reassigned to his regiment, which had been ordered to Manila and was embarking in San Francisco. On June 15, Jacob's company sailed from San Francisco on the transport *Colon.* They arrived at Honolulu, Hawaii, on June 24 and set sail again the next day.

While in Honolulu, Jacob contracted the measles, which soon developed into meningitis. He died on board the S.S. *Colon* at 7:30 a.m. on July 12, 1898, about 800 miles west of Manila, at the age of 32. His battalion arrived in Manila Bay on July 16, disembarked on the 20th, and went into camp at Camp Dewey, near Manila. Jacob's remains were interred in the bastion of the old fortress at Cavite, outside Manila, on July 17, 1898.[12]

In October, Lazelle received permission from the Assistant Adjutant General to travel to the Philippines. On November 9, he sailed on the transport *Newport,* bound for Manila by way of Japan, to retrieve Jacob's body and bring it back to the United States, where it was buried at the Presidio of San Francisco. On board the *Newport* were the last contingents of the Philippine Islands Expeditionary Forces, along with Gen. Marcus F. Miller.[13] According to Horace, his father was "very moody, either in high or low spirits" after returning from the Philippines and San Francisco. Eventually, he went down to Florida, fishing in Punta Gorda.

In the fall of 1899, Lazelle returned to New England and rented a house in Somerville, Massachusetts. Horace had graduated from medical school in April at the top of his class and had gone to Boston to "take courses" (equivalent to today's internship) at hospitals there. Martha and her mother, who were living in Andover, moved back in with the colonel.

Martha was working at Harvard. That December, Lazelle, showing a bit of his old sense of humor, wrote to Barrows:

> Well we had a lovely Christmas. Horace here and a goose—with the other things making up our Christmas dinner. Cousin Mary and Martha send love to you both as do Horace and I. Tell Sister Isabel [Barrows' wife]—you know her, I believe—that I may accept the invitation to come to Washington for a few days but not for long.

In July 1901, Horace finished his internship at Lying-In Hospital, adjacent to Harvard University and went to Cambridge Hospital for his residency. That Christmas, he and Martha were officially engaged, five years after he had first proposed to the then-18-year-old. By February, his father was restless again, wanting to return out West.

They gave up the Somerville house, and all but Horace left for California, where he would join them after his residency, settling for the moment in Oakland across the bay from San Francisco.When Horace finished his residency in July 1902, he first went to Richmond to sell his furniture that had been stored there, and then joined his father and the ladies in Oakland. Since Horace had secured a medical position in Seattle, Washington, however, their stay in Oakland was brief.

Colonel Lazelle went by boat to Seattle, and the others by train. Horace took and passed the state medical boards, and the family moved to a house on Howell Street. He and Martha were married March 3, 1903. Colonel Lazelle and Martha's mother stayed at the Howell Street house, while 33-year-old Horace and 25-year-old Martha honeymooned in Victoria, B.C. [14]

WAKE ROBIN

The day Horace and Martha returned, the restless colonel was off again, this time back to the Barrowses' camp in Quebec, on the shores of Lake Memphremagog. Samuel and Isabel had been camping there regularly since 1878 and had co-authored two books about their camping experiences. The Lazelles had first visited the Barrows family in the 1880s at the lakeshore property that came to be known as Birch Bay.

In 1887, Isabel Barrows had acquired part of a farm to the north of their property, located about halfway between the shoreline and the road connecting the towns of Georgeville and Magog. This piece of property would eventually become "Wake Robin," a common name for the trillium plant that grew on the property, called wake-robin because it would emerge as the robins flocked in the spring. In the meantime, however, the Barrowses bought another large plot of land between the Wake Robin property and the lakeshore to the north of Birch Bay. This became known as Cedar Lodge.

Having acquired the Cedar Lodge property, the Barrowses apparently felt the other lot could be used by Colonel Lazelle. No formal lease was ever signed, but Lazelle had a local handyman build a cabin, in keeping with the style of the other cedar log cabins and lodges built by the Barrows and other families in the area. Isabel Barrows named the cabin "Wake Robin."

The cabin apparently was built in 1900, while Horace was completing his internship, based on journal references that describe its construction, the transport of furniture to the cabin, and a housewarming event hosted that year. [15] In addition to the main cabin and its semi-attached kitchen building (now used for storage), there was an ice house and a sleeping cabin on the property.

Georgeville is an old village on a cove of Lake Memphremagog, about 20 miles north of the Vermont border. The general store dates to 1888, a small red church (now converted into a private residence) to 1849, and an Anglican church to 1866. The Auberge Georgeville, now a B&B and restaurant, dates as an inn (under various names) to 1889 and is the oldest inn in Quebec Province. It, the store, and the two churches would have been there when Lazelle lived there, and undoubtedly, he would have visited at least the inn and the store.

A New Wife and Peace of Mind

Once back east in 1903, Lazelle also bought a house at 11 Symmes Road in Winchester, Massachusetts. He never went west again. Through an old Army friend, he made numerous acquaintances in Winchester; and through Mrs. Barrows, he met a 33-year-old French woman, originally from Strasbourg in Alsace, Emilie Marie Monard, from whom he took French lessons. Quickly, he was smitten.

By an April 23, 1904, Act of Congress, all officers who had served in the Civil War and retired "for age or for wounds or disability incurred in the line of duty" were promoted to the next higher rank, with pay. On July 2, 1904, Henry M. Lazelle signed the formal oath of office as a Brigadier General, the rank he had sought for years. [16]

That September, after he and Emilie returned from "camp" at Memphremagog, he wrote Isabel Barrows from Boston, discussing his new love and their marriage plans. Absent was any discussion of séances and connecting with Rebecca:

> Before this I would hardly have turned my hand over to live; now I want to live to make that other sweet life happy. God help me to do so is my prayer, and it shall be my effort. I want to preserve the flower just as she comes to me; never suppressing one joyous note of her merry sweet soul nature. [17]

Brigadier General Lazelle, 72, and Emilie Monard, 33, were married November 22, 1904, in New York City. Samuel Barrows officiated. It is not known whether Horace was invited, but he did not attend. The newlyweds went first to Washington, D.C., and then on to New Orleans and Mexico. From Washington, Lazelle wrote Barrows that he had named Emilie beneficiary under his $1,500 Army Mutual Insurance Company life insurance policy. [18]

Little is known about Lazelle's life with Emilie Monard. They traveled to Jamaica in the spring of 1913 but generally spent their winters in Florida and summers at Wake Robin, with the Winchester house as their base and permanent residence. According to Horace's daughter, following his father's marriage, to which he seriously objected, Horace never saw him again.

Frank W. Fetter, who had last visited Barrows' Camp in 1909 as a ten-year-old, remembered Lazelle, the first general he had ever seen, as a "kindly old gentleman ... [who] walking across the fields with his wife was so completely different from my boyhood picture of what a general looked like and what a general did that it made an impression on me, and at the same time puzzled me. It was so different from my picture of generals from my reading about the Civil War and the Charge of the Light Brigade." [19]

Photo 34. Colonel Lazelle at Wake Robin Cabin—Barrows' Camp

Photo 35. H.M. Lazelle in Winchester, Mass.

Photo 36. General H. M. Lazelle

In May 1909, Lazelle commenced one final battle with the United States Government, filing a claim in the U.S. Court of Claims against the government for failing to take his time as a cadet at West Point into account when computing his longevity pay and rations allowances. Based on War Department calculations, he was owed the princely sum of $2,330.03. The claims court ruled against him, however, because he had filed his claim well beyond a six-year statute of limitations from his retirement date. Again, he had won a battle—he had a legitimate claim—but lost the war, this one against time. [20]

In 1911, after Lazelle had remarried, the possibility arose that Samuel and Isabel Barrows might sell their holdings, so the Lazelles undertook to secure their investment in the cabin at Wake Robin by buying the land under it. The one-acre plot of land was purchased from Isabel Barrows for $10.00 in February 1912, and was titled in Emilie M. Lazelle's name.

Although estranged from his son, the General, as he was known to the Canadian crowd, nonetheless continued to write both to Horace and his granddaughter, Barbara, who was born in 1907. In his last letter to Horace, dated February 28, 1917, from Winchester, Massachusetts, with an enclosed photograph, he wrote:

> My dear boy,
>
> The friend with me is Colonel Stanton of the Engineers, who was stationed at West Point when we were there. These or this was a shot taken by his daughter who was here with us. They are now very healthy and industrious—of course, for an Army officer never got sick any other way—and I look "old and worn"? 84 years.
>
> Always affectionately, Pop.[21]

Six months later, on July 21, 1917, Horace received a cryptic telegram from "Lazelle" in Magog, Quebec: "Father passed away at three thirty this AM." According to the death certificate, the cause of death was arterial sclerosis. He was buried on the property of Wake Robin.[22]

When he died, General Lazelle left everything to his wife, and Horace had no communication with her after his father's death. In October 1917, she applied for his Army pension, as his widow. Col. William S. Stanton and his wife, Katharine, witnessed her application.

Emilie Monard Lazelle lived for only seven more years, passing away on December 23, 1923. Although her probate documents did not include the home in Winchester, Massachusetts (it may have been sold prior to her death), they did include Wake Robin as part of her estate. According to her will, all of her personal property went to friends and two Monard family members. In November 1924, her estate sold the property in Georgeville for the sum of $900.

According to the current owners of Wake Robin, Emilie was known for swimming—and perhaps sunbathing—"au naturel" on the beach by Cedar Lodge to "ward off tuberculosis." When the property went on the market after Emilie's death, the owners of Cedar Lodge, which had become a children's summer camp, started to bid on it to prevent any future nude swimming on their beach. The eventual buyer assured them that, rather than get into a bidding war, if they would sell him a small strip of lake-front on the far edge of their property, he and his family would not follow Emilie's unacceptable practices. The deed to Wake Robin still guarantees the owners' access to the lakeshore.

Wake Robin remains in that buyer's family today, and Emilie is buried on the property—next to her husband.

Notes

Chapter 1—A Five-Year Man

1. Henry would change the spelling of his last name to "Lazelle" sometime in 1852, influenced perhaps by his French language instruction and French Huguenot heritage. The academy used both "Lazell" and "Lazelle" interchangeably. The annual *Official Register of the Officers and Cadets of the U.S. Military Academy* consistently used "Lazell," the name on his nomination and appointment documents, as well as on some official orders. However, other official correspondence as early as March 1852 used "Lazelle."

2. Horatio G. Wright, "West Point and Cadet Life," *Putnam's Monthly*, August 1854, pp. 192-204. Copy found in Lazelle Family Papers.

3. Caleb A. Wall, *Reminiscences of Worcester from the Earliest Period* (Worcester, MA: Tyler & Seagrave, 1877), 211. See also Friends of Hope Cemetery web site @ http://www.friendsofhopecemetery.com and *Proceedings of the Worcester Society of Antiquity, 1897*, Worcester Historical Society, Worcester, MA. @ http://books.google.com.

4. U.S. Military Academy Cadet Application Papers, 1805-1916, Record Group (RG) 94 (National Archives Microfilm Publication M688), National Archives and Records Administration, National Archives Building, Washington, DC (hereafter NARA).

5. Gordon H. Fleming, *James Abbott McNeill Whistler, a Life* (New York: St. Martin's Press, 1991), 38.

6. Wright, 193-194.

7. U.S. Military Academy website: http://www.usma.edu/wphistory/SitePages/Home.aspx.

8. Ibid.

9. "Post Orders No. 36, June 24, 1850," *Military Academy Post Orders 1846-1852, Vol. 3.* U.S. Military Academy (USMA) Archives.

10. *Circumstances of the Parents of the Cadets, 1842-1879, Vol. I,* USMA Archives.

11. "Inst." was the abbreviation of the Latin term "instante mense," meaning "this month," commonly used in nineteenth-century letters and memos. Its counterparts were: "ult," for *ultimo mense* (last month) and "prox" for *proximo mense* (next month).

12. Letter to George Lazelle, dated July 19, 1850, Military Academy Letters, Engineer Department Records Relating to the U.S. Military Academy, Records of the Adjutant General's Office, 1780s-1917, RG 94.2.6 (M91, Roll 17), NARA. Brewerton served as Superintendent from 1845 to 1852, when he was replaced by then-Brevet Colonel Robert E. Lee.

13. Oliver Otis Howard, *Autobiography of Oliver Otis Howard, Major General, United States Army, Vol. I* (New York: Baker & Taylor, 1908), 49. (Available at openlibrary.org)

14. Peggy Hoffman, "Henry M. Lazelle, U.S. Army," unpublished manuscript, September, 1969, Lazelle Family Papers.

15. *Official Register of the Officers and Cadets of the U.S. Military Academy,* June 1851. USMA Archives. (USMA online records @ http://digital-library.usma.edu/cdm/landingpage/collection/p16919coll3.)

16. Wright, *West Point and Cadet Life,* 198.

17. Wright, 199.

18. Lazelle, H. M., "Whistler at West Point," *The Century* 90, 1915. Also quoted in Fleming's *Whistler: A Life.*

19. Ronald Anderson and Anne Koval, *James McNeill Whistler: Beyond the Myth* (New York: Carroll & Graf, 1994), 23.

20. Lazelle, "Whistler at West Point."

21. James S. Robbins, *Last in Their Class: Custer, Pickett and the Goats of West Point* (New York: Encounter Books, 2006), 14.

22. Lazelle, "Whistler at West Point."

23. Letter, dated March 2, 1852, from Captain Henry Brewerton, Superintendent, USMA, to Brig. Gen. G. Totten, Chief of Engineers, Washington DC. USMA Archives.

24. It was not uncommon for cadets at the time to appeal punishments and suspensions to the Chief of Engineers, Secretary of War and, ultimately, the President. There are numerous examples in the West Point archives.

25. "Orders dated May 1, 1852," Order Book No. 3, USMA Archives.

26. Letter, dated 7 January 1853, from Bvt. Col. Robert E. Lee to Gen. Joseph G. Totten, Chief of Engineers. USMA Library Occasional Paper No. 5, "The Daily Correspondence of Robert E. Lee, Superintendent, USMA, 1852-1855." USMA Archives.

27. "Official Record of the U.S. Military Academy, West Point, New York," June 1852. USMA Archives.

28. Philip H. Sheridan, *Personal Memoirs of P. H. Sheridan, Volume I* (New York: Charles L. Webster & Co., 1888), 12.

29. John M. Schofield, *Forty-Six Years in the Army* (New York: The Century Co. 1897), 10-13.

30. University of Glasgow Library, Scotland, Special Collections, MS Whistler L32 (BP II 36/3) and MS Whistler L33 (BP II 36/4).

31. Fleming, *Whistler: A Life*, 47.

32. "Post Orders, No. 4, November 13, 1852–November 30, 1856," USMA Archives.

33. Lazelle, "Whistler at West Point."

34. "Academic Board Meeting, June 20, 1854," U.S. Military Academy Staff Records, Vol. 5, 1851-1854, USMA Archives.

35. Margaret F. McDonald, *James McNeill Whistler: Drawings, Pastels, and Watercolours—A Catalogue Raisonné* (New Haven, CT: Yale University Press, 1995), 43-44.

36. Hoffman, "Henry M. Lazelle, U.S. Army," Lazelle Family Papers.

CHAPTER 2—OPERATIONS AGAINST THE APACHES

1. Fort Bliss, Monthly Returns, January—March 1856, Returns from U.S. Military Posts, 1800-1916 (hereafter Post Returns), RG94 (M617, roll 116), NARA.

2. A distant relative of Colonel William Wallace Smith Bliss for whom the fort was named.

3. Thomas T. Smith, et al., eds., *The Reminiscences of Major General Zenas R. Bliss, 1854-1876* (Austin: Texas State Historical Association, 2007), 4-11.

4. Large, usually flat-bottomed boats used to transfer passengers and cargo between anchored vessels and the shore.

5. Fort Bliss website @ www.bliss.army.mil/garrison/sites/about/history.asp. See also Donald B. Sanger, Major, Signal Corps, US Army, *The Story of Fort Bliss* (Carlisle Barracks, PA: US Army Heritage Center), 1933.

6. Ibid.

7. Lydia Spencer Lane, *I Married a Soldier or Old Days in the Old Army* (Philadelphia: J.B. Lippincott, 1893), 68-73.

8. "Eighth United States Infantry," *The Handbook of Texas Online*, Texas State Historical Association, @ www.tshaonline.org.

9. Thomas Wilhelm, *History of the Eighth U.S. Infantry From Its Organization in 1838, Vol. II* (NP: Headquarters, Eighth Infantry, 1873), 47-50.

10. Robert M. Utley, *Frontiersmen in Blue: The United States Army and the Indian, 1848-1865* (Lincoln: University of Nebraska Press, 1967), 22. See also Fort Bliss Monthly Returns, July 1856, Post Returns, RG94 (M617, roll 116), NARA.

11. Fort Bliss Monthly Returns, July 1856, Post Returns, RG94 (M617, roll 116), NARA and Correspondence from Lt. H.M. Lazelle, Quartermaster, Fort Bliss, Texas, Quartermaster Records, RG 92, Box 87, NARA.

12. "Known by the Bullet Patching—An Incident of a Falcon Hunt in the Fifties—Lieutenant Jackson's Shot," *The Times*, Philadelphia, February 10, 1895.

13. Ibid.

14. "A Night Encounter—Another Reminiscence of the Famous and Unterrified Kit Carson," *The Algona Upper Des Moines*, Algona, Iowa, 11 January 1893, pg. 3.

15. Ibid.

16. Ibid.

17. Utley, *Frontiersmen in Blue*, 155.

18. Frank D. Reeve, "Puritan and Apache: A Diary," *The New Mexico Historical Review* 23, no. 4 (October 1948): 273-74. The December 7, 1857, edition of the *New York Times* also carried a partial account of the Bonneville expedition, "Severe Fights with the Indians: Interesting News from New Mexico—Colonel Bonneville's Late Expedition," available online in the newspaper archives.

19. Ibid.

20. In the October 1948 and January 1949 editions of the *New Mexico Historical Review*, Professor Reeve, then editor, published an annotated

transcription of Lieutenant Henry M. Lazelle's diary. The original of the diary is held in the University of New Mexico Library Archives.

21. Reeve, October 1948, pg. 276.

22. Du Bois's comment reflects the superiority that members of the "mounted infantry" felt over the "regular" infantry.

23. John Van Deusen DuBois, *Campaigns in the West—1856–1861: The Journal and Letters of Colonel John Van Deusen Du Bois* (Tucson: Arizona Historical Society, 1949 and 2003), 6.

24. Lazelle's great-grandson, the author, married one of those hated Roman Catholics and became one himself.

25. For further information on the Know Nothings, see Tyler Anbinder, *Nativism and Slavery: The Northern Know Nothings and the Politics of the 1850s* (New York: Oxford University Press, 1992).

26. Du Bois, 7.

27. Du Bois, 12.

28. In the passage Lazelle was quoting, from 2 Kings in the Old Testament, a watchman announced, "He came even unto them, and comes not back; and the driving is like the driving of Jehu the son of Nimshi; for he drives furiously." This is but one of numerous biblical references throughout his journal, typical of well-educated Protestants.

29. General Orders No. 14, Headquarters of the Army, New York, November 13, 1857, H.M. Lazelle File, 2624 ACP 1874, RG94, NARA; and *The Centennial of the United States Military Academy at West Point, New York. 1802-1902, Volume I, Addresses and Histories* (West Point, NY: United States Military Academy, 1904), 555.

30. Du Bois, 20-30.

31. Ibid., 36.

32. Du Bois, 39.

33. *The Times-Picayune*, New Orleans, December 3, 1857, pg. 1.

34. General Orders No. 5, Headquarters of the Army, New York, November 10, 1859, H. M. Lazelle File 2624 ACP 1874, RG94, NARA.

35. Fort Bliss Monthly Return, January 1859, Post Returns, RG94 (M617, roll 116), NARA. See also Wilhelm's *Synopsis*, 55-60.

36. Sources used in this account: (1) *The Desert Magazine*, January 1949; (2) "History" of Fort Bliss, Fort Bliss website @ www.bliss.army.mil/Garrison/sites/about/history.asp; (3) "Apache Battleground," *New Mexico Magazine*, April 1941; (4) Headquarters of the Army, New York, Nov. 10, 1859, General Orders No. 5, official accounting of the battle (original signed copy—Lazelle Family Papers); (5) Leon Metz, *Desert Army: Fort Bliss on the Texas Border* (El Paso: Mangan Books, 1988), 44-45.

37. Local hiker's description @ www.rozylowicz.com/retirement/dogcanyon/dogcanyon.html.

38. "Message from the President of the United States to the Two Houses of Congress at the Commencement of the First Session of the Thirty-Sixth Congress, December 27, 1859," Serial Set Vol. No. 1024-2, S. Exec. Doc. 2, Pt.2, January 19, 1860, pp. 287-291. (Source: *GenealogyBank.com.*)

39. Ibid.

40. Ibid.

41. *The National Era*, Washington D.C., June 30, 1859.

42. Headquarters of the Army, New York, Nov. 10, 1859, General Orders No. 5. Lazelle Family Papers.

43. Du Bois, 89-90. The two classmates killed were: 2nd Lt. Jesse K. Allen, 28 years old, 9th Infantry, killed by Indians August 15, 1858, in Upper Yakima, Washington; and 2nd Lt. Cornelius Van Camp, 24 years old, 2nd Cavalry, killed by Indians October 1, 1858, at Wichita Village, Texas.

44. A.B. Bender, "Government Explorations in the Territory of New Mexico, 1846-1859," *New Mexico Historical Review* 9 (1934): 30.

45. Fort Bliss Monthly Returns, November 1859–October 1860, Post Returns, RG94 (M617, roll 116); Fort Fillmore Monthly Returns, November 1859–October 1860, Post Returns, RG94 (M617, roll 366); and 8th Infantry Regiment Monthly Returns, November 1859–October 1860, Returns from Regular Army Infantry Regiments, June 1821–December 1916, RG94 (M665, roll 92), NARA.

46. Du Bois, 110.

CHAPTER 3—FROM PRISONER OF WAR TO PRISONER EXCHANGE AGENT

1. Reeve, *The New Mexico Historical Review,* October 1948, p. 295.

2. Undated letter to the Governor and Lieutenant Governor of Massachusetts, signed H.M. Lazelle, Capt. 8th Infantry, U.S. Army, Lazelle Family Papers.

3. Major John T. Sprague, U.S.A., "The Treachery of Texas, the Secession of Texas, and the Arrest of the United States Officers and Soldiers Serving in Texas, Read before the New York Historical Society, June 25, 1861," Press of the Rebellion Record, New York, 1862. Texas History Online @ http://texashistory.unt.edu/ark:/67531/metapth6102/m1/1/.

4. Metz, *Desert Army,* 47.

5. "Reports of Bvt. Lieut. Col. L. V. D. Reeve, Eighth U. S. Infantry, of the surrender of his command at San Lucas Spring, Tex.," Operations in Texas and New Mexico, No. 15, Official Records of the War of the Rebellion (hereafter O.R.), Series I—Vol. 1 (S# 1) Chapter VII, pp. 567-568, NARA. The Official Records are available on-line (and fully searchable) through the Cornell University Library @ http://digital.library.cornell.edu/m/moawar/waro.html.

6. Smith, *Reminiscences of Major General Zenas R. Bliss,* 230-234.

7. Ibid., 237-238.

8. Ibid., 239.

9. Richard B. McCaslin, "United Stated Regulars in Gray: Edward Ingraham and Company A, 1st Regular Confederate Cavalry," *Southwestern Historical Quarterly* 118 (July 2014): 27-31.

10. Ibid., 32.

11. Smith, 250.

12. See Maj. Gary D. Brown, "Prisoner of War Parole: Ancient Concept, Modern Utility," *Military Law Review* 156 (June 1998): 200-223. Brown defines parole as "the agreement of personnel who have been taken prisoner by an enemy that they will not again take up arms against those who captured them, either for a limited time or during the continuance of the war," and traces the practice of paroling captives back to the Carthaginians.

13. The Texas Surrender, Disposition and Negotiations for the Release and Exchange of the Union Prisoners, Confederate Correspondence, letter dated July 30, 1861, O.R., Series II, Volume 1 (S#114), pg. 89.

14. Letters Received by the Office of the Adjutant General Main Series 1861-1870, RG94 (M619, roll 34-35), NARA.

15. The *New York Times*, August 31, 1861, pg. 8

16. Brooks continued to live in the Northeast, became embroiled in questionable business deals and legal problems, and died penniless in Hartford, Connecticut, in 1900.

17. Letters Received by the Office of the Adjutant General Main Series 1861-1870, RG94 (M619, roll 34-35), NARA.

18. Ibid.

19. Correspondence, Orders, Etc., Relating to Prisoners of War and State from February 19, 1861, to June 12, 1862, #8, O.R., Series II, Volume III (S#116), Union pg. 204.

20. The U.S. Coast Survey, established in 1806 as a geodetic survey, conducted topographic and hydrographic surveys and mapping along America's coastlines. It was staffed, in part, with Army and Navy officers. During the Civil War it played an important role, especially in supporting the naval blockade of the Confederate states. For more information see "The U.S. Coast Survey in the Civil War," John Cloud, Ph.D., June 2011, U.S. Department of Commerce, National Oceanic and Atmospheric Administration.

21. Letters Received by the Office of the Adjutant General Main Series 1861-1870, RG94 (M619, roll 112-113), NARA.

22. Special Orders No. 153, War Department, Adjutant General's Office, June 13, 1862, O.R., Series II, Volume IV (S#117), pg. 1: "Capt. H.M. Lazelle, Eighth Infantry, will report for such duty as he can perform to Colonel Hoffman, commissary-general of prisoners, at New York City."

23. "Administrative History," Records of the Commissary General of Prisoners, RG249, NARA @ http://www.archives.gov/research/guide-fed-records/groups/249.html#249.2.

24. Letter, dated March 31, 1866, to Recorder, Board of Adjudication, Lazelle Family Papers.

25. Ohio History Central @ http://www.ohiohistorycentral.org/entry.php?rec=662.

26. Letters Received by the Office of the Adjutant General Main Series 1861-70, RG94 (M-619, roll 112-113), NARA.

27. Ibid.

28. The *New York Times*, January 11, 1862.

29. Union Correspondence, Orders, Etc., Relating to Prisoners of War and State from June 13, 1862, to November 30, 1862, O.R.—Series II, Vol. IV, #17, pp. 266-268.

30. Ibid., pg. 414.

31. Ibid., pp. 419-424.

32. Ibid., pg. 459.

33. O.R.—Series II, Vol. IV, S#117, #17—19.

34. *The Baltimore Sun*, November 13, 1861, pg. 4.

35. The Handbook of Texas Online @ http://www.tshaonline.org/handbook/online/articles/SS/fsp30.html.

36. Letter to Sprague, dated February 10, 1862, H. M. Lazelle File, 2624 ACP 1874, RG94, NARA.

37. Letters Received by the Office of the Adjutant General Main Series 1861-1870, RG94 (M619, roll 112-113), NARA.

38. Ibid.

39. Sykes, then a division commander, had been promoted to major general after the Battle of Antietam. In late June 1863, when Maj. Gen George Meade replaced Joseph Hooker in command of the Army of the Potomac, Sykes took over command of the Corps. However, he had not yet been confirmed by the President when he made his request for Lazelle's services in August.

40. H. M. Lazelle File, 2624 ACP 1874, RG94, NARA.

41. Letters Received by the Office of the Adjutant General Main Series 1861–1870, RG94 (M619, roll 183-184), NARA.

42. H. M. Lazelle File, 2624 ACP 1874, RG94, NARA.

43. Smith et. al., *The Reminiscences of Major General Zenas R. Bliss*, pp. xviii–xix

Chapter 4—Defending Washington

1. H. M. Lazelle File, 2624 ACP 1874, RG94, NARA.

2. "Mustering" was the term used for officially registering soldiers and officers as members of a unit. The term also applied to adding units to the official rolls of the Army.

3. H. M. Lazelle File, 2624 ACP 1874, RG94, NARA.

4. "Saw the Elephant" was a term used by both Confederate and Union troops to describe battle. If you were in a battle (or skirmish), you "saw the elephant."

5. New York State Military Museum and Veterans Research Center web site @ www.dmna.state.ny.us/historic/reghist/civil/cavalry/16thCav/16thCavCWN.htm.

6. The *New York Times*, May 25, 1863, pg. 1.

7. *The Albany Evening Journal*, Albany, N.Y., June 22, 1863, pg. 2.

8. New York State Military Museum and Veterans Research Center @ www.dmna.state.ny.us/historic/reghist/civil/cavalry/16thCav/16thCavCWN.htm.

9. John F. Walter, "Sixteenth New York Cavalry," unpublished monograph, July 1982, revised March 1997. Courtesy of the author.

10. Genealogy website maintained by Rod A. MacDonald, Ed.D., Niagara Falls, Ontario, Canada @ www.r-a-macdonald.ca.

11. Ibid.

12. Ibid.

13. Return of the Cavalry Forces, Defences of Washington South of the Potomac, Dept. of Washington for the Month of October 1863: H. M. Lazelle, Col., 16th Reg't N.Y. Cav, Commanding Camp, Vienna, Va., Records of Named Departments 1821-1920, RG 393.4, NARA.

14. Connie P. Stuntz and Mayo S. Stuntz, *This Was Vienna, Virginia: Facts and Photos* (Vienna, VA: Self-Published, 1987), 117.

15. Stuntz, 119. The Convention was called by the loyal "Restored" state government, meeting in Alexandria, where it adopted a new state constitution that, among other things, abolished slavery.

16. St. John's Parish was founded in the 1700s. The church of brick and stone in which Henry and Rebecca were wed, on the northeast corner of Jonathan Street (now Summit Avenue) and Antietam Street, was finished in 1832 and consecrated two years later by the second Bishop of Maryland. The original sanctuary was destroyed by fire in 1871 and rebuilt in 1872, where it stands today.

17. Letters Received by the Office of the Adjutant General, 1861-1870, RG94 (M619, roll 271-273), NARA.

18. Charles A. Humphries, *Field, Camp, Hospital and Prison in the Civil War, 1863-1865* (Boston: Press of Geo. E. Ellis Co., 1918), 3-4.

19. Stuntz, 95, 123.

20. Stuntz, 123-126.

21. Charles Wells Russell, ed., *The Memoirs of Colonel John S. Mosby* (Boston: Little Brown & Co., 1917). Available online @ http://www.pattonhq.com/militaryworks/mosby.html.

22. Ibid.

23. James J. Williamson, *Mosby's Rangers: A Record of the Operations of the 43d Battalion Virginia Cavalry* (New York: Ralph B. Kenyon, Pub., 1896; repr. Time-Life Books, 1982), 146.

24. Ibid., 147.

25. February 25-26, 1864 Scout from Vienna to Farmwell Station, Va. Report of Maj. Casper Crowninshield, 2nd Mass. Cavalry, O.R. Series I, Volume 51/1 (S#107), pp. 214-215.

26. Williamson, *Mosby's Rangers,* 149.

27. Timothy Swenson, *Charles S. Eigenbrodt, Alvarado Civil War Hero,* Creative Commons, Attribution-Non-Commerical-Share-Alike, 2005, @ www.museumoflocalhistory.org/pages/eigenbrodt.pdf.

28. The Second Mass and Its Fighting Californians web page @ http://2mass.omnica.com/References/ormsby.html.

29. Stuntz, *This Was Vienna,* 119-120 and Miller, *Informal History.*

30. "Roster of the New York Cavalry Regiments During the Civil War," New York State Military Museum and Veterans Research Center @ http://dmna.state.ny.us/historic/reghist/civil/rosters/rosterscavalry.htm.

31. Ibid.

32. Carol Bundy, *The Nature of Sacrifice: A Biography of Charles Russell Lowell, Jr., 1835-64* (New York: Farrar, Straus and Giroux, 2005), 322. For a more complete account of Hollister's transgressions, see Thomas P. Lowry, *Sexual Misbehavior in the Civil War* (Xlibris: Self Published, 2006), 196–200.

33. "New York Civil War Muster Roll Abstracts, 1861-1900," Archive Collections # 13775-83, New York State Archives, Albany, New York (also available on-line @ Ancestry.com).

34. "Roster of the New York Cavalry Regiments During the Civil War," 826. See also *British Medical Journal,* February 25, 1865, pg. 207.

35. "Roster of New York Cavalry Regiments During the Civil War," 900. See also *United States Service Magazine* 2, pg. 498.

36. *United States Service Magazine* 2, p. 396.

37. Ibid., 495.

38. Ibid., 497.

39. Williamson, *Mosby's Rangers,* 110-111.

40. Ibid.

41. Williamson, *Mosby's Rangers,* 116.

42. Thomas J. Evans and James M. Moyer, *Mosby Vignettes, Volume I* (NP: Privately printed, 1993), 80.

43. *Intelligence in the Civil War*, p. 13, Central Intelligence Agency @ www.cia.gov.

44. Ibid., 23.

45. Ibid., 17-18.

46. Williamson, *Mosby's Rangers*, 177.

47. The Second Mass and Its Fighting Californians web page @ http://2mass.omnica.com/References/ParkerLetter.htm

48. "Skirmishes nears Falls Church and Centreville, Va. Reports of Col. Charles R. Lowell, Jr., 2nd Mass Cavalry, Commanding Cavalry Brigade," O.R. Series I, Volume 37/1 (S#70), June 23-24, 1864. pp. 167-169.

49. Fort Buffalo was constructed in 1862 near Falls Church in the area now known as Seven Corners, at the intersection of the current-day Leesburg Pike (Route 7) and Sleepy Hollow Road. Along with Fort Ramsay on the adjacent Upton's Hill, it was one of the area's two "first-class" fortifications with earthworks and gun emplacements. For more information, see Bradley E. Gemand, *A Virginia Village Goes to War: Falls Church During the Civil War* (Virginia Beach, VA: The Donning Company Pub., 2002).

50. "Union Correspondence, Orders, and Returns Relating Specially to Operations in Northern Virginia, West Virginia, Maryland and Pennsylvania, July 1 to August 3, 1864," O.R., Series I, Volume 37/2 (S#71), pp. 387-390.

51. Russell, *Mosby's Memoirs*.

52. Williamson, *Mosby's Rangers*, 204.

53. Ibid., 206-207.

54. O.R. Series I, Volume 43/1 (S#90), pg. 777.

55. Williamson, *Mosby's Rangers,* 218.

56. "August 24, 1864, Skirmish at Annandale, Va., No. 2, Report of Capt. Joseph Schneider, Sixteenth New York Cavalry," O.R. Series I, Volume 43/1 (S#90), pp. 638-639.

57. Russell, *Mosby's Memoirs.*

58. Williamson, *Mosby's Rangers,* 233.

59. "Union Correspondence, Orders, and Returns Relating Specially to Operations in Northern Virginia, West Virginia and Pennsylvania, September 1, 1864, to December 31, 1864, #6," O.R. Series I, Volume 43/2 (S#91), pg. 145.

60. Wells, *Mosby's Memoirs.*

61. "Union Correspondence, Orders, and Returns Relating Specially to Operations in Northern Virginia, West Virginia and Pennsylvania, September 1, 1864, to December 31, 1864, #6," O.R. Series I, Volume 43/2 (S#91), pp. 133-134.

62. Ibid.

63. Ibid.

64. Letter dated April 15, 1866 from Lazelle to Captain Eugene Carter, Recorder, Board of Adjudication, Washington, DC, H.M. Lazelle File, 2624 ACP 1874, RG94, NARA.

65. O.R. Series I, Vol. 43/1 (S#91), pp. 165-166.

66. Ibid., 211.

67. Ibid., 165.

68. "August 9–October 14, 1864, Mosby's Operations. No. 2," O.R. Series I, Volume 43/1 [S#90), pg. 618.

69. Devine, John. E., "Joseph Hancock Blackwell," *News and Notes from The Fauquier Historical Society,* Warrenton, Virginia, Vol. 11, No. 4, Fall, 1989, pp. 1-5.

70. O.R. Series I, Vol. 43/1 (S#91), pg. 178.

71. John Minor Botts, a longtime Whig congressman from Virginia, had opposed secession and, although he refused to fight against Virginia, he remained a staunch Unionist throughout the war. He was jailed briefly for his pro-Union views in 1862 and remained under house arrest in Richmond for several months. Once released, he retired to "Auburn," his family farm in Culpeper County. In his memoirs, Botts vowed that he arrived at Auburn with "a firm determination to stand aside and take no part in a war that the people had no agency in making," and he was known to entertain officers and troops from both sides. While it's not clear that Botts "spied" for the Union side, it is quite possible he passed on information and rumors to Lazelle and other Union officers who passed by.

72. "Union Correspondence, Orders, and Returns Related Specially to Operations in Northern Virginia, West Virginia, Maryland, and Pennsylvania, September 1, 1864 to December 31, 1864, #12," O.R. Series I, Volume 3 43/1 (S#91), pp. 291-292.

73. Scheel, Eugene M., *The Civil War in Fauquier* (Waterford, VA: Self-published, 1985), 79.

74. Ibid.

75. Williamson, *Mosby's Rangers*, 251.

76. "Union Correspondence, Orders, and Returns Related Specially to Operations in Northern Virginia, West Virginia, Maryland, and Pennsylvania, September 1, 1864 to December 31, 1864, #13," O.R. Series I, Volume3 43/1 (S#91), pp. 310 and 319.

77. Ibid.

78. Williamson, *Mosby's* Rangers, 271.

79. Evans and Moyer, *Mosby Vignettes*, 46-51. For an additional account of John Read's death, see Gernand, *A Virginia Village Goes to War*, "Mosby Raids Again; John Read's Tale Concludes," pp. 205-209.

80. Ibid.

81. "Union Correspondence, Orders, and Returns Related Specially to Operations in Northern Virginia, West Virginia, Maryland, and Pennsylvania, September 1, 1864 to December 31, 1864, #17," O.R. Series I, Volume 3 43/1 (S#91), pp. 414-415.

82. H. M. Lazelle File, 2624 ACP 1874, RG94, NARA.

83. Ibid.

84. According to William F. Fox's *Regimental Losses in the American Civil War (1861-1865)*, a substantial number of regiments suffered more than 10 percent killed during the regiment's entire term of service. Of these, however, fewer than half were 15 percent or higher.

85. Sweitzer, according to all accounts, shared little in the immediate glory of Booth's capture, but he was brevetted to Brigadier General of U.S. Volunteers in September 1865 for meritorious service during the war. Following the war, he returned to the regular Army and commanded the 2nd U.S. Cavalry. He retired as a colonel in 1888. Lazelle also retired as a colonel in 1894.

Lazelle's 13th New York Cavalry counterpart, Col. Henry S. Gansevoort, remained with his regiment until the war ended and also was brevetted to the rank of Brigadier General of U.S. Volunteers and lieutenant colonel in the regular Army. Following the war, he returned to duty as an artillery officer, serving at Fort Monroe, Virginia; Fort Barrancas, near Pensacola, Florida; and Fort Independence in Boston. Along the way, he contracted a chronic fever, which eventually claimed his life in 1871.

Colonel Lowell's 2nd Massachusetts went on to serve gallantly in General Sheridan's Shenandoah Valley campaign and in the final battles of the Army of the Potomac, including the Battle of Petersburg and the capture of General Lee's supply trains at Appomattox Station in April 1865. Lowell, however, would not follow his men to Petersburg and Appomattox. He was mortally wounded during the Union counterattack at the Battle of Cedar Creek near Middletown, Virginia, on October 19, 1864.

86. "Col. H.M. Lazelle to Adjutant General of the Army, dated October 18, 1864," Letters Received by the Office of the Adjutant General Main Series 1861-70 (M619, roll 273, L804), NARA.

87. "Halleck to Grant, October 4, 1864," O.R. Vol. 43, Part 2, pp. 272-273.

Chapter 5—The Pride of Mecklenburg County

1. Letter from Bvt. Brig. Gen. William Hoffman, Commissary General of Prisoners, to the Assistant Adjutant General, dated October 31, 1864, Letters Received by the Adjutant General's Office Main Series 1861-70, RG94 (M619, roll 273, H1223), NARA.

2. Special Order No. 10, dated November 10, 1864, War Department Orders 1864-1865, RG107 (M444, roll 8), NARA.

3. H. M. Lazelle File, 2624 ACP 1874, RG94, NARA.

4. War Department, Adjutant General's Office, Special Orders No. 425, paragraph 34, dated December 1, 1864, RG107 (M444, roll 8), NARA.

5. O.R., Dyers Compendium.

6. Special Orders No. 6, Headquarters, Military Division of West Mississippi, New Orleans, dated January 6, 1865, O.R. Series 1, Volume 48/1 (S# 101), pg. 428.

7. Special Orders No. 43, Headquarters, Military Division of West Mississippi, New Orleans, dated February 12, 1865, O.R. Series 1, Volume 48/1 (S# 101), pg. 824.

8. *New York Times*, March 5, 1865.

9. Ronald Craig, "Evolution of the Office of the Provost Marshal General," *Military Police*, April, 2004.

10. "The Provost-Marshal and the Citizen in the American Civil War," Home of the American Civil War website @ http://www.civilwarhome.com/ProvostMarshal.htm.

11. Sefton, James E., *The United States Army and Reconstruction, 1865-1877* (Baton Rouge: Louisiana State University Press, 1967), 7.

12. Family records include only written notes of his assignment and an envelope postmarked June 17, 1865, addressed to Mrs. H. M. Lazelle, care of Lieut. Col. W. H. Wood, Provost Marshal Genl., New Orleans, Louisiana, "via New York." Colonel Wood was the Provost Marshal General under whom Lazelle served.

13. Records of Provost Marshal Field Organizations (Civil War), 1861-70. RG 393.12, NARA.

14. Allan Pinkerton, Chief of the United States Secret Service, *The Spy of the Rebellion: A True History of the Spy System of the United States Army During the Late Rebellion* (New York: G.W. Carlton & Co., 1884).

15. Eighth Infantry Regiment Monthly Return, March 1866, Returns from Regular Army Infantry Regiments (hereafter Regimental Returns), June 1821–December 1916 RG94, (665, roll 93), NARA.

16. Sefton, 25.

17. Craig J. Currey, "The Role of the Army in North Carolina Reconstruction, 1865-1877," Master's Thesis, University of North Carolina at Chapel Hill, 1991, pg. 17.

18. Ibid., 31.

19. Ibid., 29-30.

20. Eighth Infantry Regiment Return, April 1866, Regimental Returns, RG94, (M665, roll 93), NARA.

21. Mark Bradley, *Bluecoats and Tar Heels: Soldiers and Civilians in Reconstruction North Carolina* (Lexington: University Press of Kentucky, 2009), 29.

22. Legett Blythe and Charles R. Brockman, *Hornets' Nest: The Story of Charlotte and Mecklenburg County* (Charlotte, NC: McNally, 1961). (Also available on-line through the Public Library of Charlotte and Mecklenburg County @ http://www.cmstory.org/history/hornets/.)

23. Bradley, 73.

24. Charlotte, NC, Post Report, April 15, 1866, Post Returns, RG94 (M617, roll 201), NARA.

25. Ibid., May 15 and May 31, 1866.

26. Letters Received by the Office of the Adjutant General, Main Series, 1861-1870, RG 94 (M619, roll 491, L440), NARA.

27. Undated, unidentified newspaper clipping, Lazelle Family Papers.

28. Undated newspaper clipping, Lazelle Family Papers.

29. Letters Received by the Office of the Adjutant General, Main Series, 1861-1870, RG94 (M619, roll 558, L2), NARA.

30. Letters Received by the Office of the Adjutant General, Main Series, 1861-1870, RG94 (M619, roll 558, L77), NARA.

31. Ibid.

32. Undated clipping from *The Western Democrat* (identified from partial heading), Lazelle Family Papers.

33. Undated newspaper clipping, Lazelle Family Papers.

34. Ibid.

35. Bradley, *Blue Coats and Tar Heels*, 184.

36. *Anderson Intelligencer*, June 3, 1868, Library of Congress, Chronicling America website @ www.chroniclingamerica.loc.gov.

37. *Anderson Intelligencer*, June 10, 1868.

38. Ibid.

39. Wilhelm, *Synopsis*, 135.

40. H. M. Lazelle File, 2624 ACP 1874, RG94, NARA.

41. *The Washington Post*, April 2, 2012.

42. Letter dated February 6, 1873, to Capt. H. M. Lazelle, 8th U.S. Infantry, Omaha, signed W.T. Sherman, General, Lazelle Family Papers.

43. *The Nation*, Number 419, July 10, 1873, pg. 29.

44. Undated clippings, Lazelle Family Papers.

CHAPTER 6—INDIAN TERRITORY

1. Eighth Infantry Regiment Monthly Return, July, 1872, Regimental Returns, RG94 (M665, roll 93), NARA.

2. For further information, see "Union Pacific History and Chronologies," @ up.com and Jackson Peters, "The Northern Pacific Railway," @ psmre.org.

3. Robert W. Larson, *Red Cloud: Warrior-Statesman of the Lakota Sioux* (Norman: University of Oklahoma Press, 1997), 67.

4. John D. McDermot, "Brule Sioux Chief Spotted Tail," *Wild* West, February, 2006, pg. 12.

5. Larson, 88.

6. Robert M. Utley, *Frontier Regulars: The United States Army and the Indian, 1866-1891* (Lincoln: University of Nebraska Press, 1973), 99.

7. Ibid., 100.

8. Ibid., 102-103.

9. Dee Brown, *The Fetterman Massacre* (Lincoln: University of Nebraska Press, 1962), 170-189.

10. Utley, *Frontier Regulars*, 113-114.

11. Larson, 116-117.

12. Larson, 120ff.

13. At the time, Federal management of local Indian affairs was handled by agents of the Office of Indian Affairs, created by an act of Congress in June 1834. When the Department of the Interior was established in March 1849, the Office of Indian Affairs was transferred to it from the War Department. The compounds (often trading posts) of Federal Indian agents were known as "agencies." Some were named after the chief of the band or nation for which the reservation was established. Others were named for the tribe they served or their physical location.

14. John M. Lubetkin, *Jay Cooke's Gamble: The Northern Pacific Railroad, the Sioux, and the Panic of 1873* (Norman: University of Oklahoma Press, 2006), 80.

15. Eighth Infantry Regiment Monthly Return, July, 1872, Regimental Returns, RG94 (M665, roll 93), NARA.

16. Lubetkin, 121.

17. Eighth Infantry Regiment Monthly Return, August, 1872, Regimental Returns, RG94 (M665, roll 93), NARA.

18. Lubetkin, 123.

19. Lubetkin, 149-150, and Eighth Infantry Monthly Returns, August–October 1872, Regimental Returns, RG94 (M665, roll 93), NARA.

20. Eighth Infantry Monthly Returns, August–October 1872, Regimental Returns, RG94 (M665, roll 93), NARA.

21. Meanwhile, the 8th Infantry's Headquarters, band, and two companies had relocated to Fort D. A. Russell, Wyoming Territory, three miles northwest of Cheyenne on the Union Pacific Railroad line. Three other companies were stationed at Beaver, Utah, one of a string of Mormon settlements established in the 1850s. The rest of the regiment remained officially stationed at Omaha Barracks.

22. *New York Times*, July 17, 1873. See also Richard W. Stewart, ed., *American Military History, Volume 1: The United States Army and the Forging of a Nation, 1775-1917* (Washington, DC: Center of Military History, 2005), 335.

23. Eighth Infantry Monthly Returns, May–October 1873, Regimental Returns, RG94 (M665, roll 93), NARA.

24. "Fifth Annual Report of the Board of Indian Commissioners to the President of the United States, 1873," Government Printing Office, 1874, pg. 163.

25. Lubetkin, 175.

26. Ibid.

27. Eighth Infantry Regiment Monthly Return, July 1873, Regimental Returns, RG94 (M665, roll 93), NARA; Lubetkin, 189.

28. Lubetkin, 192.

29. Eighth Infantry Regiment Monthly Return, August 1873 Regimental Returns, RG94 (M665, roll 93), NARA; Lubetkin, 256-264.

30. Eighth Infantry Regiment Monthly Returns, September–October 1873, Regimental Returns, RG94 (M665, roll 93), NARA.

31. Lubetkin, 193.

32. Larson, 156-157.

33. Thomas Wilhelm, *Memorandum from The Adjutant's Office, 8th Infantry*, n.p., 1875 (in the collection of the U.S. Army Military History Institute, Carlisle, PA), pp. 8-9. Also, Eighth Infantry Regiment Monthly Return, February, 1874, Regimental Returns, RG94 (M665, roll 94), NARA.

34. Eighth Infantry Regiment Monthly Return, March, 1874, Regimental Returns, RG94 (M665, roll 94), NARA. In March 1874, Washington authorized the establishment of a military camp at the Red Cloud Agency, to be named Camp Robinson.

35. *New York Herald*, April 16, 1874.

36. "Report of the Sioux Commission," Papers Accompanying the Annual Report of the Commissioner of Indian Affairs to the Secretary of the Interior for the Year 1874, Government Printing Office, Washington, 1874, pp. 87-97. (University of Wisconsin Library @ http://images.library.wisc.edu/History/EFacs/CommRep/AnnRep74/reference/history.annrep74.i0008.pdf.)

37. Letter, postmarked April 6, 1874, Camp at Spotted Tail's Agency, to General John E. Smith, U.S.A., Commanding Sioux Expedition, Camp Robinson, Red Cloud Agency, Letters Received by the Office of the Adjutant General, Main Series, 1871-1880. RG94 (M666, roll 149), NARA.

38. "Report of the Sioux Commission," 87-97.

39. Eighth Infantry Regiment Monthly Returns, May–June, 1874, Regimental Returns, RG94 (M665, roll 94), NARA.

40. Ray Brandes, *Frontier Military Posts of Arizona* (Globe, AZ: D.S. King, 1960), 81-83.

41. Martha Summerhayes, *Vanished Arizona: Recollections of the Army Life of a New England Woman* (Salem, MA: The Salem Press, 1911), 32-45.

42. Written notes prepared by Horace Lazelle, and oral history prepared by his daughter, Barbara Lazelle, Lazelle Family Papers.

43. First Infantry Regiment Monthly Return, June, 1875, Regimental Returns, RG94 (M665, roll 7), NARA.

44. Harold H. Schuler, *Fort Sully: Guns at Sunset* (Vermillion: University of South Dakota Press, 1992), 54.

45. Written notes prepared by Horace Lazelle, and oral history prepared by his daughter, Barbara Lazelle, Lazelle Family Papers.

46. First Infantry Regiment Monthly Returns, June–August 1876, Regimental Returns, RG94 (M665, roll 7), NARA.

47. Utley, *Frontier Regulars*, 244–245.

48. *Report of the Secretary of War—Being Part of the Message and Documents Communicated to the Two Houses of Congress at the Beginning of the Second Session of the Forty-Fifth Congress, Volume I* (Washington, DC: Government Printing Office, 1877), 565-566, (hereafter *Report of the Secretary of War, 1877*).

49. Letters Received by the Office of the Adjutant General Main Series 1871-1880, RG94 (M666, roll 307, file 6154), NARA.

50. In a proclamation, dated August 3, 1891, the City Council of Fargo acknowledged receipt of the sketch from Col. H. M. Lazelle, noting that it was believed to be "the only drawing in existence of the first house erected on the site of the present City of Fargo." Lazelle Family Papers.

51. Robert Wooster, *Nelson A. Miles and the Twilight of the Frontier Army* (Lincoln: University of Nebraska Press, 1993), 81.

52. *Report of the Secretary of War, 1877*, 487.

53. Theophilus F. Rodenbough and William L. Haskin, eds., *The Army of the United States, Historical Sketches of Staff and Line with Portraits of Generals-in-Chief*, "The Fifth Regiment of Infantry" (New York: Maynard, Merrill & Co., 1896), 475-476. See also: Fifth Infantry Regiment Monthly Return, November 1876, Regimental Returns, RG94 (M665, roll 58), NARA.

54. *Report of the Secretary of War, 1877*, 55.

55. Ibid., 498-499.

56. Ibid., 499.

57. First Infantry Regiment Monthly Returns, April–May, 1877, Regimental Returns, RG94 (M665, roll 7), NARA.

58. *Report of the Secretary of War, 1877*, 499.

59. Ibid., 543.

60. Ibid., 574 and First Infantry Regiment Monthly Returns, June–July 1877, Regimental Returns, RG94 (M665, roll 7), NARA.

61. *Report of the Secretary of War, 1877,* 574.

62. Ibid., 575.

63. Letters Received by the Office of the Adjutant General, Main Series, 1871-1880, RG94 (M666, roll 334, file 3241), NARA.

64. *The Bismarck Tribune,* June 29 and July 6, 1877.

65. Letters Received by the Office of the Adjutant General, Main Series, 1871-1880, RG94 (M666, roll 334, file 3241), NARA.

66. First Infantry Regiment Monthly Returns, September–December 1877, Regimental Returns, RG94 (M665, roll 7), NARA.

67. Robert Lee, *Fort Meade and the Black Hills* (Lincoln: University of Nebraska Press, 1991), 4-17. Lee provides a detailed account of the events and politics that drove the decisions on establishing and locating the fort.

68. Lee, 23–30; First Infantry Regiment Monthly Returns, July–August, 1878, Regimental Returns, RG94 (M665, roll 7), NARA.

69. Hand-written notes prepared by Horace G. Lazelle and oral history taken by Barbara Lazelle, Lazelle Family Papers.

70. Letters Received by the Office of the Adjutant General, Main Series, 1871-1880, RG94 (M666, roll 446, file 8086), NARA.

71. Lee, *Fort Meade and the Black Hills,* 42.

72. *New York Times,* April 2, 1880.

73. First Infantry Regiment Monthly Returns, May-June 1879, Regimental Returns, RG94 (M665, roll7), NARA.

74. The Correspondence of James McNeill Whistler, University of Glasgow Library, MS Whistler L34.

75. Flemming, *Whistler: A Life,* 168-175.

CHAPTER 7—WEST POINT—A NEW BATTLEGROUND

1. According to 1880 Census records, two Irish maids, Henrietta Denye (aged 18) and Katty Lynch (aged 21) also lived with them at West Point.

2. A grand-nephew of Napoleon Bonaparte.

3. John McAllister Schofield, *Forty-Six Years in the Army* (New York: The Century Co., 1897), 7-8.

4. Ibid., 6.

5. Ibid., 10-13.

6. Thomas J. Fleming, *West Point: The Men and Times of the United States Military Academy* (New York: William Morrow and Co., 1969), 246.

7. "Directive to the Commandant of Cadets," dated August 27, 1878, John McAllister Schofield Papers (hereafter Schofield Papers), Box 50: "John M. Schofield, Letters Sent, US Military Academy, West Point, 1877-1881 (Letters Sent, March 3, 1877–January 18, 1881, USMA, West Point—Also: Letters Received, 1871 from W.T Sherman), pp. 54-55, Library of Congress, Manuscript Division.

8. July 12, 1879, Letter to the Adjutant General; "Special Orders No. 172," Headquarters of the Army Adjutant General's Office, July 25, 1879; Letter to the Adjutant General, July 28, 1879, pp. 84-117, Schofield Papers, Letters Sent, March 3, 1877–January 18, 1881.

9. Ibid., 91-96.

10. "Annual Report, Department of West Point, United States Military Academy, for the Year 1880, West Point, N.Y., October 5, 1880," Box 93, Schofield Papers.

11. Fleming, 246.

12. Fleming, 245.

13. Ibid.

14. Headquarters, U.S. Corps of Cadets, West Point, N.Y., January 3, 1880, Special Orders No. 1, USMA Archives.

15. George W. Cullum, *Biographic Register of the Officers and Graduates of the U.S. Military Academy,* 3rd ed., vol. 3 (Boston: Houghton, Mifflin & Co., 1891), 328-341.

16. April 11, 1880, letter to General of the Army William T. Sherman, Letters Sent, USMA, March 7 –November 29, 1880, pp. 43-45, Box 50, Schofield Papers.

17. The "calls" were a collection of specific drum rolls, done at specific times during the day to announce events, such as meals and formations.

18. Memorandum from Lazelle to the Adjutant General, USMA, September 10, 1880. Records of the Adjutant General's Office, 1780s-1917, Records Relating to the U.S. Military Academy, RG 94.2.6, NARA.

19. Robert Cowley, and Thomas Guinzburg, eds., *West Point: Two Centuries of Honor and Tradition* (New York: Warner Books, 2002), 119. See also, Charles M. Robinson III, *The Fall of a Black Army Officer: Racism and the Myth of Henry O. Flipper* (Norman: University of Oklahoma Press, 2008), 4.

20. "Annual Report, Department of West Point, United States Military Academy, for The Year 1880, Major General J. M. Schofield, U.S. Army, Commanding, West Point, N.Y., October 5, 1880," Schofield Papers, Box 50.

21. Albert E. Williams, *Black Warriors: Unique Units and Individuals* (West Conshohocken, PA: Infinity Publishing, 2003), 18.

22. Ibid., 19. See also: Selected Documents Related to Blacks Nominated for Appointment to the US Military Academy During the 19th Century, 1870-1887, Vol. 21, Record Groups 94, 107 and 153 (Hereafter, "Selected Documents") (M1002, roll 1), NARA.

23. *Hartford Daily Courant*, "Letter from Colored Cadet Smith," July 2, 1870, pg. 2.

24. War Department, Office of the Superintendent of the Military Academy, Orders No. 12, August 11, 1870, Selected Documents (M1002, roll 1), NARA.

25. General Court Martial Orders No. 52, War Department, Adjutant General's Office, November 14, 1870, Selected Documents (M1002, roll 1), NARA.

26. Judge Advocate General Letter to the Secretary of War, dated November 20, 1870, Selected Documents (M1002, roll 1), NARA.

27. Special Orders No. 385, War Department, Adjutant General's Office, Washington, December 31, 1870, Selected Documents (M1002, roll 1), NARA.

28. "The Colored Cadet: Smith Again in Trouble—Another Trial on New Charges—A Plot to Disgrace Him—Organized Persecution on the Part of His Associates," *New York Times*, January 5, 1871.

29. Ibid.

30. "White Paper: The United States Military Academy, Cadet Honor Code and Honor System," William E. Simon Center for the Professional Military Ethic, West Point, New York, February 10, 2000.

31. James Webster Smith, January 1871 Court Martial Record, pg. 108, Selected Documents (M1002, roll 1), NARA.

32. General Court Martial Orders No. 8, War Department, Adjutant General's Office, Washington, June 13, 1871, Selected Documents (M1002, roll 1), NARA.

33. General Orders No. 8, War Department, June 26, 1874, Selected Documents (M1002, roll 1), NARA.

34. Williams, *Black Warriors,* 21-22.

35. For detailed background on Whittaker, see John F. Marszalek, *Assault at West Point: The Court-Martial of Johnson Whittaker* (New York: Collier Books, Macmillan Publishing Co., 1994), 1-43.

36. Letter from General Schofield to the Adjutant General, dated January 15, 1879, Selected Documents (M1002, roll 3), NARA.

37. *New York Times*, April 7, 1880.

38. Ibid.

39. Ibid.

40. Correspondence Accompanying the Proceedings of the General Court-Martial of Cadet Whittaker, 1881-1903, Letter from the Secretary of War to Colonel Thomas F. Barr, Judge Advocate, U.S. Army, dated April 8, 1880, Selected Documents (M1002, roll 20), NARA.

41. Proceedings of the General Court Martial of Johnson C. Whittaker, USMA, Records of the Judge Advocate, RG 153, QQ1858, (Hereafter, "Proceedings."), Part XI, Appendix, pp. 1820-1824. Selected Documents (M1002, roll 7), NARA.

42. Ibid., 2825-2829.

43. Schofield Testimony, April 17, 1880, Proceedings, Part III, pp. 640-646. Selected Documents (M1002, roll 7), NARA.

44. Marszalek, 84.

45. Lazelle Testimony, April 16, 1880, Proceedings, Part III, pg. 580, Selected Documents (M1002, roll 7), NARA.

46. Lazelle Testimony, April 16, 1880, Proceedings, Part III, pp. 549-614, Selected Documents (M1002, roll 7), NARA.

47. Schofield Testimony, April 27, 1880, Proceedings, Part VIII, pg. 2032, Selected Documents (M1002, roll 6), NARA.

48. General Orders No. 14, Headquarters, Department of West Point, United States Military Academy, West Point, N.Y., April 21, 1880, Selected Documents (M1002, roll 3), NARA.

49. Report and Opinion of the Court of Inquiry, May 29, 1880, Proceedings, Part X, pp. 2812-2813, Selected Documents (M1002, roll 7), NARA.

50. Letter from General Schofield to the Adjutant General, U.S. Army, dated June 4, 1880, Selected Documents (M1002, roll 3), NARA.

51. Peter S. Michie, "Caste at West Point," *North American Review*, June 1880, pp. 116-118.

52. *New York Times*, June 25, 1880.

53. Adjutant General Memorandum, June 25, 1880, Selected Documents (M1002, roll 3), NARA.

54. *New York Times*, July 17, 1880.

55. *New York Times*, August 18, 1880.

56. Dillard, 213.

57. August 11, 1880, letter to General of the Army William T. Sherman, Box 50, Letters Sent, USMA, March 7 –November 29, 1880, Box 50, pp. 187-200, Schofield Papers.

58. Memorandum from Headquarters, U. S. Corps of Cadets, West Point, N.Y., dated August 29, 1880, to the Adjutant U.S. Military Academy, West Point, N.Y. USMA Archives.

59. Headquarters of the Army, Adjutant General's Office, Special Orders No. 278, December 31, 1880, Selected Documents (M1002, roll 8), NARA.

60. Marszalek, 165-167.

61. Letter to General Sherman, July 31, 1880, Letters Sent, USMA, March 7–November 29, 1880, pp. 178-182, Schofield Papers.

62. Court-Martial Proceedings, Part III, pp. 120-137, Selected Documents (M1002, roll 8), NARA.

63. Ibid., 158-159.

64. Ibid., 227-228.

65. *New York Times*, February 16, 1881.

66. Court-Martial Proceedings, Part X, pp. 852-869, Selected Documents (M1002, roll 9), NARA.

67. Ibid., 877-978.

68. Ibid., 961-962 and 972-973.

69. Marszalek, 219-240.

70. *New York Times*, June 17, 1881.

71. Correspondence Accompanying the Proceedings of the General Court-Martial of Cadet Whittaker, 1881-1903. War Department, Bureau Military Justice, Memorandum for the Secretary of War from the Judge Advocate General, dated December 1, 1881, Selected Documents (M1002, roll 20), NARA.

72. Ibid.

73. Correspondence Accompanying the Proceedings of the General Court-Martial of Cadet Whittaker, 1881-1903. Letter from Secretary of War Robert T. Lincoln to Attorney General Benjamin Harris Brewster, dated March 6, 1882; Letter from Attorney General Benjamin Harris Brewster to Secretary of War Robert T. Lincoln, dated March 17, 1882, Selected Documents (M1002, roll 20), NARA.

74. Correspondence Accompanying the Proceedings of the General Court-Martial of Cadet Whittaker, 1881-1903. Executive Mansion Order, dated March 21, 1882, signed by Chester A. Arthur; and Headquarters of the Army, Adjutant General's Office, General Court Martial Orders No. 18, dated March 22, 1882, Selected Documents (M1002, roll 20), NARA.

Chapter 8—A New Challenge—General Howard Takes Command

1. At Chancellorsville in May 1863, he had earned the nickname "Oh-Oh Howard." Despite warnings from General Joseph Hooker, he allowed the right flank of the Union line where his corps was positioned to remain

exposed and thus vulnerable to General Stonewall Jackson's famous attack. Howard was again criticized when his corps was routed on July 1, 1863, at Gettysburg.

2. Oliver Otis Howard, *Autobiography of Oliver Otis Howard, Major General, United States Army*, (New York: Baker & Taylor, 1908), 2: 487-490.

3. *New York Times*, December 27, 1880.

4. Oliver Otis Howard, *Autobiography of Oliver Otis Howard, Major General, United States Army* (New York: Baker & Taylor, 1907), 1: 50-55.

5. Howard, vol. 2, 486.

6. Ibid., 489-490.

7. "Oliver Otis Howard Papers: 1833-1912," M91.4, Box 15, Bowdoin College Library, Brunswick, Maine.

8. Howard, *Autobiography*, vol. 2, 489-491.

9. "Annual Report of the Board of Visitors to the United States Military Academy, made to the Secretary of War, for the Year 1881," Washington, Government Printing Office, 1881, pp. 4-5. Available online at the USMA digital archives @ http://digital-library.usma.edu.

10. *The Stevens Point Journal*, Stevens Point, Wisconsin, December 22, 1906.

11. Oliver Otis Howard Papers, Box 15.

12. Letters Received by the Adjutant General, No. 1190 and 1192, August 30, 1881, No. 1251, September 2, 1881, USMA Archives.

13. Letters Received by the Adjutant General's Office Main Series 1881-1889, RG94 (M-689, roll 51, item 5553), NARA.

14. Stephen E. Ambrose, *Upton and the Army* (Baton Rouge: Louisiana State University Press, 1964), 22.

15. Ibid., 33.

16. Ibid., 61.

17. David J. Fitzpatrick, "Emory Upton and the Army of a Democracy," *The Journal of Military History* 77 (April 2013): 463-464. Also see Fitzpatrick's earlier discussion of Upton's studies of military organizational reforms in the armies of Asia and Europe, "Emory Upton and the Citizen Solider," *The Journal of Military History* 65 (April 2001): 355-383.

18. *The Army and Navy Journal*, November 26, 1881, pp. 359-360.

19. *The Army and Navy Journal*, November 16, 1878, pg. 234.

20. *The Army and Navy Journal*, November 26, 1881, pg. 363.

21. Perry D. Jamieson, *Crossing the Deadly Ground: United States Army Tactics 1865-1899* (Tuscaloosa: The University of Alabama Press, 1994), 73.

22. Ibid., 93.

23. The Military Service Institution of the United States, modeled on Great Britain's Royal United Services Institute, was founded in September 1878 for the purpose of "professional unity and improvement by correspondence, discussion, the reading and publication of papers, the ultimate establishment of a military library and museum, and generally the promotion of the military interests of the United States." *New York Times*, September 29, 1878.

24. *Journal of the Military Service Institution of the United States* 3, no. 9 (1882): 374-375, U.S. Army Military History Institute, Carlisle Barracks.

25. Ibid., 343-373.

26. Ibid., 375.

27. *The Army and Navy Journal*, undated clipping, Lazelle Family Papers. A later edition of the *Journal* noted that the essay had received "extended notice by the public press, and all the journals commend its excellence and thoroughness."

28. *New York Times*, December 23, 1882.

29. Letter dated April 28, 1882 to the Adjutant General, U.S. Army, through Headquarters, U.S. Military Academy, from H. M. Lazelle, Lieut. Colonel, US Army, Commanding Corps of Cadets. War Department, May 2, 1882, Letters Received by the Office of the Adjutant General Main Series 1881-1889, RG94 (M689, roll 77, file 394), NARA.

30. Ibid.

31. *New York Times*, "Revels at West Point," June 10, 1882.

32. *Army and Navy Journal* 20 (August 5, 1882–July 28, 1883), September 9, 1882, pg. 125.

33. Correspondence from Headquarters, U.S. Corps Cadets, West Point, N.Y., Commandant Cadets, H. M. Lazelle, Lieut. Colonel, dated July 3, 1882, Letters Received by the Office of the Adjutant General Main Series 1881-1889, RG94 (M689, roll 82, file 679), NARA.

34. Ibid.

35. Ibid.

36. Letter dated July 20, 1882, from Lazelle to the Adjutant General, RG94, Lazelle File, 2624 ACP 1874, NARA.

37. Letter dated July 22, 1882, from Lazelle to the Adjutant General, RG94, Lazelle File, 2624 ACP 1874, NARA.

38. "Oliver Otis Howard Papers," Box 16.

39. West Point/Military Academy Post Return, January 1881–December 1890, Post Returns, RG94 (M617, roll 1417), NARA.

Chapter 9—First to Purgatory, Then to India

1. He had been promoted into the position in June 1881.

2. *Fort Craig: 1854-1885*, Bureau of Land Management, U.S. Department of the Interior, Washington DC. Today, the ruins of the fort are preserved at the Fort Craig National Historic Site.

3. Marion Cox Grinstead, "Back at the Fort," *Fort Craig: The United States Fort on the Camino Real—Collected Papers of the First Fort Craig Conference*, U.S. Department of the Interior, Bureau of Land Management, 2000, pp. 28-31.

4. *Las Vegas [New Mexico] Daily Gazette*, March 23, 1883, pg. 4.

5. Darlis A. Miller, *Captain Jack Crawford: Buckskin Poet, Scout, and Showman* (Albuquerque: University of New Mexico Press, 1993), 17-65. See also, *Black Hills Visitor Magazine*, Winter 2011 @ http://blackhillsvisitor.com.

6. Miller, 74-77.

7. Miller, 89-94. See also, "Western Poet-Scout Was a Picturesque Character," *Deadwood Magazine*, Black Hills, South Dakota, Sept-Oct, 1998 @ www.deadwoodmagazine.com/archivedsite/Archives/CaptJack.htm

8. Letter from Capt. Jack Crawford to Horace G. Lazelle, December 18, 1911, Lazelle Family Papers. One of the enclosures was a pamphlet titled "Souvenir of The Camp Fire Club, Buckskin Night, December 4, '09, at Hotel Astor, New York," with a reprint of several of his poems.

9. Henry M. Lazelle File, USMA Archives. Howard was commanding the Department of the Platte.

10. Undated, unattributed news clipping, Lazelle Family Papers.

11. "Report to the Secretary of the Inspector-General," September 17, 1885, Annual Report of the Secretary of War to Congress, Serial Set Vol. No. 2369, H. Exec.Doc. 1 pt. 2, v. 1, January 1, 1886. Library of Congress.

12. Ibid.

13. Ibid.

14. Adjutant General to Lieut. Colonel Henry M. Lazelle, November 25, 1885, Letters Received by the Office of the Adjutant General Main Series 1881-1889, RG94 (M689, roll 398, file 6832), NARA.

15. Undated, unattributed transcription of newspaper article, Lazelle Family Papers.

16. Lord Roberts of Kandahar, V.C., *Forty-One Years in India from Subaltern to Commander-in-Chief* (London: Richard Bentley & Son, 1898), Chap. 64. Also available at Complete Books, Academy of the Punjab in North America web site @ http://www.apnaorg.com/books/fortyone-years/.

17. Lieut. Colonel Henry M. Lazelle, "India," *Journal of the Military Service Institution of the United States* 9, pp. 355-384.

18. Parsees were adherents of a pre-Islamic, monotheistic religion, also known as Zoroastrianism, founded by a Persian prophet in the 6th century BC. They were driven out of Persia by the Muslims in the 8th century AD, and many ended up in India.

19. Sir Edwin Arnold, M.A., *India Revisited* (London: Trubner & Co., 1886), 179-180. Also available from Googlebooks.

20. According to historians at Britain's National Army Museum, "Army pegs" probably were either brandy and soda water or whisky and soda. In India, such drinks also were known as "chota pegs."

21. *The Ipswich Journal,* January 23, 1886; *The Glasgow Herald,* January 22, 1886.

22. Lazelle, "India," *Journal of the Military Service Institution of the United States.*

23. Lt. Col. Henry M. Lazelle, "The Strengths and Weaknesses of England in India," *Journal of the Military Service Institution of the United States* 8 (1887): 247-258. Copies of both of his reports were requested by the House of Representatives: House of Representatives, 49th Congress, 1st Session, Mis. Doc. No. 345 and No. 363. Library of Congress.

24. Headquarters, Department of the Columbia, Office Acting Inspector General, Vancouver Barracks, W.T., to the Adjutant General, U.S. Army, Washington, D.C., March 31, 1886, Letters Received by the Office of

the Adjutant General Main Series 1881-1889, RG94 (M689, roll 495, file 6832), NARA.

Chapter 10—Back to Washington and Controversy

1. *The Morning Oregonian*, Portland, Oregon, October 3, 1886, pg. 3.

2. Harold E. Mahan, "The Arsenal of History: The Official Records of The War of the Rebellion," *Civil War History* (Kent State University Press), 29, no. 1, pg. 10.

3. O.R., Series I, Volume 37/1 (S#70), Preface.

4. Mahan, 12-18.

5. *The Chicago Daily Tribune*, March 12, 1887, pg. 2 and March 19, pg. 4.

6. *The Evening Star*, Washington, D.C., April 2, 1887, pg. 1 and April 19, pg. 3.

7. Telegram, datelined Vancouver Barracks, April 23, 1887, to General R. O. Drum, Adjutant General, U.S. Army, RG 94, H.M. Lazelle File, 2624 ACP 1874.

8. *The Chicago Daily Tribune*, April 30, 1887, pg. 7.

9. Letters Received by the Appointment Commission and Personal Branch, Adjutant General's Office, 1871-1894. Special Orders No. 105, Headquarters of the Army, Adjutant General's Office, dated May 7, 1887, RG94 (Microfiche 1395), NARA.

10. *The Morning Oregonian*, Portland, Oregon, May 29, pg. 3 and June 7, 1887, pg. 3. Available at Newspapers.com.

11. Alyn Brodsky, *Grover Cleveland: A Study in Character* (New York: St. Martin's Press, 2000), 75.

12. Henry F. Graff, *Grover Cleveland: The American Presidents Series*, Times Books (New York: Henry Holt and Co., 2002), 68.

13. Records of the War Records Office of the War Department, Letters Received, 1877-1894 (hereafter WRO Letters Received), RG 94.13, Entry 710, Box 8, Item 143, NARA.

14. *The Cincinnati Commercial Gazette,* December 26, 1887, pg. 4.

15. WRO Letters Sent, Entry 708, Book 6, pp. 55-56 and 63; and Records of the War Records Office of the War Department, Letters Received, Entry 710, Box 8, Item 221, NARA.

16. *New York Times*, December 31, 1887, pg. 5.

17. *New York Times*, April 4, 1888, pg. 4

18. Mis. Doc. No. 54, December 18, 1887; and Ex. Doc. No. 155, February 14, 1888, U.S. House of Representatives, 50th Congress, 1st Session.

19. Ex. Doc. No. 155, February 14, 1888, pg. 4, U.S. House of Representatives, 50th Congress, 1st Session.

20. Report No. 4153, *Records of the Rebellion,* February 28, 1889 (hereafter House Report 4153), pg. 25, U.S. House of Representatives, 50th Congress, 2nd Session.

21. House Report 4153, pg. 1. See also Ex. Doc. No. 155, "War Records, Letter from the Secretary of War," U.S. House of Representatives, 50th Congress, 1st Session.

22. House Report 4153, pp. 31-34.

23. WRO Letters Received, Entry 710, Box 8, Item 143.

24. House Report 4153, pg. 6.

25. *Cincinnati Commercial Gazette,* March 1, 1888, pg. 1.

26. Ibid.

27. *The Boston Daily Globe,* July 28, 1888, pg. 3.

28. 50 Cong. Rec. H2026 (March 13, 1888).

29. House Report 4153, pg. 39.

30. House Report 4153, pp. 5-10.

31. Ibid., 10-15 and 25-26

32. Ibid., 31.

33. *The Washington Post*, April 6, 1888, pg. 2.

34. House Report 4153, pp. 38-40

35. *The Washington Post*, April 28, 1888, pg. 5; see also House Report 4253, pp. 50-51.

36. *The Washington Post*, May 1, 1888, pg. 2.

37. House Report 4153, pp. 446-47.

38. Mis. Doc. No. 356, House of Representatives, 50th Congress, 1st Session.

39. WRO Letters Received, Entry 710, Box 8, Item 338.

40. *New York Times*, July 4, 1888.

41. WRO Letters Sent, Book 7, pg. 29. While many regard Lee's surrender at Appomattox Court House on April 9, 1865 as the end of the war, it was not until August 20, 1866, that President Andrew Johnson issued "Proclamation 157—Declaring that Peace, Order, Tranquility, and Civil Authority Now Exists in and Throughout the Whole of the United States of America." The America Presidency Project, University of California at Santa Barbara @ http://www.presidency.ucsb.edu/ws/?pid=71992.

42. Letter to the Secretary of War, December 4, 1888, WRO Letters Sent, Book 7, pp. 114-118.

43. Report to Accompany Bill H. R. 12008, February 14, 1889, (S. Rep. 2-8) Committee on Appropriations, Sundry Civil Appropriations. Serial Set Vol. No. 2619, S. Rpt. 2613.

44. Ibid., 94.

45. Ibid., 97.

46. Ibid., 101.

47. Letter to the Secretary of War, March 5, 1889, pp. 190-191, WRO Letters Sent, Book 7.

48. House Report 4153, pg. 4.

49. WRO Letters Received, Entry 710, Box 8, Item 487.

50. *The Washington Post*, May 7, 1889, pg. 1.

51. Barrows Family Papers (MS Am 1807-1807.5). Houghton Library, Harvard University.

52. Ibid.

53. Ibid.

54. Letters Received by the Adjutant General's Office, Main Series, 1881-1889, RG94 (M689, roll 716, file 5432), NARA.

55. Letter from Col. H. M. Lazelle, dated October 20, 1889, to the Adjutant General, U. S. Army, RG94, Lazelle File, 2624 ACP 1874.

56. Letter to General J. C. Kelton, Adjutant General, U. S. Army, postmarked Fort Clark, Texas, dated October 20, 1889, Letters Received by the Appointment Commission and Personal Branch, Adjutant General's Office, 1871-1894, RG94 (Microfiche No. 1395), NARA.

CHAPTER 11—FORT CLARK, THE 18TH INFANTRY AND RETIREMENT

1. *1873 Infantry Barracks, Fort Clark, Texas*, undated pamphlet, Kinney County Historical Commission, Brackettville, Texas.

2. R.B. Marcy, Inspector General, *Posts and Stations of Troops in the Geographical Divisions and Departments of the United States* (Washington, DC: Government Printing Office, 1872), 177.

3. R. Christopher Goodwin and Associates, *National Historic Context for Department of Defense Installations, 1790-1940, Volume II*, Prepared for the U. S. Army Corps of Engineers, Baltimore District, August 1995, pp. 372 and 395.

4. *Narrative History of the Commanding Officer's Quarters (Wainwright House)*, Fort Clark Historical Society, 1963. Courtesy of William F. Haenn, Lt. Col., US Army (Ret.).

5. *Regulations for the Army of the United States—1889* (Washington, DC: U. S. War Department, Government Printing Office, 1889), 124.

6. Letters Received by the Adjutant General's Office, Main Series, 1881-1889, RG94 (M689, roll 716, file 5432), NARA.

7. *The Kansas City Times*, Kansas City, Missouri, December 13, 1889, pg. 6

8. In August 1872, a group of "Seminole-Negroes," formed into the Seminole-Negro Indian Scout Detachment, moved from Fort Duncan at Eagle Pass to a settlement two miles south of Fort Clark along Las Moras Creek. These Seminole-Negroes were descendants of freed or escaped slaves taken in by the Seminole Indian tribe in Spanish Florida and had made their way into Texas from the Oklahoma Indian territory in 1850. (*Seminole-Negro Indian Scout Camp, Fort Clark, Texas*, Kinney County Historical Commission, 2007.)

9. Fort Clark Post Returns, January–December 1890, Post Returns, RG94 (M617, roll 215) and 18th Infantry Regiment Monthly Returns, January–December 1890, Regimental Returns, RG94 (M665, roll 196), NARA.

10. Edward M. Coffman, *The Old Army: A Portrait of the American Army in Peacetime, 1784-1898* (New York: Oxford University Press, 1986), 281.

11. *The Times-Picayune*, New Orleans, December, 22, 1890, pg. 2.

12. *The Kansas City Times*, Kansas City, Missouri, January 20, 1891, pg. 6.

13. Coffman, 350 and 360.

14. *Regulations for the Army of the United States—1889* (Washington, DC: Government Printing Office, 1889), 33.

15. Coffman, 374.

16. Col. Lazelle would eventually establish Minneapolis and the West Hotel as his initial official residence when he retired on disability in 1894.

17. Letter to the Adjutant General, U. S. Army, postmarked Fort Clark, Texas, October 4, 1891, RG94, Lazelle File, 2624 ACP 1874.

18. "The Handbook of Texas History Online," Texas State Historical Association, website @ http://www.tshaonline.org/handbook/online/articles/jcgwk.

19. Ibid.

20. 18th Infantry Regiment Monthly Return, December 1891, Regimental Returns, RG94, (665, roll 196), NARA.

21. *The Christian Register*, February 25, 1892, 125-126. Lazelle Family Papers. It is not uncommon for military history buffs to complain about the poor quality or complete lack of maps in military histories, most often, especially today, the victims of cost-cutting by editors and publishers.

22. Medical Certificate to Accompany Application for Leave of Absence, dated May 4, 1892, Letters Received by the Appointment Commission and Personal Branch, Adjutant General's Office, 1871-1894, RG94 (Microfiche No. 1395), NARA.

23. *New York Times*, June 7 and June 10, 1892.

24. *Official Register of the Officers and Cadets of the U. S. Military Academy*, West Point, N. Y., June, 1892, pp. 7, 10 and 24. USMA Archives.

25. *Minneapolis Star Tribune*, January 15, 2008.

26. H.M. Lazelle File, 2624 ACP 1874, RG94, NARA.

27. Special Order No. 54, Headquarters, Army Adjutant General's Office, dated March 11, 1893, Letters Received by the Appointment Commission and Personal Branch, Adjutant General's Office, 1871-1894, RG94 (Microfiche No. 1395), NARA.

28. Letter Postmarked Fort Clark to the Secretary of War through the Adjutant General, dated March 10, 1863, with endorsement dated March 16, 1893, Letters Received by the Appointment Commission and Personal Branch, Adjutant General's Office, 1871-1894, RG94 (Microfiche No. 1395), NARA.

29. *The Charlotte Observer*, April 19, 1893.

30. Ibid.

31. Fort Clark Monthly Return, April 1893, Post Returns, RG94, (M617, roll 216), NARA.

32. Barrows Family Papers (MS Am 1807-1807.5). Houghton Library, Harvard University.

33. "Guardians of the Pass—The Story of the U.S. Army in El Paso," *Fort Bliss Monitor*, El Paso, Texas, June 29, 2006, pg. 36-38.

34. Metz, *Desert Army*, 65-70.

35. Ibid. See also: Matthew H. Thomlinson, *The Garrison of Fort Bliss 1849-1916* (El Paso, TX: Hertzog & Resler, Printers, 1945); and Perry Jamieson, *A Survey History of Fort Bliss 1890-1940*, Historic and Natural Resources Report No. 5, Cultural Resources Management Program, Director of Environment, United States Army Air Defense Artillery Center, Fort Bliss, Texas, 1993.

36. Richard T. Cassidy, MG US Army, *The Story of Fort Bliss*, undated monograph, p. 21. Courtesy Fort Bliss and Old Ironsides Museum.

37. Arthur Van Voorhis Crego, "City on the Mesa—The New Fort Bliss 1890–1895," unpublished manuscript, July 1969, pp. 39-40. Courtesy of the Fort Bliss and Old Ironsides Museum.

38. Letter marked "Personal," dated November 27, 1893, Letters Received by the Appointment Commission and Personal Branch, Adjutant General's Office, 1871-1894, RG94 (Microfiche No. 1395), NARA.

39. Crego, 40.

40. 18th Regiment Monthly Returns, June-July 1894, Regimental Returns, RG94 (M665, roll 196), NARA, and New Fort Bliss Monthly Returns, June-July 1894, Post Returns, RG94 (M617, roll 118), NARA.

41. 18th Regiment Monthly Returns, January 1895–June 1898, Regimental Returns, RG 94, (M665, rolls 196-197), NARA.

42. Letters Received by the Appointment Commission and Personal Branch, Adjutant General's Office, 1871-1894, RG94 (Microfiche No. 1395), NARA.

43. Ibid.

44. Ibid.

CHAPTER 12—A LOST SOUL

1. In a letter dated March 13, 1895, from the Assistant Adjutant General, and addressed to Colonel Lazelle at 202 West Washington Street in Hagerstown, he was granted permission "to go beyond sea" but also informed he must request permission each time he desired to go abroad. Lazelle Family Papers.

2. Unattributed, *Some Account of the Vampires of Onset, Past and Present* (Boston: Press of S. Woodberry & Co., 1892), 2.

3. *The Boston Herald*, Boston, Mass., March 20, 1884.

4. Barrows Family Papers (MS Am 1807-1807.5). Houghton Library, Harvard University.

5. Ibid.

6. *Matter, Force, and Spirit or Scientific Evidence of a Supreme Intelligence* (New York: G. P. Putnam's Sons, The Knickerbocker Press, 1895).

7. Barrows Family Papers. No record of a review has been found.

8. *The Algona Courier*, Algona, Iowa, June 21, 1885, pg. 7. Can be found on Newspapers.com.

9. Oral and written family history notes, Lazelle Family Papers.

10. Robert A. Lancaster, *Historic Virginia Homes and Churches* (Philadelphia, PA: J. B. Lippincott, 1915), 165-166.

11. The University College of Medicine—originally known as the College of Physicians and Surgeons—was founded in 1893 by Dr. Hunter Holmes McGuire of Hampton-Sydney College. In 1913, it merged with the Medical College of Virginia, which is now part of Virginia Commonwealth University.

12. 18th Infantry Regiment Monthly Returns, June–July 1898, Regimental Returns, RG 94 (M665, roll 197), NARA. See also: Record of the Annual Reunion, U.S. Military Academy, June 8, 1901, pg. 15., USMA Archives.

13. *Annual Reports of the War Department for the Fiscal Year Ended June 30, 1899*, Report of the Major-General Commanding the Army, Part 2 (Washington, DC: Government Printing Office, 1899), 204. The sailing of the *Newport* was reported in the November 9 edition of *The San Francisco Call.*

14. Oral and written family history notes, Lazelle Family Papers.

15. Information drawn from research completed by Steven A. Moore, President of the Georgeville Historical Society.

16. Oath of Office dated July 2, 1904, H.M. Lazelle File, 2624 ACP 1874, RG94, NARA.

17. Barrows Family Papers.

18. Ibid.

19. Letter, dated July 21, 1971, from Frank W. Fetter, to Mrs. Arnold Hoffman, historian. Lazelle Family Papers.

20. Document No. 196, December 20, 1911, U.S. Senate Committee on Claims, 62nd Congress, 2nd Session.

21. Lazelle Family Papers.

22. Ibid.

Bibliography

Archives and collections

Barrows Family Papers (MS Am 1807-1807.5). Houghton Library, Harvard University.

Howard, Oliver Otis Papers: 1833-1912, Bowdoin College Library (M91.4, Box 15). Bowdoin College, Brunswick, ME.

Lazelle Family Papers, Vienna, Virginia. Available from author upon request.

Lazelle, Henry M., "Manuscript Diary of Lt. Henry Martyn Lazelle, 2nd Lieutenant, 8th Infantry, April 20, 1857 to June 13, 1857," University of New Mexico Library, Coronado Room (L458g), University of New Mexico, Albuquerque, NM.

New York State Archives. *New York Civil War Muster Roll Abstracts, 1861-1900* (Archive Collections # 13775-83). Albany, New York.

New York State Military Museum and Veterans Research Center, "16th New York Volunteer Cavalry Regiment," newspaper clipping files and photos. Saratoga, NY.

Schofield, John McAllister Papers, Manuscript Division, Library of Congress, Washington, DC.

US Army Heritage Center, Carlisle, PA. Sanger, Donald B., Major, Signal Corps, US Army. "The Story of Fort Bliss" (unpublished manuscript, 1933).

_____. Wilhelm, Thomas. *History of the Eighth U.S. Infantry From Its Organization in 1838, Vol. II.* Headquarters, Eighth Infantry, 1873.

_____. "Memorandum from the Adjutant's Office, 8th Infantry," 1875.

US Military Academy Archives, West Point, NY: "Annual Report of the Board of Visitors to the United States Military Academy, made to the Secretary of War, for the Year 1881."

_____. "Circumstances of the Parents of the Cadets, 1842-1879, Vol. I."

_____. "Official Record of the U. S. Military Academy," various months and years.

_____. "Order Books," various months and years.

_____. "Post Orders," various dates.

_____. "Record of the Annual Reunion, U.S. Military Academy," various years.

_____. "The Daily Correspondence of Robert E. Lee, Superintendent, USMA, 1852-1855," USMA Library Occasional Paper No. 5.

_____. "U.S. Military Academy Staff Records, Vol. 5, 1851-1854."

U.S. National Archives, Washington, DC. "Letters Received by the Adjutant General's Office, 1860-1870," Microfiche M619.

_____. "Letters Received by the Appointment Commission and Personal Branch, Adjutant General's Office, 1871-1894," Microfiche M1395.

_____. "Letters Received by the Office of the Adjutant General, 1812-1889," Microfilm M711.

_____. "Letters Received by the Office of the Adjutant General, 1871-1880," Microfilm M666.

_____. "Post Returns, West Point/Military Academy, January 1881-December 1890," Microfilm M617.

_____. Record Group 92, "Quartermaster Records," Box 87.

_____. Record Group 94, "H. M. Lazelle File," 2624 ACP 1874.

_____. Record Group 94, "Records of the Adjutant General's Office, 1780s—1917, Returns from Regular Army Infantry Regiments, June 1821—December 1916," Microfilm M665A & B.

_____. Record Group 94, "Records of the Adjutant General's Office, 1780s—1917, Returns from U.S. Military Posts, 1800-1916," Microfilm M617H.

_____. Records of the War Records Office of the War Department, Letters Received, 1877-1894," RG 94.13, Entry 710.

_____. Records of the War Records Office of the War Department, Letters Sent, 1877-1894," RG 94.13, Entry 708.

_____. "Records Relating to the U.S. Military Academy, Records of the Adjutant General's Office, 1780's-1917," RG 94.2.6.

_____. "Selected Documents Related to Blacks Nominated for Appointment to the US Military Academy During the 19th Century, 1870-1887," Vol. 21, Record Groups 94, 107, and 153, Microfilm M1002.

_____. "U.S. Military Academy Cadet Application Papers, 1805-1916," Microfilm M688.

_____. "War Department Orders, 1864-1865," Microfilm M444.

Whistler, James McNeill, "The Correspondence of James McNeill Whistler" (MS Whistler). University of Glasgow Library, Special Collections, Glasgow, Scotland.

U.S. Government Documents

Carroll, Charles, and Lynne Sebastian, eds. *Fort Craig: The United States Fort on the Camino Real—Collected Papers of the First Fort Craig Conference.* Washington, DC: U.S. Department of the Interior, Bureau of Land Management, 2000.

"Fifth Annual Report of the Board of Indian Commissioners to the President of the United States, 1873." Washington, DC: Government Printing Office, 1874.

"Fort Craig: 1854-1885." Washington, DC: U.S. Department of the Interior, Bureau of Land Management, undated.

Goodwin, R. Christopher and Associates, *National Historical Context for Department of Defense Installations, 1790-1940, Vol. II*, Prepared for the U.S. Army Corps of Engineers, Baltimore District, August 1995.

Jamieson, Perry D. *A Survey History of Fort Bliss 1890-1940, Historic and Natural Resources Report No. 5.* Fort Bliss, TX: Cultural Resources

Management Program, Director of Environment, United States Army Air Defense Artillery Center, 1993.

Marcy, R.B., Inspector General. *Posts and Stations of Troops in the Geographical Divisions and Departments of the United States.* Washington DC: Government Printing Office, 1872.

Munden, Kenneth W., and Henry Putney Beers. *The Union: A Guide to Federal Archives Relating to the Civil War.* Washington, DC: National Archives and Records Administration, 1986.

"Report of the Secretary of War—Being Part of the Message and Documents Communicated to the Two Houses of Congress at the Beginning of the Second Session of the Forty-Fifth Congress, Volume I, 1877." Washington, DC: Government Printing Office, 1877.

"Report of the Sioux Commission," Papers Accompanying the Annual Report of the Commissioner of Indian Affairs to the Secretary of the Interior for the Year 1874. Washington, DC: Government Printing Office, 1874.

Fort Craig: The United States Fort on the Camino Real—Collected Papers of the First Fort Craig Conference. Washington DC: United States Department of the Interior, Bureau of Land Management, 2000.

United States Congress. "Congressional Record-House," March 13, 1888.

_____. House of Representatives, "Official Records of the War of the Rebellion—Resolution," 50th Congress, 1st Session, Mis. Doc. No. 54, December 19, 1887.

____. House of Representatives, "Records of the Rebellion—Resolution," 50th Congress, 1st Session, Mis. Doc. No. 308, March 5, 1888.

_____. House of Representatives, "Report of the Select Committee on the Pacific Railroad and Telegraph," 36th Congress, 1st Session, No. 358, August 16, 1856.

_____. House of Representatives, "Report No. 4153, Records of the Rebellion," 50th Congress, 1st Session, February 28, 1889.

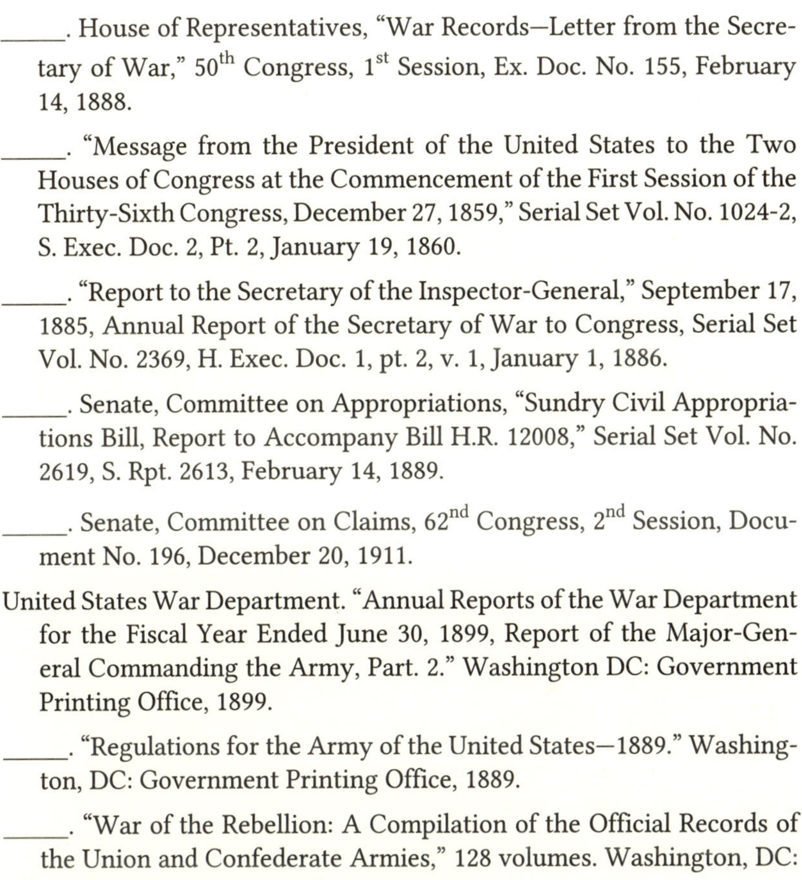

_____. House of Representatives, "War Records—Letter from the Secretary of War," 50th Congress, 1st Session, Ex. Doc. No. 155, February 14, 1888.

_____. "Message from the President of the United States to the Two Houses of Congress at the Commencement of the First Session of the Thirty-Sixth Congress, December 27, 1859," Serial Set Vol. No. 1024-2, S. Exec. Doc. 2, Pt. 2, January 19, 1860.

_____. "Report to the Secretary of the Inspector-General," September 17, 1885, Annual Report of the Secretary of War to Congress, Serial Set Vol. No. 2369, H. Exec. Doc. 1, pt. 2, v. 1, January 1, 1886.

_____. Senate, Committee on Appropriations, "Sundry Civil Appropriations Bill, Report to Accompany Bill H.R. 12008," Serial Set Vol. No. 2619, S. Rpt. 2613, February 14, 1889.

_____. Senate, Committee on Claims, 62nd Congress, 2nd Session, Document No. 196, December 20, 1911.

United States War Department. "Annual Reports of the War Department for the Fiscal Year Ended June 30, 1899, Report of the Major-General Commanding the Army, Part. 2." Washington DC: Government Printing Office, 1899.

_____. "Regulations for the Army of the United States—1889." Washington, DC: Government Printing Office, 1889.

_____. "War of the Rebellion: A Compilation of the Official Records of the Union and Confederate Armies," 128 volumes. Washington, DC: Government Printing Office, 1880-1900.

Books

Ambrose, Stephen E. *Upton and the Army.* Baton Rouge: Louisiana State University Press, 1964.

Anbinder, Tyler. *Nativism and Slavery: The Northern Know Nothings and the Politics of the 1850s.* New York: Oxford University Press, 1992.

Anderson, Ronald, and Anne Koval. *James McNeill Whistler: Beyond the Myth.* New York: Carroll & Graf, 1994.

Arnold, Sir Edwin, M.A. *India Revisited.* London: Trubner & Co., 1886.

Bradley, Mark. *Bluecoats and Tar Heels: Soldiers and Civilians in Reconstruction North Carolina.* Lexington: University Press of Kentucky, 2009.

Brandes, Ray. *Frontier Military Posts of Arizona.* Globe, AZ: D.S. King, 1960.

Brodsky, Alyn. *Grover Cleveland: A Study in Character.* New York: St. Martin's Press, 2000.

Brown, Dee. *The Fetterman Massacre.* Lincoln: University of Nebraska Press, 1962.

Bundy, Carol. *The Nature of Sacrifice: A Biography of Charles Russell Lowell, Jr., 1835-64.* New York: Farrar, Straus and Giroux, 2005.

Coffman, Edward M. *The Old Army—A Portrait of the American Army in Peacetime, 1784-1898.* New York: Oxford University Press, 1986.

Cooling, Benjamin Franklin, III. *Symbol, Sword and Shield: Defending Washington During the Civil War.* Shippensburg, PA: White Main Publishing Co., 1991.

______, and Walton H. Owen, II. *Mr. Lincoln's Forts: A Guide to the Civil War Defenses of Washington.* Shippensburg, PA: White Main Publishing Co., 1988.

Cowley, Robert, and Thomas Guinzburg, ed. *West Point—Two Centuries of Honor and Tradition.* New York: Warner Books, 2002.

Crawford, J. Marshall. *Mosby and His Men: A Record of the Adventures of That Renowned Partisan Ranger, John S. Mosby.* New York: G. W. Carleton & Co., 1867.

Crouch, Howard R. *Like a Hurricane: The Men, Mounts, Arms, and Tactics of Colonel John S. Mosby's Command.* Catlett, VA: SCS Publications, 2013.

Cullum, George W. *Biographic Register of the Officers and Graduates of the U.S. Military Academy, Third Edition, Vol. III.* Boston: Houghton, Mifflin & Co., 1891.

Custer, Elizabeth B. *Boots and Saddles or Life in Dakota with General Custer.* Lincoln: University of Nebraska Press, 2010.

DuBois, John Van Deusen. *Campaigns in the West—1856–1861: The Journal and Letters of Colonel John Van Deusen Du Bois.* Tucson: Arizona Historical Society, 1949 and 2003.

Dyer, Frederick H. *A Compendium of the War of the Rebellion.* Des Moines, IA: The Dyer Publishing Company, 1908.

Evans, Thomas J., and James M. Moyer. *Mosby Vignettes, Volume I.* Farifax, VA: Privately printed, 1993.

Fleming, Gordon H. *James Abbott McNeill Whistler, a Life.* New York: St. Martin's Press, 1991.

Fleming, Thomas J. *West Point: The Men and Times of the United States Military Academy.* New York: William Morrow & Company, 1969.

Fort Clark Historical Society. *Narrative History of the Commanding Officer's Quarters (Wainwright House).* Fort Clark, TX, 1963.

Fox, William F., Lt. Col., U.S.V. *Regimental Losses in the American Civil War, 1861-1865.* Albany, NY: Albany Publishing Company, 1889.

Gemand, Bradley E. *A Virginia Village Goes to War: Falls Church During the Civil War.* Virginia Beach, VA: The Donning Company Publishers, 2002.

Graff, Henry F. *Cleveland: The American Presidents Series.* New York: Henry Holt and Co., Times Books, 2002.

Greene, Jerome A. *Yellowstone Command: Colonel Nelson A. Miles and the Great Sioux War, 1876-1877.* Norman: University of Oklahoma Press, 2006.

Hathaway, Herman, and Ethan S. Rafuse, eds. *The Ongoing Civil War: New Versions of Old Stories.* Columbia: University of Missouri Press, 2004.

Haenn, William F. *Fort Clark and Brackettville, Land of Heroes.* Charleston, SC: Arcadia Publishing, 2002.

Herr, John K., and Edward S. Wallace. *The Story of the U.S. Cavalry, 1775-1942.* Boston: Little, Brown and Company, 1953.

Hoadley, J. C., Ed. *Memorial of Henry Sanford Gansevoort.* Boston: Franklin Press, Rand, Avery, & Co., 1875. Reprint: Forgotten Books, 2012.

Horgan, Paul. *Great River: The Rio Grande in North American History.* Hanover, NH: Wesleyan University Press, 1984.

Howard, Oliver Otis. *Autobiography of Oliver Otis Howard, Major General, United States Army, Vol. I & II.* New York: Baker & Taylor, 1908.

Humphries, Charles A. *Field, Camp, Hospital and Prison in the Civil War, 1863-1865.* Boston: Press of Geo. E. Ellis Co., 1918.

Hutton, Paul Andrew. *Phil Sheridan and His Army.* Lincoln: University of Nebraska Press, 1985.

______, ed. *Soldiers West: Biographies from the Military Frontier.* Lincoln: University of Nebraska Press, 1987.

Jamieson, Perry D. *Crossing the Deadly Ground: United States Army Tactics, 1865-1899.* Tuscaloosa: The University of Alabama Press, 1994.

Jones, Virgil Carrington. *Gray Ghosts and Rebel Raiders.* New York: Henry Holt & Co., 1956.

______. *Ranger Mosby.* McLean, VA: EPM Publications, Inc., 1972.

Kinney County Historical Commission. *1873 Infantry Barracks, Fort Clark, Texas.* Fort Clark, TX, undated.

_____. *Seminole-Negro Indian Scout Camp, Fort Clark, Texas.* Fort Clark, TX: Self-published, 2007.

Lancaster, Robert A. *Historic Virginia Homes and Churches.* Philadelphia: J.B. Lippincott Co., 1915.

Lane, Lydia Spencer. *I Married a Soldier or Old Days in the Old Army.* Philadelphia: J.B. Lippincott Co., 1893.

Larson, Robert W. *Red Cloud: Warrior-Statesman of the Lakota Sioux.* Norman: University of Oklahoma Press, 1997.

Lazelle, Henry M. *Matter, Force, and Spirit or Scientific Evidence of a Supreme Intelligence.* New York: G. P. Putnam's Sons, The Knickerbocker Press, 1895.

______. *One Law in Nature—A New Corpuscular Theory, Comprehending Unity of Force, Identity of Matter, and Its Multiple Atom Constitution: Applied to The Physical Affections or Modes of Energy.* New York: D. Van Nostrand, 1872.

Lee, Robert. *Fort Meade and the Black Hills.* Lincoln: University of Nebraska Press, 1991.

Leech, Margaret. *Reveille in Washington, 1860-1865.* New York: Harper & Brothers, 1941.

Long, E. B. *The Civil War Day by Day: An Almanac 1861-1865.* Garden City: Doubleday & Company, 1971.

Lubetkin, John M. *Jay Cooke's Gamble: The Northern Pacific Railroad, the Sioux, and the Panic of 1873.* Norman: University of Oklahoma Press, 2006.

McDonald, Margaret F. *James McNeill Whistler: Drawings, Pastels, and Watercolours—A Catalogue Raisonné.* New Haven: Yale University Press, 1995.

McLean, James. *California Sabers: The 2nd Massachusetts Cavalry in the Civil War.* Bloomington: Indiana University Press, 2000.

Marszalek, John F. *Assault at West Point: The Court-Martial of Johnson Whittaker.* New York: Collier Books, Macmillan Publishing Company, 1972.

Metz, Leon C. *Desert Army: Fort Bliss on the Texas Border.* El Paso: Mangan Books, 1988.

Miller, Darlis A. *Captain Jack Crawford—Buckskin Poet, Scout, and Showman.* Albuquerque: University of New Mexico Press, 1993.

Morris, R. Rebecca. *A Low, Dirty Place: The Parole Camps of Annapolis, MD, 1862-1865.* Linthicum, MD: Ann Arundel County Historical Society, 2012.

Phisterer, Frederick. *New York in the War of the Rebellion*, 3rd ed. Albany: J.B. Lyon Company, 1912.

Pinkerton, Allan. *The Spy of the Rebellion: A True History of the Spy System of the United States Army During the Late Rebellion.* New York: G.W. Carlton & Co., 1884.

Quaife, Milo Milton, ed. *Kit Carson's Autobiography.* Lincoln: University of Nebraska Press, 1966.

Ramage, James A. *Gray Ghost: The Life of Col. John Singleton Mosby.* Lexington: The University Press of Kentucky, 1999.

Rapp, Kenneth W. *West Point: Whistler in Cadet Gray and Other Stories About the United States Military Academy.* Great Barrington, MA: North River Press, 1978.

Robbins, James S. *Last in Their Class: Custer, Pickett and the Goats of West Point.* New York: Encounter Books, 2006.

Robinson, Charles M., III. *The Fall of a Black Army Officer—Racism and the Myth of Henry O. Flipper.* Norman: University of Oklahoma Press, 2008.

Roberts, Lord of Kandahar, V.C. *Forty-One Years in India from Subaltern to Commander-in-Chief.* London: Richard Bentley & Son, 1898.

Rodenbough, Theophilus F., and William L. Haskin, eds., *The Army of the United States, Historical Sketches of Staff and Line with Portraits of Generals-in-Chief.* New York: Maynard, Merrill & Co., 1896.

Russell, Charles Wells, ed. *The Memoirs of Colonel John S. Mosby.* Boston: Little Brown & Co., 1917.

Scheel, Eugene M. *The Civil War in Fauquier.* Waterford, VA: privately printed, 1985.

Schofield, John M. *Forty-Six Years in the Army.* New York: The Century Co., 1897.

Schuler, Harold H. *Fort Sully: Guns at Sunset.* Vermillion, SD: University of South Dakota Press, 1992.

Sefton, James E. *The United States Army and Reconstruction, 1865-1877.* Baton Rouge: Louisiana State University Press, 1967.

Sheridan, Philip H. *Personal Memoirs of P. H. Sheridan, Volume I.* New York: Charles L. Webster & Co., 1888.

Sides, Hampton. *Blood and Thunder: The Epic Story of Kit Carson and the Conquest of the American West.* New York: Random House, 2006.

Smith, Thomas T., et al., eds. *The Reminiscences of Major General Zenas R. Bliss, 1854-1876.* Austin: Texas State Historical Association, 2007.

Some Account of the Vampires of Onset, Past and Present. Boston: Press of S. Woodberry & Co., 1892.

Stewart, Richard W., ed. *American Military History, Volume 1: The United States Army and the Forging of a Nation, 1775-1917.* Washington, DC: Center of Military History, U.S. Army, 2005.

Stuntz, Connie P., and Mayo S. Stuntz. *This Was Vienna, Virginia: Facts and Photos.* Vienna, VA: Privately printed, 1987.

Summerhayes, Martha. *Vanished Arizona: Recollections of the Army Life of a New England Woman.* Salem, MA: The Salem Press, 1911.

The Centennial of the United States Military Academy at West Point, New York, 1802-1902, Volume I, Addresses and Histories. West Point: U.S. Military Academy, 1904.

Thomlinson, Matthew H. *The Garrison of Fort Bliss 1849-1916.* El Paso, TX: Hertzog & Resler, Printers,1945.

Utley, Robert M. *Frontier Regulars: The United States Army and the Indian, 1866-1891.* Lincoln: University of Nebraska Press, 1973.

_______. *Frontiersmen in Blue: The United States Army and the Indian, 1848-1865.* Lincoln: University of Nebraska Press, 1967.

Wall, Caleb A. *Reminiscences of Worcester from the Earliest Period.* Worcester, MA: Tyler & Seagrave, 1877.

Weigley, Russell F. *The American Way of War: A History of United States Military Strategy and Policy.* Bloomington: Indiana University Press, 1973.

Welcher, Frank J. *The Union Army, 1861-1865, Organization and Operations, Vol. I, The Eastern Theater.* Bloomington: Indiana University Press, 1989.

Williams, Albert E. *Black Warriors: Unique Units and Individuals.* West Conshohocken, PA: Infinity Publishing, 2003.

Williamson, James J. *Mosby's Rangers: A Record of the Operations of the 43d Battalion Virginia Cavalry.* New York: Ralph B. Kenyon, Publisher, 1896.

Wooster, Robert. *Nelson A. Miles and the Twilight of the Frontier Army.* Lincoln: University of Nebraska Press, 1993.

Zimmer, William F., and Jerome A. Greene. *Frontier Soldier: An Enlisted Man's Journal of the Sioux and Nez Perce Campaigns, 1877.* Helena: Montana Historical Society Press, 1998.

ARTICLES

Bender, A.B. "Government Explorations in the Territory of New Mexico, 1846-1859," *New Mexico Historical Review* 9, 1934.

Brown, Maj. Gary D. "Prisoner of War Parole: Ancient Concept, Modern Utility," *Military Law Review* 156 (June 1998): 200-223.

Center for the Professional Military Ethic, "White Paper: The United States Military Academy, Cadet Honor Code and Honor System," West Point, NY, February 10, 2000.

Craig, Ronald. "Evolution of the Office of the Provost Marshal General," *Military Police*, April, 2004.

Devine, John. E. "Joseph Hancock Blackwell," *News and Notes from The Fauquier Historical Society,* Warrenton, Virginia, Vol. 11, no. 4 (Fall, 1989): 1-5. Available at the Fairfax County Library, Virginia Room Collection, Fairfax, Virginia.

Fitzpatrick, David J. "Emory Upton and the Army of a Democracy," *The Journal of Military History* 77 (April 2013): 463-490.

______. "Emory Upton and the Citizen Soldier," *The Journal of Military History* 65 (April, 2001): 355-390.

Lazelle, Lieut. Colonel Henry M., "India," *Journal of the Military Service Institution of the United States* 9 (1888): 355-384.

______. "The Strengths and Weaknesses of England in India," *Journal of the Military Service Institution of the United States* 8 (1887): 247-258.

______. "Whistler at West Point," *The Century* 90 (1915).

Mahan, Harold E. "The Arsenal of History: The Official Records of the War of the Rebellion, *Civil War History* 29 (March 1983): 5-27.

Marszalek, John F. "A Black Cadet at West Point," *American Heritage Magazine*, August 1971.

McCaslin, Richard B., "United States Regulars in Gray: Edward Ingraham and Company A, 1st Regular Confederate Cavalry," *Southwestern Historical Quarterly* 118 (July 2014): 25-45.

McDermot, John D. "Brule Sioux Chief Spotted Tail," *Wild West*, February 2006: 10-14.

Michie, Peter S. "Caste at West Point," *North American Review*, June 1880.

Reeve, Frank D. "Puritan and Apache: A Diary," *The New Mexico Historical Review* 23 (December 1948): 269-301; and 24 (January 1949): 12-53.

Wright, Horatio G. "West Point and Cadet Life," *Putnam's Monthly*, August 1854: 192-204.

NEWSPAPERS AND JOURNALS

Albany Evening Journal, Albany, NY

Algona Courier, Algona, IA

Algona Upper Des Moines, Algona, IA

Anderson Intelligencer, Anderson, SC

Baltimore Sun, Baltimore, MD

Boston Daily Globe, Boston, MA

Boston Herald, Boston, MA

Charlotte Observer, Charlotte, NC

Chicago Daily Tribune, Chicago, IL

Cincinnati Commercial Gazette, Cincinnati, OH

Daily Gazette, Las Vegas, NM

Evening Star, Washington, DC

Fort Bliss Monitor, El Paso, TX

Glasgow Herald, Scotland

Hartford Daily Courant, Hartford, CT

Ipswich Journal, UK

Journal of the Military Service Institution of the United States, New York, NY

Kansas City Times, Kansas City, MO

Minneapolis Star Tribune, Minneapolis, MN

Morning Oregonian, Portland, OR

New York Times, New York, NY

San Francisco Call, San Francisco, CA

Stevens Point Journal, Stevens Point, WI

The Army and Navy Journal, New York, NY

The Christian Register, Boston, MA

The Nation, New York, NY

The National Era, Washington, DC

The Times, Philadelphia, PA

The United States Service Magazine, New York, NY

Times-Picayune, New Orleans, LA

Washington Post, Washington, DC

WEBSITES

Central Intelligence Agency, "Intelligence in the Civil War," https://www.cia.gov/library/publications/additional-publications/civil-war/index.html,August 2014.

Fold3, "US Military Records by War," www.fold3.com, August 2014.

Home of the American Civil War, "The Provost Marshal and the Citizen in the American Civil War," www.civilwarhome.com/ProvostMarshal.htm, August 2014.

Library of Congress, "Chronicling America," chronicling america.loc.gov, August 2014.

Making of America. "The War of the Rebellion: A Compilation of the Official Records of the Union and Confederate Armies," http://ebooks.library.cornell.edu/m/moawar/waro.html, August 2014.

Museum of Local History. *Charles S. Eigenbrodt, Alvarado Civil War Hero*, Timothy Swenson, 2005, http://www.museumoflocalhistory.org/pages/eigenbrodt.pdf, August 2014.

National Archives and Records Administration, "Records of the Commissary General of Prisoners," http://www.archives.gov/research/guide-fed-records/groups/249.html, August 2014.

New York State Military Museum and Veterans Research Center, "Roster of the New York Cavalry Regiments During the Civil War" http://dmna.state.ny.us/historic/reghist/civil/rosters/rosterscavalry.htm, August 2014.

Ohio History Central, "Camp Chase," http://www.ohiohistorycentral.org/w/Camp_Chase?rec=662, August 2014.

Ronald A. MacDonald's Website, "The Life of William Jeremiah Keays," www.r-a-macdonald.ca, August 2014.

Texas History Online, "The Treachery of Texas, the Secession of Texas, and the Arrest of the United States Officers and Soldiers Serving in Texas, Read before the New York Historical Society, June 25, 1861," by Major John T. Sprague, U.S. Army (Press of the Rebellion Record, New York, 1862), http://texashistory.unt.edu/ark:/67531/metapth6102/m1/1/, August 2014.

Texas State Historical Association. *The Handbook of Texas Online*, "Eighth United States Infantry," http://www.tshaonline.org/handbook/online/articles/qzemw, August 2014.

The Public Library of Charlotte and Mecklenburg County, "Hornets' Nest: The Story of Charlotte and Mecklenburg County," http://www.cmstory.org/history/hornets/content.htm, August 2014.

The Second Mass and Its Fighting Californians, http://www.2mass.reunioncivilwar.com/index.htm, August 2014.

U.S. Military Academy Digital Collections, "Annual Reports of the Board of Visitors," http://digital-library.usma.edu/cdm/search/collection/bovreports/order/date, August 2014.

U.S. Military Academy Digital Collections, "Official Register of the Officers and Cadets of the U.S. Military Academy," http://digital-library.usma.edu/cdm/search/collection/p16919coll3/searchterm/Official%20register%20of%20the%20officers%20and%20cadets/mode/all/order/date, August 2014.

U.S. Military Academy, "History," http://www.usma.edu/wphistory, August 2014.

UNPUBLISHED PAPERS AND INTERVIEWS

Cassidy, Richard T., MG US Army. "The Story of Fort Bliss" (unpublished, undated manuscript). Fort Bliss and Old Ironsides Museum Archives, Fort Bliss, Texas.

Crego, Arthur Va Voorhis. "City on the Mesa—The New Fort Bliss 1890—1895" (unpublished manuscript, July 1969). Fort Bliss and Old Ironsides Museum Archives, Fort Bliss, Texas.

Currey, Craig J. "The Role of the Army in North Carolina Reconstruction, 1865-1877" (Masters thesis, University of North Carolina at Chapel Hill, 1991).

Dillard, Walter Scott. "The United States Military Academy, 1865-1900: The Uncertain Years" (PhD dissertation, University of Washington, 1972).

Fetter, Frank W., Letter to Mrs. Arnold Hoffman, historian and author: memories of General Lazelle, July 21, 1971.

Lazelle, Horace G., and Barbara H. Lazelle, Lazelle Family History: written notes and transcript of oral history.

Miller, Steven G. "An Informal History of the 16th New York Volunteer Cavalry" (unpublished manuscript, Mundelein, IL: March, 1997), courtesy of the author.

Moore, Steven A., President, Georgeville Historical Society: Genealogic and historic research notes and documentation related to Henry M. Lazelle, Emilie Monard, and Wake Robin cabin, Georgeville, Quebec, Canada.

Oliver, Captain Matt, "Society's Sacrifice: The First Black Cadet at West Point, James Webster Smith" (history paper, United States Military Academy, December 1993). USMA Library, West Point, NY.

Walter, John F. "Sixteenth New York Cavalry" (unpublished monograph, July, 1982, revised March, 1997), courtesy of the author.

Index